UNITED NATIONS HANDBOOK 2012│2013

UNITED NATIONS HANDBOOK

AN ANNUAL GUIDE FOR THOSE WORKING WITH AND WITHIN THE UNITED NATIONS

First published in 1961 and reprinted annually as a revised edition
(with the exception of 1970 and 1976).

Fiftieth edition

© Crown Copyright Reserved 2012

ISSN: 0110-1951

Published by the Ministry of Foreign Affairs and Trade/Manatū Aorere,
Private Bag 18–901, Wellington, New Zealand

Editorial services by Ann Howarth, New Zealand

Cover design and typesetting by *typeface*, Wellington, New Zealand

Printed by Printlink, Wellington, New Zealand

Copies may be purchased from:
Ministry of Foreign Affairs and Trade/Manatū Aorere, Private Bag 18–901, Wellington, New Zealand
Website: www.mfat.govt.nz
Telephone: (64 4) 439 8000, Fax: (64 4) 439 8855
Email: cmd@mfat.govt.nz
Selected bookstores and New Zealand Embassies, High Commissions and Consulates-General
An electronic version of this Handbook can be found on the New Zealand Ministry of Foreign Affairs and Trade website,
www.mfat.govt.nz.

CONTENTS

LIST OF ABBREVIATIONS

Country names

The following abbreviations of the names of UN Member States are used throughout this Handbook.

Andorra	Principality of Andorra
Bahrain	Kingdom of Bahrain
Bolivia	Plurinational State of Bolivia
Congo	Republic of the Congo
DPRK	Democratic People's Republic of Korea
DR Congo	Democratic Republic of the Congo
Iran	Islamic Republic of Iran
Lao PDR	Lao People's Democratic Republic
Mauritania	Islamic Republic of Mauritania
Micronesia	Federated States of Micronesia
Monaco	Principality of Monaco
Morocco	Kingdom of Morocco
Netherlands	Kingdom of the Netherlands
Oman	Sultanate of Oman
ROK	Republic of Korea
South Sudan	Republic of South Sudan
Sri Lanka	Democratic Socialist Republic of Sri Lanka
Syrian AR	Syrian Arab Republic
UAE	United Arab Emirates
UK or United Kingdom	United Kingdom of Great Britain and Northern Ireland
UR of Tanzania	United Republic of Tanzania
USA	United States of America
Venezuela	Bolivarian Republic of Venezuela
Viet Nam	Socialist Republic of Viet Nam

Other abbreviations

ECOSOC	UN Economic and Social Council
GA	UN General Assembly
Res.	Resolution
SC	UN Security Council
UN	United Nations

FOREWORD

New Zealand Minister of Foreign Affairs

In 1961, New Zealand produced the first edition of the United Nations Handbook, a short collection of reference notes that had previously only been used by the New Zealand Mission to the UN. Over the years, it has steadily grown to become a valuable aide for governments and their UN delegations as they navigate the complex United Nations system. In yet another milestone of its evolution, this 50th edition is accompanied by the introduction of the UN Handbook 'e-Book', giving users access to both hard and soft copy versions of the publication.

The UN remains the world's pre-eminent international organisation. While we can be proud of its successes, it still has the potential to do much more. The turbulent events of the past year, political and economic, have highlighted and tested the strengths and the limitations of an organisation founded in the middle of the 20th Century. Sixty-seven years after its creation, the UN must draw on its wealth of experience, including its successes and its shortcomings, to address issues of international peace and security, to set standards of international behaviour, and to advance the reforms needed to meet the challenges of the 21st Century.

One of the UN's greatest strengths is that all states, no matter their size, wealth, or military might, are empowered with an equal voice. Every state has a chance to speak, an opportunity to listen and a role to play. As a small nation in the Pacific, but one which has always sought to play an active, independent and constructive role in the United Nations, New Zealand understands the importance of that multilateralism and of the UN's goals and values.

New Zealand is a firm believer in the United Nations and in doing our share. We demonstrate this commitment in our continuing role in producing this Handbook, and in New Zealand's decision to seek a non-permanent seat on the UN Security Council in 2014, for the 2015–16 term.

For more than 50 years, this UN Handbook has offered an annually revised and detailed resource for those of us who strive towards the UN's goals, and who seek to further the efficient functioning of this essential global institution.

In the words of our indigenous people:

He waka eke noa
We are all in this canoe together; in this we are the same.

Hon Murray McCully
NEW ZEALAND MINISTER OF FOREIGN AFFAIRS

WHAT THIS BOOK DOES

The *United Nations Handbook* is published by the New Zealand Government as a ready reference guide. The Handbook provides current information on all the UN family organisations, including their purpose, evolution, structure, membership and an overview of activities. It is not intended to be a historical record.

The book has at its heart information about the six principal UN organs established by the UN Charter: the General Assembly, Security Council, Economic and Social Council, Trusteeship Council, International Court of Justice and the Secretariat.

It also contains information about subsidiary organs established in accordance with the Charter, related UN organs and programmes, specialised agencies and autonomous bodies related to the UN, and various ad hoc organs and programmes. Some bodies are shown as subsidiary to, or associated with, one or other of the principal organs, while others are shown under the heading 'Other Bodies Subsidiary or Related to the UN'. The specialised agencies of the UN are included under this heading.

Non-governmental organisations with UN connections are not included; neither, generally, are other inter-governmental (but non-UN) organisations or political groupings.

All money values are in US dollars unless otherwise stated.

Website, email and postal/physical addresses are included where possible, along with telephone and fax numbers. Agencies without specified contact details can be reached through UN Headquarters in New York:

United Nations Plaza
New York, NY 10017
United States of America
Telephone: (+1 212) 963 1234
Fax: (+1 212) 963 4879

The main UN website is www.un.org; many UN websites are indexed at www.unsystem.org; and many documents can be found at www.undocs.org.

The publishers are indebted to the UN bodies and agencies that provide considerable assistance each year to ensure the Handbook is as up to date and comprehensive as possible.

The information in this Handbook is intended to be accurate as at 31 May 2012, unless otherwise stated.

THE UNITED NATIONS SYSTEM – PRINCIPAL ORGANS

SECURITY COUNCIL

Subsidiary Bodies

Counter-terrorism committees

International Criminal Tribunal for Rwanda (ICTR)

International Criminal Tribunal for the former Yugoslavia (ICTY)

Military Staff Committee

Peacekeeping operations and missions

Sanctions commitees (ad hoc)

Standing committees and ad hoc bodies

Advisory Subsidiary Body

UN Peacebuilding Commission

GENERAL ASSEMBLY

Subsidiary Bodies

Main and other sessional committees

Disarmament Commission

Human Rights Council

International Law Commission

Standing committees and ad hoc bodies

Related Organisations

CTBTO Preparatory Commission for the Comprehensive Nuclear-Test-Ban Treaty Organization

IAEA[2] International Atomic Energy Agency

OPCW Organisation for the Prohibition of Chemical Weapons

WTO[3] World Trade Organization

Programmes and Funds

UNCTAD UN Conference on Trade and Development

- **ITC** International Trawde Centre (UNCTAD/WTO)

UNDP UN Development Programme

- **UNCDF** UN Capital Development Fund
- **UNV** UN Volunteers

UNEP UN Environment Programme

UNFPA UN Population Fund

UN-HABITAT UN Human Settlements Programme

UNHCR Office of the UN High Commissioner for Refugees

UNICEF UN Children's Fund

UNODC UN Office on Drugs and Crime

UNRWA[1] UN Relief and Works Agency for Palestine Refugees in the Near East

UN Women UN Entity for Gender Equality and the Empowerment of Women

WFP World Food Programme

Research and Training Institutes

UNICRI UN Interregional Crime and Justice Research Institute

UNIDIR[1] UN Institute for Disarmament Research

UNITAR UN Institute for Training and Research

UNRISD UN Research Institute for Social Development

UNSSC UN System Staff College

UNU UN University

Other UN Entities

UNAIDS Joint UN Programme on HIV/AIDS

UNISDR UN International Strategy for Disaster Reduction

UNOPS United Nations Office for Project Services

INTERNATIONAL COURT OF JUSTICE

TRUSTEESHIP COUNCIL[5]

Notes

1 UNRWA and UNIDIR report only to the General Assembly.

2 IAEA reports to the Security Council and the General Assembly.

3 WTO has no reporting obligation to the General Assembly (GA) but contributes on an ad-hoc basis to GA and ECOSOC work inter alia on finance and developmental issues.

4 Specialised agencies are autonomous organisations working with the UN and each other through the coordinating machinery of the Economic and Social Council at the inter-governmental level, and through the Chief Executives Board for Coordination (CEB) at the inter-secretariat level. This section is listed in order of establishment of these organisations as specialised agencies of the UN.

5 The Trusteeship Council suspended operation on 1 November 1994 with the independence of Palau, the last remaining UN Trust Territory, on 1 October 1994.

As illustrated, some UN organisations have linkages to more than one principal organ. For example, General Assembly Programmes and Funds, Research and Training Institutes, and Other Entities also have linkages with ECOSOC.

This is not an official UN document, nor is it intended to be all-inclusive.

ECONOMIC & SOCIAL COUNCIL

SECRETARIAT

Specialised Agencies[4]

ILO International Labour Organization

FAO Food and Agriculture Organization of the UN

UNESCO UN Educational, Scientific and Cultural Organization

WHO World Health Organization

World Bank Group

- **IBRD** International Bank for Reconstruction and Development
- **IDA** International Development Association
- **IFC** International Finance Corporation
- **MIGA** Multilateral Investment Guarantee Agency
- **ICSID** International Centre for Settlement of Investment Disputes

IMF International Monetary Fund

ICAO International Civil Aviation Organization

IMO International Maritime Organization

ITU International Telecommunication Union

UPU Universal Postal Union

WMO World Meterological Organization

WIPO World Intellectual Property Organization

IFAD International Fund for Agricultural Development

UNIDO UN Industrial Development Organization

UNWTO World Tourism Organization

Functional Commissions

Crime Prevention and Criminal Justice

Narcotic Drugs

Population and Development

Science and Technology for Development

Social Development

Statistics

Status of Women

Sustainable Development

UN Forum on Forests

Other Bodies

Committee for Development Policy

Committee of Experts on Public Administration

Committee on Non-Governmental Organizations

Permanent Forum on Indigenous Issues

UN Group of Experts on Geographical Names

Other sessional and standing committees and expert, ad hoc and related bodies

Departments and Offices

EOSG Executive Office of the Secretary-General

DESA Department of Economic and Social Affairs

DFS Deparment of Field Support

DGACM Department for General Assembly and Conference Management

DM Department of Management

DPA Department of Political Affairs

DPI Department of Public Information

DPKO Department of Peacekeeping Operations

DSS Department of Safety and Security

OCHA Office for the Coordination of Humanitarian Affairs

OHCHR Office of the UN High Commissioner for Human Rights

OIOS Office of Internal Oversight Services

OLA Office of Legal Affairs

OSAA Office of the Special Adviser on Africa

OSRSG/CAAC Office of the Special Representative of the Secretary-General for Children and Armed Conflict

UNOAU UN Office to the African Union

UNODA Office for Disarmament Affairs

UNOG UN Office at Geneva

UN-OHRLLS Office of the High Representative for the Least Developed Countries, Landlocked Developing Countries and Small Island Developing States

UNON UN Office at Nairobi

UNOV UN Office at Vienna

Regional Commissions

ECA Economic Commission for Africa

ECE Economic Commission for Europe

ECLAC Economic Commission for Latin America and the Caribbean

ESCAP Economic and Social Commission for Asia and the Pacific

ESCWA Economic and Social Commission for Western Asia

GENERAL ASSEMBLY

GENERAL ASSEMBLY

CHARTER PROVISIONS

The General Assembly consists of all the members of the UN. It may discuss any questions or matters within the scope of the UN Charter, or relating to the powers and functions of any organ provided for in the Charter. It may make recommendations to UN members or the Security Council or both, on any such questions or matters, except disputes or situations in respect of which the Security Council is currently exercising its functions.

General Assembly decisions on important questions are made by a two-thirds majority of the members present and voting, and on other questions by a simple majority. Categories of questions requiring a two-thirds majority are listed in article 18 of the Charter. This article also provides that decisions on other questions, including the determination of additional categories of questions to be decided by a two-thirds majority, are made by a simple majority.

The General Assembly receives and considers reports from the other organs of the UN. It elects the 10 non-permanent members of the Security Council and the 54 members of the Economic and Social Council. Together with the Security Council, but voting independently, it elects the members of the International Court of Justice. On the recommendation of the Security Council it appoints the Secretary-General. The General Assembly considers and approves the regular budgets of the UN and apportions expenses among members.

The Charter provisions concerning the General Assembly are contained in Chapter IV (articles 9–22), which defines its composition, functions and powers, voting and procedures. Other provisions relating to the General Assembly are contained in articles 1, 2, 4–7, 23, 24, 35, 60–64, 66, 85–88, 93, 96, 97, 98, 101, 105, 108 and 109 of the Charter, and articles 4, 7–15, 32, 33 and 69 of the Statute of the International Court of Justice.

MEMBERSHIP

As at 31 July 2012, 193 states were represented in the General Assembly. These states, together with their dates of admission to the UN, are:

Afghanistan	19 Nov 1946[1]	Bangladesh	17 Sep 1974
Albania	14 Dec 1955	Barbados	9 Dec 1966
Algeria	8 Oct 1962	Belarus	24 Oct 1945*
Andorra	28 Jul 1993	Belgium	27 Dec 1945*
Angola	1 Dec 1976	Belize	25 Sep 1981
Antigua and Barbuda	11 Nov 1981	Benin	20 Sep 1960
Argentina	24 Oct 1945*	Bhutan	21 Sep 1971
Armenia	2 Mar 1992	Bolivia	14 Nov 1945*
Australia	1 Nov 1945*	Bosnia and Herzegovina	22 May 1992[3]
Austria	14 Dec 1955	Botswana	17 Oct 1966
Azerbaijan	2 Mar 1992	Brazil	24 Oct 1945*
Bahamas	18 Sep 1973	Brunei Darussalam	21 Sep 1984
Bahrain	21 Sep 1971[2]	Bulgaria	14 Dec 1955

Burkina Faso	20 Sep 1960	Guyana	20 Sep 1966
Burundi	18 Sep 1962	Haiti	24 Oct 1945*
Cambodia	14 Dec 1955	Honduras	17 Dec 1945*
Cameroon	20 Sep 1960	Hungary	14 Dec 1955
Canada	9 Nov 1945*	Iceland	19 Nov 1946
Cape Verde	16 Sep 1975	India	30 Oct 1945*
Central African Republic	20 Sep 1960	Indonesia	28 Sep 1950[7]
Chad	20 Sep 1960	Iran	24 Oct 1945*
Chile	24 Oct 1945*	Iraq	21 Dec 1945*
China	24 Oct 1945*[4]	Ireland	14 Dec 1955
Colombia	5 Nov 1945*	Israel	11 May 1949
Comoros	12 Nov 1975	Italy	14 Dec 1955
Congo	20 Sep 1960	Jamaica	18 Sep 1962
Costa Rica	2 Nov 1945*	Japan	18 Dec 1956
Côte d'Ivoire	20 Sep 1960	Jordan	14 Dec 1955
Croatia	22 May 1992[3]	Kazakhstan	2 Mar 1992
Cuba	24 Oct 1945*	Kenya	16 Dec 1963
Cyprus	20 Sep 1960	Kiribati	14 Sep 1999
Czech Republic	19 Jan 1993*[5]	Kuwait	14 May 1963
DPRK	17 Sep 1991	Kyrgyzstan	2 Mar 1992
DR Congo	20 Sep 1960	Lao PDR	14 Dec 1955
Denmark	24 Oct 1945*	Latvia	17 Sep 1991
Djibouti	20 Sep 1977	Lebanon	24 Oct 1945*
Dominica	18 Dec 1978	Lesotho	17 Oct 1966
Dominican Republic	24 Oct 1945*	Liberia	2 Nov 1945*
Ecuador	21 Dec 1945	Libya	14 Dec 1955[8]
Egypt	24 Oct 1945*	Liechtenstein	18 Sep 1990
El Salvador	24 Oct 1945*	Lithuania	17 Sep 1991
Equatorial Guinea	12 Nov 1968	Luxembourg	24 Oct 1945*
Eritrea	28 May 1993	Madagascar	20 Sep 1960
Estonia	17 Sep 1991	Malawi	1 Dec 1964
Ethiopia	13 Nov 1945*	Malaysia	17 Sep 1957
Fiji	13 Oct 1970	Maldives	21 Sep 1965
Finland	14 Dec 1955	Mali	28 Sep 1960
France	24 Oct 1945*	Malta	1 Dec 1964
Gabon	20 Sep 1960	Marshall Islands	17 Sep 1991
Gambia	21 Sep 1965	Mauritania	27 Oct 1961
Georgia	31 Jul 1992	Mauritius	24 Apr 1968
Germany	18 Sep 1973[6]	Mexico	7 Nov 1945*
Ghana	8 Mar 1957	Micronesia	17 Sep 1991
Greece	25 Oct 1945*	Monaco	28 May 1993
Grenada	17 Sep 1974	Mongolia	27 Oct 1961
Guatemala	21 Nov 1945*	Montenegro	28 Jun 2006[3]
Guinea	12 Dec 1958	Morocco	12 Nov 1956
Guinea-Bissau	17 Sep 1974	Mozambique	16 Sep 1975

Myanmar	19 Apr 1948
Namibia	23 Apr 1990
Nauru	14 Sep 1999
Nepal	14 Dec 1955
Netherlands	10 Dec 1945*
New Zealand	24 Oct 1945*
Nicaragua	24 Oct 1945*
Niger	20 Sep 1960
Nigeria	7 Oct 1960
Norway	27 Nov 1945*
Oman	7 Oct 1971
Pakistan	30 Sep 1947
Palau	15 Dec 1994
Panama	13 Nov 1945*
Papua New Guinea	10 Oct 1975
Paraguay	24 Oct 1945*
Peru	31 Oct 1945*
Philippines	24 Oct 1945*
Poland	24 Oct 1945*
Portugal	14 Dec 1955
Qatar	21 Sep 1971
ROK	17 Sep 1991
Republic of Moldova	2 Mar 1992
Romania	14 Dec 1955
Russian Federation	24 Oct 1945*[9]
Rwanda	18 Sep 1962
Saint Kitts and Nevis	23 Sep 1983
Saint Lucia	18 Sep 1979
Saint Vincent and the Grenadines	16 Sep 1980
Samoa	15 Dec 1976
San Marino	2 Mar 1992
Sao Tome and Principe	16 Sep 1975
Saudi Arabia	24 Oct 1945*
Senegal	28 Sep 1960
Serbia	1 Nov 2000[3]
Seychelles	21 Sep 1976
Sierra Leone	27 Sep 1961
Singapore	21 Sep 1965
Slovakia	19 Jan 1993*[5]

Slovenia	22 May 1992[3]
Solomon Islands	19 Sep 1978
Somalia	20 Sep 1960
South Africa	7 Nov 1945*
South Sudan	14 July 2011[10]
Spain	14 Dec 1955
Sri Lanka	14 Dec 1955
Sudan	12 Nov 1956
Suriname	4 Dec 1975
Swaziland	24 Sep 1968
Sweden	19 Nov 1946
Switzerland	10 Sep 2002
Syrian AR	24 Oct 1945*[11]
Tajikistan	2 Mar 1992
Thailand	16 Dec 1946
The former Yugoslav Republic of Macedonia	8 Apr 1993[3]
Timor-Leste	27 Sep 2002
Togo	20 Sep 1960
Tonga	14 Sep 1999
Trinidad and Tobago	18 Sep 1962
Tunisia	12 Nov 1956
Turkey	24 Oct 1945*
Turkmenistan	2 Mar 1992
Tuvalu	5 Sep 2000
Uganda	25 Oct 1962
Ukraine	24 Oct 1945*
UAE	9 Dec 1971
UK	24 Oct 1945*
UR of Tanzania	14 Dec 1961[12]
USA	24 Oct 1945*
Uruguay	18 Dec 1945*
Uzbekistan	2 Mar 1992
Vanuatu	15 Sep 1981
Venezuela	15 Nov 1945*
Viet Nam	20 Sep 1977
Yemen	30 Sep 1947[13]
Zambia	1 Dec 1964
Zimbabwe	25 Aug 1980

Notes

* Original members, i.e., those that participated in the UN Conference on International Organisation at San Francisco or had previously signed the UN Declaration of 1 January 1942, and that signed and ratified the Charter. Although Poland was not represented at San Francisco, it was agreed that it should sign the Charter subsequently as an original member.

continued next page

1. On 22 December 2001, the Islamic State of Afghanistan informed the UN it had changed its name to Afghanistan.

2. On 14 February 2002, the State of Bahrain informed the UN it had changed its name to the Kingdom of Bahrain.

3. The Socialist Federal Republic of Yugoslavia was an original member of the UN (the Charter having been signed on its behalf on 26 June 1945 and ratified on 19 October 1945) until its dissolution following the establishment and subsequent admission as new members of Bosnia and Herzegovina, the Republic of Croatia, the Republic of Slovenia, the former Yugoslav Republic of Macedonia and the Federal Republic of Yugoslavia. The Federal Republic of Yugoslavia did not automatically succeed to memberships held by the former Socialist Federal Republic of Yugoslavia. On 4 February 2003, the Federal Republic of Yugoslavia informed the UN that it had changed its name to Serbia and Montenegro. On 3 June 2006, the Republic of Serbia notified the UN that the membership of the State Union of Serbia and Montenegro in the UN, including all organs and organisations of the UN system, was continued by the Republic of Serbia on the basis of article 60 of the Constitutional Charter of Serbia and Montenegro, activated by the Declaration of Independence adopted by the National Assembly of Montenegro on 3 June 2006. The Republic of Montenegro was admitted as a member of the UN on 28 June 2006. In February 2008, the Assembly of Kosovo declared independence although it has yet to seek UN membership.

4. By GA res. 2758 (XXVI) (1971), the General Assembly decided to restore all its rights to the People's Republic of China and to recognise the representatives of its government as the only legitimate representatives of China in the UN.

5. Formerly part of Czechoslovakia, an original member of the UN from 24 October 1945.

6. Through the accession of the German Democratic Republic to the Federal Republic of Germany, with effect from 3 October 1990, the two German states united to form one sovereign state. As from the date of reunification, the Federal Republic of Germany acts in the UN under the designation 'Germany'.

7. Indonesia withdrew from membership of the UN in 1965, but resumed full participation in 1966.

8. In September 2011, the UN recognised the change of state name from 'Libyan Arab Jamahiriya' to 'Libya'.

9. The USSR was an original member of the UN from 24 October 1945. In 1991, the Russian Federation informed the Secretary-General that the membership of the Soviet Union in the Security Council and all other UN organs was being continued by the Russian Federation with the support of the 11 member countries of the Commonwealth of Independent States.

10. The Republic of South Sudan was admitted as the 193rd UN member on 14 July 2011.

11. Syria withdrew in 1958 to unite with Egypt as the United Arab Republic, but resumed its independent status and separate membership of the UN in 1961.

12. Tanganyika was a member of the UN from 1961 and Zanzibar from 1963. After 1964, they continued as a single member, the United Republic of Tanganyika and Zanzibar, which later became the United Republic of Tanzania.

13. On 22 May 1990, Democratic Yemen and the Arab Republic of Yemen became a single sovereign state called the Republic of Yemen. Both had previously been members of the UN, Democratic Yemen since 14 December 1967 and the Arab Republic of Yemen since 30 September 1947.

MEMBERS OF THE GENERAL ASSEMBLY ARRANGED IN CURRENT REGIONAL GROUPS

African states

Algeria	DR Congo	Liberia
Angola	Djibouti	Libya
Benin	Egypt	Madagascar
Botswana	Equatorial Guinea	Malawi
Burkina Faso	Eritrea	Mali
Burundi	Ethiopia	Mauritania
Cameroon	Gabon	Mauritius
Cape Verde	Gambia	Morocco
Central African Republic	Ghana	Mozambique
Chad	Guinea	Namibia
Comoros	Guinea-Bissau	Niger
Congo	Kenya	Nigeria
Côte d'Ivoire	Lesotho	Rwanda

Sao Tome and Principe
Senegal
Seychelles
Sierra Leone
Somalia

South Africa
South Sudan
Sudan
Swaziland
Togo

Tunisia
Uganda
UR of Tanzania
Zambia
Zimbabwe

Asia–Pacific

Afghanistan
Bahrain
Bangladesh
Bhutan
Brunei Darussalam
Cambodia
China
Cyprus
DPRK
Fiji
India
Indonesia
Iran
Iraq
Japan
Jordan
Kazakhstan
Kuwait

Kyrgyzstan
Lao PDR
Lebanon
Malaysia
Maldives
Marshall Islands
Micronesia
Mongolia
Myanmar
Nauru
Nepal
Oman
Pakistan
Palau
Papua New Guinea
Philippines
Qatar
ROK

Samoa
Saudi Arabia
Singapore
Solomon Islands
Sri Lanka
Syrian AR
Tajikistan
Thailand
Timor-Leste
Tonga
Turkmenistan
Tuvalu
UAE
Uzbekistan
Vanuatu
Viet Nam
Yemen

Eastern European states

Albania
Armenia
Azerbaijan
Belarus
Bosnia and Herzegovina
Bulgaria
Croatia
Czech Republic

Estonia
Georgia
Hungary
Latvia
Lithuania
Montenegro
Poland
Republic of Moldova

Romania
Russian Federation
Serbia
Slovakia
Slovenia
The former Yugoslav Republic
   of Macedonia
Ukraine

Latin American and Caribbean states

Antigua and Barbuda
Argentina
Bahamas
Barbados
Belize
Bolivia
Brazil
Chile
Colombia
Costa Rica
Cuba
Dominica

Dominican Republic
Ecuador
El Salvador
Grenada
Guatemala
Guyana
Haiti
Honduras
Jamaica
Mexico
Nicaragua

Panama
Paraguay
Peru
Saint Kitts and Nevis
Saint Lucia
Saint Vincent and the
   Grenadines
Suriname
Trinidad and Tobago
Uruguay
Venezuela

continued next page

Western European and Other states

Andorra	Iceland	Norway
Australia	Ireland	Portugal
Austria	Israel	San Marino
Belgium	Italy	Spain
Canada	Liechtenstein	Sweden
Denmark	Luxembourg	Switzerland
Finland	Malta	
France	Monaco	Turkey
Germany	Netherlands	UK
Greece	New Zealand	

Notes

The United States of America is not a member of any regional group, but attends meetings of the Western European and Other States Group (WEOG) as an observer and is considered to be a member of that group for electoral purposes.

Turkey participates fully in both the Asia–Pacific group and WEOG but, for electoral purposes, is considered a member of WEOG only.

Israel became a full member of WEOG on a temporary basis on 28 May 2000.

As at 31 May 2012, Kiribati was not a member of any regional group.

The Holy See is a non-Member State that has observer status in the UN.

By GA res. 52/250 (1998) the General Assembly conferred upon Palestine, in its capacity as observer, additional rights and privileges of participation. These included the right to participation in the general debate of the General Assembly but did not include the rights to vote or put forward candidates.

SESSIONS AND OFFICERS

RULES GOVERNING SESSIONS

GA res. 57/301 (2002) amended rule 1 of the rules of procedure of the Assembly to read: "The General Assembly shall meet every year in regular session commencing on the Tuesday of the third week in September, counting from the first week that contains at least one working day". It was further decided that, with effect from the 58th regular session, the general debate of the General Assembly should open on the Tuesday following the opening of the regular session and should be held without interruption over a period of nine working days. Sessions are held at UN Headquarters (New York), unless convened elsewhere following a decision of the General Assembly at a previous session, or at the request of a majority of UN members.

Special sessions may be summoned by the General Assembly, at the request of the Security Council, or at the request or concurrence of a majority of UN members. Unless the date for a special session has been fixed by the General Assembly, it must be held within 15 days of receipt by the Secretary-General of the request or notification of concurrence. The Secretary-General must notify members at least 14 days in advance of the opening of a special session summoned at the request of the Security Council; otherwise 10 days' notice is required.

Emergency special sessions must be convened within 24 hours of receipt by the Secretary-General of a request from the Security Council, on the vote of any nine of its members, or of a request or notification of concurrence from a majority of UN members. Members must be given at least 12 hours' notice.

SESSIONS AND PRESIDENTS OF THE GENERAL ASSEMBLY SINCE 1946

The President of the General Assembly and the 21 Vice-Presidents are elected by the General Assembly. They hold office until the close of the session at which they are elected.

1st Regular, 1946:
Paul-Henri Spaak, Belgium

1st Special, Apr 1947
Question of Palestine:
Oswaldo Aranha, Brazil

2nd Regular, 1947:
Oswaldo Aranha, Brazil

2nd Special, Apr 1948
Question of Palestine:
Jose Arce, Argentina

3rd Regular, 1948–49:
H V Evatt, Australia

4th Regular, 1949:
Brigadier-General
Carlos P Romulo, Philippines

5th Regular, 1950–51:
Nasrollah Entezam, Iran

6th Regular, 1951–52:
Luis Padilla Nervo, Mexico

7th Regular, 1952–53:
Lester B Pearson, Canada

8th Regular, 1953:
Vijaya Lakshmi Pandit, India

9th Regular, 1954:
E N van Kleffens,
Netherlands

10th Regular, 1955:
Jose Maza, Chile

1st Emergency Special,
Nov 1956
Suez Canal:
Rudecindo Ortega, Chile

2nd Emergency Special,
Nov 1956
Situation in Hungary:
Rudecindo Ortega, Chile

11th Regular, 1956–57:
Prince Wan Waithayakon,
Thailand

12th Regular, 1957:
Sir Leslie Munro,
New Zealand

3rd Emergency Special,
Aug 1958
Situation in Lebanon:
Sir Leslie Munro,
New Zealand

13th Regular, 1958:
Charles Malik, Lebanon

14th Regular, 1959:
V A Belaunde, Peru

4th Emergency Special,
Sep 1960
*Situation in the Congo
(Leopoldville):*
V A Belaunde, Peru

15th Regular, 1960–61:
Frederick Boland, Ireland

3rd Special, Aug 1961
Grave Situation in Tunisia:
Frederick Boland, Ireland

16th Regular, 1961–62:
Mongi Slim, Tunisia

17th Regular, 1962:
Sir M Zafrulla Khan, Pakistan

4th Special, May 1963
*Consideration of the Financial
Situation of the Organisation:*
Sir M Zafrulla Khan, Pakistan

18th Regular, 1963:
C Sosa Rodriguez, Venezuela

19th Regular, 1964–65:
Alex Quaison-Sackey, Ghana

20th Regular, 1965:
Amintore Fanfani, Italy

21st Regular, 1966:
Abdul Rahman Pazhwak,
Afghanistan

5th Special, Apr 1967
*South West Africa and the
Postponement to 1968 of
the UN Conference on the
Exploration and Peaceful
Uses of Outer Space:*
Abdul Rahman Pazhwak,
Afghanistan

5th Emergency Special,
Jun 1967
*Humanitarian Assistance:
Question of the Middle East:*
Abdul Rahman Pazhwak,
Afghanistan

22nd Regular, 1967–68:
Corneliu Manescu, Romania

23rd Regular, 1968:
E Arenales, Guatemala

24th Regular, 1969:
Angie Brooks, Liberia

25th Regular, 1970:
Edvard Hambro, Norway

26th Regular, 1971:
Adam Malik, Indonesia

27th Regular, 1972:
Stanislaw Trepczynski, Poland

28th Regular, 1973:
Leopoldo Benites, Ecuador

6th Special, Apr 1974
*New International Economic
Order:*
Leopoldo Benites, Ecuador

29th Regular, 1974:
Abdelaziz Boutefliika, Algeria

7th Special, Sep 1975
*Development and International
Economic Cooperation and
Establishment of a New
International Economic Order:*
Abdelaziz Boutefliika, Algeria

30th Regular, 1975:
Gaston Thorn, Luxembourg

31st Regular, 1976:
H Shirley Amerasinghe,
Sri Lanka

32nd Regular, 1977:
Lazar Mojsov, Yugoslavia

8th Special, Apr 1978
*Financing of UN Interim
Force in Lebanon:*
Lazar Mojsov, Yugoslavia

9th Special, Apr 1978
Namibia:
Lazar Mojsov, Yugoslavia

10th Special, Jun 1978
Disarmament:
Lazar Mojsov, Yugoslavia

33rd Regular, 1978–79:
I Lievano, Colombia

34th Regular, 1979–80:
Salim A Salim,
UR of Tanzania

6th Emergency Special,
Jan 1980
Situation in Afghanistan:
Salim A Salim,
UR of Tanzania

7th Emergency Special,
Jul 1980
Question of Palestine:
Salim A Salim,
UR of Tanzania

11th Special, Aug 1980
*Critical Economic Situation
of Many Developing Countries:*
Salim A Salim, UR of
Tanzania

35th Regular, 1980–81:
Rüdiger von Wechmar,
FR Germany

8th Emergency Special,
Sep 1981
Question of Namibia:
Rüdiger von Wechmar,
FR Germany

36th Regular, 1981–82:
Ismat T Kittani, Iraq

9th Emergency Special,
Jan 1982
*Situation in the Occupied
Arab Territories, the
Syrian Golan Heights:*
Ismat T Kittani, Iraq

7th Emergency Special
(resumed), Apr, Jun, Aug,
Sep 1982
Question of Palestine:
Presided over by:
Ismat T Kittani, Iraq,
Apr, Jun, Aug 1982
Imre Hollai, Hungary,
Sep 1982

12th Special, Jun 1982
Disarmament:
Ismat T Kittani, Iraq

37th Regular, 1982–83:
Imre Hollai, Hungary

38th Regular, 1983–84:
Jorge E Illueca, Panama

39th Regular, 1984–85:
Paul J F Lusaka, Zambia

40th Regular, 1985–86:
Jaime de Pinies, Spain

13th Special, May 1986
*Critical Economic Situation
in Africa:*
Jaime de Pinies, Spain

41st Regular, 1986–87:
H R Choudhury, Bangladesh

14th Special, Sep 1986
Namibia:
H R Choudhury, Bangladesh

42nd Regular, 1987–88:
Peter Florin, German DR

15th Special, May–Jun 1988
Disarmament:
Peter Florin, German DR

43rd Regular, 1988–89:
Dante M Caputo, Argentina

44th Regular, 1989–90:
Joseph N Garba, Nigeria

16th Special, 1989
*Apartheid and its Destructive
Consequences in Southern Africa:*
Joseph N Garba, Nigeria

17th Special, Feb 1990
*Question of International
Cooperation Against Illicit
Production, Supply, Demand,
Trafficking and Distribution
of Narcotic Drugs:*
Joseph N Garba, Nigeria

18th Special, Apr 1990
*Devoted to International
Economic Cooperation,
in particular to the
Revitalisation of Economic
Growth and Development
of Developing Countries:*
Joseph N Garba, Nigeria

45th Regular, 1990–91:
Guido de Marco, Malta

46th Regular, 1991–92:
Samir Shihabi, Saudi Arabia

47th Regular, 1992–93:
Stoyan Ganev, Bulgaria

48th Regular, 1993–94:
Samuel R Insanally, Guyana

49th Regular, 1994–95:
Amara Essy, Côte d'Ivoire

50th Regular, 1995–96:
Diogo Freitas do Amaral,
Portugal

51st Regular, 1996–97:
Razali Ismail, Malaysia

10th Emergency Special,
Apr 1997
*Illegal Israeli Actions in Occupied
East Jerusalem and the Rest of the
Occupied Palestinian Territory:*
Razali Ismail, Malaysia

19th Special, Jun 1997
*Review and Appraisal of the
Implementation of Agenda 21:*
Razali Ismail, Malaysia

10th Emergency Special
(resumed), Jul, Nov 1997,
Mar 1998, Feb 1999,
Oct 2000
*Illegal Israeli Actions in
Occupied East Jerusalem and the
Rest of the Occupied Palestinian
Territory:*
Presided over by:
Razali Ismail, Malaysia,
Jul 1997

Hennadiy Udovenko,
Ukraine, Nov 1997, Mar 1998

Didier Opertti Badan,
Uruguay, Feb 1999

Harri Holkeri, Finland,
Oct 2000

52nd Regular, 1997–98:
Hennadiy Udovenko, Ukraine

20th Special, Jun 1998
*Devoted to Countering the
World Drug Problem Together:*
Hennadiy Udovenko, Ukraine

53rd Regular, 1998–99:
Didier Opertti Badan,
Uruguay

21st Special, Jun–Jul 1999
*Review and Appraisal of
the Implementation of the
Programme of Action of
the International Conference
on Population and Development:*
Didier Opertti Badan,
Uruguay

54th Regular, 1999–2000:
Theo-Ben Gurirab, Namibia

22nd Special, Sep 1999
*Review and Appraisal of
the Implementation of the
Programme of Action for
the Sustainable Development
of Small Island Developing
States:*
Theo-Ben Gurirab, Namibia

23rd Special, 5–9 Jun 2000
*Women 2000: Gender Equality,
Development and Peace for the
Twenty-First Century:*
Theo-Ben Gurirab, Namibia

24th Special, 26–30 Jun 2000
*World Summit for Social
Development and Beyond:
Achieving Social Development
for All in a Globalising World:*
Theo-Ben Gurirab, Namibia

55th Regular, 2000–01:
Harri Holkeri, Finland

25th Special, 6–8 Jun 2001
*Overall Review and Appraisal
of the Implementation of the
Outcome of the UN Conference
on Human Settlements
(Habitat II):*
Harri Holkeri, Finland

26th Special, 25–27 Jun 2001
HIV/AIDS:
Harri Holkeri, Finland

56th Regular, 2001–02:
Han Seung-Soo, ROK

10th Emergency Special
(resumed), Dec 2001,
May 2002, Aug 2002
*Illegal Israeli Actions in Occupied
East Jerusalem and the Rest of the
Occupied Palestinian Territory:*
Han Seung-Soo, ROK

27th Special, 8–10 May 2002
Children:
Han Seung-Soo, ROK

57th Regular, 2002–03:
Jan Kavan, Czech Republic

58th Regular, 2003–04:
Julian Hunte, Saint Lucia

10th Emergency Special
(resumed), Sep, Oct, Dec 2003
*Illegal Israeli Actions in Occupied
East Jerusalem and the Rest of the
Occupied Palestinian Territory:*
Julian Hunte, Saint Lucia

59th Regular, 2004–05:
Jean Ping, Gabon

60th Regular, 2005–06:
Jan Eliasson, Sweden

61st Regular, 2006–07:
Haya Rashed Al Khalifa,
Bahrain

62nd Regular, 2007–08:
Srgjan Kerim, the former
Yugoslav Republic of
Macedonia

63rd Regular, 2008–09:
Miguel D'Escoto Brockmann,
Nicaragua

64th Regular, 2009–10:
Ali Abdussalam Treki, Libya

65th Regular, 2010–11:
Joseph Deiss, Switzerland

66th Regular, 2011–12:
Nassir Abdulaziz Al-Nasser,
Qatar

67th Regular, 2012–13:
Vuk Jeremić, Serbia

OFFICE HOLDERS: 67TH REGULAR SESSION

Session dates

From 18 September 2012. The General Debate is scheduled to be held from 25 to 28 September and 1 October 2012.

President

Vuk Jeremić, Serbia

21 Vice-Presidents

Comprising the representatives of the five permanent members of the Security Council (China, France, Russian Federation, UK and USA) and:

Afghanistan	Honduras	Palau
Algeria	Israel	Peru
Angola	Kenya	Sierra Leone
Bangladesh	Lebanon	Trinidad and Tobago
Congo	Nepal	
Ghana	Netherlands	

First Committee: Disarmament and International Security

Chair	Vice-Chairs	Rapporteur
Not confirmed at the time of printing	Not confirmed at the time of printing	Not confirmed at the time of printing

Second Committee: Economic and Financial

Chair	Vice-Chairs	Rapporteur
Not confirmed at the time of printing	Not confirmed at the time of printing	Not confirmed at the time of printing

Third Committee: Social, Humanitarian and Cultural

Chair	Vice-Chairs	Rapporteur
Not confirmed at the time of printing	Not confirmed at the time of printing	Not confirmed at the time of printing

Fourth Committee: Special Political and Decolonization

Chair	Vice-Chairs	Rapporteur
Not confirmed at the time of printing	Not confirmed at the time of printing	Not confirmed at the time of printing

Fifth Committee: Administrative and Budgetary

Chair	Vice-Chairs	Rapporteur
Not confirmed at the time of printing	Not confirmed at the time of printing	Not confirmed at the time of printing

Sixth Committee: Legal

Chair	Vice-Chairs	Rapporteur
Not confirmed at the time of printing	Not confirmed at the time of printing	Not confirmed at the time of printing

OFFICE HOLDERS: 66TH REGULAR SESSION

Session dates

From 13 September 2011. The General Debate was held from 21 to 24 and 26 to 27 September 2011.

President

Nassir Abdulaziz Al-Nasser, Qatar

21 Vice-Presidents

Comprising the representatives of the five permanent members of the Security Council (China, France, Russian Federation, UK and USA) and:

Australia	Haiti	Mauritius
Austria	Hungary	Morocco
Benin	Iran	ROK
Bolivia	Kuwait	Uruguay
Chad	Liberia	
Fiji	Malawi	

First Committee: Disarmament and International Security

Chair	Vice-Chairs	Rapporteur
Jarmo Viinanen, Finland	Amr Aljowaily, Egypt	Archil Gheghechkori, Georgia
	Mohammad Al Mutairi, Kuwait	
	Ayesha Borland, Belize	

Second Committee: Economic and Financial

Chair	Vice-Chairs	Rapporteur
Abulkalam Abdul Momen, Bangladesh	Philippe Donckel, Luxembourg	Raymond Landeveld, Suriname
	Bitrus Vandy Yohanna, Nigeria	
	Denis Zdorov, Belarus	

Third Committee: Social, Humanitarian and Cultural

Chair	Vice-Chairs	Rapporteur
Hussein Haniff, Malaysia	Donnette Critchlow, Guyana	Kadra Ahmed Hassan, Djibouti
	Carolina Popovici, Republic of Moldova	
	Luca Zelioli, Italy	

Fourth Committee: Special Political and Decolonization

Chair	Vice-Chairs	Rapporteur
Simona-Mirela Miculescu, Romania	Mansor Ciss, Senegal	Hasan Abulhasan, Kuwait
	Jim Kelly, Ireland	
	María Waleska Vivas Mendoza, Venezuela	

Fifth Committee: Administrative and Budgetary

Chair	Vice-Chairs	Rapporteur
Michel Tommo Monthe, Cameroon	Mariam Saif Abdulla Al-Shamisi, UAE	Noel González Segura, Mexico
	Paul Ballantyne, New Zealand	
	Jelena Plakalović, Serbia	

Sixth Committee: Legal

Chair	Vice-Chairs	Rapporteur
Hernán Salinas Burgos, Chile	Mattanee Kaewpanya, Thailand	Jacqueline K Moseti, Kenya
	Ceta Noland, Netherlands	
	Petr Válek, Czech Republic	

STRUCTURE

The following are established under the General Assembly's rules of procedure:
- Main committees
- Procedural committees
- Standing committees
- Subsidiary bodies.

Treaty bodies established by human rights conventions also report to the General Assembly on their activities.

MAIN COMMITTEES

Internet: www.un.org/ga (follow link to 'Main Committees')

Purpose

The Main Committees consider agenda items referred to them by the General Assembly and prepare recommendations and draft resolutions for submission to the General Assembly plenary. The Committees correspond to the General Assembly's major fields of responsibility:

- First Committee (Disarmament and International Security Committee)
- Second Committee (Economic and Financial Committee)
- Third Committee (Social, Humanitarian and Cultural Committee)
- Fourth Committee (Special Political and Decolonization Committee)
- Fifth Committee (Administrative and Budgetary Committee)
- Sixth Committee (Legal Committee).

Evolution

GA res. 2837 (XXVI) (1971) increased the number of Main Committee vice-chairs to two per committee. By GA res. 47/233 (1993) the General Assembly decided to merge the Special Political Committee and the Fourth Committee, thereby reducing the number of Main Committees from seven to six. In GA res. 48/264 (1994) the General Assembly decided on a pattern for election of the six Chairs, reviewing this arrangement at its 53rd session. By GA res. 52/163 (1997) the General Assembly decided that each Main Committee would elect a chair, three vice-chairs and a rapporteur. GA res. 56/509 (2002) provided for the election of the President, Vice-Presidents and Chairs at least three months before the session over which they were to preside. GA res. 58/126 (2003) provided for the election of the full bureaux three months in advance of the next session.

Structure

All UN members have the right to be represented on each of these committees. Each committee elects its own officers, and decisions are made by a majority of the members present and voting. A majority of the committee constitutes a quorum.

Although it is usual practice to refer most items to a committee, the General Assembly may decide to deal with certain items without doing so.

PROCEDURAL COMMITTEES

General Committee

Internet: www.un.org/ga (follow links from 'Main Committees')

Purpose

The General Committee considers the provisional agenda, supplementary list and requests for the inclusion of additional items on the agenda; allocates items to committees; and submits its report for the approval of the General Assembly. It assists the President in drawing up the agenda for plenary meetings, determining the priority of agenda items, coordinating the proceedings of the committees and in the general conduct of the work of the General Assembly that falls within the President's competence. The General Committee may also make recommendations to the General Assembly concerning the closing date of the session. It may not decide any political question.

Membership

The General Committee comprises the General Assembly President, the 21 Vice-Presidents and the Chairs of the six Main Committees. No two members of the General Committee can be members of the same delegation and the Committee is constituted to ensure its representative character.

Credentials Committee

Internet: www.un.org/ga (follow links from 'Main Committees')

Purpose

The Credentials Committee examines and reports on the credentials of representatives. Any representative to whose admission a member has objected is seated provisionally in the General Assembly, with the same rights as other representatives, until the Committee has reported and the Assembly has given its decision.

Membership

The Committee consists of nine members appointed at the beginning of each session by the General Assembly on the proposal of the President. Members appointed at the 66th session were:

China	Italy	Russian Federation
Costa Rica	Maldives	Senegal
Egypt	Panama	USA

STANDING COMMITTEES

Advisory Committee on Administrative and Budgetary Questions (ACABQ)

Internet: www.un.org/ga/acabq

Purpose

The Advisory Committee on Administrative and Budgetary Questions (ACABQ) was set up at the first session of the General Assembly by GA res. 14(I) A (1946). It examines and reports on the regular and peacekeeping budgets, UN accounts and administrative budgets of the specialised agencies. The Committee also advises the General Assembly on other administrative and financial matters referred to it.

Membership

ACABQ's membership has been expanded a number of times, most recently by GA res. 32/103 (1977), and now stands at 16. Members are appointed by the General Assembly, on the recommendation of the Fifth Committee, on the basis of broad geographical representation, personal qualifications and experience. Members serve for three years, retire by rotation and are eligible for reappointment. Rules 155 and 156 of the rules of procedure state that the Committee shall include at least three financial experts of recognised standing and that these experts may not retire simultaneously. The 16 members of the 2012 Committee are:

Bruno Brant, Brazil	Stafford Oliver Neil, Jamaica
Pavel Chernikov, Russian Federation	Jean Christian Obame, Gabon
Jasminka Dinic, Croatia	Carlos G Ruiz Massieu, Mexico (Vice-Chair)
Collen V Kelapile, Botswana (Chair)	Akira Sugiyama, Japan
Namgya C Khampa, India	Mohammad Mustafa Tal, Jordan
Dietrich Lingenthal, Germany	David Traystman, USA
Peter Maddens, Belgium	Nonye Udo, Nigeria
Richard Moon, UK	Zhang Wanhai, China

Committee on Contributions

Internet: www.un.org/ga/contributions

Purpose

The Committee on Contributions, established by GA res. 14(I) (1946), advises the General Assembly on the apportionment among members of UN expenses, assessments for new members, appeals by members for a change of assessment and application of article 19 in cases of arrears in the payment of assessments.

Meetings

The Committee meets annually for three to four weeks, usually in June. Its 72nd session was held in New York from 4 to 29 June 2012.

Membership

Membership has been expanded a number of times, most recently by GA res. 31/96 (1976), and now stands at 18. Members are selected by the General Assembly, on the recommendation of the Fifth Committee, on the basis of broad geographical representation, personal qualifications and experience. They serve for three years, retire by rotation and are eligible for reappointment. The members are:

Term ending 31 Dec 2012	Term ending 31 Dec 2013	Term ending 31 Dec 2014
Andrzej Abraszewski, Poland	Joseph Acakpo-Satchivi, Benin	NneNne Iwuji-Eme, UK
Meshal Al-Mansour, Kuwait	Gordon Eckersley, Australia (Vice-Chair)	Nikolay Lozinskiy, Russian Federation
Elmi Ahmed Duale, Somalia		Dae-jong Yoo,[3] ROK
Ihor V Humenny, Ukraine	Bernardo Greiver, Uruguay (Chair)	Henrique da Silveira Sardinha Pinto, Brazil
Susan McLurg,[1] USA	Juan Mbomio Ndong Mangue, Equatorial Guinea	Gonke Roscher, Germany
Kazuo Watanabe,[2] Japan	Pedro Luis Pedroso Cuesta, Cuba	Sun Xudong, China
	Thomas Schlesinger, Austria	

Notes

1   Susan McLurg replaced Lisa Spratt who resigned effective from 3 May 2012.

2   Kazuo Watanabe replaced Shigeki Sumi who resigned effective from 1 February 2012.

3   Dae-jong Yoo replaced Hae-Yun Park who resigned effective from 6 February 2012.

SUBSIDIARY AND AD HOC BODIES OF THE GENERAL ASSEMBLY

INTER-GOVERNMENTAL BODIES

Human Rights Council (HRC)

Secretariat of the Human Rights Council
OHCHR
Palais Wilson
52 Rue des Pâquis
CH-1201 Geneva
Switzerland
Telephone: (+41 22) 917 9219
Fax: (+41 22) 917 9011
Internet: www2.ohchr.org/english/bodies/hrcouncil; www2.ohchr.org/english/bodies/chr/special
(HRC Special Procedures)

Purpose

The Human Rights Council (HRC) was established by GA res. 60/251 (2006). It replaced the Commission on Human Rights. The Council is responsible for promoting universal respect for the protection of all human rights and fundamental freedoms for all, without distinction of any kind and in a fair and equal manner. It is mandated to consider violations of human rights, including gross and systemic violations, and to make recommendations. The Council is also expected to promote the effective coordination and mainstreaming of human rights within the UN system.

Structure

The Council is a subsidiary body of the General Assembly. Among the Council's elements is the Universal Periodic Review (UPR) mechanism, which assesses the human rights situations in all 193 UN Member States. Other features include the Advisory Committee, which serves as the Council's 'think tank' to provide it with expertise and advice on thematic human rights issues; and the revised Complaint Procedure mechanism, which allows individuals and organisations to bring complaints about human rights violations to the Council's attention. The Council's Special Procedures are its independent expert mechanisms, which have fact-finding and reporting mandates that provide global coverage of major thematic human rights issues, and currently 10 countries or territories.

Meetings

The Council meets for at least 10 weeks a year over three regular sessions. It is able to convene special sessions at the request of a Council member and with the support of one-third of the Council membership. Working groups of the Council, such as the UPR Working Group, meet separately throughout the year.

Membership

The Council comprises 47 members elected by a majority of General Assembly members (97 votes), whether or not they are present and voting. In order to be suspended, two-thirds of the full electorate is needed.

Membership is based on equitable geographical distribution as follows: Africa 13 seats, Asia–Pacific 13, Eastern Europe six, Latin America and Caribbean eight, Western European and Other states seven. The standard term of membership is three years. After two consecutive terms, members are not eligible for immediate re-election. Memberships expire in December of the last year of the term.

The President for the ongoing cycle of the Council is Laura Dupuy Lasserre, Uruguay. (A new president will be elected in December 2012 or early January 2013 for the 2013 year.)

Membership from 20 June 2011 to 31 December 2012 is as follows. Elections for the 2013–15 term were expected to be held in November 2012.

African states

Angola	2010–13	Libya	2010–13
Benin	2011–14	Mauritania	2010–13
Botswana	2011–14	Mauritius	2009–12
Burkina Faso	2011–14	Nigeria	2009–12
Cameroon	2009–12	Senegal	2009–12
Congo	2011–14	Uganda	2010–13
Djibouti	2009–12		

Asia–Pacific

Bangladesh	2009–12	Malaysia	2010–13
China	2009–12	Maldives	2010–13
India	2011–14	Philippines	2011–14
Indonesia	2011–14	Qatar	2010–13
Jordan	2009–12	Saudi Arabia	2009–12
Kuwait	2011–14	Thailand	2010–13
Kyrgyzstan	2009–12		

Eastern European states

Czech Republic	2011–14	Republic of Moldova	2010–13
Hungary	2009–12	Romania	2011–14
Poland	2010–13	Russian Federation	2009–12

Latin American and Caribbean states

Chile	2011–14	Guatemala	2010–13
Costa Rica	2011–14	Mexico	2009–12
Cuba	2009–12	Peru	2011–14
Ecuador	2010–13	Uruguay	2009–12

Western European and Other states

Austria	2011–14	Spain	2010–13
Belgium	2009–12	Switzerland	2010–13
Italy	2011–14	USA	2009–12
Norway	2009–12		

Universal Periodic Review

Internet: www2.ohchr.org/english/bodies/hrcouncil (follow link to 'Universal Periodic Review')

Purpose

The General Assembly agreed in its resolution 60/251 (2006) that the Human Rights Council (HRC) would "undertake a universal periodic review, based on objective and reliable information, of the fulfilment by each State of its human rights obligations and commitments in a manner which ensures universality of coverage and equal treatment with respect to all States".

Evolution

The Council adopted the Universal Periodic Review (UPR) modalities in June 2007 (A/HRC/RES/5/1). This included decisions that the review of each state would be conducted in a working group chaired by the Council President and composed of Council members. Up to one hour would be set aside in the HRC plenary for adoption of the Working Group's report in respect of each state under review.

The Working Group convenes three two-week sessions a year that are open to participation by HRC members and observer states, and may be observed by other stakeholders. The initial review cycle (2008–11) was four years, with 48 countries reviewed each year.

In 2011, as foreseen when the HRC was created, the Council reviewed its methods of work, including for UPR. The Council subsequently adopted resolution 16/21 and decision 17/119, which introduced adjustments to UPR modalities from the second cycle, which started in May 2012. The second cycle is four-and-a-half years, with the review of 42 countries each year.

The review in the Working Group is a three-and-a-half hour interactive dialogue. Half an hour is allocated to the adoption of the Working Group report. The review is based on information prepared by the state under review. In addition, the Office of the UN High Commissioner for Human Rights compiles information from UN documents and a summary of information provided by other relevant stakeholders. Working Group reports are submitted to the Council for its consideration in plenary. The Council plenary adopts an outcome report in respect of each state.

At its sixth regular session, in September 2007, the HRC adopted a calendar in relation to the (then) 192 UN Member States to be considered during the first four-year cycle of the UPR mechanism. The exact same order of review of the first cycle will be used for the second cycle.[1] The existing general guidelines for the information to be submitted by states under review were adjusted (HRC decision 17/119).

At its 19th regular session, in March 2012, the HRC adopted outcome decisions in respect of the last 28 states reviewed, thus marking the formal closure of the first UPR cycle and the adoption of outcome documents for 193 states.[2]

Meetings

As at 31 May 2012, the Working Group had concluded the first cycle, having held 12 sessions and reviewed all UN states members. The 13th session, the start of the second cycle, was held from 21 May to 4 June 2012.

Notes

1   South Sudan, which formally became a UN Member State in July 2011, was included at the end of the calendar and will be reviewed as the last country in the second cycle.

2   At the time of the review of Sudan, South Sudan was not yet an independent state. However, at the time of the consideration and adoption of the UPR outcome in the Council plenary, South Sudan had become a UN Member State. A specific outcome document was thus adopted for South Sudan.

Human Rights Council Advisory Committee (HRCAC)

Internet: www2.ohchr.org/english/bodies/hrcouncil (follow link to 'Advisory Committee')

Purpose

The Human Rights Council Advisory Committee (HRCAC) provides thematic expertise to the Human Rights Council (HRC), mainly through studies and research-based advice. It is intended to function as a think tank to the Council and to work at its direction.

Evolution

In its decision A/HRC/5/1 of June 2007, the HRC established the Advisory Committee to replace the former Sub-commission on the Promotion and Protection of Human Rights, which was a subsidiary body of the former Commission on Human Rights.

Structure

The Advisory Committee comprises 18 experts, acting in their personal capacity and elected by the HRC. Members serve for three years and are eligible for re-election once. The geographic distribution of experts is: Africa five, Asia–Pacific five, Eastern Europe two, Latin America and Caribbean three, Western European and Others three.

The Committee may convene up to two sessions a year for a maximum of 10 days a year. Additional sessions may be scheduled on an ad hoc basis with the prior approval of the Council. The Advisory Committee may not adopt resolutions or decisions.

Meetings

The Advisory Committee held its inaugural 10-day meeting in 2008. The Committee's first annual session is now convened immediately prior to the Council's March session, while the second session is held in August (Council res. 16/21). The ninth session was scheduled to be held in Geneva from 6 to 10 August 2012. The Committee's annual report is submitted to the Council at its September session and is the subject of an interactive dialogue with the Committee Chair (Council res. 16/21).

Membership

The Advisory Committee's cycle runs from 1 October to 30 September (Council res. 16/21). Elections for the four experts whose term of membership ends in 2012 were to be held at the Council's September 2012 session.

Membership and year of term expiry:

Miguel d'Escoto Brockmann, Nicaragua (2012)

José Antonio Bengoa Cabello, Chile (2013)

Laurence Boisson de Chazournes, France (2014)

Chen Shiqiu, China (2012)

Chung Chinsung, ROK (2013)

Wolfgang Stefan Heinz, Germany (2013)

Latif Hüseynov, Azerbaijan (2014)

Alfred Ntunduguru Karokora, Uganda (2013)

Vladimir Kartashkin, Russian Federation (2013)

Obiora Chinedu Okafor, Nigeria (2014)

Cecilia Rachel V Quisumbing, Philippines (2014)

Anantonia Reyes Prado, Guatemala (2014)

Shigeki Sakamoto, Japan (2013)

Dheerujlall Seetulsingh, Mauritius (2014)

Ahmer Bilal Soofi, Pakistan (2014)

Halima Embarek Warzazi, Morocco (2012)

Jean Ziegler, Switzerland (2012)

Mona Zulficar, Egypt (2013)

Working Groups on Communications and Situations (Complaint Procedure)

Internet: www2.ohchr.org/english/bodies/hrcouncil (follow link to 'Complaint Procedure')

Purpose

The complaint procedure of the Human Rights Council (HRC) addresses consistent patterns of gross and reliably attested violations of all human rights and all fundamental freedoms occurring in any part of the world and under any circumstances. It is based on the former Commission's 1503 procedure, improved to ensure that the procedure is impartial, objective, efficient, victim-oriented and conducted in a timely manner.

The HRC complaint procedure is the only universal complaint procedure covering all human rights and fundamental freedoms in all states. Communications under it are not tied to the acceptance of treaty obligations by the country concerned or the existence of a special procedures mandate.

Structure and complaint procedure

The HRC's complaint procedure comprises two working groups, established in June 2007.

- The Working Group on Communications (WGC) decides on the admissibility of communications in accordance with criteria set out in the Council's resolution A/HRC/RES/5/1, and assesses the merits of allegations of violations, including whether a communication alone or in combination with other communications appears to reveal a consistent pattern of gross and reliably attested violations of human rights and fundamental freedoms. The WGC examines complaints and any replies received from governments with a view to bringing to the attention of the Working Group on Situations any particular situation that appears to reveal a consistent pattern of gross and reliably attested violations of human rights and fundamental freedoms.
- The Working Group on Situations (WGS), on the basis of information and recommendations provided by the WGC, presents the Council with a report on consistent patterns of gross and reliably attested violations of human rights and fundamental freedoms, and makes recommendations to the Council on the course of action to take. Alternatively, it may decide to keep a situation under review or to dismiss a case.

Both working groups, to the greatest extent possible, work on the basis of consensus. In the absence of consensus, decisions are taken by simple majority of the votes. The complaint procedure is confidential so as to enhance cooperation with the state concerned.

The HRC considers, in two closed plenary meetings, situations brought to its attention by the WGS as frequently as needed, but at least once a year.

Meetings

Both working groups meet in private twice a year for five working days each session. The WGC 11th session was scheduled to be held in August 2012. The WGS 10th session was held in June 2012.

Membership

The WGC is composed of five members of the HRC Advisory Committee appointed for three years, renewable once. The members are:

José Bengoa, Chile

Shiqiu Chen, China

Wolfgang Heinz, Germany

Vladimir Kartashkin, Russian Federation

Halima Warzazi, Morocco

The WGS is composed of five representatives of HRC Member States appointed by each regional group to serve in their personal capacity. Members may be re-elected once. The members are:

Siti Hajjar Adnin, Malaysia (Asia–Pacific states)

Christian Guillermet-Fernández, Costa Rica (Latin American and Caribbean states)

Mariusz Lewicki, Poland (Eastern European states)

Mothusi Bruce Rabasha Palai, Botswana (African states)

Ana-Maria Menéndez Pérez, Spain (Western European and Other states)

Expert Mechanism on the Rights of Indigenous Peoples (EMRIP)

Internet: www2.ohchr.org/english/bodies/hrcouncil (follow links to 'Other Subsidiary Bodies' and 'Expert Mechanism on the Rights of Indigenous People')

Purpose

The Expert Mechanism on the Rights of Indigenous Peoples (EMRIP) is a subsidiary expert mechanism of the Human Rights Council (HRC). It was established by the HRC in resolution A/HRC/RES/6/36 of 14 December 2007, and consists of five independent expert members selected by the HRC to provide thematic expertise on the rights of indigenous peoples in the manner and form requested.

Evolution

The Expert Mechanism completed its first study, on the right of indigenous peoples to education, and submitted it to the HRC (A/HRC/12/33) in 2009. It completed its second study, on indigenous peoples and the right to participate in decision making, in 2011. The Expert Mechanism is currently focused on a study on indigenous peoples' languages and cultures.

Meetings

EMRIP meets annually for up to five days, usually in July. Meetings may be open or private and are open to the participation of observers. The fifth session took place from 9 to 13 July 2012.

Membership

Members serve for three years and are eligible for re-election once. There is a strong recommendation that the HRC give due regard to experts of indigenous origin in the selection and appointment process. The members are:

Anastasia Chukhman, Russian Federation
(term expires in 2013)

José Carlos Morales, Costa Rica
(term expires in 2013)

Jannie Lasimbang, Malaysia
(term expires in 2014)

Daniel Titus, South Africa
(term expires in 2015)

Wilton Littlechild, Canada
(term expires in 2014)

Forum on Minority Issues

Internet: www2.ohchr.org/english/bodies/hrcouncil (follow links to 'Other Subsidiary Bodies' and 'Forum on Minority Issues')

Purpose

The Human Rights Council (HRC) established the Forum on Minority Issues in resolution A/HRC/RES/6/15 of 28 September 2007. The Forum is intended to provide a platform for promoting dialogue and cooperation on issues relating to the human rights of people belonging to national or ethnic, religious and linguistic minorities. It provides thematic contributions and expertise to the work of the Independent Expert on minority issues, and identifies best practices, challenges, opportunities and initiatives for implementation of the Declaration on the Rights of Persons Belonging to National or Ethnic, Religious and Linguistic Minorities. The HRC reviewed the Forum's work after four years, as required by resolution 6/15, at its 19th session in March 2012 and adopted resolution A/HRC/RES/19/23 renewing the mandate of the Forum as an annual meeting.

Meetings

The Forum meets each year for two days, which are allocated to thematic discussions. In 2008, the Forum considered minorities and the right to education; in 2009, minorities and effective political participation; in 2010, issues relating to minorities and their effective participation in economic life; and in 2011 focused on guaranteeing the rights of minority women and girls.

The Independent Expert on minority issues is required by resolution 19/23 to guide the Forum's work and prepare its annual meetings. In addition, the Independent Expert is invited to report on the Forum's thematic recommendations, along with recommendations for future thematic subjects, for consideration by the HRC. The fifth session is scheduled to be held from 27 to 28 November 2012 in Geneva.

In accordance with resolution A/HRC/RES/19/23, the Forum is open to participants including: UN Member States; UN mechanisms, bodies and specialised agencies, funds and programmes; inter-governmental organisations, regional organisations and mechanisms in the field of human rights; national human rights institutions and other relevant national bodies; academics; and non-governmental organisations. Experts in the thematic areas covered by the Forum who are members of minorities are particularly encouraged to attend.

A chair, who is an expert on minority issues, is appointed by the HRC President for each session on the basis of regional rotation and in consultation with regional groups. The Chair is also responsible for preparing a summary of the Forum's discussion. Chairs have included Viktória Mohácsi, a Roma and former member of the European Parliament from Hungary; Barbara Lee, USA House of Representatives member (second session); Gita Sen, Professor of Public Policy at the Indian Institute of Management (third session); and Graciela Dixon, former Chief Justice of the Supreme Court of Panama (fourth session).

The Independent Expert on minority issues is Rita Izsák, Hungary, who was appointed in 2011 by the UN High Commissioner for Human Rights.

Social Forum
Internet: www2.ohchr.org/english/bodies/hrcouncil (follow links to 'Other Subsidiary Bodies' and 'Social Forum')

Purpose
The Social Forum serves as a space for dialogue between the UN human rights machinery and Member States, global and regional inter-governmental organisations, non-governmental and civil society organisations and the private sector on issues linked with the environment needed for the promotion of human rights. Since its operation began in 2002, the issue of poverty in all its aspects has dominated the theme and focus of the Social Forum. Since 2008, the reformed Social Forum has focused on emerging and challenging thematic issues such as human rights and climate change, people-centred development and globalisation.

Evolution
The Social Forum was initially set up as a subsidiary body of the former Sub-Commission on the Promotion and Protection of Human Rights, which was the main subsidiary body of the former Commission on Human Rights. The Human Rights Council (HRC) decided, in its resolution 6/13 of 28 September 2007, to preserve the Social Forum and upgraded its status to be a subsidiary body of the HRC, not of its Advisory Committee that replaced the former Sub-Commission.

Meetings
The Social Forum meets annually for three working days. Its 2012 meeting is scheduled to take place from 1 to 3 October in Geneva.

Membership
The Forum is open to a wide range of participants listed in the relevant paragraphs of the HRC's resolution on the Social Forum. The Chair–Rapporteur is appointed for each forum by the HRC's President from candidates nominated by regional groups. Minelik Alemu Getahun, Ethiopia, chaired the 2012 Forum.

Thematic Working Groups of the Human Rights Council

Working Group on the Right to Development

Internet: www2.ohchr.org/english/bodies/hrcouncil (follow links from 'Other Subsidiary Bodies' and 'Intergovernmental Working Groups')

Purpose

The Working Group was set up to:

- Monitor and review progress made in the promotion and implementation of the right to development as elaborated in the Declaration on the Right to Development, providing recommendations and further analysing obstacles to its full enjoyment
- Review reports and any other information submitted by states, UN agencies, other relevant international organisations and non-governmental organisations on the relationship between their activities and the right to development
- Present for the consideration of the Human Rights Council (HRC) a report on its deliberations, including advice to the Office of the UN High Commissioner for Human Rights (OHCHR) with regard to the implementation of the right to development; and suggesting possible programmes of technical assistance, at the request of interested countries, with the aim of promoting the implementation of the right to development.

Evolution

The Working Group was established by the Commission on Human Rights, in its resolution 1998/72, and by the Economic and Social Council (ECOSOC), in its decision 1998/269. The HRC, in its resolution 9/3, renewed the Working Group's mandate until it completes the tasks entrusted to it by the Council in its resolution 4/4. Expert assistance was provided to the Working Group by the Independent Expert on the Right to Development from 1998 to 2004, followed by a five-member High-level Task Force on the Implementation of the Right to Development until May 2010. At its 13th session, in May 2012, the Working Group focused on the refinement of the criteria and operational sub-criteria developed by the Task Force for assessment of the effective implementation of the right to development.

Meetings

The Working Group meets once a year for five working days. The 14th session is scheduled to be held in May 2013.

Membership

The Working Group is open to all UN Member States and observers including UN agencies and civil society organisations. The open-ended Working Group is chaired by a government representative (Tamara Kunanayakam, Sri Lanka).

Intergovernmental Working Group on the Effective Implementation of the Durban Declaration and Programme of Action

Internet: www2.ohchr.org/english/bodies/hrcouncil (follow links from 'Other Subsidiary Bodies' and 'Intergovernmental Working Groups')

Purpose

The Intergovernmental Working Group was created in 2002 as a follow-up mechanism to the World Conference against Racism, Racial Discrimination, Xenophobia and Related Intolerance (Durban, South Africa, 2001).

Evolution

During its inaugural session, 21 to 31 January and 21 March 2003, the Working Group decided to adopt a thematic approach in its future sessions, focusing on critical areas affecting the well-being of the victims of racism (E/CN.4/2003/20).

The Working Group's mandate was transferred from the Commission on Human Rights to the Human Rights Council (HRC) in June 2006 (GA res. 60/251) and extended for three years by HRC resolution 11/12 of 18 June 2009.

Meetings

The Working Group usually meets once a year. Its 10th session is scheduled to take place from 8 to 19 October 2012.

Membership

Membership is open to all UN Member States and observers. The Chair–Rapporteur is Mohamed Siad Douale, Djibouti, who was elected in 2009 and re-elected in 2010 and 2011.

Ad Hoc Committee on the Elaboration of Complementary Standards

Internet: www2.ohchr.org/english/bodies/hrcouncil (follow links from 'Other Subsidiary Bodies' and 'Intergovernmental Working Groups')

Purpose

The Ad Hoc Committee on the Elaboration of Complementary Standards was established by Human Rights Council (HRC) decision 3/103 of 8 December 2006. Its mandate is "to elaborate, as a matter of priority and necessity, complementary standards in the form of either a convention or additional protocol(s) to the International Convention on the Elimination of All Forms of Racial Discrimination, filling the existing gaps in the Convention and also providing new normative standards aimed at combating all forms of contemporary racism, including incitement to racial and religious hatred". The HRC reiterated the mandate of the Ad Hoc Committee in its resolution 6/21 of 28 September 2007.

Meetings

Ad Hoc Committee annual meetings are often held in two parts. The fifth session is scheduled to take place in 2013.

During the third session, preliminary substantive discussions took place on 'Xenophobia' and 'Establishment, Designation or Maintaining of National Mechanisms with Competences to Protect Against and Prevent All Forms and Manifestations of Racism, Racial Discrimination, Xenophobia and Related Intolerance'. At the fourth session, these two topics and a third topic 'Procedural gaps with regard to the International Convention on the Elimination of All Forms of Racial Discrimination' were considered in more depth. These topics and others will be considered at future sessions.

Membership

Membership is open to all Member States and observers. Abdul Samad Minty, South Africa, was elected Chair–Rapporteur of the fourth session.

Group of Independent Eminent Experts (IEE)

Internet: www2.ohchr.org/english/issues/racism/groups/eminent-experts

Purpose

The World Conference against Racism, Racial Discrimination, Xenophobia and Related Intolerance, held in Durban in 2001, adopted the Durban Declaration and Programme of Action (DDPA). This document records a commitment by governments, inter-governmental organisations, national human rights institutions and civil society organisations, including non-governmental organisations, to work together to eradicate racism, racial discrimination, xenophobia and related intolerance.

The DDPA requested the UN High Commissioner for Human Rights cooperate with five independent eminent experts, one from each region, appointed by the UN Secretary-General.

GA res. 56/266 (2002) requested the UN Secretary-General, in accordance with the DDPA, to appoint the experts, one from each region, from among candidates proposed by the (then) Commission on Human Rights Chair, after consultation with the regional groups, to follow implementation of the DDPA provisions.

The Secretary-General appointed the five experts on 16 June 2003, with the Commission defining their terms of reference in its resolution 2002/68. The terms of reference were later adjusted by resolution 2003/30.

GA res. 59/177 (2005) emphasised the central role to be played by the Group in mobilising the necessary political will required for the successful implementation of the DDPA.

The General Assembly has requested the Secretary-General to provide the necessary resources for the effective fulfilment of the mandates of all the follow-up mechanisms, including the Group, on implementation of the DDPA.

Meetings

The Group of Independent Eminent Experts (IEE) has met twice, once in 2003 and once in 2005 (E/CN.4/2005/125). At its second meeting, the experts discussed how best to follow, in cooperation with the UN High Commissioner for Human Rights, implementation of the DDPA provisions. Individual members have participated in seminars, meetings and other UN initiatives in the field of human rights and non-discrimination.

Membership[1]

Prince El Hassan bin Talal, Jordan

Salim Ahmed Salim, former Prime Minister of the UR of Tanzania, former Secretary-General of the Organization of African Unity and former President of the UN General Assembly

Edna Maria Santos Roland, Brazil, General Rapporteur of the World Conference against Racism, Racial Discrimination, Xenophobia and Related Intolerance

Hanna Suchocka, former Prime Minister of Poland

Note

1   Martti Ahtisaari, a former President of Finland, resigned from the Group in 2006 following his appointment by the UN Secretary-General as Special Envoy for Kosovo. As of 31 May 2012, he had not been replaced.

Special Procedures of the Human Rights Council

Internet: www2.ohchr.org/english/bodies/hrcouncil (follow link from 'Special Procedures (Human Rights Experts)')

Purpose

The UN Human Rights Council's 'Special Procedures' are independent human rights experts who investigate and report on thematic or country-specific human rights issues. They cover all sets of rights, including civil, cultural, economic, political and social, and are core to the UN human rights machinery. As independent experts who are able to monitor and rapidly respond to allegations of violations occurring anywhere in the world, they play a critical role in promoting and protecting human rights.

The mandate holders – known as Special Rapporteurs, Independent Experts or Working Group members – serve in their personal capacities. With their mandates established by the Human Rights Council, they are not UN staff members and do not receive salaries or any other financial remuneration for their work. They carry out their mandates through independence, probity, impartiality, equity, honesty and good faith.

Mandate holders conduct studies, visit countries, provide advice, engage in advocacy, raise public awareness and work in partnership with non-governmental organisations. They regularly prepare written submissions, or 'communications', addressed to governments, drawing attention to individual cases or situations where human rights have allegedly been violated. They interact regularly with actual and potential victims of human rights violations, and constitute a unique link between governments, national institutions and civil society.

The Office of the UN High Commissioner for Human Rights (OHCHR) supports 46 Special Procedures mandates (36 thematic and 10 relating to countries or territories) as well as a committee designed to promote greater coordination between the various mandates. OHCHR's Special Procedures Branch provides direct support for the majority of thematic mandates. It also works closely with other parts of OHCHR that service the country mandates and other thematic Special Procedures, and supports their work in the field. OHCHR provides thematic, fact-finding, policy and legal expertise, conducts research and analysis and provides assistance with logistical and administrative matters.

The Special Procedures mandate holders are as follows. Lists can also be found at www2.ohchr.org (follow links from 'Human rights bodies', 'Special Procedures of the Human Rights Council', 'thematic' and 'country' mandates).

Special Rapporteurs, Independent Experts and Working Groups

Mandate	Established	Mandate-holder
Country mandates		
Special Rapporteur on the situation of human rights in Myanmar	1992	Tomás Ojea Quintana, Argentina
Special Rapporteur on the situation of human rights in the Palestinian territories occupied since 1967	1993	Richard Falk, USA

Mandate	Established	Mandate-holder
Independent Expert on the situation of human rights in Somalia	1993	Shamsul Bari, Bangladesh
Special Rapporteur on the situation of human rights in Cambodia	1993	Surya Prasad Subedi, Nepal
Independent Expert on the situation of human rights in Haiti	1995	Michel Forst, France
Special Rapporteur on the situation of human rights in the Democratic People's Republic of Korea	2004	Marzuki Darusman, Indonesia
Independent Expert on the situation of human rights in the Sudan	2009	Mashood Baderin, Nigeria
Special Rapporteur on the situation of human rights in Iran	2011	Ahmed Shaheed, Maldives
Independent Expert on the situation of human rights in Côte d'Ivoire	2011	Doudou Diene, Senegal
Special Rapporteur on the situation of human rights in the Syrian AR	2011	Paulo Pinheiro, Brazil (once the mandate of the Commission of Inquiry on the Syrian AR ends)

Thematic mandates

Mandate	Established	Mandate-holder
Working Group on Enforced or Involuntary Disappearances	1980	Olivier de Frouville, France (Chair–Rapporteur) Ariel Dulitzky, Argentina/USA Jasminka Dzumhur, Bosnia and Herzegovina Osman El-Hajjé, Lebanon Jeremy Sarkin, South Africa
Special Rapporteur on extrajudicial, summary or arbitrary executions	1982	Christof Heyns, South Africa
Special Rapporteur on torture and other cruel, inhuman or degrading treatment or punishment	1985	Juan Mendez, Argentina
Special Rapporteur on freedom of religion or belief	1986	Heiner Bielefeldt, Germany
Special Rapporteur on the sale of children, child prostitution and child pornography	1990	Najat Maalla M'jid, Morocco
Working Group on Arbitrary Detention	1991	El Hadji Malick Sow, Senegal (Chair–Rapporteur) Shaheen Sardar Ali, Pakistan Roberto Garretón, Chile Mads Andenas, Norway Vladimir Tochilovsky, Ukraine
Special Rapporteur on the promotion and protection of the right to freedom of opinion and expression	1993	Frank La Rue, Guatemala

Mandate	Established	Mandate-holder
Special Rapporteur on contemporary forms of racism, racial discrimination, xenophobia and related intolerance	1993	Mutuma Ruteere, Kenya
Special Rapporteur on the independence of judges and lawyers	1994	Gabriela Knaul, Brazil
Special Rapporteur on violence against women, its causes and consequences	1994	Rashida Manjoo, South Africa
Special Rapporteur on the human rights obligations related to environmentally sound management and disposal of hazardous substances and waste	1995	Calin Georgescu, Romania
Special Rapporteur on the right to education	1998	Kishore Singh, India
Special Rapporteur on extreme poverty and human rights	1998	Maria Magdalena Sepúlveda Carmona, Chile
Special Rapporteur on the human rights of migrants	1999	François Crépeau, Canada
Special Rapporteur on adequate housing as a component of the right to an adequate standard of living, and on the right to non-discrimination in this context	2000	Raquel Rolnik, Brazil
Independent Expert on the effects of foreign debt and other related international financial obligations of States on the full enjoyment of human rights, particularly economic, social and cultural rights	2000	Cephas Lumina, Zambia
Special Rapporteur on the right to food	2000	Olivier De Schutter, Belgium
Special Rapporteur on the situation of human rights defenders	2000	Margaret Sekaggya, Uganda
Special Rapporteur on the rights of indigenous peoples	2001	James Anaya, USA
Special Rapporteur on the right of everyone to the enjoyment of the highest attainable standard of physical and mental health	2002	Anand Grover, India
Working Group on people of African descent	2002	Mirjana Najcevska, the former Yugoslav Republic of Macedonia (Chair–Rapporteur) Monorama Biswas, Bangladesh Mireille Fanon-Mendes-France, France Maya Sahli, Algeria Verene Shepherd, Jamaica
Special Rapporteur on the human rights of internally displaced persons	2004	Chaloka Beyani, Zambia
Special Rapporteur on trafficking in persons, especially in women and children	2004	Joy Ngozi Ezeilo, Nigeria

Mandate	Established	Mandate-holder
Working Group on the use of mercenaries as a means of impeding the exercise of the right of peoples to self-determination	2005	Faiza Patel, Pakistan (Chair–Rapporteur) Patricia Arias, Chile Elzbieta Karska, Poland Anton Katz, South Africa Gabor Rona, USA/Hungary
Independent Expert on human rights and international solidarity	2005	Virginia Dandan, Philippines
Special Rapporteur on the promotion and protection of human rights and fundamental freedoms while countering terrorism	2005	Ben Emmerson, UK
Independent Expert on minority issues	2005	Rita Izsák, Hungary
Special Rapporteur on contemporary forms of slavery, including its causes and consequences	2007	Gulnara Shahinian, Armenia
Special Rapporteur on the human right to safe drinking water and sanitation	2008	Catarina de Albuquerque, Portugal
Special Rapporteur in the field of cultural rights	2009	Farida Shaheed, Pakistan
Working Group on the issue of discrimination against women in law and in practice	2010	Kamala Chandrakirana, Indonesia (Chair–Rapporteur) Emna Aouij, Tunisia Mercedes Barquet, Mexico Frances Raday, Israel/UK Eleonora Zielinska, Poland
Special Rapporteur on the rights to freedom of peaceful assembly and of association	2010	Maina Kiai, Kenya
Independent Expert on the promotion of a democratic and equitable international order	2011	Alfred De Zayas, USA
Special Rapporteur on the promotion of truth, justice, reparation and guarantees on non-recurrence	2011	Pablo De Greiff, Colombia
Working Group on the issue of human rights and transnational corporations and other business enterprises	2011	Margaret Jungk, USA (Chair–Rapporteur) Michael K Addo, Ghana Alexandra Guaqueta, Colombia/USA Puvan J Selvanathan, Malaysia Pavel Sulyandziga, Russian Federation
Independent Expert on the issue of human rights obligations related to the enjoyment of a safe, clean, healthy and sustainable environment	2012	John Knox, USA

OTHER INTER-GOVERNMENTAL BODIES

Ad Hoc Committee on the Indian Ocean

Internet: www.un.org/en/ga/about/subsidiary/committees (see under 'Ad hoc Committees')

Purpose

The Ad Hoc Committee on the Indian Ocean was established by GA res. 2992 (XXVII) (1972) to study the implications of the Declaration of the Indian Ocean as a Zone of Peace (GA res. 2832 (XXVI) (1971)).

Evolution

Following GA res. 32/86 (1977), a meeting of the Indian Ocean coastal and hinterland states was held in New York in 1979 as a step towards convening a conference on the Indian Ocean. However, efforts at reaching a consensus on when the conference should be held have not been successful. GA res. 46/49 (1991) decided the conference should be structured in more than one stage and that the first stage should be convened in Colombo, Sri Lanka, in 1993 or as soon as possible. The Committee has not yet been able to reach consensus on the implementation of the Declaration.

GA res. 66/22 (2011) requested the Committee Chair to continue informal consultations with members and report through the Committee to the General Assembly at its 68th session.

Membership

Originally 15 members, the Committee has been progressively enlarged, most recently by GA res. 34/80 (1979). Further changes to membership were brought about by the reunification of Germany; General Assembly resolutions regarding the Socialist Federal Republic of Yugoslavia; and the 6 April 1990 withdrawal from the Committee of France, UK and USA. The Committee now comprises 43 members:

Australia (Vice-Chair)	Japan	Russian Federation
Bangladesh	Kenya	Seychelles
Bulgaria	Liberia	Singapore
Canada	Madagascar (Rapporteur)	Somalia
China	Malaysia	Sri Lanka (Chair)
Djibouti	Maldives	Sudan
Egypt	Mauritius	Thailand
Ethiopia	Mozambique (Vice-Chair)	Uganda
Germany	Netherlands	UAE
Greece	Norway	UR of Tanzania
India	Oman	Yemen
Indonesia (Vice-Chair)	Pakistan	Zambia
Iran	Panama	Zimbabwe
Iraq	Poland	
Italy	Romania	

Observers

Nepal	South Africa	Sweden

Ad Hoc Committee established by the General Assembly in its resolution 51/210 of 17 December 1996

Internet: www.un.org/law/terrorism

Purpose

GA res. 51/210 (1996) established an ad hoc committee to develop an international convention for the suppression of terrorist bombings and, subsequently, an international convention for the suppression of acts of nuclear terrorism. These were intended to supplement related existing international instruments and address ways of further developing a comprehensive legal framework of conventions dealing with international terrorism.

Evolution

The Ad Hoc Committee has negotiated several texts resulting in the adoption of three treaties:

- The International Convention for the Suppression of Terrorist Bombings (1997)
- The International Convention for the Suppression of the Financing of Terrorism (1999)
- The International Convention for the Suppression of Acts of Nuclear Terrorism (2005).

In 2000, the Committee began preparing a draft comprehensive convention on international terrorism. In accordance with GA res. 65/34 (2010), the Committee was to continue to elaborate the draft and discuss the question of convening a high-level conference under the auspices of the UN to formulate an international community response to terrorism in all its forms and manifestations (GA res. 51/210 (1996) and 54/110 (1999)).

The Committee will not be convened in 2012, but will be reconvened in 2013, on dates to be decided at the General Assembly 67th session, to continue to elaborate the draft convention and discuss the question of a high-level conference.

The General Assembly also decided (res. 66/105) that, at its 67th session, the Sixth Committee would establish a working group with a view to finalising the draft convention and continue discussions on a conference.

Membership

Membership of the Committee is open to all Member States, members of the specialised agencies and International Atomic Energy Agency. The officers of the Committee are:

Chair	Vice-Chairs	Rapporteur
Rohan Perera, Sri Lanka	Ana Cristina Rodríguez-Pineda, Guatemala	Petr Válek, Czech Republic
	Maria Telalian, Greece	
	Dire David Tladi, South Africa	

UN Counter-Terrorism Implementation Task Force (CTITF)

United Nations
1 United Nations Plaza
TB-08004A
New York, NY 10017
United States of America
Telephone: (+1 212) 963 4134
Fax: (+1 212) 963 4199
Email: trezza@un.org
Internet: www.un.org/en/terrorism/ctitf
Chair: Robert Orr, USA (appointed by the UN Secretary-General in 2011)

Purpose

The Counter-Terrorism Implementation Task Force (CTITF) was established by the UN Secretary-General in 2005 to enhance the UN system's coordination and coherence of counter-terrorism efforts. The Task Force consists of 31 international entities that have a stake in counter-terrorism matters at the multilateral level. In 2009, the CTITF was institutionalised with a secretariat office to coordinate UN counter-terrorism related activities (GA res. A/RES/64/235).

While the primary responsibility for implementation of the UN Global Counter-Terrorism Strategy (GA res. A/RES/60/288) rests with Member States, CTITF ensures the UN system is attuned to the needs of Member States in order to provide them with the necessary support. CTITF also undertakes initiatives and activities that require multi-agency support or are not part of existing mandates of CTITF entities on counter-terrorism matters. CTITF also engages Member States on technical assistance delivery, promoting in-depth knowledge of the Strategy amongst national and regional stakeholders and promoting integrated implementation of the Strategy in key countries. CTITF's mandate in this regard emanates from reviews of the Global Strategy, which were adopted under GA resolutions A/RES/62/272 and A/RES/64/297. The next review was scheduled to take place in June 2012.

The primary goal of CTITF is to maximise each entity's comparative advantage by delivering as one to help Member States implement the four pillars of the Global Strategy, which are measures to: address the conditions conducive to the spread of terrorism; prevent and combat terrorism; build states' capacity to prevent and combat terrorism, and to strengthen the role of the UN system in that regard; and ensure respect for human rights for all and the rule of law as the fundamental basis for the fight against terrorism.

Structure

CTITF organises its work through working groups and counter-terrorism related projects and initiatives. The working groups are:
- Preventing and Resolving Conflict
- Supporting and Highlighting Victims of Terrorism
- Preventing and Responding to WMD (weapons of mass destruction) Terrorist Attacks
- Tackling the Financing of Terrorism
- Countering the Use of the Internet for Terrorist Purposes
- Strengthening the Protection of Vulnerable Targets
- Protecting Human Rights while Countering Terrorism
- Border Management related to Countering Terrorism.

CTITF initiatives are:

- Integrated Assistance for Countering Terrorism (I-ACT) – through which CTITF aims to enhance capacity within the UN system to help interested Member States, upon their request and in a user-friendly way, to implement the UN Global Counter-Terrorism Strategy in an integrated manner.
- Project to Promote the Implementation of the UN Global Counter-Terrorism Strategy at the Regional Level – which aims to familiarise national governments, experts and practitioners on all provisions of the Global Strategy in an in-depth manner in order to develop a multi-stakeholder whole-of-government approach consistent with regional priorities.

CTITF entities

Counter-Terrorism Committee Executive Directorate (CTED)

Department of Peacekeeping Operations (DPKO)

Department of Political Affairs (DPA)

Department of Public Information (DPI)

Department of Safety and Security (UNDSS)

Expert Staff of 1540 Committee

International Atomic Energy Agency (IAEA)

International Civil Aviation Organization (ICAO)

International Maritime Organization (IMO)

International Monetary Fund (IMF)

International Criminal Police Organization (INTERPOL)

Monitoring Team of 1267 Committee

Office for Disarmament Affairs (UNODA)

Office of the UN High Commissioner for Human Rights (OHCHR)

Office of Legal Affairs (OLA)

Office of the Secretary-General (OSG)

Organization for the Prohibition of Chemical Weapons (OPCW)

Special Rapporteur on the promotion and protection of human rights while countering terrorism

UN Development Programme (UNDP)

UN Educational, Scientific and Cultural Organization (UNESCO)

UN Interregional Crime and Justice Research Institute (UNICRI)

UN Office on Drugs and Crime (UNODC)

World Customs Organization (WCO)

World Bank

World Health Organization (WHO)

Observers

Department of Economic and Social Affairs (DESA)

International Organization for Migration (IOM)

Office for the Coordination of Humanitarian Affairs (OCHA)

UN Office of the Special Adviser on Africa (UNOSAA)

UN High Commissioner for Refugees (UNHCR)

UN Alliance of Civilizations

UN Counter-Terrorism Centre

In September 2011, the UK and Saudi Arabia signed a contribution agreement establishing the UN Counter-Terrorism Centre (UNCCT) within the CTITF office.

The UNCCT has four strategic priorities: engaging with Member States on counter-terrorism capacity building issues; facilitating the implementation of all four pillars of the Strategy in an integrated manner; fostering international counter-terrorism cooperation and promoting collaboration between national, regional and international counter-terrorism centres; and generating political support for UN counter-terrorism efforts.

The CTITF Chair is also the UNCCT Executive Director. An Advisory Board of 21 Member States and one international organisation, representing all regions of the world, provides guidance to the Executive Director.

UNCCT members

Saudi Arabia (Chair)	European Union	Norway
Algeria	(guest member)	Pakistan
Argentina	France	Russian Federation
Belgium	Germany	Spain
Brazil	India	Switzerland
China	Indonesia	Turkey
Egypt	Morocco	UK
	Nigeria	USA

Ad Hoc Committee on the Criminal Accountability of United Nations Officials and Experts on Mission

Internet: www.un.org/law/criminalaccountability

Purpose

The General Assembly (res. 61/29 (2006)) established an ad hoc committee to consider the report of the Group of Legal Experts, established by the Secretary-General under GA res. 59/300 (document A/60/980), in particular its legal aspects.

Evolution

The Committee held its first session in April 2007. It recommended that the Sixth Committee, at the General Assembly 62nd session, establish a working group with a view to continuing consideration of the Group of Legal Experts' report, taking into account the views expressed in the Ad Hoc Committee. In its resolution 62/63, the General Assembly decided to reconvene the Committee to continue its consideration of the report, taking into account the views of Member States and the information contained in the Note prepared by the Secretariat (A/62/329).

The Ad Hoc Committee last met in April 2008.

The Committee, in its report (A/63/54), decided to reiterate its recommendation that the Sixth Committee, at the General Assembly 63rd session, establish a working group to continue consideration of the Group of Legal Experts' report, also taking into account the views expressed in the Ad Hoc Committee. Since the 63rd session, the item "criminal accountability of United Nations officials and experts on mission" has been included on the Sixth Committee's agenda for each General Assembly session.

GA res. 66/93 (2011) decided the item would be included on the provisional agenda of the 67th session, and that consideration of the Group of Legal Experts' report, in particular its legal aspects, would be continued at the 67th session in the framework of a working group of the Sixth Committee.

Membership

Membership of the Committee is open to all Member States, members of the specialised agencies and International Atomic Energy Agency. Bureau officers elected at the Committee's April 2008 meeting were:

Chair	Vice-Chairs	Rapporteur
Maria Telalian, Greece	El Hadj Lamine, Algeria	Minna-Liina Lind, Estonia
	Ruddy José Flores Monterrey, Bolivia	
	Zainol Rahim Zainuddin, Malaysia	

Committee on Conferences

Internet: www.un.org/en/ga/conferences

Purpose

The Committee on Conferences recommends to the General Assembly, after consultation, a draft calendar of conferences and meetings. Overlapping of meetings in the same sector of activity is avoided wherever possible. The Committee is also mandated to:

- Recommend the best use of conference-servicing resources, including the introduction of new technology for interpretation, translation and documentation
- Advise on current and future requirements
- Monitor the organisation's publications policy.

Evolution

The Committee was established by GA res. 3351 (XXIX) (1974). GA res. 43/222(B) (1988) retained the Committee as a permanent subsidiary organ and set the membership at 21, on the basis of six members from African states, five from Asia–Pacific states, four from Latin American and Caribbean states, two from Eastern European states, and four from Western European and Other states.

Members are appointed by the General Assembly President, after consultations with the regional group Chairs, for terms of three years. One-third of the Committee's membership retires annually. Retiring members are eligible for reappointment. The Committee agreed at its 1999 substantive session to a procedure for the participation of observers in its work.

Meetings

The Committee holds a substantive session annually. The 2012 session was scheduled to be held from 4 to 10 September.

Membership[1]

Membership of the Committee is:

Term ending 31 Dec 2012	Term ending 31 Dec 2013	Term ending 31 Dec 2014
Côte d'Ivoire	Austria	Congo
Germany	China	France
Nigeria	Ethiopia	Namibia
Panama	Japan	Philippines
Republic of Moldova	Libya	Russian Federation
Syrian AR	USA	
Venezuela	Uruguay	

The officers of the Committee for 2012 are:

Chair	Vice-Chairs[2]	Rapporteur
Carolina Popovici, Republic of Moldova	Carmen Avila, Panama	Felix Ayibanuah Datuowei, Nigeria
	Maria Angela Holzmann, Austria	

Notes

1   As of May 2012, one member from Asia–Pacific states and one member from Latin American and Caribbean states were to be appointed.

2   One vice-chair from Asia–Pacific states was to be nominated.

Committee on Information

Internet: www.un.org/ga/coi

Purpose

GA res. 33/115C (1978) established a committee to review UN public information policies and activities. The Committee comprised 41 Member States appointed by the President of the General Assembly, after consultation with regional groups, on the basis of equitable geographical distribution. It was mandated to report to the General Assembly on the policies and activities of the UN public information services.

Evolution

GA res. 34/182 (1979) changed the Committee's name to the UN Committee on Information, and its membership was increased to 66. By this resolution, the Committee was also requested to:

- Continue to examine UN public information policies and activities in the light of the evolution of international relations, particularly during the past two decades, and the imperatives of the establishment of the new international economic order and a new world information and communication order
- Evaluate and follow up the efforts made and progress achieved by the UN system in the field of information and communications
- Promote the establishment of a new, more just and more effective world information and communication order, intended to strengthen peace and international understanding. This would be based on the principles of free circulation and wider and better-balanced dissemination of information. Recommendations would be made to the General Assembly.

At its organisational session in 1980, the Committee reached an agreement to apply the principle of geographical rotation to all officers and that they would be elected to two-year terms.

Meetings

The Committee meets annually in April/May. The 34th session was held from 23 April to 4 May 2012.

Membership

Membership has increased over the years and now stands at 113. The members are:

African states	Libya	Asia–Pacific states
Algeria	Madagascar	Bangladesh
Angola	Morocco	China
Benin	Mozambique	Cyprus
Burkina Faso	Niger	DPRK
Burundi	Nigeria	India
Cape Verde	Senegal	Indonesia
Congo	Sierra Leone	Iran
Côte d'Ivoire	Somalia	Japan
DR Congo	South Africa	Jordan
Egypt	Sudan	Kazakhstan
Ethiopia	Togo	Lebanon
Gabon	Tunisia	Mongolia
Ghana	UR of Tanzania	Nepal
Guinea	Zambia	Pakistan
Kenya	Zimbabwe	Philippines
Liberia		Qatar

continued next page

ROK
Saudi Arabia
Singapore
Solomon Islands
Sri Lanka
Syrian AR
Thailand
Viet Nam
Yemen

Eastern European states

Armenia
Azerbaijan
Belarus
Bulgaria
Croatia
Czech Republic
Georgia
Hungary
Poland
Republic of Moldova
Romania
Russian Federation
Slovakia
Ukraine

Latin American and
Caribbean states

Antigua and Barbuda
Argentina
Belize
Brazil
Chile
Colombia
Costa Rica
Cuba
Dominican Republic
Ecuador
El Salvador
Guatemala
Guyana
Jamaica
Mexico
Peru
Saint Vincent and the
  Grenadines
Suriname
Trinidad and Tobago
Uruguay
Venezuela

Western European and
Other states

Austria
Belgium
Denmark
Finland
France
Germany
Greece
Iceland
Ireland
Israel
Italy
Luxembourg
Malta
Monaco
Netherlands
Portugal
Spain
Switzerland
Turkey
UK
USA

The Holy See, Palestine and the UN Educational, Scientific and Cultural Organization (UNESCO) participated in the session as observers.

Office holders for the two years 2011–12 are:

Chair

Eduardo Ulibarri, Costa Rica

Vice-Chairs

Guillaume Dabouis, France

Gheorghe Leuca, Moldova

Moses Sayela Walubita, Zambia

Rapporteur

Mohammad Reza Sahraei, Iran

Committee on Relations with the Host Country

Internet: follow link from www.un.org/en/ga/about/subsidiary/committees

Purpose

In general, the Committee deals with questions of the security of missions accredited to the UN and the safety of their staff; issues arising in connection with implementation of the agreement between the UN and USA regarding UN Headquarters; and, more generally, questions regarding privileges and immunities, including the Convention on the Privileges and Immunities of the UN, and other relevant instruments.

If requested by missions accredited to the UN, the UN Secretary-General is authorised to bring to the Committee's attention cases involving infringement of their status.

Evolution

GA res. 2819 (XXVI) (1971) established the Committee by replacing the Informal Joint Committee on Host Country Relations, which was reconvened under GA res. 2618 (XXIV) (1969).

In May 1992, the Committee adopted a detailed list of topics for its consideration. This was modified slightly in March 1994. The list is set out in annex I to the Committee's annual report.

Membership

Until 1998, the Committee comprised the host country and 14 Member States chosen by the General Assembly President. GA res. 53/104 (1998) increased the Committee's membership by four (one each from African, Asia–Pacific, Latin American and Caribbean, and Eastern European states), bringing the total membership to 19.

Meetings

The Committee meets every two months, although emergency meetings can be requested by UN Member States at any time. It has been chaired since 1971 by successive permanent representatives of Cyprus. The members are:

African states	Eastern European states	Western European and Other states
Côte d'Ivoire (Vice-Chair)	Bulgaria (Vice-Chair)	Canada (Vice-Chair)
Libya	Hungary	France
Mali	Russian Federation	Spain
Senegal		UK
	Latin American and	USA
Asia–Pacific states	Caribbean states	
China	Costa Rica (Rapporteur)	
Cyprus (Chair)	Cuba	
Iraq	Honduras	
Malaysia		

Committee on the Exercise of the Inalienable Rights of the Palestinian People

Internet: http://unispal.un.org/unispal.nsf/com.htm

Purpose

By GA res. 3376 (XXX) (1975), the General Assembly established a 20-member committee to consider and recommend to it a programme that would enable the Palestinian people to exercise the rights recognised in GA res. 3236 (XXIX) (1974).

Evolution

By GA res. 66/14 of 30 November 2011, the General Assembly requested that the Committee continue to exert all efforts to promote the realisation of the inalienable rights of the Palestinian people, support the Middle East peace process, and mobilise international support for, and assistance to, the Palestinian people. The General Assembly authorised the Committee to adjust its approved work programme as it considered appropriate and necessary, and report to the General Assembly. It requested the Committee to continue to keep under review the question of Palestine, and to report and make suggestions to the General Assembly, the Security Council or the Secretary-General as appropriate.

The General Assembly also requested the Committee to continue to extend its cooperation and support to Palestinian and other civil society organisations in order to mobilise international solidarity and support for the Palestinian people's achievement of their inalienable rights and a peaceful settlement of the question of Palestine, and to involve additional civil society organisations in its work.

Meetings

The Committee's 2012 opening session and election of its officers (Bureau) took place on 13 February.

Membership

Since 1976, membership has expanded and now consists of 25 Member States[1] and 24 observers. The members of the Committee are:

Afghanistan	Lao PDR	Senegal
Belarus	Madagascar	Sierra Leone
Cuba	Malaysia	South Africa
Cyprus	Mali	Tunisia
Ecuador[1]	Malta	Turkey
Guinea	Namibia	Ukraine
Guyana	Nicaragua	Venezuela
India	Nigeria	
Indonesia	Pakistan	

In December 2011, the Committee approved Saudi Arabia's request to become an observer.

The following elected officers comprise the Bureau of the Committee:

Chair	Vice-Chairs	Rapporteur
Abdou Salam Diallo, Senegal	Pedro Núñez Mosquera, Cuba Zahir Tanin, Afghanistan	Christopher Grima, Malta

Note

1 Ecuador approved for full membership by the Committee on the Exercise of the Inalienable Rights of the Palestinian People, to be confirmed by the General Assembly.

Committee on the Peaceful Uses of Outer Space (COPUOS)

United Nations Office for Outer Space Affairs (UNOOSA)
Vienna International Centre
PO Box 500
A–1400 Vienna
Austria
Telephone: (+43 1) 26060 4950
Fax: (+43 1) 26060 5830
Email: oosa@unoosa.org
Internet: www.unoosa.org
Director: Mazlan Othman, Malaysia (appointed by the UN Secretary-General in 2007)

Purpose

The Committee on the Peaceful Uses of Outer Space (COPUOS) is mandated to:
- Review the scope of international cooperation in peaceful uses of outer space
- Devise programmes in this field that would be undertaken under UN auspices
- Encourage continued research and disseminate information on research
- Study legal problems arising from the exploration of outer space.

Evolution

The General Assembly established COPUOS as a permanent body by GA res. 1472 (XIV) (1959). It succeeded the 18-nation ad hoc committee of the same name established by GA res. 1348 (XIII) (1958).

The General Assembly has authorised the convening of three conferences on the exploration and peaceful uses of outer space. All three were held in Vienna, in 1968, 1982 and 1999. The third, UNISPACE III, adopted The Space Millennium: Vienna Declaration on Space and Human Development, which was endorsed by the General Assembly in GA res. 54/68 (1999).

The Committee has two standing subcommittees:
- Scientific and Technical Subcommittee
- Legal Subcommittee.

Meetings

The Committee meets annually in June.

Membership

The Committee originally comprised 24 members whose terms of office expired at the end of 1961. By GA res. 1721 (XVI) (1961), the General Assembly decided to continue the membership of the Committee and increase it to 28. The membership has since increased further, most recently from 70 to 71 by GA res. 66/71 (2012). The 71 members of COPUOS are:

African states
Algeria
Benin
Burkina Faso
Cameroon
Chad
Egypt
Kenya
Libya
Morocco
Niger
Nigeria
Senegal
Sierra Leone
South Africa
Sudan
Tunisia

Asia–Pacific states
Azerbaijan
China
India
Indonesia
Iran
Iraq
Japan
Kazakhstan

Lebanon
Malaysia
Mongolia
Pakistan
Philippines
ROK
Saudi Arabia
Syrian AR
Thailand
Viet Nam

Eastern European states
Albania
Bulgaria
Czech Republic
Hungary
Poland
Romania
Russian Federation
Slovakia
Ukraine

Latin American and Caribbean states
Argentina
Bolivia
Brazil
Chile

Colombia
Cuba
Ecuador
Mexico
Nicaragua
Peru
Uruguay
Venezuela

Western European and Other states
Australia
Austria
Belgium
Canada
France
Germany
Greece
Italy
Netherlands
Portugal
Spain
Sweden
Switzerland
Turkey
UK
USA

At its 55th session (2012), the Bureau of the Committee comprised the following office holders:

Chair
Yasushi Horikawa, Japan

First Vice-Chair
Filipe Duarte Santos, Portugal

Second Vice-Chair and Rapporteur
Piotr Wolanski, Poland

Chair of the Scientific and Technical Subcommittee
Félix Clementino Menicocci, Argentina

Chair of the Legal Subcommittee
Tare Brisibe, Nigeria

Conference on Disarmament (CD)

Palais des Nations
1211 Geneva 10
Switzerland
Telephone: (+41 22) 917 2281
Fax: (+41 22) 917 0034
Email: cd@unog.ch
Internet: www.unog.ch (follow link from 'Disarmament')
CD Secretary-General and Personal Representative of the UN Secretary-General to the CD: Kassym-Jomart Tokayev, Kazakhstan (appointed by the UN Secretary-General in May 2011)

Purpose

The Conference on Disarmament (CD) is the single multilateral forum for negotiating disarmament.

Evolution

Agreement on establishing the Conference was reached at the General Assembly's First Special Session on Disarmament in 1978 (UNSSOD I res. S10/2). It succeeded the Conference of the Eighteen-Nation Committee on Disarmament (GA res. 1722 (XVI) (1961)) and the Conference of the Committee on Disarmament (GA res. 2602 (XXIV) (1969)), which had met annually in Geneva since 1962 under the co-chairing of the former USSR and the USA.

In 1979, following UNSSOD I, the Conference committed itself to promoting general and complete disarmament under effective international control. It also decided that it would deal with the arms race and disarmament in 10 areas (the 'decalogue'):
- Nuclear weapons in all aspects
- Chemical weapons
- Other weapons of mass destruction
- Conventional weapons
- Reduction of military budgets
- Reduction of armed forces
- Disarmament and development
- Disarmament and international security
- Collateral measures, confidence-building measures and effective verification methods in relation to appropriate disarmament measures, acceptable to all parties concerned
- Comprehensive programme of disarmament leading to general and complete disarmament under effective international control.

Between 1979 and 1984, the Conference was known as the Committee on Disarmament.

The Conference draws its annual agenda from the decalogue, taking into account the recommendations made to it by the General Assembly, proposals presented by Member States of the Conference and the decisions of the Conference. Item 2 of the decalogue ceased to be current after the completion of negotiations on the Chemical Weapons Convention in 1992.

In 1996, the Conference completed negotiations on a Comprehensive Nuclear-Test-Ban Treaty.

The Conference has its own rules of procedure and a special relationship with the UN. It is funded from the UN regular budget, holds its meetings on UN premises and is serviced by the UN staff of the Office for Disarmament Affairs, Geneva branch. It conducts its work by consensus and reports annually to the General Assembly.

Meetings

The Conference's annual session is divided into three parts of 10, seven and seven weeks respectively, under a presidency that rotates among the membership every four working weeks. The Conference pursues its mandate in plenary meetings and through subsidiary bodies or special coordinators established under individual agenda items.

Membership

The 65 members are:

Algeria	Germany	Peru
Argentina	Hungary	Poland
Australia	India	ROK
Austria	Indonesia	Romania
Bangladesh	Iran	Russian Federation
Belarus	Iraq	Senegal
Belgium	Ireland	Slovakia
Brazil	Israel	South Africa
Bulgaria	Italy	Spain
Cameroon	Japan	Sri Lanka
Canada	Kazakhstan	Sweden
Chile	Kenya	Switzerland
China	Malaysia	Syrian AR
Colombia	Mexico	Tunisia
Cuba	Mongolia	Turkey
DPRK	Morocco	Ukraine
DR Congo	Myanmar	UK
Ecuador	Netherlands	USA
Egypt	New Zealand	Venezuela
Ethiopia	Nigeria	Viet Nam
Finland	Norway	Zimbabwe
France	Pakistan	

Special Committee on Peacekeeping Operations

Internet: www.un.org/en/peacekeeping/ctte/CTTEE

Purpose

GA res. 2006 (XIX) (1965) authorised the President of the General Assembly to establish a special committee to undertake a comprehensive review of all issues relating to peacekeeping.

Evolution

GA res. 51/136 (1996) expanded the Committee's membership to include all past or present personnel contributors to UN peacekeeping operations and observers. It also decided that Member States that became personnel contributors in the future, or that participated as observers for three consecutive years, could become members.

Membership

At the Committee's 2012 session, convened in Substantive Session from 21 February to 16 March, membership comprised the following Member States:

Afghanistan	Germany	Norway
Albania	Ghana	Pakistan
Algeria	Greece	Palau
Angola	Grenada	Paraguay
Argentina	Guatemala	Peru
Armenia	Guinea	Philippines
Australia	Guyana	Poland
Austria	Haiti	Portugal
Azerbaijan	Honduras	Qatar
Bangladesh	Hungary	ROK
Belarus	Iceland	Republic of Moldova
Belgium	India	Romania
Benin	Indonesia	Russian Federation
Bolivia	Iran	Rwanda
Bosnia and Herzegovina	Iraq	Samoa
Brazil	Ireland	Saudi Arabia
Bulgaria	Israel	Senegal
Burkina Faso	Italy	Serbia
Burundi	Jamaica	Sierra Leone
Cambodia	Japan	Singapore
Cameroon	Jordan	Slovakia
Canada	Kazakhstan	Slovenia
Central African Republic	Kenya	South Africa
Chad	Kuwait	Spain
Chile	Kyrgyzstan	Sri Lanka
China	Lao PDR	Sudan
Colombia	Lebanon	Swaziland
Congo	Lesotho	Sweden
Costa Rica	Libya	Switzerland
Côte d'Ivoire	Lithuania	Syrian AR
Croatia	Luxembourg	Thailand
Cuba	Madagascar	The former Yugoslav Republic
Cyprus	Malawi	of Macedonia
Czech Republic	Malaysia	Timor-Leste
DR Congo	Mali	Togo
Denmark	Mauritania	Tunisia
Djibouti	Mauritius	Turkey
Dominican Republic	Mexico	Uganda
Ecuador	Mongolia	Ukraine
Egypt	Montenegro	UK
El Salvador	Morocco	UR of Tanzania
Eritrea	Mozambique	USA
Estonia	Namibia	Uruguay
Ethiopia	Nepal	Vanuatu
Fiji	Netherlands	Venezuela
Finland	New Zealand	Viet Nam
France	Nicaragua	Yemen
Gabon	Niger	Zambia
Gambia	Nigeria	Zimbabwe
Georgia		

Observers

Brunei Darussalam	European Community	International Organisation
Comoros	Holy See	de la Francophonie
DPRK	International Committee	Organization of the Islamic
Liberia	of the Red Cross	Conference
Myanmar	International Criminal Court	Sovereign Military Order
Papua New Guinea	(ICC)	of Malta
African Union	International Criminal Police	
	Organization (INTERPOL)	

Chair	Vice-Chairs	Rapporteur
U Joy Ogwu, Nigeria	Kazutoshi Aikawa, Japan	Mohamed Sarwat Selim,
	Mateo Estreme, Argentina	Egypt
	Gilles Rivard, Canada	
	Zbigniew Szlek, Poland	

Special Committee on the Charter of the UN and on the Strengthening of the Role of the Organization

Internet: www.un.org/law/chartercomm

Purpose

The Ad Hoc Committee on the Charter of the UN was established in 1974 under GA res. 3349 (XXIX). It was reconvened under GA res. 3499 (XXX) (1975) as the Special Committee on the Charter. The resolution requested the Special Committee to examine in detail suggestions and proposals received from governments concerning:
- The Charter
- The strengthening of the role of the UN with regard to the maintenance and consolidation of international peace and security
- The development of cooperation among all nations and the promotion of the rules of international law in relations between states
- Any additional specific proposals made by governments with a view to enhancing the ability of the UN to achieve its purpose.

Most recently, the Special Committee has been considering, amongst other things, the maintenance of international peace and security in all its aspects; implementation of the provisions of the Charter of the UN related to assistance to third states affected by the application of sanctions under Chapter VII of the Charter; and peaceful settlement of disputes between states.

The Special Committee's mandate has been renewed in successive years, most recently in GA res. 66/101 (2011).

Meetings

The Special Committee's 2012 session was held in February/March in New York.

Membership

Under GA res. 50/52 (1995) the Committee's membership was expanded to include all Member States. Bureau officers elected at the Committee's 2012 meeting were:

Chair	Vice-Chairs	Rapporteur
Garen Nazarian, Armenia	Hilding Lundkvist, Sweden	Juan Manuel Sánchez
	Pham Vinh Quang, Viet Nam	Contreras, Mexico
	Ibrahim Salem, Egypt	

Special Committee on the Situation with Regard to the Implementation of the Declaration on the Granting of Independence to Colonial Countries and Peoples (Committee of Twenty-Four)

Internet: follow link from www.un.org/Depts/dpi/decolonization

Purpose

GA res. 1654 (XVI) (1961) established a special committee of 17 members to examine the application of the Declaration on the Granting of Independence to Colonial Countries and Peoples (GA res. 1514 (XV) (1960)), and to make suggestions and recommendations on the implementation of the Declaration.

The Special Committee's Sub-committee on Small Territories, Petitions, Information and Assistance was integrated into the Special Committee in January 1997.

Membership

GA res. 1810 (XVII) (1962) enlarged the membership of the Special Committee to 24. The General Assembly extended membership to Dominica and Timor-Leste on 10 December 2004, to Ecuador on 5 December 2008 (Decision 63/526) and to Nicaragua in 2010. Total membership now stands at 29, although the Committee continues to be known as the 'Committee of 24'. The members are:

Antigua and Barbuda	Fiji	Saint Kitts and Nevis
Bolivia	Grenada	Saint Lucia
Chile	India	Saint Vincent and the
China	Indonesia	Grenadines
Congo	Iran	Sierra Leone
Côte d'Ivoire	Iraq	Syrian AR
Cuba	Mali	Timor-Leste
Dominica	Nicaragua	Tunisia
Ecuador	Papua New Guinea	UR of Tanzania
Ethiopia	Russian Federation	Venezuela

Chair	Vice-Chairs	Rapporteur
Diego Morejón Pazmino, Ecuador	Pedro Nunez Mosquera, Cuba	Bashar Ja'afari, Syrian AR
	Shekou M Touray, Sierra Leone	

Territories on the Committee's agenda are:

American Samoa	Gibraltar	St Helena
Anguilla	Guam	Tokelau
Bermuda	Montserrat	Turks and Caicos Islands
British Virgin Islands	New Caledonia	United States Virgin Islands
Cayman Islands	Pitcairn Islands	Western Sahara
Falkland Islands (Malvinas)		

Special Committee to Investigate Israeli Practices Affecting the Human Rights of the Palestinian People and Other Arabs of the Occupied Territories

Purpose

GA res. 2443 (XXIII) (1968) established the Special Committee to Investigate Israeli Practices Affecting the Human Rights of the Palestinian People and Other Arabs of the Occupied Territories, composed of three Member States appointed by the General Assembly President.

The Occupied Territories within the scope of the Special Committee's terms of reference are the occupied Syrian Golan Heights and the occupied Palestinian territory, which comprises the West Bank, including East Jerusalem, and the Gaza Strip.

The Special Committee's mandate has been renewed annually, most recently by GA res. 66/76 (January 2012).

Membership

The Committee members are:

Hussein Haniff, Malaysia   Palitha T B Kohona,   Fodé Seck, Senegal
                               Sri Lanka (Chair)

UN Conciliation Commission for Palestine

Purpose

GA res. 194 (III) (1948) established the UN Conciliation Commission for Palestine to:
- Help with the repatriation of refugees
- Arrange for compensation for the property of those choosing not to return
- Assist Israel and the Arab states to achieve a final settlement of all questions outstanding between them.

GA res. 66/72 (2011) requested the Commission to continue its work.

Membership

The members of the Commission are France, Turkey and the USA. As set out in GA res. 194 (III) (1948), they were selected by a committee of the General Assembly consisting of the five permanent members of the Security Council.

UN Disarmament Commission (UNDC)

Internet: follow link from www.un.org/disarmament

Purpose

The General Assembly established the UN Disarmament Commission (UNDC) in 1978 (GA res. S-10/2 para. 118) as successor to the Commission established by GA res. 502 (VI) (1952). The General Assembly decided the UNDC should be a deliberative body required to consider and make recommendations on disarmament problems, and to follow up decisions and recommendations of the 10th Special Session.

Evolution

GA res. 37/78H (1982) requested the Commission direct its attention to specific subjects, taking into account the relevant General Assembly resolutions, and to make concrete recommendations to each General Assembly session. In 1998, by its decision 52/492, the General Assembly decided that from 2000 the Commission's agenda would normally comprise two substantive items.

Meetings

The UNDC normally meets in one three-week session annually in the northern hemisphere spring (most recently in April 2012 in New York), and operates by way of plenary meetings and working groups. The number of working groups depends on the number of substantive items on its agenda. The five regional groups take turns chairing the Commission. Working group chairs are selected in accordance with the principle of equitable geographical representation.

Membership

Membership consists of all Member States. The Chair and other officers elected for the 2012 session are:

Chair	Vice-Chairs	Rapporteur
Enrique Román-Morey, Peru	Algeria	Fikry Cassidy, Indonesia
	Mexico	
	Morocco	
	Norway	
	Poland	
	Saudi Arabia	
	Serbia	
	Sweden	

Chair of Working Group I (Recommendations for achieving the objective of nuclear disarmament and non-proliferation of nuclear weapons)

Naifbin Bandar Al-Sudairy, Saudi Arabia

Chair of Working Group II (Practical confidence-building measures in the field of conventional weapons)

Veronique Pepin-Halle, Canada

UN Scientific Committee on the Effects of Atomic Radiation (UNSCEAR)

Vienna International Centre
PO Box 500
A–1400 Vienna
Austria
Telephone: (+43 1) 26060 4330
Fax: (+43 1) 26060 5902
Internet: www.unscear.org
Secretary: Malcolm Crick, UK (selected by the UN Environment Programme (UNEP) Executive Director in 2005)

Purpose

The UN Scientific Committee on the Effects of Atomic Radiation (UNSCEAR) was established by GA res. 913 (X) (1955). The resolution requested the Committee receive and evaluate radiological information furnished by UN Member States or members of the specialised agencies, and summarise reports received on radiation levels and radiation effects.

The Committee submits annual progress reports to the General Assembly and periodically publishes comprehensive reports. These contain systematic assessments of all the major sources of exposure to ionising radiation. They have prompted significant worldwide reductions in unnecessary radiation exposure, and continue to underpin the risk management programmes of international bodies such as the International Atomic Energy Agency (IAEA), World Health Organization (WHO), International Labour Organization (ILO) and UN Environment Programme (UNEP).

The Committee also conducts systematic evaluations of the evidence for radiation-induced health effects from survivors of the atomic bombings in Japan in 1945 and other exposed groups. It has evaluated advances in scientific understanding of the mechanisms by which radiation effects can occur. These assessments provide the scientific foundation used by the relevant agencies in the UN system in formulating international radiation protection standards and other instruments.

Meetings

The Committee usually meets annually in Vienna, Austria, for about five days (most recently in May 2012).

Membership

Originally 15, the membership of UNSCEAR has been increased, most recently by GA res. 66/70 (2011), to 27. The General Assembly decided in November 2011 to increase the membership to 27 states on the understanding that the increase could be achieved from within existing resources for the biennium 2012–13. It invited Belarus, Finland, Pakistan, ROK, Spain and Ukraine to become members.

Scientists representing the 27 states members are from:

African states	Eastern European states	Western European and Other states
Egypt	Belarus	
Sudan	Poland	Australia
	Russian Federation	Belgium
Asia–Pacific states	Slovakia	Canada
China	Ukraine	Finland
India		France
Indonesia	Latin American and	Germany
Japan	Caribbean states	Spain
Pakistan	Argentina	Sweden
ROK	Brazil	UK
	Mexico	USA
	Peru	

Working Group on the Financing of the UN Relief and Works Agency for Palestine Refugees in the Near East

Purpose

The General Assembly established the Working Group (GA res. 2656 (XXV) of 7 December 1970) to study all aspects of the financing of the UN Relief and Works Agency for Palestine Refugees in the Near East.

Each year, the General Assembly has endorsed the Working Group's efforts and requested it to continue, most recently in GA res. 66/74 (2012).

Membership

The nine members designated by the Secretary-General are:

France	Lebanon	Turkey (Chair)
Ghana	Norway (Rapporteur)	UK
Japan (Vice-Chair)	Trinidad and Tobago	USA

UN Open-Ended Informal Consultative Process on Oceans and the Law of the Sea (Informal Consultative Process)

Division for Ocean Affairs and the Law of the Sea
Office of Legal Affairs
Room DC2-0450
UN New York
New York, NY 10017
United States of America
Telephone: (+1 212) 963 5915, (+1 917) 367 3085, (+1 917) 367 4506
Fax: (+1 212) 963 5847
Email: doalos@un.org
Internet: www.un.org/Depts/los (follow link under 'Oceans and the law of the sea in the General Assembly')

Purpose

Following a 1999 review by the Commission on Sustainable Development of the sectoral theme of 'Oceans and Seas', the General Assembly decided (GA res. 54/33 (1999)) to establish an open-ended informal consultative process to facilitate its annual review of developments in ocean affairs.

The Informal Consultative Process meets once a year to consider a theme or topic(s) identified in the annual General Assembly resolution on oceans and the law of the sea, and based particularly on information in the Secretary-General's annual report on oceans and the law of the sea. It carries out three inter-related tasks:
• Studying developments in ocean affairs consistent with the legal framework provided by the Convention on the Law of the Sea and the goals of chapter 17 of the global sustainable development environmental action plan Agenda 21
• Identifying particular issues to be considered by the General Assembly against the backdrop of overall developments of all relevant oceans issues
• Placing emphasis on areas where coordination and cooperation at inter-governmental and inter-agency levels should be enhanced.

Evolution

GA resolutions 57/141 (2002) and 60/30 (2005) extended the Informal Consultative Process for further periods of three years, GA res. 63/111 (2008) for two years and, most recently, GA res. 65/37 A (2011) for a further two years.

Meetings

The Informal Consultative Process meets annually, most recently in New York from 29 May to 1 June 2012, where the topic of focus was 'marine renewable energies'.

Membership

The Informal Consultative Process is open to all UN Member States, states members of the specialised agencies and all parties to the Convention. It is also open to entities that have received a standing invitation to participate as observers in the work of the General Assembly and to inter-governmental organisations with competence in ocean affairs. Discussion panels allow input from representatives of the major groups identified in Agenda 21.

The two Co-Chairs appointed by the President of the General Assembly for the 13th meeting were Don MacKay, New Zealand, and Milan Jaya Meetarbhan, Mauritius.

Ad Hoc Open-ended Informal Working Group to study issues relating to the conservation and sustainable use of marine biological diversity beyond areas of national jurisdiction

Division for Ocean Affairs and the Law of the Sea
Office of Legal Affairs
Room DC2-0450
UN New York
New York, NY 10017
United States of America
Telephone: (+1 212) 963 5915, (+1 917) 367 3085, (+1 917) 367 4506
Fax: (+1 212) 963 5847
Email: doalos@un.org
Internet: www.un.org/Depts/los (follow link under 'Oceans and the law of the sea in the General Assembly')

Purpose

The Ad Hoc Open-ended Informal Working Group was established by GA res. 59/24 (2004) to study issues relating to the conservation and sustainable use of marine biological diversity beyond areas of national jurisdiction. The Working Group was mandated to:

- Survey the past and present activities of the UN and other relevant international organisations with regard to the conservation and sustainable use of marine biological diversity beyond areas of national jurisdiction
- Examine the scientific, technical, economic, legal, environmental, socio-economic and other aspects of these issues
- Identify key issues and questions where more detailed background studies would facilitate consideration by states of these issues
- Indicate, where appropriate, possible options and approaches to promote international cooperation and coordination for the conservation and sustainable use of marine biological diversity beyond areas of national jurisdiction.

Evolution

GA res. 66/231 (2011) decided to initiate within the Working Group a process "with a view to ensuring that the legal framework for the conservation and sustainable use of marine biological diversity in areas beyond national jurisdiction effectively addresses those issues by identifying gaps and ways forward, including through the implementation of existing instruments and the possible development of a multilateral agreement under the United Nations Convention on the Law of the Sea".

The process will address the conservation and sustainable use of marine biodiversity in areas beyond national jurisdiction, in particular, together and as a whole:

- Marine genetic resources, including questions on the sharing of benefits

- Measures such as area-based management tools, including marine protected areas, and environmental impact assessments
- Capacity building and the transfer of marine technology.

The process will take place in the Working Group and in inter-sessional workshops.

Members

The Working Group is open to all UN Member States and parties to the UN Convention on the Law of the Sea, with others invited as observers. It is also open to participation from the major groups, in accordance with the practice of meetings on oceans and the law of the sea.

Meetings

The Working Group's fifth meeting was held in May 2012. The two Co-Chairs appointed by the President of the General Assembly for the fifth meeting were Palitha T B Kohona, Sri Lanka, and Liesbeth Lijnzaad, Netherlands.

Ad Hoc Working Group of the Whole on the Regular Process for Global Reporting and Assessment of the State of the Marine Environment, including Socio-economic Aspects

Division for Ocean Affairs and the Law of the Sea
Office of Legal Affairs
Room DC2-0450
UN New York
New York, NY 10017
United States of America
Telephone: (+1 212) 963 5915, (+1 917) 367 3085, (+1 917) 367 4506
Fax: (+1 212) 963 5847
Email: doalos@un.org
Internet: www.un.org/Depts/los (follow link under 'Oceans and the law of the sea in the General Assembly')

Purpose

Following the 2002 World Summit on Sustainable Development, held in Johannesburg, South Africa, the General Assembly established a regular process for global reporting and assessment of the state of the marine environment, including socio-economic aspects, both current and foreseeable, building on existing regional assessments (GA res. 57/141). The Ad Hoc Working Group of the Whole was established in 2008 (GA res. 63/111) to oversee and guide the UN's 'Regular Process'.

Evolution

In accordance with GA resolutions 58/240 (2003) and 60/30 (2005), the General Assembly launched the 'Assessment of Assessments' as the start-up phase of the Regular Process.

In December 2009, the General Assembly endorsed the recommendations adopted by the Ad Hoc Working Group of the Whole that proposed a framework for the Regular Process (GA res. 64/71). In December 2010, the General Assembly endorsed recommendations that proposed modalities for the implementation of the Regular Process, including the key features, institutional arrangements, capacity-building and financing (GA res. 65/37 A). The deadline for the first integrated assessment is 2014.

The Regular Process is overseen and guided by the Ad Hoc Working Group of the Whole. The General Assembly also established a group of experts to be an integral part of the Regular Process.

In December 2011, the General Assembly adopted criteria for the appointment of experts and guidelines for regional workshops to assist the Regular Process (GA res. 66/231). To date, regional workshops have been hosted by Chile (September 2011) and China (February 2012).

Bureau

The Working Group has established a 15-member bureau to put into practice its decisions and guidance during the inter-sessional period between meetings.

Meetings

The Ad Hoc Working Group of the Whole held its first two meetings in 2011 and third in April 2012. All have been in New York.

Membership

The Working Group is open to UN Member States and observers; relevant inter-governmental and non-governmental organisations in consultative status with ECOSOC; and relevant scientific institutions and major groups identified in Agenda 21 that request an invitation to participate.

The two Co-Chairs appointed by the President of the General Assembly in January 2011 were Donatus Keith St Aimee, Saint Lucia, and Renée Sauvé, Canada. In April 2012, the President of the General Assembly appointed Gonçalo da Motta, Portugal, to replace Ms Sauvé, who stepped down after the June 2011 meeting.

Independent Audit Advisory Committee (IAAC)

United Nations
Committee Room IN-03014B
300 East 42nd Street
New York, NY 10017
United States of America
Telephone: (+1 212) 963 0788
Fax: (+1 212) 963 0600
Email: bamuwamye@un.org
Internet: www.un.org/ga/iaac
Executive Secretary: Moses Bamuwamye

Purpose

The Independent Audit Advisory Committee (IAAC) was established by GA res. 60/248 (2005) as a subsidiary body of the General Assembly to serve in an expert advisory capacity and to assist the General Assembly in fulfilling its oversight responsibilities.

The Committee's responsibilities are to provide independent advice to the General Assembly on: the scope, results and effectiveness of audit as well as other oversight functions, especially the Office of Internal Oversight Services (OIOS); measures to ensure the compliance of management with audit and other oversight recommendations; and on various risk management, internal control, operational, accounting and disclosure issues.

Evolution

The terms of reference for the IAAC were established in GA res. 61/275 (2007) and the new body started functioning in January 2008. The General Assembly reviewed the terms of reference in 2011 (GA res. 65/250) and no change was made. The next review is scheduled for the General Assembly's 70th session in 2015.

Meetings

The IAAC meets up to four times a year.

Membership

The IAAC consists of five members, who serve three-year terms, renewable at least once.

Term ending 31 Dec 2013

Vadim Vadimovich Dubinkin, Russian Federation
Vinod Rai, India
Adrian Patrick Strachan, Jamaica (Vice-Chair)

Term ending 31 Dec 2014

J Christopher Mihm, USA
John F S Muwanga, Uganda (Chair)

Open-ended Working Group on Ageing for the purpose of strengthening the protection of the human rights of older persons

Secretariat: Division for Social Policy and Development
Department for Economic and Social Affairs
2 United Nations Plaza, Room DC2–1382
New York, NY 10017
United States of America
Telephone: (+1 212) 963 5090
Fax: (+1 212) 963 3062
Email: ageing-working-group@un.org
Internet: http://social.un.org/ageing-working-group
Focal Point on Ageing: Rosemary Lane, USA

Purpose

The Open-ended Working Group on Ageing for the purpose of strengthening the protection of the human rights of older persons was established by GA res. 65/182 on 21 December 2010. Its role is to consider the existing international framework of the human rights of older persons and identify possible gaps and how best to address them, including by considering, as appropriate, the feasibility of further instruments and measures.

Meetings

The Working Group's third session was scheduled to be held from 21 to 24 August 2012.

Bureau

Latin American and Caribbean states	Western European and Other states	Eastern European states
Jorge Martin Agüello, Argentina (Chair)	Léo Faber, Luxembourg	Ervin Nina, Albania
Asia–Pacific states	African states	
Alya Ahmed S Al-Thani, Qatar	Vacant	

Open-Ended Working Group on the Question of Equitable Representation and Increase in the Membership of the Security Council

GA res. 48/26 (1993) established an open-ended working group to consider all aspects of the question of an increase in the membership of the Security Council and other matters related to the Security Council.

The Working Group's mandate was renewed in 2011 for the General Assembly's 66th session, but the Group was only to convene if Member States so decided. As of May 2012, the Group had not convened and no formal decision had been made on who would chair it.

ADVISORY BODIES

Advisory Board on Disarmament Matters

United Nations
405 East 42nd Street, Room DN 2510
New York, NY 10017
United States of America
Telephone: (+1 212) 963 3022
Fax: (+1 212) 963 4066
Email: UNODA-web@un.org
Internet: www.un.org/disarmament (follow link from 'Secretary-General's Advisory Board')
Secretary: Tam Chung

Purpose

The functions of the Advisory Board on Disarmament Matters are to:
- Advise the Secretary-General on arms limitation and disarmament matters, including studies and research under the auspices of the UN or institutions within the UN
- Serve as the Board of Trustees of the UN Institute for Disarmament Research (UNIDIR)
- Advise the Secretary-General on implementation of the UN Disarmament Information Programme.

Evolution

The Advisory Board was established in 1978 under paragraph 124 of the Final Document of the 10th Special Session of the General Assembly (GA res. S10/2, para. 124). The Board received its current mandate through GA res. 54/418 of 1 December 1999.

Meetings

The Advisory Board usually holds two sessions each year, alternating between New York and Geneva.

Membership

The Secretary-General chooses the members of the Board from all regions of the world for their knowledge and experience in the field of disarmament and international security. Members serve an initial two-year term.

continued next page

There are 16 members (including the Director of UNIDIR) in 2012:

Nobuyasu Abe, Japan

Dewi Fortuna Anwar, Indonesia

Desmond Bowen, UK

Cheng Jingye, China

Kate Dewes, New Zealand

István Gyarmati, Hungary

Mônica Herz, Brazil

Togzhan Kassenova, Kazakhstan

Sergey M Koshelev, Russian Federation

H M G S Palihakkara, Sri Lanka (Chair)

Olga Pellicer, Mexico

Marcie Berman Ries, USA

François Rivasseau, France

S E Cheikh Sylla, Senegal

Carlo Trezza, Italy

Ex Officio Member: Theresa Hitchens, USA (Director Of UNIDIR)

Advisory Committee of the UN Programme of Assistance in the Teaching, Study, Dissemination and Wider Appreciation of International Law

United Nations
M-13076, 380 Madison Avenue
New York, NY 10017
United States of America
Telephone: (+1 917) 367 5284
Fax: (+1 212) 963 1963
Internet: www.un.org/law/programmeofassistance
Secretary: Virginia Morris

Purpose

The General Assembly established a programme of assistance and exchange in the field of international law through GA res. 2099 (XX) (1965). This resolution set up the Committee to advise the Secretary-General on substantive aspects of the programme. The following year, by GA res. 2204 (XXI) (1966), the Advisory Committee was given its current title.

The Programme of Assistance was established to contribute to a better knowledge of international law and provide direct assistance by means of:
• Fellowship programmes, regional courses and symposia in international law
• The preparation and dissemination of publications and other information relating to international law.

The General Assembly authorised the programme's continuation annually until its 26th session, then every two years. Since its 64th session, the General Assembly has considered this agenda item annually (GA res. 64/113). The Secretary-General reports to the General Assembly on the implementation of the programme and is then authorised to carry out activities in subsequent years.

Evolution

A UN Audiovisual Library of International Law website (www.un.org/law/avl) was launched in October 2008. The website is maintained by the Office of Legal Affairs Codification Division.

General Assembly resolution 66/97 (2011) authorised the provision of fellowships for participants from developing countries to attend the International Law Fellowship Programme in The Hague in 2012 and 2013. The Assembly also authorised fellowships for participants from developing countries to attend regional courses in international law in 2012 and 2013. The numbers are to be determined in light of the programme's overall resources. The regional courses are financed by Members States' voluntary contributions. The General Assembly also authorised the award of a minimum of one scholarship, in both

2012 and 2013, under the Hamilton Shirley Amerasinghe Memorial Fellowship on the Law of the Sea, subject to the availability of voluntary contributions made for this fellowship.

Membership

GA res. 66/97 (2011) appointed 25 Member States to serve on the Committee for a four-year period from 1 January 2012 to 31 December 2015.

African states
Ethiopia
Ghana
Kenya
Nigeria
Sudan
UR of Tanzania

Asia–Pacific states
Cyprus
Iran
Lebanon
Malaysia
Pakistan

Latin American and Caribbean states
Argentina
Chile
Mexico
Suriname
Trinidad and Tobago

Eastern European states
Czech Republic
Russian Federation
Ukraine

Western European and Other states
Canada
France
Germany
Italy
Portugal
USA

EXPERT BODIES

Board of Auditors

1 United Nations Plaza, Room DC1-2680A
New York, NY 10017
United States of America
Telephone: (+1 212) 963 5623
Fax: (+1 212) 963 3684
Email: dasa@un.org
Internet: www.un.org/auditors/board
Executive Secretary: Anjana Das

Purpose

GA res. 74 (I) (1946) established the Board of Auditors to serve as external auditor of UN accounts, funds and programmes, and the International Court of Justice. It submits reports to the General Assembly annually or every two years, depending on the financial periods of the respective organisations.

Structure

The Board is composed of the Auditors-General (or officers holding equivalent title) of three UN Member States. Each member provides an audit staff of about 50 professional officers for four months a year and a full-time director.

To enable the Board to carry out its mandate, an Audit Operations Committee was established at UN Headquarters. This comprises three full-time Directors of External Audit, each representing a member of the Board.

Meetings

The Board meets twice a year. The 2012 regular session and special session were scheduled to be held in New York from 24 to 25 July and on 11 December respectively.

Membership

Board members are appointed by the General Assembly on the recommendation of the Fifth Committee and retire by rotation. GA res. 55/248 (2001) approved a change in the term of office for Board members to a non-consecutive term of six years beginning 1 July 2002. Previously, members were appointed for a three-year term, which was renewable.

The three Board of Auditors members, or their equivalents, are:

China (until 30 June 2014)	UK (until 30 June 2016)	Tanzania (until 30 June 2018)
Auditor-General of the General Audit Office of China	Comptroller and Auditor-General of the National Audit Office of the UK	Auditor-General of Tanzania

International Civil Service Commission (ICSC)

ICSC Headquarters
2 United Nations Plaza, 10th Floor
New York, NY 10017
United States of America
Telephone: (+1 212) 963 5465
Fax: (+1 212) 9630159
Email: icscmail@un.org
Internet: http://icsc.un.org

Purpose

The International Civil Service Commission (ICSC) was established by GA res. 3357 (XXIX) (1974). It is responsible for the regulation and coordination of staff conditions of service within the UN, the specialised agencies and other international organisations that participate in the UN common system and accept the Commission's statute. The Commission also has some decision-making functions with respect to post-adjustment indices, daily subsistence allowances, methodologies to determine salary levels and job classification standards. For other compensation issues and on human resource matters, it makes recommendations to the General Assembly or the executive heads of the participating organisations.

Membership

The Commission comprises 15 independent experts appointed in their individual capacities by, and answerable as a body to, the General Assembly. Only the Chair and Vice-Chair serve in a full-time capacity. Members are appointed for four years by the General Assembly, on the recommendation of the Fifth Committee, from a list of candidates compiled by the Secretary-General. Members may be reappointed. The members are:

Term ending 31 Dec 2012	Term ending 31 Dec 2013	Term ending 31 Dec 2014
Fatih Bouayad-Agha, Algeria	Minoru Endo, Japan	Marie-Françoise Bechtel, France
Shamsher Chowdhury, Bangladesh	Luis Mariano Hermosillo, Mexico	Emmanuel Oti Boateng, Ghana
Sergei Garmonin, Russian Federation	Lucretia Myers, USA	Carleen Gardner, Jamaica
Xiaochu Wang, China	Wolfgang Stöckl, Germany (Vice-Chair)	Kingston P Rhodes, Sierra Leone (Chair)
El Hassane Zahid, Morocco	Gian Luigi Valenza, Italy	Eugeniusz Wyzner, Poland

International Law Commission (ILC)

405 East 42nd Street, Room M-13065[1]
New York, NY 10017
United States of America
Telephone: (+1 212) 963 5331
Fax: (+1 212) 963 1963
Email: ilcweb@un.org
Internet: www.un.org/law/ilc

Purpose

The International Law Commission (ILC), with a membership of 15 international law experts, was established by the General Assembly (GA res. 174 (II) (1947)) to encourage the progressive development and codification of international law.

The eighth edition of the publication *Work of the International Law Commission*, issued in April 2012, reviews the Commission's work over nearly seven decades. Items currently on its programme of work are:

- Expulsion of aliens
- The obligation to extradite or prosecute (*aut dedere aut judicare*)
- Protection of persons in the event of disasters
- Immunity of state officials from foreign criminal jurisdiction
- Treaties over time
- The Most-Favoured-Nation clause.

Meetings

The Commission's 64th session was held in Geneva from 7 May to 1 June 2012 and was scheduled to continue from 2 July to 3 August 2012.

Membership

The Commission's membership has been increased a number of times, most recently by GA res. 36/39 (1981), and now stands at 34. By GA res. 36/39 (1981), the General Assembly decided the members should be elected according to the following pattern: eight from African states, seven from Asia–Pacific states, three from Eastern European states, six from Latin American and Caribbean states, and eight from Western European and Other states. They would be joined by one from African or Eastern European states in rotation, and one from Asia–Pacific or Latin American and Caribbean states in rotation.

The regional group allocation for the current five-year term is: nine from African states, eight from Asia–Pacific states, three from Eastern European states, six from Latin American and Caribbean states, and eight from Western European and Other states.

Commission members are elected by the General Assembly for a five-year term and are eligible for re-election. They are elected on a personal basis and sit in their personal capacity as experts. Casual vacancies during the term, following resignation or death, are filled by the Commission.

The members elected for the term 1 January 2012 to 31 December 2016 are:

Mohammed Bello Adoke, Nigeria

Ali Mohsen Fetais Al-Marri, Qatar

Lucius C Caflisch, Switzerland

Enrique J A Candioti, Argentina

Pedro Comissário Afonso, Mozambique

Abdelrazeg El-Murtadi Suleiman Gouider, Libya

Concepción Escobar Hernández, Spain

Mathias Forteau, France

Kirill Gevorgian, Russian Federation

Juan Manuel Gómez-Robledo, Mexico

Hussein A Hassouna, Egypt

Mahmoud D Hmoud, Jordan

Huikang Huang, China

Marie G Jacobsson, Sweden

Maurice Kamto, Cameroon

Kriangsak Kittichaisaree, Thailand

Ahmed Laraba, Algeria

Donald M McRae, Canada

Shinya Murase, Japan

Sean D Murphy, USA

Bernd H Niehaus, Costa Rica

Georg Nolte, Germany

Ki Gab Park, ROK

Chris M Peter, UR of Tanzania

Ernest Petric, Slovenia

Gilberto V Saboia, Brazil

Narinder Singh, India

Pavel Šturma, Czech Republic

Dire D Tladi, South Africa

Eduardo Valencia-Ospina, Colombia

Stephen C Vasciannie, Jamaica

S Amos Wako, Kenya

Nugroho Wisnumurti, Indonesia

Michael Wood, UK

Note

1   Address expected to change in March 2013.

Investments Committee

Internet: www.unjspf.org (follow link to 'Investments')

Purpose

The Investments Committee was established by the General Assembly (GA res. 155 (II) (1947)) to advise the Secretary-General on the investment of the UN Joint Staff Pension Fund, the UN Library Endowment Fund and the UN University Endowment Fund.

Meetings

The Committee meets four or five times a year, including one meeting held in conjunction with the UN Pension Board. The meetings are normally held in New York and, on occasion, in another UN member country.

Membership

Committee members are appointed by the Secretary-General for three-year terms, following consultation with the UN Joint Staff Pension Board and Advisory Committee on Administrative and Budgetary Questions. Appointments are subject to confirmation by the General Assembly. In addition to the nine regular members, the Secretary-General may appoint additional members to ensure geographical representation and expertise in specific sectors and markets. Such additional members are referred to as ad hoc members. The regular members are eligible for reappointment with a limit of five terms of three years each, while the ad hoc member appointments are renewed every year.

Membership has been expanded a number of times and now stands at nine, although extra ad hoc members can be appointed if required (see GA res. 31/196 (1976)). The members are:

Term ending 31 Dec 2012
Emilio Cárdenas, Argentina
Linah Mohohlo, Botswana

Ad Hoc Members ending 31 Dec 2012
Hilda Ochoa-Brillembourg, Venezuela
Ivan Pictet, Switzerland

Term ending 31 Dec 2013
Simon Jiang, China
Achim Kassow, Germany
William McDonough, USA

Term ending 31 Dec 2014
Masakazu Arikawa, Japan
Madhav Dhar, India
Nemir Kirdar, Iraq
Dominique Senequier, France

Joint Inspection Unit (JIU)

Palais des Nations
Room D-507
CH 1211 Geneva 10
Switzerland
Telephone: (+41 0) 22 917 3044
Fax: (+41 0) 22 917 06 27
Email: jiu@unog.ch
Internet: www.unjiu.org
Executive Secretary: Susanne Frueh

Purpose

The Joint Inspection Unit (JIU) began work in 1968 following recommendations by the Ad Hoc Committee of Experts to Examine the Finances of the United Nations and the Specialized Agencies (A/6635) (GA res. 2150 (XXI) (1966) and further confirmed in GA res. 2360 (XXII) (1967)). After eight years, the General Assembly gave the JIU its Statute as the annex of GA res. 31/192 (1976).

The JIU's mandate covers the UN, its separately administered funds and programmes, and the specialised agencies that have accepted the Statute. The Unit reports to the General Assembly and the relevant organs of other participating organisations.

Articles 5 and 6 of the Statue include that the Unit shall satisfy itself that activities undertaken by the organisations are carried out in the most economical manner and that optimum use is made of the resources available. The Statute also includes that inspectors have the broadest powers of investigation in all matters having a bearing on efficiency and proper use of funds; provide an independent view aimed at improving management and methods, and achieving greater coordination between organisations; may propose reforms or make recommendations; and, acting singly or in small groups, make on-the-spot inquiries and investigations, some of which may be without prior notification, in any of the organisations' services.

Structure

The Unit, located in Geneva, is assisted by an executive secretary, and evaluation and inspection, research and support staff. Its budget is included in the regular UN budget as a jointly financed activity, with expenditure shared by participating organisations.

Membership

The Unit consists of not more than 11 inspectors with special experience in administrative and financial matters, serving in their personal capacity for five-year terms that can be renewed once.

Inspectors are appointed by the General Assembly on the nomination of its President, after appropriate consultations, and with due regard to the principles of equitable geographical distribution and reasonable rotation. The inspectors are:

Term ending 31 Dec 2012
Nikolay V Chulkov, Russian Federation
Even Fontaine Ortiz, Cuba
Deborah Wynes, USA
Mohamed M Zahran, Egypt (Chair)
Yishan Zhang, China

Term ending 31 Dec 2014
Tadanori Inomata, Japan (Vice-Chair)

Term ending 31 Dec 2015
Gérard Biraud, France
Papa Louis Fall, Senegal
István Posta, Hungary
Cihan Terzi, Turkey

Term ending 31 Dec 2018
Jorge Flores Callejas, Honduras

Panel of External Auditors

1 United Nations Plaza, Room DC1-2680A
New York, NY 10017
United States of America
Telephone: (+1 212) 963 5623
Fax: (+1 212) 963 3684
Email: dasa@un.org
Internet: www.un.org/auditors/panel
Executive Secretary: Anjana Das

Purpose

The General Assembly established the Panel of External Auditors (GA res. 1438 (XIV) (1959)) to further coordinate and exchange information on the audits for which its members are responsible, and to achieve a greater degree of uniformity of audit practices and use of common accounting principles within the UN system. The Panel may submit to the executive heads of participating organisations observations or recommendations in relation to the accounts and financial procedures of their organisations. The executive heads of participating organisations may, through their external auditors, submit requests to the Panel for its advice or opinion.

Meetings

The Panel meets annually. Its 2012 session is scheduled to be held at UN Headquarters in New York from 10 to 11 December.

Membership

The membership, which stands at 10, comprises the members of the UN Board of Auditors, along with the appointed external auditors of the specialised agencies and International Atomic Energy Agency (IAEA).

UN Appeals Tribunal (UNAT) and UN Dispute Tribunal (UNDT)

Internet: www.un.org/en/internaljustice (follow links to 'Appeals Tribunal' for UNAT and 'Dispute Tribunal' for UNDT)

Purpose

The UN Appeals Tribunal (UNAT) and the UN Dispute Tribunal (UNDT) were established by the General Assembly (GA res. 62/228 (2008)) to judge allegations of non-compliance with the terms and conditions of appointment of UN staff members.

Evolution

The system of internal justice in the UN has undergone significant reform in recent years. GA res. 62/228 reaffirmed an intention to establish a "new, independent, transparent, professionalized, adequately resourced and decentralized system of administration of justice". The resolution established a two-tier formal system comprising a first instance UNDT, located in New York, Geneva and Nairobi, and an appellate instance, the UNAT, the registry of which is based in New York. The statutes for the new bodies were adopted by the General Assembly in res. 63/253 (2008). This resolution also abolished the former UN Administrative Tribunal as of 31 December 2009. The two new bodies became operational from 1 July 2009.

Membership

Judges are appointed to both tribunals by the General Assembly on the recommendation of the Internal Justice Council.

UNAT judges

Sophia Adinyira, Ghana (seven-year term starting 1 July 2009, ending 2016)

Inès Weinberg de Roca, Argentina (seven-year term starting 1 July 2009, ending 2016)

Luis Maria Simón, Uruguay (seven-year term starting 1 July 2009, ending 2016)

Mary Faherty, Ireland (appointed 2011 to serve the remainder of a seven-year term starting 1 July 2009, ending 2016)

Rosalyn M Chapman, USA (non-renewable seven-year term starting 1 July 2012, ending 2019)

Richard Lussick, Samoa (non-renewable seven-year term starting 1 July 2012, ending 2019)

Jean Courtial, France (initial three-year term, reappointed for a non-renewable seven-year term starting 1 July 2012, ending 2019)

UNDT full-time judges

Geneva: Thomas Laker, Germany (seven-year term starting 1 July 2009, ending 2016)

Nairobi: Vinod Boolell, Mauritius (seven-year term starting 1 July 2009, ending 2016)

New York: Memooda Ebrahim-Carstens, Botswana (initial three-year term, reappointed for a non-renewable seven-year term starting 1 July 2012, ending 2019)

UNDT half-time judges

Geneva: Coral Shaw, New Zealand (seven-year term starting 1 July 2009, ending 2016)

Nairobi: Goolam Hoosen Kader Meeran, UK (initial three-year term, reappointed for a non-renewable seven-year term starting 1 July 2012, ending 2019)

continued next page

UNDT ad litem judges[1]

Alessandra Greceanu, Romania[2] (term ends 31 December 2012)

Jean-François Cousin, France (term ends 31 December 2012)

Nkemdilim Amelia Izuako, Nigeria (term ends 31 December 2012)

Notes

1   Initially appointed to the UNDT for one year until 30 June 2010 and subsequently extended. The latest extension expires 31 December 2012.

2   Alessandra Greceanu was appointed in February 2012. She replaced Marilyn Kaman, USA, who resigned in July 2011.

UN Commission on International Trade Law (UNCITRAL)

Vienna International Centre
PO Box 500
A–1400 Vienna
Austria
Telephone: (+43 1) 26060 4060
Fax: (+43 1) 26060 5813
Email: uncitral@uncitral.org
Internet: www.uncitral.org
Secretary: Renaud Sorieul, France (appointed by the UN Secretary-General in 2008)

Purpose

The General Assembly established the UN Commission on International Trade Law (UNCITRAL) to promote the harmonisation and unification of the law of international trade (GA res. 2205 (XXI) (1966)). The Commission has since become the core legal body in the UN system in the field of international trade law. The Commission pursues its mandate through preparation of texts dealing with the substantive law that governs trade transactions or other aspects of business law that have an impact on international trade. The Commission also undertakes a range of technical assistance activities to promote the use and adoption of the texts it has developed. It also ensures coordination of the work of organisations active in the international trade law field to encourage cooperation, avoid duplication of effort, and promote efficiency, consistency and coherence.

Evolution

Under GA res. 57/20 (2003), the General Assembly increased the Commission's membership to 60 states. The additional members were elected during the 58th session of the General Assembly in November 2003. By GA res. 31/99 (1976), the General Assembly altered the dates of commencement and termination of membership, so that members take office at the beginning of the first day of the regular annual session of the Commission immediately following their election, and that their terms of office expire on the day prior to the opening of the regular annual session following their election.

Since the first day of the Commission's 37th session (14 June 2004), when the additional members took office, the Commission has observed the following distribution of seats: 14 members from African states, 14 from Asia–Pacific states, eight from Eastern European states, 10 from Latin American and Caribbean states, and 14 from Western European and Other states.

Structure

UNCITRAL's work is organised and conducted at three levels. The first level is the Commission itself. The second is inter-governmental working groups, which to a large extent undertake the development of the topics on UNCITRAL's work programme. The third is the Secretariat, which assists the Commission and its working groups in the preparation and conduct of their work.

Meetings

The Commission holds an annual plenary session (most recently in New York from 25 June to 6 July 2012).

Membership[1]

Member States are elected for a term of six years, with the terms of half the members expiring every three years. The members of UNCITRAL, and the expiry of their terms of membership, are:

African states

Algeria	2016	Mauritius	2016
Benin	2013	Morocco	2013
Botswana	2016	Namibia	2013
Cameroon	2013	Nigeria	2016
Egypt	2013	Senegal	2013
Gabon	2016	South Africa	2013
Kenya	2016	Uganda	2016

Asia–Pacific states

Bahrain	2013	Malaysia	2013
China	2013	Pakistan	2016
Fiji	2016	Philippines	2016
India	2016	ROK	2013
Iran	2016	Singapore	2013
Japan	2013	Sri Lanka	2013
Jordan	2016	Thailand	2016

Eastern European states[1]

Armenia	2013	Latvia	2013
Bulgaria	2013	Russian Federation	2013
Croatia	2016	Ukraine	2014
Czech Republic	2013		

continued next page

Latin American and Caribbean states

Argentina	2016	El Salvador	2013
Bolivia	2013	Honduras	2013
Brazil	2016	Mexico	2013
Chile	2013	Paraguay	2016
Colombia	2016	Venezuela	2016

Western European and Other states

Australia	2016	Italy	2016
Austria	2016	Malta	2013
Canada	2013	Norway	2013
France	2013	Spain	2016
Germany	2013	Turkey	2016
Greece	2013	UK	2013
Israel	2016	USA	2016

Note

1   On 3 November 2009, the General Assembly held elections to fill the vacancies in UNCITRAL for a six-year term beginning on 21 June 2010 and expiring on the last day prior to the beginning of the 49th session of the Commission in 2016. At that time, the following six states members were also elected to alternate their membership during the same period: Belarus, Croatia, Czech Republic, Georgia, Poland and Ukraine. Therefore, for six years the membership of the Commission will change every year. Changes will occur on the first day of each session of the Commission. This pattern will continue until the opening of the Commission's 49th session in 2016.

Belarus: alternating membership 2010–11, 2013–16. Croatia: alternating membership 2012–16. Czech Republic: alternating membership 2010–13, 2015–16. Georgia: alternating membership 2011–15. Poland: alternating membership 2010–12, 2014–16. Ukraine: alternating membership 2010–14.

UN Joint Staff Pension Fund

PO Box 5036
New York, NY 10017
United States of America
Telephone: (+ 1 212) 963 6931
Fax: (+1 212) 963 3146
Email: unjspf@un.org
Internet: www.unjspf.org

Palais des Nations
1211 Geneva 10
Switzerland
Telephone: (+41 0) 22 928 8800
Fax: (+41 0) 22 928 9099
Email: unjspf.gva@unjspf.org

Purpose

The Joint Staff Pension Fund was established under regulations adopted by the General Assembly in GA res. 248 (III) (1948) to provide retirement, death, disability and related benefits for staff upon cessation of their services with the UN. The regulations, which have been amended at various times, provide for the admission of other organisations to the Fund. Twenty-three organisations, including the UN, are members.

Evolution

GA res. 42/222 (1987) amended the regulations of the Fund, together with the composition and size of the Board. These changes took effect on 1 January 1989.

Structure

The member organisations jointly administer the Fund through the UN Joint Staff Pension Board, which has 33 members. Twelve members are from the UN (four chosen by the General Assembly, four by the Secretary-General and four by the participants) and 21 are from the other member organisations.

The Board reports to the General Assembly every two years on the operations of the Fund and the investment of its assets, and, when necessary, recommends amendments to the regulations governing its activities. Expenses incurred by the Board in the administration of the Fund, principally the cost of its central secretariat at UN Headquarters in New York and the management expenses of its investments, are met by the Fund.

Membership

The UN Staff Pension Committee, consisting of 12 members and their alternates, serves the UN participants in the Fund. The terms of those appointed by the General Assembly are four years. The terms are due to end on 31 December 2012.

Appointed by the General Assembly

Members	Alternates
Valeria Maria González Posse, Argentina	Dmitry Chumakov, Russian Federation
Gerhard Küntzle, Germany	Muhammad Muhith, Bangladesh
Lovemore Mazemo, Zimbabwe	Thomas Repasch, USA
Philip Richard Okanda Owade, Kenya	

Appointed by the Secretary-General

Members	Alternates
Eugenia Casar, Mexico	Arnab Roy, India
Angela Kane, Germany	Dennis Thatchaichawalit, Thailand
Catherine Pollard, Guyana	
Jay William Pozenel, USA	

Elected by the participants and serving until successors elected*

Members	Alternates
Adebowale Adeniyi, Nigeria	Vacant
Ajay Lakhanpal, India	Vacant
Carlos Santos Tejada, Ecuador	
Vacant	

Note

* The representatives of the UN participants were elected for four-year terms expiring on 31 December 2008. The representatives remain in office, in accordance with article 6(b) of the UN Joint Staff Pension Fund Regulations, "until the election of their successors".

UN Register of Damage Caused by the Construction of the Wall in the Occupied Palestinian Territory (UNRoD)

Vienna International Centre
Wagramer Strasse 5
PO Box 500
A–1400 Vienna
Austria
Internet: www.unrod.org
Executive Director: Vladimir Goryayev, Russian Federation (appointed by the UN Secretary-General in 2007)

Purpose

General Assembly resolution ES-10/17 of January 2007 established the UN Register of Damage (UNRoD) to serve as a record, in documentary form, of the damage caused to all natural and legal persons concerned as a result of the construction of the Wall by Israel in the Occupied Palestinian Territory, including in and around East Jerusalem. UNRoD is not a compensation commission, claims-resolution facility, judicial or quasi-judicial body.

To fulfil its mandate, UNRoD undertakes outreach activities in the Occupied Palestinian Territory to inform potential claimants of the existence and purpose of UNRoD, and the procedure for filing a claim for registration of damage. UNRoD also assists claimants in completing the official UNRoD claim forms, and collects completed claims forms for processing in Vienna. UNRoD's three-member board has the ultimate authority to decide, based on criteria established by it, whether or not a loss or damage claimed is to be included in the UN Register of Damage.

As of May 2012, more than 27,500 claims and 300,000 supporting documents had been collected in 105 out of 240 affected Palestinian municipalities with more than 420,000 affected Palestinians. Claim intake activities in four out of nine affected governorates have been completed (Tubas, Jenin, Tulkarem and Qalqiliya) and were ongoing in Salfit governorate. A total of 5108 of the collected claims have been reviewed by the UNRoD Board for its inclusion in the Register.

Structure

UNRoD is a subsidiary organ of the UN General Assembly and operates under the administrative authority of the Secretary-General. It is based at the UN Office in Vienna (UNOV).

Board membership

Board members are appointed by the UN Secretary-General. The Executive Director is also an ex officio member. The three appointed members are:

Ronald Bettauer, USA (since 2008)	Harumi Hori, Japan (since 2007)	Matti Pellonpää, Finland (since 2007)

United Nations Office for Partnerships (UNOP)

1 United Nations Plaza, Room DC1–1330
New York, NY 10017
United States of America
Telephone: (+1 212) 963 1000
Fax: (+1 212) 963 1486
Email: partner@un.org
Internet: www.un.org/partnerships
Officer-in-Charge: Roland Rich, Australia (since 2010)

Purpose

The UN Office for Partnerships (UNOP) promotes alliances and partnerships worldwide. Working with corporations, philanthropic foundations and civil society organisations, the Office seeks ways to leverage their skills in leadership, management, technology and innovative delivery systems to help achieve the Millennium Development Goals and other UN objectives. It also provides a platform for policy dialogues to effectively address global challenges.

UNOP also supports the UN Democracy Fund (UNDEF) and the UN Fund for International Partnerships (UNFIP). UNDEF funds projects that strengthen the voice of civil society, promote human rights and encourage the participation of all groups in democratic processes around the world. UNFIP works with the United Nations Foundation to support its role as founder of projects delivered by the UN, an advocate for the UN and a platform for connecting people, ideas and resources to help the UN solve global problems.

The UNFIP Advisory Board comprises UN high-level representatives and outside experts from the fields of philanthropy and academia. Members are appointed by the UN Secretary-General and generally serve for two years.

United Nations Democracy Fund (UNDEF)

1 United Nations Plaza, Room DC1–1300
New York, NY 10017
United States of America
Telephone: (+1 212) 963 3399
Fax: (+1 212) 963 1486
Email: democracyfund@un.org
Internet: www.un.org/democracyfund
Executive Head: Roland Rich, Australia (since 2007)

Purpose

The UN Democracy Fund (UNDEF) was established by the UN Secretary-General in July 2005 as a UN trust fund to support democratisation efforts in developing countries and in societies in transition. UNDEF finances and manages projects, implemented by civil society organisations, that build and strengthen democratic institutions, promote human rights and ensure the participation of all groups in democratic processes.

Structure

The UNDEF Advisory Board is appointed by the UN Secretary-General and comprises 13 Member States (the seven largest contributors to UNDEF and six countries representing geographical diversity as well as a commitment to democratic principles); two representatives of non-governmental organisations; and four representatives serving in an individual capacity. Members serve for two years.

SECURITY COUNCIL

SECURITY COUNCIL

CHARTER PROVISIONS

Pursuant to article 24 of the UN Charter, the members of the UN have conferred on the Security Council primary responsibility for the maintenance of international peace and security. The functions of the Council fall mainly under two headings:
- Pacific settlement of disputes
- Action with respect to threats to the peace, breaches of the peace, and acts of aggression.

Decisions on procedural matters are made by an affirmative vote of any nine members. Decisions on other matters are made by an affirmative vote of nine members, including the concurring votes of the five permanent members of the Council. Parties to a dispute must abstain from voting on measures for the pacific settlement of that dispute.

The Charter provisions relating to the Security Council are contained in chapter V (articles 23–32), chapter VI (articles 33–38), chapter VII (articles 39–51), chapter VIII (articles 52–54), and articles 76 and 82–84 of chapter XII. Other provisions are found in articles 1, 2, 4–7, 10–12, 15, 18, 20, 65, 93, 94, 96–99, 106, 108 and 109 of the Charter and articles 4, 7–15, 35, 41 and 69 of the Statute of the International Court of Justice.

MEMBERSHIP

The Security Council consists of five permanent members and 10 non-permanent members. Five of the non-permanent members are elected each year by the General Assembly for a term of two years. Membership terms of each non-permanent member end on 31 December of the year indicated. China, France, the Russian Federation, the UK and the USA are the permanent members.

In electing the Security Council's non-permanent members, the General Assembly is required by the Charter to pay due regard, in the first instance, to the contribution of UN members to the maintenance of international peace and security, the other purposes of the organisation, and also to equitable geographical distribution. A retiring member is not eligible for immediate re-election.

The Presidency is held in turn by Security Council members in the English alphabetical order of their country names, each holding office for one month.

By GA res. 1991A (XVIII) (1963), the General Assembly adopted, and submitted for ratification by Member States of the UN, amendments to the Charter provisions relating to membership of the Security Council (articles 23 and 27). It was decided to increase the number of non-permanent members from six to 10, and that the 10 non-permanent members should be elected according to the following pattern: five from African and Asia–Pacific states, one from Eastern European states, two from Latin American and Caribbean states, and two from Western European and Other states.

These amendments took effect in 1965, having been ratified by more than two-thirds of UN Member States, including all the permanent members of the Security Council. The first expanded Council was elected in 1965.

African and Asia–Pacific states

	Previous membership	Current membership
Algeria	1968–69 88–89 2004–05	
Angola	2003–04	
Bahrain	1998–99	
Bangladesh	1979–80 2000–01	
Benin	1976–77 2004–05	
Botswana	1995–96	
Burkina Faso	1984–85 2008–09	
Burundi	1970–71	
Cameroon	1974–75 2002–03	
Cape Verde	1992–93	
Congo	1986–87 2006–07	
Côte d'Ivoire	1964–65 90–91	
DR Congo	1982–83 90–91	
Djibouti	1993–94	
Egypt	1946 49–50 61–62 84–85 96–97	
Ethiopia	1967–68 89–90	
Gabon	1978–79 98–99 2010–11	
Gambia	1998–99	
Ghana	1962–63 86–87 2006–07	
Guinea	1972–73 2002–03	
Guinea-Bissau	1996–97	
India	1950–51 67–68 72–73 77–78 84–85 91–92	2011–12
Indonesia	1973–74 95–96 2007–08	
Iran	1955–56	
Iraq	1957–58 74–75	
Japan	1958–59 66–67 71–72 75–76 81–82 87–88 92–93 97–98 2005–06 09–10	
Jordan	1965–66 82–83	
Kenya	1973–74 97–98	
Kuwait	1978–79	
Lebanon	1953–54 2010–11	
Liberia	1961[1]	
Libya	1976–77 2008–09	
Madagascar	1985–86	
Malaysia	1965[1] 89–90 1999–2000	
Mali	1966–67 2000–01	
Mauritania	1974–75	
Mauritius	1977–78 2001–02	
Morocco	1963–64 92–93	2012–13
Namibia	1999–2000	
Nepal	1969–70 88–89	
Niger	1980–81	
Nigeria	1966–67 78–79 94–95 2010–11	
Oman	1994–95	
Pakistan	1952–53 68–69 76–77 83–84 93–94 2003–04	2012–13
Philippines	1957[1] 63[1] 80–81 2004–05	
Qatar	2006–07	
ROK	1996–97	
Rwanda	1994–95	
Senegal	1968–69 88–89	
Sierra Leone	1970–71	
Singapore	2001–02	
Somalia	1971–72	

	Previous membership	Current membership
South Africa	2007–08	2011–12
Sri Lanka	1960–61	
Sudan	1972–73	
Syrian AR[2]	1947–48 70–71 2002–03	
Thailand	1985–86	
Togo	1982–83	2012–13
Tunisia	1959–60 80–81 2000–01	
Uganda	1966 81–82 2009–10	
UAE	1986–87	
UR of Tanzania	1975–76 2005–06	
Viet Nam	2008–09	
Yemen	1990–91	
Zambia	1969–70 79–80 87–88	
Zimbabwe	1983–84 91–92	

Eastern European states[3, 4]

	Previous membership	Current membership
Azerbaijan		2012–13
Belarus	1974–75	
Bosnia and Herzegovina	2010–11	
Bulgaria	1966–67 86–87 2002–03	
Czech Republic	1994–95	
Croatia	2008–09	
Hungary	1968–69 92–93	
Poland	1946–47[1] 60 70–71 82–83 96–97	
Romania	1962[1] 76–77 90–91 2004–05	
Slovakia	2006–07	
Slovenia	1998–99	
Ukraine	1948–49 84–85 2000–01	

Latin American and Caribbean states

	Previous membership	Current membership
Argentina	1948–49 59–60 66–67 71–72 87–88 94–95 1999–2000 05–06	
Bolivia	1964–65 78–79	
Brazil	1946–47 51–52 54–55 63–64 67–68 88–89 93–94 98–99 2004–05 10–11	
Chile	1952–53 61–62 96–97 2003–04	
Colombia	1947–48 53–54 57–58 69–70 89–90 2001–02	2011–12
Costa Rica	1974–75 97–98 2008–09	
Cuba	1949–50 56–57 90–91	
Ecuador	1950–51 60–61 91–92	
Guatemala		2012–13
Guyana	1975–76 82–83	
Honduras	1995–96	
Jamaica	1979–80 2000–01	
Mexico	1946 80–81 2002–03 09–10	
Nicaragua	1970–71 83–84	
Panama	1958–59 72–73 76–77 81–82 2007–08	
Paraguay	1968–69	
Peru	1955–56 73–74 84–85 2006–07	
Trinidad and Tobago	1985–86	
Uruguay	1965–66	
Venezuela	1962–63 77–78 86–87 92–93	

Western European and Other states

Country	Previous membership	Current membership
Australia	1946–47 56–57 73–74 85–86	
Austria	1973–74 91–92 2009–10	
Belgium	1947–48 55–56 71–72 91–92 2007–08	
Canada	1948–49 58–59 67–68 77–78 89–90 1999–2000	
Denmark	1953–54 67–68 85–86 2005–06	
Finland	1969–70 89–90	
Germany[5]	1977–78 87–88 95–96 2003–04	2011–12
Greece	1952–53 2005–06	
Ireland	1962[1] 81–82 2001–02	
Italy	1959–60 71–72 75–76 87–88 95–96 2007–08	
Malta	1983–84	
Netherlands	1946 51–52 65–66 83–84 1999–2000	
New Zealand	1954–55 66[6] 93–94	
Norway	1949–50 63–64 79–80 2001–02	
Portugal	1979–80 97–98	2011–12
Spain	1969–70 81–82 93–94 2003–04	
Sweden	1957–58 75–76 97–98	
Turkey	1951–52 54–55 61[1] 2009–10	

Countries that have never served on the Security Council are not listed.

Notes

1 Split term.

2 The United Arab Republic served on the Council in 1961.

3 Czechoslovakia served on the Council in 1964 and 1978–79.

4 The Socialist Federal Republic of Yugoslavia served on the Council in 1950–51, 1956 (split term), 1972–73 and 1988–89. It was not succeeded by any of the new states following its dissolution.

5 The German Democratic Republic served a term on the Council in 1980–81.

6 One-year term pursuant to elections held in accordance with article 23(2) of the Charter.

STRUCTURE

- Standing committees
- Working groups
- Ad hoc working groups
- Military Staff Committee
- Counter-Terrorism Committee
- SC Res. 1540 Committee – Non-proliferation of Weapons of Mass Destruction
- Sanctions committees
- Peacekeeping operations
- Political and peacebuilding missions
- Commissions
- International tribunals
- Other organisations

STANDING COMMITTEES

The Committee of Experts on Rules of Procedure, the Committee on Council Meetings away from Headquarters and the Committee on the Admission of New Members each comprises representatives of all the members of the Security Council. The Presidency of the Council provides the Chair in each case.

WORKING GROUPS

Working Group on Children and Armed Conflict (CAAC)

Internet: http://childrenandarmedconflict.un.org (follow link from 'Our Work')

The Working Group on Children and Armed Conflict (CAAC) was established in July 2005 pursuant to Security Council res. 1612 (2005) to:
- Review the reports of the monitoring and reporting mechanism referred to in paragraph 3 of res. 1612 (2005)
- Review progress in the development and implementation of the action plans mentioned in paragraph 5(a) of res. 1539 (2004) and paragraph 7 of res. 1612 (2005)
- Consider other relevant information presented to it
- Make recommendations to the Security Council on possible measures to promote the protection of children affected by armed conflict, including through recommendations on appropriate mandates for peacekeeping missions and recommendations with respect to parties to the conflict
- Address requests, as appropriate, to other bodies within the UN system for action to support implementation of res. 1612 (2005) in accordance with their respective mandates.

Security Council res. 1882 (2009) and 1998 (2011) paragraphs 7 and 9 respectively, requested enhanced communication between the Working Group and relevant Security Council sanctions committees, including through the exchange of pertinent information on violations and abuses committed against children in armed conflict.

The Chair of the Working Group is Peter Wittig, Germany, who was re-elected to serve for the year to 31 December 2012 (S/2012/2).

AD HOC WORKING GROUPS

Security Council Informal Working Group on Documentation and Other Procedural Questions

Internet: www.un.org/sc/wgdocs

Established in June 1993, the Informal Working Group is concerned with the Security Council's documentation and other procedural questions. It comprises representatives of all Security Council members.

The Group Chair is José Filipe Moraes Cabral, Portugal, who was elected to serve from 3 January until 31 December 2012 (S/2012/2).

Working Group on Peacekeeping Operations

Established on 31 January 2001 (S/PRST/2001/3), the Working Group addresses both generic peacekeeping issues relevant to the responsibility of the Security Council and technical aspects of individual peacekeeping operations. This is done without prejudice to the competence of the General Assembly's Special Committee on Peacekeeping Operations.

The Chair is Mohammed Loulichki, Morocco, who was elected to serve the year to 31 December 2012 (S/2012/2).

Ad Hoc Working Group on Conflict Prevention and Resolution in Africa

The Working Group was established on 1 March 2002 (S/2002/207) to monitor and implement the recommendations contained in Presidential Statement S/PRST/2002/2, and previous presidential statements and resolutions regarding conflict prevention and resolution in Africa. The Group is also mandated to propose recommendations on the enhancement of cooperation between the Security Council and the Economic and Social Council (ECOSOC), as well as with other UN agencies dealing with Africa. In particular, it is asked to examine regional and cross-conflict issues that affect the Council's work on African conflict prevention and resolution, and to propose recommendations to the Security Council to enhance cooperation on conflict prevention and resolution among the UN, regional (African Union) and sub-regional organisations.

The Chair is Baso Sangqu, South Africa, who was re-elected to serve the year to 31 December 2012 (S/2012/2).

Working Group Established Pursuant to Resolution 1566 (2004)

Internet: www.un.org/sc/wg/1566

By res. 1566 (2004), the Security Council established the Working Group to examine:
- Practical measures to be imposed on individuals, groups or entities involved in or associated with terrorist activities, other than those designated by the Al-Qaida/Taliban Sanctions Committee (now two committees)
- The possibility of establishing an international fund to compensate victims of terrorist acts and their families.

The Chair is Hardeep Singh Puri, India, who was re-elected to serve for the year to 31 December 2012 (S/2012/2).

MILITARY STAFF COMMITTEE

The Military Staff Committee, established under article 47 of the Charter, consists of representatives of the Chiefs of Staff of the Permanent Members of the Security Council. Its function is to advise and assist the Security Council on all questions relating to:
- The military requirements for maintaining international peace and security
- The employment and command of forces placed at its disposal
- The regulation of armaments and possible disarmament.

The Committee's advice and assistance is expected to be sought for:
- Actions requiring the use of military forces under article 42
- Agreements to provide military forces to the Security Council under articles 43 and 44
- The readiness of immediately available air force contingents for combined international enforcement action under article 45

- Planning for the application of armed force under article 46. The Committee's task in assisting the Security Council in formulating plans for the regulation of armaments is addressed under article 26.

GA res. 1235 (XII) (1957) authorised the integration of the Military Staff Committee civilian staff with the UN Secretariat.

In accordance with the remit placed on the Security Council by paragraph 178 of the 2005 World Summit Outcome (A/RES/60/1), the Military Staff Committee has considered its composition, mandate and working methods. These discussions are ongoing.

The Military Staff Committee generally meets every fortnight. Certain Committee meetings also include informal participation by military representatives from the elected members of the Security Council.

COUNTER-TERRORISM COMMITTEE (CTC)

Internet: www.un.org/sc/ctc

The Counter-Terrorism Committee (CTC) was established by SC res. 1373 (2001), which was adopted unanimously on 28 September 2001 in the wake of the 11 September terrorist attacks in the USA.

The Committee, comprising all 15 Security Council members, was tasked with monitoring implementation of the resolution, which requested countries to implement measures intended to enhance their legal and institutional ability to counter terrorist activities at home, in their regions and around the world, including taking steps to:
- Criminalise the financing of terrorism
- Freeze without delay any funds related to persons involved in acts of terrorism
- Deny all forms of financial support for terrorist groups
- Suppress the provision of safe haven, sustenance or support for terrorists
- Share information with other governments on any groups practising or planning terrorist acts
- Cooperate with other governments in the investigation, detection, arrest, extradition and prosecution of those involved in such acts, and
- Criminalise active and passive assistance for terrorism in domestic law and bring violators to justice.

The resolution also calls on states to become parties, as soon as possible, to the relevant international counter-terrorism legal instruments.

In 2005, the Security Council directed the CTC to include resolution 1624 (2005), on incitement to commit acts of terrorism, in its ongoing dialogue with countries on their efforts to counter terrorism.

Under resolution 1535 (2004), the Security Council established the Counter-Terrorism Committee Executive Directorate (CTED) to assist the CTC and coordinate the process of monitoring the implementation of resolution 1373 (2001). CTED's mandate was extended by SC res. 1963 (2010) until 31 December 2013.

Chair for 2012	Vice-Chairs	CTED Executive Director
Hardeep Singh Puri, India	France	Mike Smith, Australia
	Morocco	
	Russian Federation	

SC RES. 1540 COMMITTEE – NON-PROLIFERATION OF WEAPONS OF MASS DESTRUCTION

Internet: www.un.org/sc/1540

On 28 April 2004, the Security Council unanimously adopted resolution 1540 (2004) under chapter VII of the UN Charter aimed at preventing the proliferation of weapons of mass destruction (WMDs) and their means of delivery to non-state actors. The resolution obliges states, amongst other things, to refrain from supporting by any means non-state actors from developing, acquiring, manufacturing, possessing, transporting, transferring or using nuclear, chemical or biological weapons and their means of delivery.

Resolution 1540 (2004) imposes binding obligations on all states to adopt legislation to prevent the proliferation of nuclear, chemical and biological weapons, and their means of delivery, and to establish appropriate domestic controls over related materials to prevent their illicit trafficking.

Paragraph 4 of SC res 1540 (2004) established a committee, comprising all Security Council members, tasked with reporting to the Council on the implementation of the resolution by Member States. The Council called on Member States to report to the Committee on steps they have taken, or intend to take, to implement the resolution. The Committee established three sub-committees, each chaired by one of the Committee's Vice-Chairs, to consider the implementation of reports received from Member States.

The Committee is assisted by experts appointed by the Secretary-General with the consent of the Committee. In 2009, the Committee established four working groups on a trial basis to focus on important and recurring issues:
- Monitoring and national implementation
- Assistance
- Cooperation with international organisations, including the Security Council committees established pursuant to resolutions 1267 (1999) and 1373 (2001)
- Transparency and media outreach.

By SC res. 1673 (2006), the Security Council reiterated its call to Member States to present reports on their implementation of resolution 1540 (2004) and encouraged them to provide additional information. The Council decided the Committee should intensify its efforts to promote the full implementation of the resolution.

By SC res. 1810 (2008), the Security Council extended the Committee's mandate until 25 April 2011. The Council also requested the Committee to consider a comprehensive review of the status of the implementation of resolution 1540 (2004). The "Final document on the 2009 comprehensive review of the status of implementation of Security Council resolution 1540 (2004): key findings and recommendations" was issued on 1 February 2010 (S/2010/52).

By SC resolution 1977 (2011), the Security Council further extended the Committee's mandate for a period of 10 years until 25 April 2021. The Council also decided the Committee would conduct a comprehensive review on implementation of resolution 1540 (2004), both after five years (before December 2016) and prior to the renewal of its mandate; include, if necessary, recommendations on adjustment to the mandate; and submit a report on the conclusion of these reviews to the Security Council. The Council further requested the Secretary-General to establish, in consultation with the 1540 Committee, a group of up to eight experts to assist the Committee in carrying out its mandate under resolutions 1540 (2004), 1673 (2006), 1810 (2008) and 1977 (2011).

Chair for 2012

Baso Sangqu, South Africa

Vice-Chairs

Azerbaijan
Portugal
UK

Coordinators of working groups

Monitoring and national implementation: Germany

Assistance: France

Cooperation with international organisations, including the Security Council committees established pursuant to resolutions 1267 (1999) and 1373 (2001): Togo

Transparency and media outreach: USA

SANCTIONS COMMITTEES

Internet: www.un.org/sc/committees

There are 13 Security Council sanctions committees, each comprising all 15 Security Council members and meeting in closed session. Office holders are normally elected by the Security Council in early January for terms that run to 31 December. The work of each committee and related expert groups, as well as the specifics of the sanctions measures currently in effect, are detailed on committee websites. Because of the frequent changes to the various sanctions regimes, up-to-date information on all Security Council sanctions should be sought from the website and applicable Security Council resolutions.

The Security Council adopted SC res. 1730 on 19 December 2006 in an attempt to ensure fair and clear procedures exist for placing individuals and entities on sanctions lists and for removing them, as well as for granting humanitarian exemptions. The resolution requested the Secretary-General to establish a focal point to receive delisting requests and to perform the tasks described in the annex to that resolution. Contact details for the focal point can be found at www.un.org/sc/committees/dfp.

In 2009, the Security Council established the Office of the Ombudsperson (SC res. 1904 (2009)) to review requests from individuals, groups, undertakings or entities seeking to be removed from the Security Council's Al-Qaida Sanctions Committee sanctions list. The Ombudsperson's mandate was extended for a further 18 months from 17 June 2011 by SC res. 1989.

SC Res. 751/1907 Committee – Somalia and Eritrea

Internet: www.un.org/sc/committees/751

The Committee was established by SC res. 751 (1992) on 24 April 1992 to oversee the arms embargo imposed on Somalia under SC res. 733 (1992). A series of resolutions have since modified the sanctions (all are available on the website).

Under SC res. 1844 (2008), the Security Council decided to impose individual targeted sanctions (arms embargo, including training and financial assistance, on individuals and entities; travel ban on individuals; and assets freeze on individuals and entities, as designated by the Committee). The same resolution provided exemptions from the measures and expanded the Committee's mandate.

SC res. 1916 (2010) established for 12 months an exemption to the assets freeze imposed by resolution 1844 (2008) in connection with the delivery of humanitarian assistance in Somalia, which was extended for 16 months by resolution 1972 (17 March 2011). On 12 April 2010, the Committee established a list of individuals and entities subject to the targeted sanctions imposed by resolution 1844 (2008).

SC res. 2002 (2011) expanded the criteria for designation to include individuals and entities found to be recruiting or using children in armed conflicts in Somalia or found to be responsible for the targeting of civilians including children and women in situations of armed conflict.

In 2009, the Security Council (SC res. 1907 (2009)) decided to impose a ban on the sale and supply to and from Eritrea of arms and related material as well as targeted sanctions (arms embargo, including training and financial assistance, on individuals and entities; travel ban on individuals; and assets freeze on individuals and entities, as designated by the Committee). The resolution also provided exemptions to the travel ban and assets freeze.

A panel of experts was established by SC res. 1425 (2002) to generate information on violations of the arms embargo with a view toward strengthening it. In 2003, the Panel was succeeded by a monitoring group to focus on the ongoing arms embargo violations. The Group's mandate was expanded and extended for 12 months by SC res. 2002 (29 July 2011).

Chair for 2012	Vice-Chairs
Hardeep Singh Puri, India	Pakistan
	Togo

SC Res. 1267/1989 Committee – Al-Qaida Sanctions Committee

Internet: www.un.org/sc/committees/1267

The Committee was originally established by SC res. 1267 on 15 October 1999 to oversee aviation and financial sanctions imposed on the Taliban regarding Taliban-controlled territory in Afghanistan under that same resolution. The aim was to secure the surrender of Osama bin Laden to the appropriate authorities for prosecution and to close down terrorist camps in Afghan territory. The demise of Osama bin Laden in May 2011 does not affect the continued application of the Al-Qaida assets freeze, travel ban and arms embargo sanctions measures.

The sanctions regime has been expanded considerably since 1999, and on 17 June 2011, the Committee was split in two to form the:
- Committee pursuant to resolutions 1267 (1999) and 1989 (2011) concerning Al-Qaida and associated individuals and entities – known as the 'Al-Qaida Sanctions Committee'
- Committee established pursuant to resolution 1988 (2011) – known as the '1988 Sanctions Committee' – to oversee sanctions against individuals and entities associated with the Taliban in constituting a threat to the peace, stability and security of Afghanistan (see below and the next entry for more information).

A list of the individuals and entities subject to the assets freeze, travel ban and arms embargo sanctions measures is maintained by the Al-Qaida Sanctions Committee on the basis of information provided by Member States and regional organisations.

Evolution

As part of its commitment to ensure fair and clear procedures for placing individuals and entities on sanctions lists and for removing them, the Security Council (SC res. 1904 (2009)) decided to establish the Office of the Ombudsperson to assist the Committee when it considered requests from individuals and entities for removal from the then Consolidated List, now Al-Qaida Sanctions List. For the first time, petitioners seeking delisting could present their case to an independent and impartial ombudsperson appointed by the Secretary-General, who, after consultations with both relevant states and the petitioner, would present a comprehensive report to the Committee with his or her observations.

As of May 2012, the Ombudsperson had received 27 requests for delisting and had submitted comprehensive reports to the Committee on 18 of these.

On 17 June 2011, the Security Council adopted resolutions 1988 (2011) and 1989 (2011) as successors to res. 1904 (2009), splitting the Al-Qaida and Taliban sanctions regime. On 30 June 2011, the 1267 Committee changed its name to the Al-Qaida Sanctions Committee.

SC res. 1989 (2011) stipulated that the sanctions list maintained by the Security Council Committee pursuant to resolutions 1267 (1999) and 1989 (2011) would be known as the 'Al-Qaida Sanctions List' and include only individuals and entities associated with Al-Qaida.

SC res. 1989 also expanded the mandate of the Ombudsperson to enable the making of recommendations on either retaining the listing or for the Committee to consider delisting; extended the Ombudsperson for a further period of 18 months; and further enhanced the fairness and transparency of how the sanctions measures are applied.

SC res. 1988 (2011) created a new sanctions regime targeting those associated with the Taliban in constituting a threat to the peace, stability and security of Afghanistan, as designated on the List established pursuant to that resolution. The 1988 Committee was established to oversee the newly established sanctions regime. The 1267 Monitoring Team (now called the Analytical Support and Sanctions Monitoring Team) continues to provide support for the work of both the 1988 and 1267/1989 Committees.

The other two terrorism-related subsidiary bodies established by the Security Council are the Counter-Terrorism Committee (CTC) and the 1540 Committee (Non-proliferation of Weapons of Mass Destruction). The terrorism-related committees and their experts coordinate their work, cooperate closely and, when possible, jointly brief the Security Council on their activities.

Chair for 2012	Vice-Chairs
Peter Wittig, Germany	Guatemala
	Russian Federation

SC Res. 1988 Sanctions Committee

Internet: www.un.org/sc/committees/1988

The Security Council established the 1988 Sanctions Committee on 17 June 2011 when, by resolutions 1988 (2011) and 1989 (2011), it split the work of the SC res. 1267 Committee (Al-Qaida and the Taliban) into two.

SC res. 1988 (2011) requires all states to take the following measures in connection with any individuals, groups, undertakings and entities associated with the Taliban in constituting a threat to the peace, stability and security of Afghanistan as designated by the Committee:

- Freeze without delay the funds and other financial assets or economic resources of designated individuals and entities (assets freeze)
- Prevent the entry into or transit through their territories by designated individuals (travel ban)
- Prevent the direct or indirect supply, sale and transfer from their territories or by their nationals outside their territories, or using their flag vessels or aircraft, of arms and related materiel of all types, spare parts, and technical advice, assistance, or training related to military activities, to designated individuals and entities (arms embargo).

SC res. 1988 (2011) also stipulated that petitioners seeking delisting without the sponsorship of a Member State are eligible to submit such requests to the Focal Point mechanism established under SC res. 1730 (2006).

The 1988 Sanctions Committee oversees the implementation of these three sanctions measures and undertakes the tasks set out in paragraph 30 of the same resolution, including establishing and maintaining the 1988 Sanctions List of individuals and entities to whom these measures apply.

Chair for 2012	Vice-Chairs
Peter Wittig, Germany	Guatemala
	Russian Federation

SC Res. 1518 Committee – Iraq

Internet: www.un.org/sc/committees/1518

The Committee was established by SC res. 1518 on 24 November 2003 as the successor body to the Security Council Committee established by SC res. 661 (1990) concerning Iraq and Kuwait. The 1518 Committee's role is to continue to identify senior officials of the former Iraqi regime and their immediate family members, including entities owned or controlled by them or by persons acting on their behalf, who are subject to the assets freeze and transfer measures imposed in SC res. 1483 (2003).

By SC res. 1546 (2004), the Security Council exempted the Government of Iraq and multi-national force from the embargo on arms and related materiel, but noted that the exemption did not include chemical, biological or nuclear weapons, or missiles or materiels related to these.

As of May 2012, an assets freeze and transfer measures concerning senior officials of the former Iraqi regime, their immediate families and related entities, as designated by the Committee, were in effect. A partial arms embargo was also in effect.

Chair for 2012	Vice-Chair
Kodjo Menan, Togo	India

SC Res. 1521 Committee – Liberia

Internet: www.un.org/sc/committees/1521

The Committee was established by SC res. 1521 on 22 December 2003 to oversee sanctions measures. It is the successor to two previous committees, the Committee established by SC res. 1343 (2001) and the Committee established by SC res. 985 (1997).

The sanctions regime and Committee's mandate have been modified by subsequent resolutions, most notably SC res. 1532 (2004), 1683 (2006) and 1903 (2009). The regime was most recently extended for 12 months by SC res. 2025 of 14 December 2011, continuing the travel ban and assets freeze on designated individuals or entities, and an arms embargo on all non-governmental entities and individuals operating in Liberia.

SC res. 1903 (2009) terminated the earlier arms embargo with regard to the Government of Liberia, but all states are under an obligation to notify the Committee in advance of any shipment of arms and related materiel to the Government of Liberia, or any provision of assistance, advice or training related to military activities.

Between 2003 and 2006, the sanctions regime included prohibitions on the import of all round logs and timber products from Liberia. Prohibitions on the import of rough diamonds from Liberia were terminated by SC res. 1753 (2007).

Chair for 2012	Vice-Chairs
Abdullah Hussain Haroon, Pakistan	Portugal
	South Africa

SC Res. 1533 Committee – Democratic Republic of the Congo
Internet: www.un.org/sc/committees/1533

The Committee was established by SC res. 1533 on 12 March 2004 to oversee the sanctions originally imposed by SC res. 1493 (2003). It has subsequently been modified by further resolutions.

The Security Council first imposed an arms embargo on all foreign and Congolese armed groups and militias operating in the territory of North and South Kivu and Ituri, and on groups not party to the Global and All-inclusive Agreement in the Democratic Republic of the Congo as at 28 July 2003. The sanctions regime has since undergone several modifications, including through resolutions 1698 (2006), 1771 (2007), 1799 (2008) and 1952 (2010).

The regime was most recently extended for 12 months by SC res. 2021 (2011), which further extended the arms embargo and targeted travel and financial sanctions until 30 November 2012.

The arms embargo applies to all non-governmental entities and individuals operating in eastern DR Congo, and all states are under an obligation to notify the Committee in advance about any shipment of arms and related materiel or provision of assistance, advice or training related to military activities.

Chair for 2012	Vice-Chairs
Agshin Mehdiyev, Azerbaijan	Morocco
	Pakistan

SC Res. 1572 Committee – Côte d'Ivoire
Internet: www.un.org/sc/committees/1572

By SC res. 1572 (2004), the Security Council imposed an arms embargo on Côte d'Ivoire and established, on 15 November 2004, a committee to oversee sanctions imposed under the same resolution.

The sanctions have subsequently been modified and extended, most notably by SC res. 1584 (2005), 1643 (2005), 1980 (2011), and most recently by SC res. 2045 (2012) until 30 April 2013. They include an arms embargo, travel ban and assets freeze on individuals designated by the Committee, and a ban on the importation of rough diamonds from Côte d'Ivoire.

The Committee is supported by a group of experts originally established by SC res. 1584 (2005) and subsequently renewed or extended, most recently by SC res. 2045 (2012) until 30 April 2013.

Chair for 2012	Vice-Chairs
Gert Rosenthal, Guatemala	Germany
	South Africa

SC Res. 1591 Committee – Sudan

Internet: www.un.org/sc/committees/1591

The Security Council first imposed an arms embargo on all non-governmental entities and individuals, including the Janjaweed militias, operating in the states of North Darfur, South Darfur and West Darfur on 30 July 2004 (SC res. 1556 (2004)).

SC res. 1591 (2005) broadened the scope of the arms embargo to include all parties to the N'Djamena Ceasefire Agreement and any other belligerents in the aforementioned states. The same resolution imposed a travel ban and/or an assets freeze on designated individuals and entities. It also established a committee to oversee the measures and a panel of experts to assist the Committee.

Subsequent resolutions, most recently SC res. 2035 (2012), have tightened the measures and extended the Panel of Expert's mandate until 17 February 2013.

Chair for 2012	Vice-Chairs
Néstor Osorio, Colombia	Azerbaijan
	India

SC Res. 1636 Committee – Lebanon

Internet: www.un.org/sc/committees/1636

The Committee was established by SC res. 1636 of 31 October 2005 to register individuals suspected of involvement in the 14 February 2005 terrorist bombing in Beirut, Lebanon – which killed former Lebanese Prime Minister Rafiq Hariri and 22 others – as subject to a travel ban and assets freeze. In the year to 31 May 2012, the Committee did not conduct any consultations or meetings.

Chair for 2012	Vice-Chairs
Kodjo Menan, Togo	Azerbaijan
	Germany

SC Res. 1718 Committee – Democratic People's Republic of Korea (DPRK)

Internet: www.un.org/sc/committees/1718

The Security Council decided by SC res. 1718 (2006) that the Democratic People's Republic of Korea (DPRK) should suspend all activities related to its ballistic missile programme, abandon all nuclear weapons and existing nuclear programmes, and abandon all other existing weapons of mass destruction (WMD) and ballistic missile programmes in a complete, verifiable and irreversible manner. The Committee was established by the same resolution, on 14 October 2006, to oversee a regime that includes an arms embargo, ban on trade and transfer of luxury goods, and an assets freeze and travel ban for designated persons or entities.

To ensure compliance with the sanctions regime, the Security Council called on all states to take cooperative action, including through inspection of cargo to and from the DPRK as necessary.

In 2009, the Security Council expanded the scope of its arms embargo, authorising Member States to inspect vessels that might carry prohibited cargo as well as to seize and dispose of prohibited items (SC res. 1874 (2009)). It also prohibited financial services or transfer of funds that might contribute to the DPRK's nuclear, ballistic missile or other WMD-related activities. By the same resolution, the Security Council created a panel of experts to assist the Committee in carrying out its mandate.

The Panel of Expert's mandate was most recently extended by SC res. 2050 (12 June 2012) until 12 July 2013.

Chair for 2012	Vice-Chairs
José Filipe Moraes Cabral, Portugal	Azerbaijan
	Togo

SC Res. 1737 Committee (2006) – Non-proliferation (Iran)

Internet: www.un.org/sc/committees/1737

The Committee was established by SC res. 1737 on 23 December 2006 to oversee the sanctions imposed under that same resolution. It now also oversees the extended sanctions imposed by resolutions 1747 (2007), 1803 (2008) and 1929 (2010). Under SC res. 1737, the sanctions included a nuclear and ballistic missile programmes-related embargo, and an assets freeze and travel notification requirements on persons and entities designated by the Security Council or Committee. In addition, the Council called on all states to prevent specialised teaching or training of Iranian nationals in disciplines that would contribute to Iran's proliferation of sensitive nuclear activities and development of nuclear weapon delivery systems.

SC res. 1747 (2007) imposed a ban on exports of arms and related materiel from Iran, and designated additional persons and entities as subject to the assets freeze and travel notification requirements. In addition, the Council called on all states to exercise vigilance and restraint in the provision of heavy weapons and related services to Iran. It also called on all states and international financial institutions not to enter into new commitments for grants, financial assistance and concessional loans to the Government of Iran, except for humanitarian and developmental purposes.

SC res. 1803 (2008) designated further persons and entities as subject to the assets freeze and travel notification requirements, imposed a travel ban on designated persons and expanded the scope of the embargo imposed by resolution 1737 to include additional items. The Security Council also called on states to exercise vigilance in the areas of publicly provided financial support for trade with Iran and of banking, particularly with respect to two specific Iranian banks. In addition, the resolution called for the inspection of cargo to and from Iran at national airports and seaports where there were reasonable grounds to suspect that goods prohibited under resolutions 1737, 1747 or 1803 were being transported.

SC res. 1929 (2010) strengthened the embargo on proliferation-sensitive nuclear and ballistic missile activities and imposed a partial arms embargo on imports by Iran of certain arms and related materiel. The Council also designated additional individuals and entities subject to the assets freeze and travel ban; established restrictions on business with Iranian entities; and imposed financial-related measures. In addition, the resolution sets out a ban on the provision of bunkering services and specifies a procedure for seizure and disposal of proscribed items, following inspections of cargo. The Security Council also established a panel of experts to assist the Committee in carrying out its mandate. The Panel's mandate was most recently extended to 9 June 2013 by SC res. 2049 (2012).

Chair for 2012	Vice-Chair
Néstor Osorio, Colombia	Togo

SC Res. 1970 Committee – Libya

Internet: www.un.org/sc/committees/1970

SC res. 1970 (2011) responded to violence perpetrated by Muammar Qadhafi on the Libyan people. It imposed immediate measures, including an arms embargo, and travel ban and asset freeze on key regime figures, including Muammar Qadhafi's family and certain government officials.

The Committee, established by SC res. 1970, was mandated to monitor the implementation of measures imposed in relation to the Libyan Arab Jamahiriya, to take action on information regarding alleged violations or non-compliance with the measures, and to designate additional individuals and entities as subject to the travel ban and assets freeze.

SC res. 1973 (17 March 2011) imposed additional measures and expanded the Committee's mandate to oversee them. The resolution also established a panel of experts to assist the Committee.

SC res. 2009 (2011) partly lifted the arms embargo on Libya and the asset freeze targeting entities connected to the previous regime (SC res. 1970 (2011)). SC res. 2017 (2011) mandated the Committee to consider the challenges posed to the region by the proliferation of arms from Libya.

Chair for 2012	Vice-Chair
José Filipe Moraes Cabral, Portugal	India

SC Res. 2048 Committee – Guinea-Bissau

www.un.org/sc/committees/2048

The Committee was established on 18 May 2012 by SC. res. 2048 following the military coup in Guinea-Bissau on 12 April 2012.

The Committee was established to oversee travel restrictions imposed on certain members of the military leadership. As at 31 May, there were five individuals subject to the travel restrictions.

Chair for 2012

Mohammed Loulichki, Morocco

Past sanctions committees

A list of terminated sanctions committees can be found towards the end of the web page www.un.org/sc/committees.

PEACEKEEPING OPERATIONS

Internet: www.un.org/en/peacekeeping/contributors

Sixty-seven UN peacekeeping operations have been deployed since 1948. They have involved more than 1.2 million military, police and civilian personnel, and cost more than $61 billion. As at 31 May 2012, there were 98,695 uniformed personnel (troops, police and military observers) and, as of 29 February 2012, 18,075 international and local civilian personnel serving in peacekeeping operations, along with 2445 UN Volunteers. The budget for UN peacekeeping operations for the year 1 July 2011 to 30 June 2012 was about $7.84 billion. On 21 June 2012, the General Assembly adopted a peacekeeping budget of just more than $7 billion for the period 1 July 2012 to 30 June 2013.

Two operations, the UN Truce Supervision Organization (UNTSO) and the UN Military Observer Group in India and Pakistan (UNMOGIP), are funded from the UN regular budget, while the other 14 peacekeeping missions are financed from their own separate accounts on the basis of legally binding assessments on all states.

The UN Assistance Mission in Afghanistan (UNAMA) is a UN political mission. It is, however, supported by the Department of Peacekeeping Operations (DPKO) and Department of Field Support (DFS), so is included here.

The mandates of most operations are renewed periodically or are subjected to reviews. Figures for operational strength, which may include military, police and civilian personnel, vary from month to month because of the rotation of contingents and personnel. Monthly figures are listed on the website.

Operations follow in chronological order of establishment.

UN Truce Supervision Organization (UNTSO)

Headquarters: Jerusalem, Israel
Telephone: (+1 917) 367 5340 (New York general enquiries for peacekeeping missions)
Internet: www.un.org/en/peacekeeping/missions/untso
Chief of Staff: Major-General Juha Kilpia, Finland (appointed by the UN Secretary-General in March 2011)

SC res. 50 (1948) formed the basis of what would become the UN Truce Supervision Organization (UNTSO). It provided for military observers to help the UN Mediator in Palestine, in concert with the Truce Commission, to supervise observance of the truce in Palestine.

Since then, UNTSO has performed various tasks entrusted to it by the Security Council, including supervision of the General Armistice Agreements of 1949 and observation of the ceasefire in the Suez Canal area and the Golan Heights following the Arab–Israeli war of June 1967.

UNTSO assists and cooperates with the UN Disengagement Observer Force (UNDOF) on the Golan Heights in the Israel–Syria sector and the UN Interim Force in Lebanon (UNIFIL) in the Israel–Lebanon sector. It is also present in the Egypt–Israel sector in the Sinai. UNTSO has liaison offices in Jerusalem, Beirut and Damascus.

The authorised uniformed strength of UNTSO is 153. As at 31 May 2012, the strength was 143 military observers and (at 29 February 2012) 99 international and 134 local civilian staff. The military personnel were from:

Argentina	Estonia	New Zealand
Australia	Finland	Norway
Austria	France	Russian Federation
Belgium	Ireland	Slovakia
Canada	Italy	Slovenia
Chile	Malawi	Sweden
China	Nepal	Switzerland
Denmark	Netherlands	USA

UN Military Observer Group in India and Pakistan (UNMOGIP)

(Nov–Apr)	(May–Oct)
UNMOGIP	UNMOGIP
Rawalpindi	Srinagar
Pakistan	India

Telephone: (+1 917) 367 5340 (New York general enquiries for peacekeeping missions)
Internet: www.un.org/en/peacekeeping/missions/unmogip
Chief Military Observer: Major-General Young-Bum Choi, ROK (appointed by the UN Secretary-General in June 2012)

SC res. 39 (1948) established a three-member UN Commission for India and Pakistan (UNCIP) to investigate and mediate the dispute over the status of Kashmir. By the terms of resolutions adopted by UNCIP on 13 August 1948 and 5 January 1949, the UN Military Observer Group in India and Pakistan (UNMOGIP) was established to supervise the ceasefire agreement of 1 January 1949. Following the termination of UNCIP, the Security Council decided UNMOGIP should continue to supervise the ceasefire in Kashmir and Jammu (SC res. 91 (1951)).

Following the outbreak of hostilities in Kashmir in 1965, the Security Council asked the Secretary-General to strengthen UNMOGIP (SC res. 210 (1965)), and a number of governments agreed to provide additional observers. As a result, the UN India–Pakistan Observation Mission (UNIPOM) was created as a temporary measure to supervise the ceasefire called for in SC res. 211 (1965) and to supervise withdrawals. After fulfilling its function, UNIPOM was disbanded and UNMOGIP reverted to its original strength.

UNMOGIP has remained in the area to observe developments pertaining to the strict observance of the ceasefire of 17 December 1971.

The authorised strength of UNMOGIP is 44 military personnel. As at 31 May 2012, its strength was 42 military observers and (at 29 February 2012) 24 international and at 50 local civilian staff. The military observers were from:

Chile	Italy	Sweden
Croatia	Philippines	Uruguay
Finland	ROK	

UN Force in Cyprus (UNFICYP)

Headquarters: Nicosia, Cyprus
Telephone: (+1 917) 367 5340 (New York general enquiries for peacekeeping missions)
Internet: www.un.org/en/peacekeeping/missions/unficyp
Special Representative of the Secretary-General: Lisa M Buttenheim (appointed by the UN Secretary-General in June 2010)
Force Commander: Major-General Chao Liu, China (appointed by the UN Secretary-General in January 2011)

In consultation with the Governments of Cyprus, Greece, Turkey and the UK, SC res. 186 (1964) established a peacekeeping force in Cyprus. The Force was declared operational on 27 March 1964, with a mandate of three months. There have been successive extensions, the latest being by SC res. 2058 (2012), which extended the mission by about six months to 31 January 2013.

The principal functions of the UN Force in Cyprus (UNFICYP) are to supervise the ceasefire and control the buffer zone in which civilian activities continue under escort. It also undertakes humanitarian work.

In earlier years, the cost of UNFICYP was met by the governments that provided military contingents and by voluntary contributions. However, by SC res. 831 (1993), the Security Council agreed that, from the time of the June 1993 mandate renewal, UNFICYP costs not otherwise met by voluntary contributions should be met from assessed contributions. This was confirmed by GA res. 47/236 (1993).

As at 31 May 2012, the strength of UNFICYP was 858 troops, 68 police, and (at 29 February 2012) 39 international and 108 local civilians. The military and police were from:

Argentina	China	Montenegro
Australia	Croatia	Paraguay
Austria	El Salvador	Serbia
Bosnia and Herzegovina	Hungary	Slovakia
Brazil	India	Ukraine
Canada	Ireland	UK
Chile	Italy	

UN Disengagement Observer Force (UNDOF)

Headquarters: Damascus, Syrian AR
Telephone: (+1 917) 367 5340 (New York general enquiries for peacekeeping missions)
Internet: www.un.org/en/peacekeeping/missions/undof
Force Commander: Major–General Iqbal Singh Singha, India (appointed by the UN Secretary-General in July 2012 to take up the role in August 2012)

By SC res. 350 (1974) and following a ceasefire agreement between Syria and Israel, the Security Council established the UN Disengagement Observer Force (UNDOF) for an initial six months. It was deployed in the Golan Heights in June 1974, with membership drawn from UN Truce Supervision Organization (UNTSO) observers in the area.

The UNDOF mandate has been renewed by successive Security Council resolutions, most recently SC res. 2052 (2012), which extended the period by about six months to 31 December 2012.

The authorised strength of UNDOF is 1047. As at 31 May 2012, its strength was 1055 troops and (at 29 February 2012) 41 international and 103 local civilians. The military were from:

Austria	Croatia	Japan
Canada	India	Philippines

UN Interim Force in Lebanon (UNIFIL)

Headquarters: Naqoura, South Lebanon
Telephone: (+1 917) 367 5340 (New York general enquiries for peacekeeping missions)
Internet: www.un.org/en/peacekeeping/missions/unifil
Force Commander: Major-General Paolo Serra, Italy (appointed by the UN Secretary-General in January 2012)

Following a request from the Government of Lebanon, the Security Council decided, by SC res. 425 (1978), to set up under its authority a UN interim force for Southern Lebanon. SC res. 426 (1978) established the UN Interim Force in Lebanon (UNIFIL) for an initial period of six months. The Force's mandate has since been extended for varying periods by successive Security Council resolutions, most recently by SC res. 2004 (2011) to 31 August 2012.

In July 2006, conflict broke out between Israel and Lebanon. On 11 August 2006, SC res. 1701 was adopted, providing a new and enhanced mandate for UNIFIL, including an authorised force of 15,000 troops and a Maritime Task Force capability. SC res. 1757 (2007) established a Special Tribunal for Lebanon.

As at 31 May 2012, UNIFIL's strength was 11,845 military personnel and (at 29 February 2012) 348 international and 657 local civilians. UNIFIL is also supported by about 50 UN Truce Supervision Organization (UNTSO) military observers of the Observer Group Lebanon. The military units and staff officers were from:

Armenia	Cambodia	Germany
Austria	China	Ghana
Bangladesh	Croatia	Greece
Belarus	Cyprus	Guatemala
Belgium	Denmark	Hungary
Brazil	El Salvador	India
Brunei	France	Indonesia

Ireland	Qatar	Sri Lanka
Italy	ROK	The former Yugoslav
Malaysia	Serbia	Republic of Macedonia
Nepal	Sierra Leone	Timor-Leste
Nigeria	Slovenia	Turkey
Portugal	Spain	UR of Tanzania

UN Mission for the Referendum in Western Sahara (MINURSO)

Headquarters: Laayoune, Western Sahara
Telephone: (+1 917) 367 5340 (New York general enquiries for peacekeeping missions)
Internet: www.un.org/en/peacekeeping/missions/minurso
Special Representative of the Secretary-General: Wolfgang Weisbrod-Weber, Germany (appointed by the UN Secretary-General in June 2012)
Force Commander: Major-General Abdul Hafiz, Bangladesh (appointed by the UN Secretary-General in July 2011)

The UN Mission for the Referendum in Western Sahara (MINURSO – a French acronym) was established by SC res. 690 (1991) in accordance with settlement proposals that provided for a transitional period for the preparation of a referendum in which the people of Western Sahara would choose between independence and integration with Morocco. The resolution also agreed a plan for a referendum involving MINURSO civilian, security and military units supervising the repatriation of Western Saharans identified as eligible to vote. Only part of MINURSO has so far been deployed.

By SC res. 973 (1995), the MINURSO Identification Commission was expanded to accelerate the voter identification and registration process. By SC res. 995 (1995), and in the context of concern at practices hampering progress towards the implementation of the Settlement Plan, the Security Council decided to send a mission to the region.

The Mission's mandate has since been extended, most recently by SC res. 2044 (2012), until 30 April 2013. This was done with the expectation that the parties, under the auspices of the Secretary-General's Personal Envoy, would continue to try to resolve the multiple problems relating to the implementation of the Settlement Plan and try to agree on a mutually acceptable political solution to their dispute over Western Sahara.

The mandated strength of MINURSO is 231 military and six police personnel. As at 31 May 2012, its strength was 27 troops, 216 military observers, six police, 19 UN Volunteers, and (at 29 February 2012) 99 international and 162 local civilians. The military and police were from:

Argentina	France	Nepal
Austria	Ghana	Nigeria
Bangladesh	Guinea	Pakistan
Brazil	Honduras	Paraguay
Chad	Hungary	Poland
China	Ireland	ROK
Croatia	Italy	Russian Federation
Djibouti	Jordan	Sri Lanka
Egypt	Malaysia	Uruguay
El Salvador	Mongolia	Yemen

UN Interim Administration Mission in Kosovo (UNMIK)

Headquarters: Skopje, Former Yugoslav Republic of Macedonia
Telephone: (+1 917) 367 5340 (New York general enquiries for peacekeeping missions)
Internet: www.un.org/en/peacekeeping/missions/unmik
Special Representative of the Secretary-General: Farid Zarif, Afghanistan (appointed by the UN
Secretary-General in October 2011)

The UN Interim Administration Mission in Kosovo (UNMIK) was established by SC res.
1244 (1999). Its mandate included: promoting the establishment, pending a final settlement,
of substantial autonomy and self-government in Kosovo; performing basic civilian
administrative functions; holding elections; facilitating a political process to determine
Kosovo's future status; supporting reconstruction; maintaining civil law and order; protecting
and promoting human rights; and assuring the safe and unimpeded return of all refugees and
displaced persons to their homes.

In August 2008, after the Kosovo Constitution was adopted, the UN reconfigured the
UNMIK mission and staff levels were reduced. Many of the UNMIK roles and tasks were
transferred to the Government of Kosovo and the European Union Rule of Law Mission in
Kosovo (EULEX).

EULEX is the largest civilian mission launched under the European Security and Defence
Policy. The central aim of the Mission is to assist and support the Kosovo authorities in
the rule of law, specifically in the police, judiciary and customs areas. EULEX is a technical
mission that will monitor, mentor and advise while retaining a limited number of executive
powers. EULEX works under the general framework of SC res. 1244 and has a unified chain
of command to Brussels.

As at 31 May 2012, the strength of UNMIK was nine military liaison officers, six police, 24
UN Volunteers, and (at 29 February 2012) 148 international civilians and 218 local staff. The
military and police were from:

Czech Republic	Norway	Romania
Germany	Pakistan	Spain
Ghana	Poland	Turkey
Italy	Portugal	Ukraine

UN Organization Stabilization Mission in the Democratic Republic of the Congo (MONUSCO)

Headquarters: Kinshasa, DR Congo
Telephone: (+1 917) 367 5340 (New York general enquiries for peacekeeping missions)
Internet: www.un.org/en/peacekeeping/missions/monusco
Special Representative of the Secretary-General: Roger A Meece, USA (appointed by the UN
Secretary-General in June 2010)
Force Commander: Lieutenant General Chander Prakash, India (appointment announced by the UN
Secretary-General in July 2010)
Police Commissioner: Abdallah Wafy, Niger (since February 2010)

DR Congo and five regional states signed the Lusaka Ceasefire Agreement in July 1999. SC
res. 1258 (1999) authorised the deployment of UN military liaison personnel and other staff
following the signing of the agreement.

To maintain liaison with the parties and carry out other tasks, the Security Council set up the
UN Organization Mission in the Democratic Republic of the Congo (MONUC – a French
acronym) on 30 November 1999 (SC res. 1279), incorporating UN personnel authorised in
earlier resolutions.

In May 2010, the Security Council decided that, in view of the new phase reached in DR Congo, MONUC would be renamed the UN Organization Stabilization Mission in the Democratic Republic of the Congo (MONUSCO) from 1 July 2010 (SC res. 1925). MONUSCO's mandate was most recently extended by one year to 30 June 2013 (SC res. 2053 (2012)), while the arms embargo and related sanctions have been renewed until 30 November 2012 (SC res. 2021 (2011)) by which time the measures in the sanction will have been reassessed.

The authorised strength of MONUSCO is 19,815 military personnel, 760 military observers, 391 police, 1050 personnel of formed police units, and appropriate civilian, judiciary and correction component. SC res. 1925 (2010) also authorised the withdrawal of up to 2000 UN military personnel by 30 June 2010 from areas where the security situation permits, and authorised MONUSCO, while concentrating its military forces in the east of DR Congo, to keep a reserve force capable of redeploying rapidly elsewhere in the country.

As at 31 May 2012, MONUSCO's strength was 17,042 military personnel, 730 military observers, 3126 police, 614 UN Volunteers, and (at 29 February 2012) 954 international and 2864 local civilians. The military and police were from:

Algeria	Indonesia	Russian Federation
Bangladesh	Ireland	Senegal
Belgium	Jordan	Serbia
Benin	Kenya	South Africa
Bolivia	Madagascar	Spain
Bosnia and Herzegovina	Malawi	Sri Lanka
Burkina Faso	Malaysia	Sweden
Cameroon	Mali	Switzerland
Canada	Mongolia	Togo
Central African Republic	Morocco	Tunisia
Chad	Mozambique	Turkey
China	Nepal	Ukraine
Côte d'Ivoire	Niger	UK
Czech Republic	Nigeria	UR of Tanzania
Egypt	Norway	USA
France	Pakistan	Uruguay
Ghana	Paraguay	Yemen
Guatemala	Peru	Zambia
Guinea	Poland	
India	Romania	

UN Assistance Mission in Afghanistan (UNAMA)

Headquarters: Kabul, Afghanistan
Telephone: (+1 917) 367 5340 (New York general enquiries for peacekeeping missions)
Internet: http://unama.unmissions.org
Head of Assistance Mission and Special Representative of the Secretary-General: Ján Kubiš of Slovakia (appointed by the UN Secretary-General in November 2011, took up the position in January 2012)

The UN Assistance Mission in Afghanistan (UNAMA) succeeds the Special Mission to Afghanistan (UNSMA), which was established by GA res. 48/208 (1993). UNAMA was established by SC res. 1401 (2002). Its original mandate was aimed at supporting the process of rebuilding and national reconciliation outlined in the Bonn Agreement of 5 December 2001 (S/2001/1154). UNAMA is a special political mission directed and supported by the Department of Peacekeeping Operations (DPKO).

The Mission's priorities include strengthening Afghan institutions and building the capacity of Afghan administration at all levels, including the development of institutions of good governance, law and order, and security.

UNAMA's mandate was most recently extended by SC res. 2041 (2012) to 23 March 2013.

UNAMA comprises a political section and a humanitarian, recovery and reconstruction section, each led by a Deputy Special Representative. The Mission, as well as parts of the Office for the Coordination of Humanitarian Affairs (OCHA), has its headquarters in Kabul, with eight regional offices throughout the country and several sub-offices. UNAMA has established two liaison offices, one in Islamabad and one in Tehran.

The strength of UNAMA, as at 30 June 2012, was 2156 UN and local civilian staff, 73 UN Volunteers, 17 military advisers and four police officers. The military and police personnel were from:

Australia	Italy	Portugal
Czech Republic	New Zealand	Sweden
Denmark	Norway	Turkey
Germany	Poland	Uruguay

UN Mission in Liberia (UNMIL)

Headquarters: Monrovia, Liberia
Telephone: (+1 917) 367 5340 (New York general enquiries for peacekeeping missions)
Internet: www.un.org/en/peacekeeping/missions/unmil
Special Representative of the Secretary-General: Karin Landgren, Sweden (appointed by the UN Secretary-General in April 2012)
Force Commander: Major-General Muhammad Khalid, Pakistan (appointed by the UN Secretary-General in October 2010)
Police Commissioner: John Nielsen, USA (since April 2012)

The UN Peace-building Support Office in Liberia (UNOL) was established on 1 November 1997 following consultations with the Government of Liberia and the Security Council. Its role was to support the Government of Liberia to consolidate peace, promote national reconciliation and strengthen its democratic institutions, as well as to strengthen the engagement of the UN system in post-conflict peacebuilding. In September 2003, UNOL ceased when the Security Council, under SC res. 1509 (2003), established the UN Mission in Liberia (UNMIL), initially for 12 months. UNMIL's mandate was most recently extended to 30 September 2012 (SC res. 2008 (2011)).

UNMIL's mission is to:
• Support implementation of the ceasefire agreement and peace process
• Protect UN staff, facilities and civilians
• Support humanitarian and human rights activities
• Assist in national security reform, including national police training and the formation of a new, restructured military.

As at 31 May 2012, UNMIL's strength was 7750 troops, 119 military observers, 1313 police, 224 UN Volunteers, and (at 29 February 2012) 480 international and 990 local civilians. Military and police were from:

Argentina	Bosnia and Herzegovina	Croatia
Bangladesh	Brazil	Czech Republic
Benin	Bulgaria	Denmark
Bolivia	China	Ecuador

Egypt	Mongolia	Rwanda
El Salvador	Montenegro	Senegal
Ethiopia	Namibia	Serbia
Fiji	Nepal	Sri Lanka
Finland	Niger	Sweden
France	Nigeria	Switzerland
Gambia	Norway	Togo
Germany	Pakistan	Turkey
Ghana	Paraguay	Uganda
India	Peru	Ukraine
Indonesia	Philippines	USA
Jordan	Poland	Uruguay
Kenya	ROK	Yemen
Kyrgyzstan	Republic of Moldova	Zambia
Malaysia	Romania	Zimbabwe
Mali	Russian Federation	

UN Operations in Côte d'Ivoire (UNOCI)

Headquarters: Abidjan, Côte d'Ivoire
Telephone: (+1 917) 367 5340 (New York general enquiries for peacekeeping missions)
Internet: www.un.org/en/peacekeeping/missions/unoci
Special Representative of the Secretary-General and Head of Mission: Albert Gerard Koenders, Netherlands (appointed by the Secretary-General in August 2011)
Force Commander: Major-General Muhammad Iqbal Asi, Pakistan (appointed by the Secretary General in March 2012)
Police Commissioner: Major-General Jean Marie Bourry, France

The UN Operations in Côte d'Ivoire (UNOCI) replaced the UN Mission in Côte d'Ivoire (MINUCI), a political mission set up by the Security Council in May 2003 with a mandate to facilitate the implementation of the peace agreement signed in January 2003.

UNOCI was established on 27 February 2004 by SC res. 1528 for an initial 12 months. MINUCI's mandate ended with the Secretary-General transferring authority from MINUCI and Economic Community of West African States (ECOWAS) forces to UNOCI in April 2004. UNOCI's mandate was most recently extended to 31 July 2013 (SC res. 2062 (2012)).

As at 31 May 2012, UNOCI's strength was 9400 troops, 196 military observers and 1337 police, 293 UN Volunteers, and (at 29 February 2012) 400 international and 458 local civilians. The military and police were from:

Argentina	Ghana	Republic of Moldova
Bangladesh	Guatemala	Romania
Benin	Guinea	Russian Federation
Bolivia	India	Senegal
Brazil	Ireland	Serbia
Burundi	Jordan	Switzerland
Cameroon	Malawi	Togo
Canada	Morocco	Tunisia
Central African Republic	Namibia	Turkey
Chad	Nepal	Uganda
China	Niger	Ukraine
DR Congo	Nigeria	UR of Tanzania
Djibouti	Pakistan	Uruguay
Ecuador	Paraguay	Yemen
Egypt	Peru	Zambia
Ethiopia	Philippines	Zimbabwe
France	Poland	
Gambia	ROK	

UN Stabilization Mission in Haiti (MINUSTAH)

Headquarters: Port-au-Prince, Haiti
Telephone: (+1 917) 367 5340 (New York general enquiries for peacekeeping missions)
Internet: www.un.org/en/peacekeeping/missions/minustah
Special Representative of the Secretary-General: Mariano Fernández, Chile (appointed by the UN Secretary-General in May 2011)
Force Commander: Major General Fernando Rodrigues Goulart, Brazil (appointed by the UN Secretary-General in March 2012)
Police Commissioner: Marc Tardif, Canada

The UN Stabilization Mission in Haiti (MINUSTAH) was established on 1 June 2004 by SC res. 1542. The mission succeeded a Multinational Interim Force (MIF) authorised by the Security Council in February 2004 after President Bertrand Aristide departed Haiti for exile in the aftermath of an armed conflict that spread to several cities across the country.

Following the devastating earthquake of 12 January 2010, SC res. 1908 (2010) increased MINUSTAH's overall force levels to support the immediate recovery, reconstruction and stability efforts in the country. Since the completion of presidential elections in 2011, MINUSTAH has been working to fulfil its original mandate to restore a secure and stable environment, promote the political process, strengthen Haiti's government institutions and rule-of-law-structures, and promote and protect human rights.

MINUSTAH's mandate was most recently extended to 15 October 2012 (SC res. 2012 (2011)).

The authorised strength is up to 7340 military and 3241 police. As at 31 May 2012, there were 7283 troops, 3126 police, 226 UN Volunteers, and (at 29 February 2012) 559 international and 1358 local civilians. The military and police were from:

Argentina	France	Peru
Bangladesh	Grenada	Philippines
Benin	Guatemala	Romania
Bolivia	Guinea	ROK
Brazil	India	Russian Federation
Burkina Faso	Indonesia	Rwanda
Burundi	Jamaica	Senegal
Cameroon	Japan	Serbia
Canada	Jordan	Sierra Leone
Central African Republic	Kyrgyzstan	Spain
Chad	Lithuania	Sri Lanka
Chile	Madagascar	Sweden
China	Mali	Thailand
Colombia	Nepal	Togo
Côte d'Ivoire	Niger	Turkey
Croatia	Nigeria	USA
Egypt	Norway	Uruguay
El Salvador	Pakistan	Yemen
Ecuador	Paraguay	

UN Mission in the Republic of South Sudan (UNMISS)

Headquarters: Juba, South Sudan
Telephone: (+1 917) 367 5340 (New York general enquiries for peacekeeping missions)
Internet: www.un.org/en/peacekeeping/missions/unmiss
Special Representative of the Secretary-General: Hilde Johnson, Norway (appointed by the UN Secretary-General in July 2011)
Force Commander: Major General Moses Bisong Obi, Nigeria (former UNMIS Force Commander, appointment announced June 2010)

The UN Mission in the Republic of South Sudan (UNMISS) was established on 9 July 2011 by SC res. 1996 (2011), the same day that South Sudan became the newest country in the world. It replaced the UN Mission in Sudan (UNMIS), which had been established by SC res. 1590 (2005).

The UNMISS mandate is to consolidate peace and security, and help establish the conditions for development in South Sudan, with a view to strengthening the Government's capacity to govern effectively and democratically, and establish good relations with its neighbours.

The mission was established for an initial period of one year from 9 July 2011, renewed by SC res. 2057 (2012) until 15 July 2013. Its authorised strength is up to 7000 military and 900 civilian police personnel.

As at 31 May 2012, there were 5157 troops, 139 military observers, 484 police, 300 UN Volunteers, and (at 29 February 2012) 779 international and 1289 local civilians. The military and police personnel were from:

Argentina	Guatemala	Philippines
Australia	Guinea	Poland
Bangladesh	India	ROK
Benin	Indonesia	Romania
Bolivia	Jamaica	Russian Federation
Bosnia and Herzegovina	Japan	Rwanda
Brazil	Jordan	Samoa
Burkina Faso	Kenya	Sierra Leone
Cambodia	Kyrgyzstan	Sri Lanka
Canada	Malaysia	Sweden
China	Mali	Switzerland
Denmark	Moldova	Timor-Leste
Ecuador	Mongolia	Turkey
Egypt	Namibia	Uganda
El Salvador	Nepal	Ukraine
Ethiopia	New Zealand	UK
Fiji	Nigeria	UR of Tanzania
Gambia	Norway	USA
Germany	Papua New Guinea	Yemen
Ghana	Paraguay	Zambia
Greece	Peru	Zimbabwe

UN Mission in Timor-Leste (UNMIT)

Headquarters: Dili, Timor-Leste
Telephone: (+1 917) 367 5340 (New York general enquiries for peacekeeping missions)
Internet: www.un.org/en/peacekeeping/missions/unmit
Acting Special Representative of the Secretary-General: Finn Reske-Nielsen, Denmark (appointed by the UN Secretary-General in June 2012)
Police Commissioner: Luis Miguel Carrilho, Portugal (since February 2009)

SC res. 1704 (2006) established the UN Mission in Timor-Leste (UNMIT) as an integrated mission. It replaced other UN operations and missions operating in Timor-Leste since 1999. SC res. 2037 (2012) extended the Mission's mandate until 31 December 2012 and endorsed the plan for its phased drawdown.

The authorised strength of UNMIT is 34 military liaison and staff officers, and 1748 UN police officers. As at 31 May 2012, there were 1242 police, 33 military liaison officers, 268 UN Volunteers, and (at 29 February 2012) 388 international and 874 local civilians.

The military liaison and police were from:

Australia		
Bangladesh	Malaysia	Sierra Leone
Brazil	Namibia	Singapore
China	Nepal	Spain
Croatia	New Zealand	Sri Lanka
Egypt	Nigeria	Thailand
El Salvador	Pakistan	Turkey
Fiji	Philippines	Uganda
Gambia	Portugal	Ukraine
India	ROK	Uruguay
Jamaica	Romania	Yemen
Japan	Russian Federation	Zambia
Jordan	Samoa	Zimbabwe
Kyrgyzstan	Senegal	

UN African Union Mission in Darfur (UNAMID)

Headquarters: El Fasher, Sudan
Telephone: (+1 917) 367 5340 (New York general enquiries for peacekeeping missions)
Internet: www.un.org/en/peacekeeping/missions/unamid
Joint AU–UN Special Representative: Ibrahim Gambari, Nigeria (appointed by the UN Secretary-General in January 2010)
Force Commander: Lieutenant General Patrick Nyamvumba, Rwanda (since September 2009)
Police Commissioner: James Oppong-Boanuh, Ghana (since August 2010)

The UN African Union Mission in Darfur (UNAMID) is a hybrid peacekeeping operation mounted by the African Union (AU) and the UN in response to the continuing violence in Sudan's Darfur region. Established by SC res. 1769 (2007), it superseded the AU Mission in Sudan (AMIS), and was given a 12-month mandate dating from 31 July 2007. SC res. 2003 (2011) extended the mandate to 31 July 2012.

UNAMID has an authorised strength of 19,555 military personnel and 6432 police. As at 31 May 2012, it had 17,364 troops, 591 military observers, 5511 police, 475 UN Volunteers, and (at 29 February 2012) 1097 international and 2923 local civilians. The military and police personnel were from:

Bangladesh	Italy	Palau
Burkina Faso	Jamaica	Philippines
Burundi	Jordan	ROK
Cameroon	Kenya	Rwanda
Canada	Kyrgyzstan	Senegal
Côte D'Ivoire	Lesotho	Sierra Leone
China	Madagascar	South Africa
Ecuador	Malaysia	Tajikistan
Egypt	Malawi	Tanzania
Ethiopia	Mali	Thailand
Fiji	Mongolia	Togo
Gambia	Niger	Turkey
Germany	Namibia	Uganda
Ghana	Nepal	UR of Tanzania
Guatemala	Netherlands	Yemen
Indonesia	Nigeria	Zambia
Iran	Pakistan	Zimbabwe

UN Interim Security Force for Abyei (UNISFA)

Headquarters: Abyei Town, Sudan
Telephone: (+1 917) 367 5340 (New York general enquiries for peacekeeping missions)
Internet: www.un.org/en/peacekeeping/missions/unisfa
Force Commander: Lieutenant-General Tadesse Werede Tesfay, Ethiopia (appointed by the UN
Secretary-General in July 2011)

SC res. 1990 (27 June 2011) established the UN Interim Security Force for Abyei (UNISFA) for an initial period of six months following renewed violence, escalating tensions and population displacement in Sudan's Abyei region, which straddles Northern and Southern Sudan and has been claimed by both. UNISFA's mandate was most recently extended by SC res. 2047 (2012) to 27 October 2012.

UNISFA monitors the border between north and south, and is authorised to use force in protecting civilians and humanitarian workers in Abyei.

The authorised strength is up to 4200 military personnel, 50 police and appropriate civilian support. As at 31 May 2012, there were 3933 troops, 120 military observers, two UN Volunteers, and (at 29 February 2012) 35 international and 12 local civilians. The military personnel were from:

Benin	Kyrgyzstan	Russian Federation
Bolivia	Mongolia	Rwanda
Brazil	Mozambique	Sierra Leone
Burundi	Namibia	Sri Lanka
Ethiopia	Nepal	UR of Tanzania
Ghana	Nigeria	Uruguay
Guatemala	Paraguay	Zambia
India	Peru	Zimbabwe
Indonesia	Philippines	

UN Supervision Mission in Syria (UNSMIS)

Headquarters: Damascus, Syria
Telephone: (+1 917) 367 5340 (New York general enquiries for peacekeeping missions)
Internet: www.un.org/en/peacekeeping/missions/unsmis
Head of Mission and Chief Military Observer: Major-General Robert Mood, Norway (since April 2012)

The UN Supervision Mission in Syria (UNSMIS) was established by SC res. 2043 (April 2012) for an initial period of 90 days, renewed on 20 July for 30 days by SC res. 2059 (2012). Its mandate includes monitoring a cessation of armed violence in all its forms in Syria, and to monitor and support the full implementation of the UN–Arab League Joint Special Envoy's six-point plan to end the conflict in Syria.

The authorised strength is up to 300 unarmed military observers as well as an appropriate civilian component. As of 14 June 2012, its strength was 298 military observers and 82 international and 30 local civilian staff. The country contributors of military personnel were:

Argentina	Cambodia	Egypt
Armenia	Chad	Fiji
Bangladesh	China	Finland
Benin	Croatia	France
Brazil	Czech Republic	Germany
Burkina Faso	Denmark	Ghana
Burundi	Ecuador	Guatemala

continued next page

SECURITY COUNCIL

Indonesia	Nepal	Russian Federation
Ireland	Netherlands	Senegal
Italy	New Zealand	Slovenia
Jordan	Niger	South Africa
Kenya	Nigeria	Switzerland
Kyrgyzstan	Norway	Togo
Malawi	Paraguay	Uruguay
Mauritania	Philippines	Yemen
Morocco	Romania	Zimbabwe

Past peacekeeping operations

See www.un.org/en/peacekeeping/operations/past for information about past peacekeeping operations.

POLITICAL AND PEACEBUILDING MISSIONS

Internet: www.un.org/depts/dpa (follow link to 'Field Operations')
Twitter: @UN_DPA

UN peacemaking and peacebuilding efforts include special representatives and envoys of the Secretary-General, as well as field-based missions and offices established for the prevention, control and resolution of conflicts, and to facilitate peacebuilding.

These missions and offices are established by the Secretary-General, and, where necessary, in consultation with the Security Council, in the exercise of the Secretary-General's global responsibilities under the UN Charter relating to the maintenance of international peace and security.

All are supported by the UN Department of Political Affairs with the exception of the UN Assistance Mission in Afghanistan (UNAMA), which is directed and supported by the Department of Peacekeeping Operations, and covered in the previous section.

As at 31 May 2012, the UN supports 13 political and peacebuilding missions (including UNAMA) comprising 469 uniformed personnel, 93 UN Volunteers, and (as at 29 February 2012) 1220 international and 2598 local civilian personnel.

UN Political Office for Somalia (UNPOS)

Headquarters: Nairobi, Kenya
Telephone: (+254) 20 762 7111
Fax: (+254) 20 762 2697
Email: unpos_pio@un.org
Internet: http://unpos.unmissions.org
Special Representative of the Secretary-General and Head of Office: Augustine P Mahiga, UR of Tanzania (appointed by the UN Secretary General in June 2010)

The UN Political Office for Somalia (UNPOS) was established on 15 April 1995 to monitor the situation in Somalia, advance national reconciliation and restore peace.

The Security Council most recently renewed the UN mandate for the African Union Mission in Somalia (AMISOM) until 31 October 2012 (SC res. 2010 (2011)), and requested the African Union (AU) to increase its force strength to its mandated level of 12,000 uniformed personnel.

UNPOS and the UN country team are charged with promoting lasting peace and stability in Somalia through the implementation of the Djibouti Peace Agreement, and with coordinating international support to these efforts.

Stepping up the UN's political support to the Somali transition, UNPOS relocated to Mogadishu from its former base in Nairobi, Kenya, in January 2012. The relocation took place against the background of major security improvements in Somalia in 2011.

As at 31 May 2012, the strength of UNPOS was 54 international and 31 local civilians, three military advisers and three police officers.

UN Integrated Peace-building Office in Guinea-Bissau (UNIOGBIS)

Headquarters: Bissau, Guinea-Bissau
Telephone: (+1 212) 963 1976 / 963 3756 / 963 8174
Fax: (+1 212) 963 1758
Internet: http://uniogbis.unmissions.org
Special Representative of the Secretary-General and Head of UNIOGBIS: Joseph Mutaboba, Rwanda (since January 2010)

The UN Integrated Peace-Building Office in Guinea-Bissau (UNIOGBIS) was established by SC res. 1876 (2009). It succeeded the UN Peace-Building Support Office in Guinea-Bissau (UNOGBIS) from 1 January 2010 for an initial 12 months, most recently extended until 28 February 2013 (SC res. 2030 (2011)).

UNIOGBIS has been mandated to support the Government of Guinea-Bissau in the areas of political reconciliation and dialogue, security sector reform, human rights and rule of law promotion, addressing drug trafficking and organised crime, and assisting the work of the Peacebuilding Commission and the Peacebuilding Fund.

As at 31 May 2012, the strength of UNIOGBIS was 53 international and 52 local civilians, two military advisers, 16 police and six UN Volunteers.

UN Integrated Peacebuilding Office in the Central African Republic (BINUCA)

Headquarters: Bangui, Central African Republic
Internet: http://binuca.unmissions.org (French-language site)
Special Representative of the Secretary-General and Head of Office: Margaret Vogt, Nigeria (appointed by the UN Secretary-General in May 2011)

The UN Integrated Peacebuilding Office in the Central African Republic (BINUCA) was established in accordance with the Security Council Presidential Statement of 7 April 2009 and became operational on 1 January 2010. BINUCA succeeded the UN Peace-building Support Office in the Central African Republic (BONUCA), which was first established in 2000 by SC Res. 1271 (1999). The BINUCA mandate was extended by SC res. 2031 (2011) to 31 January 2013.

As an integrated office, BINUCA brings together under one framework the UN's political, human rights, humanitarian and development work in the Central African Republic.

Its mandate includes helping consolidate peace and national reconciliation, strengthen democratic institutions and mobilise international political support and resources for national reconstruction and economic recovery. The Office is also tasked with promoting public awareness of human rights issues in the country and monitoring developments in this field.

The mission is also mandated to support the work of the Peacebuilding Commission and Peacebuilding Fund, and help ensure that child protection is properly addressed in the implementation of the Comprehensive Peace Agreement and the disarmament, demobilisation and reintegration (DDR) process, including by supporting the monitoring and reporting mechanism established by resolutions 1539 (2004) and 1612 (2005).

As at 31 May 2012, BINUCA's strength was 67 international and 75 local civilians, two military advisers, two police and five UN Volunteers.

UN Office for West Africa (UNOWA)

Headquarters: Dakar, Senegal
Telephone: (+221) 33 869 8585
Fax: (+221) 33 820 4638
Internet: http://unowa.unmissions.org
Special Representative of the Secretary-General: Said Djinnit, Algeria (appointed by the UN Secretary-General in February 2008)

The UN Secretary-General, in agreement with the Security Council, established both the UN Office for West Africa (UNOWA) and the position of Special Representative of the Secretary-General for West Africa in November 2001. The Security Council, on the recommendation of the Secretary-General in December 2010 (S/2010/660), extended the Office's mandate until 31 December 2013.

UNOWA was the UN's first regional conflict-prevention and peacebuilding office. Its overall mandate is to enhance the contributions of the UN towards the achievement of peace and security in West Africa.

As at 31 May 2012, UNOWA's strength was 19 international and 17 local civilians, and three military advisers.

UN Assistance Mission for Iraq (UNAMI)

Headquarters: Baghdad, Iraq
Telephone: (+962 6) 550 4700
Fax: (+962 6) 550 4705
Internet: www.uniraq.org
Special Representative of the Secretary-General: Martin Kobler, Germany (appointed by the UN Secretary-General in August 2011)

The position of Special Representative of the Secretary-General for Iraq was established by SC res. 1483 (2003). The UN Assistance Mission for Iraq (UNAMI) was established by SC Res. 1500 (2003), with an initial 12-month task of supporting the Secretary-General in the fulfilment of his mandate under SC res. 1483.

Subsequent Security Council resolutions 1546 (2003), 1557 (2004), 1619 (2005), 1700 (2006), 1770 (2007), 1830 (2008), 1883 (2009) and 1936 (2010) have modified and extended the scope of UNAMI's mandate, and have led to the expansion of UNAMI's presence and activities in Iraq. SC res. 2001 of 28 July 2011 extended the mandate for a further 12 months and reaffirmed the efforts of UNAMI in supporting the Iraqi Government and people to, amongst other things:
- Strengthen institutions for representative government
- Promote political dialogue and national reconciliation
- Engage neighbouring countries in regional dialogue
- Develop processes for holding elections and referendums

- Undertake constitutional review and the implementation of constitutional provisions
- Provide humanitarian assistance for vulnerable groups including refugees and internally displaced persons
- Promote the protection of human rights and judicial and legal reform.

As of 31 May 2012, UNAMI's strength (with staff based in Iraq, Jordan and Kuwait) was 387 international and 504 local civilians, 392 troops, eight military advisers and four police.

Office of the United Nations Special Coordinator for the Middle East Peace Process (UNSCO)

Headquarters: Jerusalem, Israel
Telephone: (+972) 2 568 7289
Fax: (+972) 2 568 7288
Internet: www.unsco.org
Special Coordinator for the Middle East Peace Process and Personal Representative of the Secretary-General to the Palestine Liberation Organization and the Palestinian Authority: Robert Serry, Netherlands (appointed by the UN Secretary-General in 2007)

The Special Coordinator represents the Secretary-General in discussions with the parties and international community on all matters relating to continuing UN support for the Middle East Peace Process. He or she is also the Secretary-General's Envoy to the Middle East Quartet (the UN, USA, European Union and Russian Federation). The Special Coordinator acts as a focal point for UN assistance relevant to the Middle East Peace Process for Jordan, Lebanon, the Occupied Palestinian Territory and the Syrian Arab Republic, and supports UN agencies in their contacts with donors in this regard.

The work of the Office of the UN Special Coordinator for the Middle East Peace Process (UNSCO) includes coordination of all UN humanitarian and development work in the Occupied Palestinian Territory.

UNSCO's strength as at 31 May 2012 consisted of 31 international and 29 local civilians operating in different component divisions, including political, coordination, public information, security and administration.

UN Office in Burundi (BNUB)

Headquarters: Bujumbura, Burundi
Telephone: (+1 212) 963 2842 (New York)
Internet: http://bnub.unmissions.org
Special Representative of the Secretary-General: Parfait Onanga-Anyanga, Gabon (appointed by the UN Secretary-General in June 2012)

The UN Office in Burundi (BNUB) succeeded the UN Integrated Office in Burundi (BINUB), which had been established by SC res. 1719 (2007) in the place of the UN Operation in Burundi. BNUB is a scaled-down operation, established by SC res. 1959 (2010) for an initial 12-month period from 1 January 2011. SC res. 2027 (2011) extended BNUB's mandate until 15 February 2013.

BNUB's role is to support the Government of Burundi in strengthening the independence, capacities and legal frameworks of key national institutions, in particular, the judiciary and parliament; promoting dialogue between national actors; fighting impunity and protecting human rights.

As at 31 May 2012, BNUB's strength was 52 international and 65 local civilians, one military adviser, one police and six UN Volunteers.

UN Regional Centre for Preventive Diplomacy for Central Asia (UNRCCA)

Headquarters: Ashgabat, Turkmenistan
Telephone: (+993 12) 48 16 12
Fax: (+993 12) 48 16 07

PO Box 4747
New York, NY
10163–4747
United States of America
Telephone: (+1 212) 963 4649

Email: unrcca-dpa@un.org
Internet: http://unrcca.unmissions.org
Special Representative of the Secretary-General: Miroslav Jenča, Slovakia (appointed by the UN Secretary-General in 2008)

The UN Regional Centre for Preventive Diplomacy for Central Asia (UNRCCA) was inaugurated in Ashgabat, Turkmenistan, on 10 December 2007. UNRCCA is an initiative of the UN and all five Central Asian countries. Its goal is to assist and support the Governments of Kazakhstan, Kyrgyzstan, Tajikistan, Turkmenistan and Uzbekistan in building their conflict-prevention capacities through enhanced dialogue, confidence-building measures and establishing genuine partnership in order to respond to existing threats and emerging challenges in the Central Asian region.

As at 31 May 2012, UNRCCA's strength was eight international and four local civilians.

Office of the United Nations Special Coordinator for Lebanon (UNSCOL)

Headquarters: Beirut, Lebanon
Telephone: (+961 1) 962 052
Fax: (+961 5) 428045
Email: unscol-website@un.org
Internet: www.unscol.unmissions.org
Special Coordinator for Lebanon: Derek Plumbly, UK (appointed by the UN Secretary-General in January 2012)

The Office of the UN Special Coordinator for Lebanon (UNSCOL) was established in February 2007. The Special Coordinator is the primary interlocutor with Lebanese authorities on all political matters and confers on a regular basis with the different political parties, with Lebanese civil society and the diplomatic community. The Special Coordinator's work includes the implementation of SC res. 1701 (2006) on Lebanon–Israel.

UNSCOL's work includes coordination of UN country team activities with the Government of Lebanon, the international donor community and international financial institutions in line with the overall UN objectives in Lebanon, with emphasis on reconstruction, development and reform. UNSCOL also provides overall political guidance to the UN country team and UN Interim Force in Lebanon (UNIFIL) peacekeeping operation.

As of 31 May 2012, UNSCOL's strength was 21 international and 61 local civilians.

UN Integrated Peacebuilding Office in Sierra Leone (UNIPSIL)

Headquarters: Freetown, Sierra Leone
Telephone: (+1 212) 963 9590 (New York)
Internet: http://unipsil.unmissions.org
Executive Representative of the Secretary-General: Jens Anders Toyberg-Frandzen, Denmark
(appointed by the UN Secretary-General in May 2012)

The UN Integrated Peacebuilding Office in Sierra Leone (UNIPSIL) succeeded two previous UN missions, the peacekeeping UN Assistance Mission in Sierra Leone (UNAMSIL), which was deployed from October 1999 to December 2005, and the UN Integrated Office in Sierra Leone (UNIOSIL), which was deployed from January 2006 to September 2008.

By SC res. 1829 (August 2008), UNIPSIL was established on 1 October 2008 with a 12-month mandate, most recently extended until 15 September 2012 (SC res. 2005 (2011)).

SC res. 1886 (2009) determined UNIPSIL should focus its efforts on supporting the Sierra Leone Government in the areas of constitutional reform and police force improvement, as well as helping it tackle corruption, illicit drug trafficking and organised crime. The Security Council emphasised the importance of UNIPSIL's assistance with youth unemployment and support in preparing for the 2012 elections (scheduled for November 2012), in conjunction with the Peacebuilding Fund and the Peacebuilding Commission, which selected Sierra Leone as one of the first two countries to receive assistance in recovering from conflict.

As of 31 May 2012, UNIPSIL's strength was 37 international and 31 local civilians, eight UN Volunteers and seven police.

UN Regional Office for Central Africa (UNOCA)

Headquarters: Libreville, Gabon
Telephone: (+241) 74 14 01
Fax: (+241) 74 14 02
Email: piounoca@un.org
Internet: www.un.org/wcm/content/site/undpa/central_africa or http://unoca.unmissions.org (French-language site)
Special Representative of the Secretary General and Head of Office: Abou Moussa, Chad (appointed by the UN Secretary-General in March 2011)

The UN Regional Office for Central Africa (UNOCA) opened on 2 March 2011. The office is designed to support the efforts of Central African nations to consolidate peace and prevent conflict, as well as to tackle cross-border challenges such as arms trafficking and organised crime.

UNOCA has an initial mandate of two years. It will work closely with the Economic Community of Central African States (ECCAS), which comprises Angola, Burundi, Cameroon, the Central African Republic, Chad, Congo, DR Congo, Equatorial Guinea, Gabon, and Sao Tome and Principe.

UNOCA is the third regional political office set up by the UN to promote preventive diplomacy and assist regions in managing shared problems and crises. The two others are the UN Office for West Africa (UNOWA) and the UN Regional Centre for Preventive Diplomacy for Central Asia (UNRCCA).

As at 31 May 2012, UNOCA's strength was 17 international and seven local civilians, and one military adviser.

United Nations Support Mission in Libya (UNSMIL)

Headquarters: Tripoli, Libya
Telephone: (+218) 92 307 0209
Internet: http://unsmil.unmissions.org
Special Representative of the Secretary-General: Ian Martin, UK (appointed by the UN Secretary-General in September 2011)

The UN Support Mission in Libya (UNSMIL) was established by SC res. 2009 (2011) for an initial period of three months, extended to 16 March 2012 by SC res. 2022 (2011). SC res. 2040 of 12 March 2012 extended UNSMIL's mandate for an additional 12 months.

UNSMIL was established to support the country's new authorities in their post-conflict efforts. SC res. 2040 (2012) modified UNSMIL's mandate to include assisting the Libyan authorities to define priorities and matching their needs with offers of strategic and technical advice, as well as supporting Libyan efforts to manage the transition of the country to an inclusive democracy, promote the rule of law, protect human rights, restore public security, counter illicit proliferation of weapons, coordinate international assistance, promote national reconciliation and hold free, fair and credible elections.

As at 31 May 2012, UNSMIL's strength was 56 international and three local civilians, and two police officers.

Past political and peacebuilding missions

For information about past political and peacebuilding missions, see http://j.mp/JNyf9c or www.un.org/depts/dpa (follow links from 'Field Operations' and 'Repertoire of the Practice of the Security Council website').

COMMISSIONS

Peacebuilding Commission (PBC)

Internet: www.un.org/en/peacebuilding

Purpose

At the UN World Summit in September 2005, leaders agreed to establish the Peacebuilding Commission (PBC) as an inter-governmental advisory body to assist countries emerging from conflict. The key objectives of the PBC are to:

- Provide advice on, and propose integrated strategies for, post-conflict peacebuilding and recovery
- Ensure predictable financing for early recovery activities and sustained financial investment over the medium to long term
- Extend the period of attention of the international community to post-conflict recovery
- Focus attention on reconstruction and institution-building efforts
- Develop best practices on issues that require collaboration and cooperation among key political, military, humanitarian and development participants.

Burundi, the Central African Republic, Guinea, Guinea-Bissau, Liberia and Sierra Leone are currently on the Commission's agenda.

Structure

The PBC's institutional structures, including its membership and procedures, were established by GA res. 60/180 (2005) and Security Council resolutions 1645 (2005) and 1646 (2005).

These resolutions provided for a review of the PBC's founding arrangements after five years to ensure they were appropriate to fulfil the agreed functions of the Commission. Such a review took place in 2010 (A/64/868 – S/2010/393). The General Assembly and Security Council requested the Peacebuilding Commission (A/RES/65/7 and S/RES/1947) to reflect in its annual reports progress made in taking forward the relevant recommendations of the review.

Membership

The PBC Organisational Committee is composed of seven members selected by the Security Council, including the five permanent members; seven members elected by the General Assembly to redress geographical imbalance and include countries with post-conflict experience; seven members elected by the Economic and Social Council (ECOSOC); five of the top 10 providers of assessed contributions to UN budgets and voluntary contributions to UN funds, programmes and agencies; and five of the top 10 providers of military personnel and civilian police to UN missions.

The Chair and Vice-Chairs for 2012 are:

Chair

A K Abdul Momen, Bangladesh

Vice-Chairs

Gert Rosenthal, Guatemala

Yuriy Sergeyev, Ukraine

Ranko Vilović Croatia

Membership

Membership of the PBC Organisational Committee:

Members selected by the Security Council

China	Morocco	UK
Columbia	Russian Federation	USA
France		

Members elected by the General Assembly

Benin	El Salvador	Tunisia
Brazil	Indonesia	Uruguay
Croatia		

Members elected by ECOSOC

Chile	Rwanda	Ukraine
Egypt	Spain	Zambia
ROK		

Top providers of assessed and voluntary contributions

Canada	Netherlands	Sweden
Japan	Norway	

Top providers of military personnel and civilian police

Bangladesh	Nepal	Pakistan
India	Nigeria	

UN Compensation Commission (UNCC)

Villa la Pelouse
Palais des Nations
1211 Geneva 10
Switzerland
Telephone: (+41 22) 917 3600
Fax: (+41 22) 917 0069
Email: unccwebmaster@uncc.ch
Internet: www.uncc.ch
Executive Head: Mojtaba Kazazi, Iran (appointed by the UN Secretary-General in 2007)

Purpose

The UN Compensation Commission (UNCC) was created in 1991 as a subsidiary organ of the Security Council. Its mandate is to process claims and pay compensation for losses and damage suffered as a direct result of Iraq's unlawful invasion and occupation of Kuwait.

SC res. 687 (1991) reaffirmed Iraq's liability under international law for any direct loss or damage, including environmental damage and the depletion of natural resources, or injury to foreign governments, nationals and corporations, resulting from Iraq's unlawful invasion and occupation of Kuwait. SC res. 692 (1991) established the UN Compensation Fund to pay compensation for claims that fell within these categories, and the Commission to administer the Fund. The Fund receives a percentage of the proceeds generated by the export sales of Iraqi petroleum and petroleum products, which was set at 5 percent under Security Council resolution 1483 (2003), and reaffirmed in subsequent resolutions, most recently SC res. 1956 (2010).

About 2.7 million claims, with an asserted value of $352.5 billion, were filed with the Commission. The total compensation awarded was $52.4 billion to approximately 1.5 million successful claimants. Nineteen panels of commissioners reviewed and evaluated the claims submitted by governments, international organisations, companies and individuals. The panels reported their recommendations to the Governing Council for approval. The processing of claims was concluded in 2007.

The Commission's principal areas of activity now relate to the payment of outstanding awards, ensuring the continued transfer of 5 percent of Iraq's oil revenues to the Compensation Fund and the management of the Follow-Up Programme for Environmental Awards, which was established by the Governing Council in 2005. This programme was set up to monitor the environmental remediation work by the participating Governments of Iran, Jordan, Kuwait and Saudi Arabia, using $4.3 billion in funds awarded for environmental damages.

As of 26 July 2012, the Commission had paid out about $37.6 billion in compensation awards to successful claimants, with about $14.7 billion outstanding to the remaining Kuwaiti awards.

Structure

The 15-member Governing Council is made up of representatives of the members of the Security Council. The Governing Council elects its own president and two vice-presidents, each for two-year terms.

The Secretariat of the Commission, headed by the Executive Head, provides support and assistance to the Governing Council.

Membership

The membership of the Governing Council is the same as the 15-member Security Council:

Permanent members

| China | Russian Federation | USA |
| France | UK | |

Non-permanent members with mandate until end of 2012

| Colombia | India | South Africa (Vice-President) |
| Germany (President) | Portugal | |

Non-permanent members with mandate until end of 2013

| Azerbaijan | Morocco (Vice-President) | Togo |
| Guatemala | Pakistan | |

INTERNATIONAL TRIBUNALS

International Criminal Tribunal for the former Yugoslavia (ICTY)

Churchillplein 1
2517 JW The Hague
The Netherlands
Telephone: (+31 70) 512 5000
Fax: (+31 70) 512 5355
Email: press@icty.org
Internet: www.icty.org
Registrar: John Hocking, Australia (appointed by the UN Secretary-General in 2009)

SECURITY COUNCIL

The Security Council in SC res. 808 (1993) established an international tribunal for the prosecution of people responsible for serious violations of international humanitarian law committed in the former Yugoslavia since 1991.

By SC res. 827 (1993), the Security Council, acting under chapter VII of the UN Charter, adopted the Statute of the International Tribunal for the former Yugoslavia.

Permanent judges

There are usually up to 16 permanent ICTY judges elected by the General Assembly or, in the event of a vacancy arising, appointed directly by the Secretary-General after consultation with the Presidents of the Security Council and General Assembly. The judges serve a term of four years and can be re-elected. As part of the Tribunal's completion strategy, one judge (Kevin Parker, Australia) was not replaced when his term expired in early 2011. As of June 2012, the 17 permanent judges[1] in order of precedence were:

Theodor Meron, USA (President) (Appeals Chamber)

Carmel A Agius, Malta (Vice-President) (Appeals Chamber)

Christoph Flügge, Germany

Alphons Martinus Maria Orie, Netherlands

O-Gon Kwon, South Korea

Patrick Lipton Robinson, Jamaica (Appeals Chamber)

Mehmet Güney, Turkey (Appeals Chamber)

Fausto Pocar, Italy (Appeals Chamber)

Liu Daqun, China (Appeals Chamber)

Arlette Ramaroson, Madagascar (Appeals Chamber)

Andrésia Vaz, Senegal (Appeals Chamber)

Khalida Rachid Khan, Pakistan (Appeals Chamber)

Jean-Claude Antonetti, France

Bakone Justice Moloto, South Africa

Burton Hall, Bahamas

Howard Morrison, UK

Guy Delvoie, Belgium

Note

1 SC res. 1993 (29 June 2011) extended the terms of the following eight permanent judges until 31 December 2012, or until the completion of their assigned cases: Jean-Claude Antonetti, Guy Delvoie, Burton Hall, Christoph Flügge, O-Gon Kwon, Bakone Justice Moloto, Howard Morrison and Alphons Orie.

Ad litem judges

In addition to the permanent judges, the Security Council decided by SC res. 1329 (2000) to establish a pool of ad litem (short-term) judges, elected by the General Assembly.

Ad litem judges are appointed by the Secretary-General, on the request of the International Tribunal President, to serve in the Trial Chambers for specific trials. SC res. 1660 (2006) increased the maximum number of ad litem judges who may serve at any one time from nine to 12.

As of June 2012,[1] the following ad litem judges, in order of precedence, were serving in the Tribunal:

Árpád Prandler, Hungary

Stefan Trechsel, Switzerland

Antoine Mindua, DR Congo

Frederick Harhoff, Denmark

Flavia Lattanzi, Italy

Michèle Picard, France

Elizabeth Gwaunza, Zimbabwe

Melville Baird, Trinidad and Tobago

Prisca Nyambe, Zambia

Note

1 SC res. 1993 (29 June 2011) extended the terms of the following ad litem judges: Melville Baird, Elizabeth Gwaunza, Frederick Harhoff, Flavia Lattanzi, Antoine Mindua, Prisca Nyambe, Michèle Picard, Árpád Prandler and Stefan Trechsel.

Structure

The Tribunal discharges its judicial functions through three Trial Chambers and an Appeals Chamber. Each Trial Chamber consists of three permanent judges. There may also be up to 12 ad litem judges in a given Trial Chamber. If ad litem judges are assigned to serve in a Trial Chamber, that Trial Chamber may be divided into a maximum of three sections of three judges each. At least one of the three judges sitting on a trial must be a permanent judge. SC res. 1660 (2006) permits the Secretary-General to appoint, at the request of the ICTY, reserve judges from the ICTY pool of ad litem judges to specific trials. Reserve judges are present at each stage of a trial and replace a judge on the bench if she or he is unable to continue sitting.

Appeals Chamber

The Appeals Chamber consists of seven judges. Only permanent judges may be members of this Chamber. Each appeal is heard by five members of the Appeals Chamber. The members of the ICTY Appeals Chamber also serve as the members of the Appeals Chamber of the International Criminal Tribunal for Rwanda (ICTR). Five ICTY Appeals Chamber judges are drawn from the permanent ICTY judges and two are drawn from the ICTR permanent judges.

Prosecutor

The Prosecutor is appointed by the Security Council, upon nomination by the Secretary-General, for a term of four years. On 28 November 2007, the Security Council appointed Serge Brammertz, Belgium, as the ICTY Prosecutor for a four-year term commencing on 1 January 2008. On 14 September 2011, the Security Council extended his term to 31 December 2014.

On 7 December 2011, Mr Brammertz reported to the Security Council that, with the arrest of the Tribunal's last remaining fugitive, Goran Hadžić, on 20 July 2011, the final impediment to the completion of the Tribunal's mandate had been removed, and the Tribunal was fully occupied with finishing trials and appeals.

International Criminal Tribunal for Rwanda (ICTR)

Arusha International Conference Centre
PO Box 6016
Arusha
United Republic of Tanzania
Telephone: (+255) 27 250 5000/256 5062
Fax: (+255) 27 250 4000/4373
Internet: www.unictr.org
Registrar: Adama Dieng, Senegal (appointed by the UN Secretary-General in 2001)

SC res. 955 (1994), adopted under chapter VII of the UN Charter, established an international tribunal for the prosecution of persons who committed genocide and other serious violations of international humanitarian law during 1994 in the territory of Rwanda, and of Rwandan citizens who committed such crimes in neighbouring territories. SC res. 955 (1994) also adopted the Statute of the International Criminal Tribunal for Rwanda under chapter VII of the UN Charter.

The Tribunal consists of three organs:
- The Trial Chambers and the Appeals Chamber
- The Office of the Prosecutor – in charge of investigations and prosecutions
- The Registry – responsible for providing overall judicial and administrative support to the Chambers and the Prosecutor.

The Tribunal is expected to complete its work by 31 December 2014.

Judges

The three Trial Chambers and the Appeals Chamber are composed of independent judges elected by the General Assembly from a list submitted by the Security Council. No two judges may be nationals of the same state. They are initially selected from a list of nominees submitted by UN Member States. Nominations must take account of adequate representation of the principal legal systems of the world. The judges are elected for a term of four years and are eligible for re-election.

Three judges sit in each of the Trial Chambers in Arusha, UR of Tanzania. Five judges sit in the Appeals Chamber in The Hague, Netherlands, which is shared with the International Tribunal for the former Yugoslavia.

As of May 2012, the permanent judges in order of precedence were:

Theodor Meron, USA
(Presiding Judge, Appeals Chamber)

Patrick Robinson, Jamaica
(Member, Appeals Chamber)

Mehmet Güney, Turkey
(Member, Appeals Chamber)

Fausto Pocar, Italy
(Member, Appeals Chamber)

Liu Daqun, China
(Member, Appeals Chamber)

Arlette Ramaroson, Madagascar
(Member, Appeals Chamber)

Andrésia Vaz, Senegal
(Member, Appeals Chamber)

Carmel Aguis, Malta
(Member, Appeals Chamber)

Khalida Rachid Khan, Pakistan
(Member, Appeals Chamber)

William H Sekule, UR of Tanzania
(Presiding Judge, Trial Chamber II)

Bakhtiyar Tuzmukhamedov, Russian Federation
(Member, Trial Chamber III)

SECURITY COUNCIL

continued next page

Notes

SC res. 1932 (2010) extended the terms of office of permanent judges Mehmet Güney and Andrésia Vaz, who are members of the Appeals Chamber, until 31 December 2012 or until the completion of the cases to which they are assigned, if sooner.

SC res. 2029 (2011) extended the term of office of the permanent judges who were members of the Trial Chamber until 30 June 2012 or the completion of the trials to which they were assigned, if sooner.

SC res. 1878 (2009) amended the ICTR Statute to permit the President to assign to the Appeals Chamber up to four additional permanent judges serving in the Trial Chambers, on the completion of the cases to which each judge is assigned. The term of office of each judge redeployed to the Appeals Chamber is the same as the term of office of the judges serving in the Appeals Chamber.

Ad litem judges[1]

By SC res. 1431 (2002) the Security Council decided to establish a pool of 18 ad litem (short-term) judges, and that a maximum of four ad litem judges might be attached to the Trial Chambers at any one time. SC res. 1512 (2003) increased the number of ad litem judges who may serve on the Tribunal at any one time from four to nine. SC res. 1855 (2008) authorised the Secretary-General to appoint up to three additional ad litem judges, which would, from time to time, temporarily exceed the maximum of nine provided for in the Tribunal's statute.

The ad litem judges serving on the Tribunal as of May 2012 were:

Vagn Joensen, Denmark
(President ICTR;
Presiding Judge, Trial Chamber III)

Florence Rita Arrey, Cameroon
(Vice-President ICTR;
Member, Trial Chamber III)

Solomy Balungi Bossa, Uganda
(Member, Trial Chamber II)

Lee Gacugia Muthoga, Kenya
(Member, Trial Chamber II)

Seon Ki Park, ROK
(Member, Trial Chamber II)

Gberdao Gustave Kam, Burkina Faso
(Member, Trial Chamber III)

Robert Fremr, Czech Republic
(Member, Trial Chamber III)

Mparany Mamy Richard Rajohnson,
Madagascar
(Member Trial Chamber I)

Notes

1   SC res. 1878 (2009) extended the term of 10 ad litem judges until 31 December 2010, or until the completion of the cases to which they are assigned, if sooner.

SC res. 1901 (2009) temporarily increased the maximum number of ad litem judges serving at any one time from nine to 12, returning to a maximum of nine by 31 December 2010 in order to enable the Tribunal to complete trials as soon as possible.

SC res. 1955 (2010) temporarily increased the maximum number of ad litem judges serving at any one time from nine to 12, returning to a maximum of nine by 31 December 2011.

SC res. 1932 (2010) extended the term of office of nine ad litem judges until 31 December 2011, or until the completion of the cases to which they are assigned, if sooner.

SC res. 2029 (2011) extended the term of office of the ad litem judges, who were members of the Trial Chamber, until 30 June 2012 or the completion of the trials to which they were assigned, if sooner.

Prosecutor

The Prosecutor, Hassan Bubacar Jallow, Gambia, was reappointed by the Security Council in SC res. 2006 (2011) for a term of four years with effect from 15 September 2011, subject to earlier termination by the Security Council upon completion of the Tribunal's work.

International Residual Mechanism for Criminal Tribunals

ICTR Branch:
Arusha International Conference Centre
PO Box 6016
Arusha
United Republic of Tanzania
Telephone: (+255) 27 250 5000/256 5062
Fax: (+255) 27 250 4000/4373
Internet: www.unictr.org

ICTY Branch:
Churchillplein 1
2517 JW The Hague
The Netherlands
Telephone: (+31 70) 512 5000
Fax: (+31 70) 512 5355
Email: press@icty.org
Internet: www.icty.org

Registrar: John Hocking, Australia (appointed by the UN Secretary-General in 2012)

Purpose

SC res. 1966 (2010), adopted under chapter VII of the UN Charter, established the International Residual Mechanism for Criminal Tribunals to finish the remaining tasks of the International Criminal Tribunals for Rwanda and for the former Yugoslavia, and maintain their respective legacies. The Mechanism will continue both tribunals' jurisdiction, rights, obligations and essential functions after they close. The same resolution also adopted the Statute of the Mechanism.

Structure

The Mechanism has two branches:
- The International Criminal Tribunal for Rwanda (ICTR), which began operations on 1 July 2012 in Arusha, UR of Tanzania
- The International Criminal Tribunal for the former Yugoslavia (ICTY), which is scheduled to begin operations on 1 July 2013 in The Hague, Netherlands.

The Mechanism consists of three organs:
- A Trial Chamber for each branch and an Appeals Chamber common to both
- The Prosecutor – in charge of investigations and prosecutions
- The Registry – to provide administrative services for the Mechanism, including the Chambers and the Prosecutor.

Judges

The Mechanism has a roster of 25 independent judges elected by the General Assembly from a list submitted by the Security Council. No two judges may be nationals of the same state. They are initially selected from a list of nominees submitted by UN Member States. As of May 2012, the judges on the roster were:

Theodor Meron, USA (President)

Liu Daqun, China

Gberdao Gustave Kam, Burkina Faso

Aydin Sefa Akay, Turkey

Carmel A Agius, Malta

Patrick Lipton Robinson, Jamaica

Lee G Muthoga, Kenya

Mparany Mamy Richard Rajohnson, Madagascar

Seon Ki Park, ROK

Burton Hall, Bahamas

Florence Arrey, Cameroon

Solomy Balungi Bossa, Uganda

Christoph Flügge, Germany

Bakone Justice Moloto, South Africa

Ivo Nelson de Caires Batista Rosa, Portugal

Vagn Prüsse Joensen, Denmark

Alphons Orie, Netherlands

José Ricardo de Prada Solaesa, Spain

Ben Emmerson, UK

Prisca Matimbe Nyambe, Zambia

Graciela Susana Gatti Santana, Uruguay

Jean-Claude Antonetti, France

Joseph E Chiondo Masanche, UR of Tanzania

William Hussein Sekule, UR of Tanzania

Aminatta Lois Runeni N'gum, Zimbabwe/ Gambia

Prosecutor

The Prosecutor, Hassan Bubacar Jallow, Gambia, was appointed by the Security Council in SC res. 2038 (2012) for a term of four years from 1 March 2012.

Note

> The President, Judges, Prosecutor and Registrar of the Mechanism may also hold the office of President, Judge, Prosecutor and Registrar, respectively, of the ICTY or ICTR.

OTHER ORGANISATIONS

UN Command in Korea

UNIT #15259, APO AP 96205–0032
Telephone: (+82 2) 7913 1110
Commander: General James D Thurman, US Army

As a signatory to the Armistice Agreement of 27 July 1953, the Commander-in-Chief of the UN Command (UNC) accepted responsibility (with the other signatories, the Supreme Commander of the Korean People's Army and the Commander of the Chinese People's Volunteers) for implementing and maintaining the Armistice until such time as the Armistice Agreement was expressly superseded either by mutually acceptable amendments and additions, or by an appropriate agreement for a peaceful settlement at a political level between both sides.

The composition of the command is not restricted or limited, except that the USA designates the commander. The 16 Member States that provided combat forces during the war are not obligated to provide support to the Commander-in-Chief of the UNC.

Coalition members actively participate in Armistice maintenance activities. For example, during 2011, UNC Special Investigation Teams, composed of UNC staff members and UNC sending state representatives, carried out 129 guard–observation post inspections in the Demilitarised Zone (DMZ), the Han River Estuary (HRE) and on the North West Islands to ensure Armistice Agreement compliance. In addition, liaison officers from sending states joined UNC staff on Special Investigation Teams to investigate 21 incidents that occurred in the DMZ, the HRE and the sea and air areas under UNC control. Sending states' representatives also took part in five North Korean People's Army (KPA)–UNC colonel level meetings and two repatriation ceremonies in Panmunjom for the return of remains of recently deceased KPA soldiers.

Some sending states provide officers to augment the Military Armistice Commission (MAC) in Armistice maintenance duties. These countries include Australia, Canada, Colombia, Denmark and New Zealand. Australia, Canada and Turkey provided officers to serve as UN Forces representatives at Headquarters, UN Command (Rear), at Yokota Air Base, Japan. In addition, Canada has posted several officers to serve on the UNC staff.

Sixteen liaison groups are accredited to the UNC. Their responsibilities include formulating policies and procedures for integration of the contingents into the UNC, and acting as their states' senior representatives to coordinate administrative, logistical and fiscal matters with the UNC. They also carry out MAC duties.

The liaison groups come from:

Australia	Greece	Thailand
Belgium	Netherlands	Turkey
Canada	New Zealand	UK
Colombia	Norway	USA
Denmark	Philippines	
France	South Africa	

Special Tribunal for Lebanon (STL)

Dokter van Stamstraat 1
2265 BC, Leidschendam
PO Box 115
2260 AC, Leidschendam
The Netherlands
Telephone: (+31 70) 800 3416
Fax: (+31 70) 800 3440
Email: stl-pressoffice@un.org
Internet: www.stl-tsl.org
Registrar: Herman von Hebel (appointed by the UN Secretary-General in December 2010)

Purpose

On 13 December 2005, the Government of Lebanon requested the UN establish a tribunal to try those responsible for the attack of 14 February 2005 in Beirut that killed the former Lebanese Prime Minister Rafiq Hariri and 22 others. Pursuant to SC res. 1664 (2006), the UN and the Lebanese Republic negotiated an agreement to establish the Special Tribunal for Lebanon (STL). Further to SC res. 1757 of 30 May 2007, the Statute of the Special Tribunal entered into force on 10 June 2007. The Tribunal began functioning on 1 March 2009.

While the STL mandate is to prosecute people responsible for the attack of 14 February 2005, the Tribunal's jurisdiction can be extended beyond that bombing if it finds other attacks that occurred in Lebanon between 1 October 2004 and 12 December 2005 are connected and are of a nature and gravity similar to the attack of 14 February 2005.

The UN Secretary-General announced in February 2012 that, pursuant to the terms of the annex to SC res. 1757 (2007), he had decided to extend the Tribunal's mandate for three years to 28 February 2015.

Structure

The STL Chambers are composed of one international pre-trial judge, a Trial Chamber (three judges: one Lebanese and two international), an Appeals Chamber (five judges: two Lebanese and three international) and two alternate judges (one Lebanese and one international).

The Secretary-General appoints the judges in consultation with the Lebanese Government and on the recommendation of a selection panel made up of two judges currently sitting on or retired from an international tribunal and a representative of the Secretary-General.

The Lebanese judges (four) are appointed by the Secretary-General from a list of 12 nominees presented by the Government of Lebanon on the proposal of the Lebanese Supreme Council of the Judiciary. The international judges (seven) are appointed by the Secretary-General from nominations received from Member States or competent persons. The judges serve for three years and are eligible for reappointment. The names of judges who are appointed to the STL are only made public when they are called upon to undertake judicial activity.

SECURITY COUNCIL

The Office of the Prosecutor (OTP) is led by a prosecutor appointed by the UN Secretary-General, after consultation with the Government of Lebanon and on the recommendation of a selection panel, for a renewable three-year term. The first prosecutor was Daniel Bellemare, Canada, who was appointed on 14 November 2007. The second is Norman Farrell, Canada, whose appointment was announced in February 2012.

Judges appointed in March 2009, and who have been called on to sit, are as follows.

David Baragwanath, New Zealand
(President, Appeals Chamber presiding judge)

Ralph Riachi, Lebanon
(Vice-President, Appeals Chamber)

Robert Roth, Switzerland
(Trial Chamber presiding judge)

Daniel Fransen, Belgium
(Pre-Trial)

Afif Chamseddine, Lebanon
(Appeals Chamber)

Kjell Erik Björnberg, Sweden
(Appeals Chamber)

Daniel Nsereko, Uganda
(Appeals Chamber)

Micheline Braidi, Lebanon
(Trial Chamber)

David Re, Australia
(Trial Chamber)

Walid Akoum, Lebanon
(Trial Chamber alternate)

Janet Nosworthy, Jamaica
(Trial Chamber alternate)

SECURITY COUNCIL

ECONOMIC AND SOCIAL COUNCIL

ECONOMIC AND SOCIAL COUNCIL

CHARTER PROVISIONS

The UN is charged by its Charter with promoting in the economic and social fields:

- Higher standards of living, full employment, and conditions of economic and social progress and development
- Solutions to international economic, social, health and related problems, and international cultural and educational cooperation
- Universal respect for, and observance of, rights and fundamental freedoms for all, without distinction as to race, sex, language or religion.

Responsibility for discharging these functions is vested in the General Assembly and, under its authority, the Economic and Social Council (ECOSOC).

ECOSOC makes or initiates studies and reports with respect to international economic, social, cultural, educational, health and related matters. It makes recommendations on these to the General Assembly, members of the UN and the specialised agencies concerned. It also makes recommendations for the purpose of promoting respect for, and observance of, human rights. ECOSOC prepares draft conventions for submission to the General Assembly and convenes international conferences when necessary. It enters into agreements with specialised agencies and makes arrangements for consultation with non-governmental organisations.

The Charter provisions relating to ECOSOC are contained in chapter IX (articles 55–60), which sets forth the objectives and functions of the UN in the sphere of international economic and social cooperation, and chapter X (articles 61–72), which defines the composition, functions and powers, and voting and procedure of the Council. Other provisions are to be found in articles 1, 2, 7, 15, 17, 18, 91, 96, 98 and 101.

MEMBERSHIP

Membership of ECOSOC, originally 18, was increased to 27 by amendment to article 61 of the UN Charter in accordance with GA res. 1991B (XVIII) (1963), which came into operation on 31 August 1965. GA res. 2847 (XXVI) (1971) enlarged the Council to 54 and amended article 61 accordingly. This enlargement took effect on 12 October 1973.

The pattern for the geographical distribution of seats was established in GA res. 2847 (XXVI) (1971): 14 members from African states, 11 from Asia–Pacific states, six from Eastern European states, 10 from Latin American and Caribbean states, and 13 from Western European and Other states.

Eighteen members of ECOSOC are elected each year. Members generally serve three-year terms of office, expiring on 31 December.

	Previous membership	Current membership

African states

Algeria	1964–66 73–81 83–85 90–92 1998–2000 07–09	
Angola	1992–94 2000–02 06–08	
Benin	1966–67 82–84 92–94 2000–08	
Botswana	1983–85 91–93	
Burkina Faso	1968–70 77–79 90–92 2000–02	2012–14
Burundi	1972–74 81–83 2002–04	
Cameroon	1966–67 78–83 89–91 2000–02 08–10	2011–13
Cape Verde	1997–99 2007–09	
Central African Republic	1978–80 96–98	
Chad	1968–70 2005–07	
Comoros	1998–2000	2010–12
Congo	1968–70 74–76 83–85 95–97 1999–2001 03–05 08–10	
Côte d'Ivoire	1974–76 95–97 09–11	
DR Congo	1971–77 80–82 84–95 1999–2001 05–07	
Djibouti	1983–88 97–99	
Egypt	1952–57 74–76 86–88 94–96 2001–03	2010–12
Ethiopia	1961–63 74–77 80–82 92–94 2001–03	2012–14
Gabon	1965–67 75–77 86–88 93–98	2011–13
Gambia	1997–99	
Ghana	1970–72 79–81 88–90 94–96 2002–04	2010–12
Guinea	1974–75 85–93 2005–07	
Guinea-Bissau	1999–2001 06–08 2009–11	
Kenya	1970–72 74–77 81–83 89–91 2003–05	
Lesotho	1978–80 88–90 1998–2000	2012–14
Liberia	1974–76 82–84 88–90	
Libya	1967–69 80–82 88–90 93–95 2002–04	2012–14
Madagascar	1971–73 92–94 2006–08	
Malawi	1980–82 2007–09	2011–13
Mali	1973–75 82–84	
Mauritania	1977–79 2006–08	
Mauritius	1998–2000 04–06 09–11	
Morocco	1966–68 79–81 85–87 91–93 1999–2001 09–11	
Mozambique	1986–88 97–99 2003–05 08–10	
Namibia	2004–06 09–11	
Niger	1971–73 89–91 2008–10	
Nigeria	1976–78 80–82 85–87 93–95 2001–06	2012–14
Rwanda	1977–79 84–92 1999–2001	2010–12
Senegal	1962–64 74–75 79–81 85–87 94–96 2003–05	2011–13
Sierra Leone	1966–69 83–88 1998–2000	
Somalia	1977–79 84–89 91–93 2007–09	
South Africa	1995–97 2001–03 05–07	
Sudan	1958–60 69–71 77–79 81–83 87–89 95–97 2000–02 07–09	
Swaziland	1982–84 92–94	
Togo	1976–78 91–98	
Tunisia	1970–72 76–78 82–84 89–91 96–98 2004–06	
Uganda	1973–78 84–86 95–97 2001–03	
UR of Tanzania	1966–69 78–80 94–96 2004–06	
Zambia	1974–76 79–81 89–91 97–99	2010–12
Zimbabwe	1985–87 94–96 2002–04	

Asia–Pacific states

State	Previous membership	Current membership
Afghanistan	1959–61 76–78	
Bahrain	1990–92 2000–02	
Bangladesh	1976–78 81–83 85–87 92–94 96–98 2004–06	2010–12
Bhutan	1993–95 2002–04	
China	1946–60 1972–2004 05–07 08–10	2011–13
Cyprus	1979–81	
Fiji	1974–75 81–83 2000–02	
India	1946–47 53–55 62–64 66–70 74 78–83 85–90 1992–2000 02–04 05–07 09–11	2012–14
Indonesia	1956–58 69–71 74–75 79–81 84–86 89–91 94–96 1999–2000 04–09	2012–14
Iran	1950–52 66–68 74–79 87–92 2001–03	
Iraq	1964–66 77–82 86–91 2007–09	2010–12
Japan	1960–65 68–70 72–80 1982–2005 06–11	2012–14
Jordan	1961–63 74–76 80–82 89–91 96–98	
Kazakhstan	2007–09	
Kuwait	1967–69 92–94	
Lebanon	1946–49 71–73 83–85 96–98	
Malaysia	1971–73 76–78 83–85 91–93 95–97 2003–05 08–10	
Mongolia	1973–75	2010–12
Nepal	1980–82 2001–03	
Oman	1987–89 1998–2000	
Pakistan	1954–59 65–67 69–71 74–77 79–84 86–88 90–92 94–96 1998–2003 05–07 08–10	2011–13
Papua New Guinea	1984–86	
Philippines	1951–53 66–68 77–79 86–88 92–97 2007–09	2010–12
Qatar	1982–84 2002–04	2011–13
ROK	1993–95 97–99 2003–06 08–10	2011–13
Saudi Arabia	1983–85 88–90 1999–2001 03–05 06–11	
Sri Lanka	1970–72 84–89 93–95 97–99 2006–08	
Syrian AR	1977–79 86–88 91–93 1999–2001	
Thailand	1974–76 80–85 89–91 95–97 2005–07	
UAE	1978–80 2004–06	
Viet Nam	1998–2000	

Eastern European states[1, 2]

State	Previous membership	Current membership
Albania	2005–07	
Armenia	2004–06	
Azerbaijan	2003–05	
Belarus	1947–49 81–83 86–88 1992–2000 07–09	2012–14
Bulgaria[3]	1959–61 68–70 75–77 80–85 87–92 94–96 1999–2001	2012–13
Croatia	2000–02	
Czech Republic	1996–2001 06–08	
Estonia	2009–11	
Georgia	2001–03	
Hungary[3]	1971–73 78–80 2002–04 11	
Latvia	1997–99	2011–13
Lithuania	2005–07	
Poland	1948–53 57–62 72–74 77–79 81–89 1992–2000 04–06 08–10	

	Previous membership	Current membership
Republic of Moldova	2008–10	
Romania	1965–67 74–76 78–80 82–87 90–98 2001–03 07–09	
Russian Federation	1947–2007 08–10	2011–13
Slovakia		2010–12
Ukraine	1946 77–79 89–91 93–95 2002–04	2010–12

Latin American and Caribbean states

	Previous membership	Current membership
Argentina	1952–57 63–65 68–70 74–86 91–93 96–98 2001–03	2010–12
Bahamas	1980–82 89–91 93–95	2010–12
Barbados	1979–81 2007–09	
Belize	1987–89 2004–06	
Bolivia	1972–74 76–78 87–89 1999–2001 07–09	
Brazil	1948–50 56–58 60–62 70–87 1989–2003 05–07 08–10	2012–14
Chile	1946–47 58–60 64–66 72–74 80–82 91–99 2002–04	2010–12
Colombia	1946 62–64 74–79 82–90 1992–2000 04–06	
Costa Rica	1958–60 84–86 94–96 2000–02 05–07	
Cuba	1946–47 52–54 76–78 88–90 93–95 1997–2008	2012–14
Dominican Republic	1955–57 78–80	2012–14
Ecuador	1954–56 64–66 79–81 83–85 90–92 2003–05	2011–13
El Salvador	1961–63 97–99 2002–04 07–09	2012–14
Guatemala	1967–69 74–75 2002–04 09–11	
Guyana	1984–86 96–98 2006–08	
Haiti	1971–73 85–87 2006–08	
Honduras	1999–2001	
Jamaica	1969–71 74–79 86–88 90–92 95–97 2003–05	
Mexico	1950–52 57–59 67–69 74–85 90–95 1997–2002 05–07	2011–13
Nicaragua	1981–83 89–91 96–98 2003–05	2011–13
Panama	1966–68 86–88 2004–06	
Paraguay	1994–96 2006–08	
Peru	1946–51 65–67 70–72 75–77 81–83 86–88 91–93 2001–03 09–11	
Saint Kitts and Nevis	2009–11	
Saint Lucia	1982–84 1998–2000 08–10	
Suriname	1983–85 92–94 2000–02	
Trinidad and Tobago	1973–75 78–80 88–93	
Uruguay	1951–53 61–63 69–71 87–89 2008–10	
Venezuela	1947–49 53–55 59–61 66–68 74–90 94–96 1999–2001 09–11	

Western European and Other states

	Previous membership	Current membership
Andorra	2001–03	
Australia[4]	1948–50 53–55 62–64 74–76 80–82 86–88 92–97 2002–06 08–10	2011–13
Austria	1963–65 76–78 82–84 91–93 2000–02 06–08	
Belgium[5]	1946 49–54 67–69 74–76 80–82 86–88 92–94 1998–2000 04–06 10–11	

	Previous membership	Current membership
Canada	1946–48 50–52 56–58 65–67 74–77 1981–2001 04–09	2010–12
Denmark	1948–50 60–62 75–77 81–83 87–89 93–95 1999–2001 05–07	
Finland[4]	1957–59 72–74 78–80 84–86 90–92 96–98 2002–04 08–10	2011–13
France	1946–2005 06–11	2012–14
Germany[6]	1974–2005 06–07 09–11	2012–14
Greece[4]	1946 56–58 66 70–72 76–78 82–84 88–90 94–96 2000 03–05 07–09	
Iceland	1985–87 97–99 2005–07	
Ireland	1968–70 79–81 88–90 94–96 2003–05	2012–14
Italy	1961–63 70–72 74–82 86–94 1998–2003 04–06	2010–12
Liechtenstein[6, 8]	2008 09–10	
Luxembourg	1964–66 83–85 95–97 2007–09	
Malta[4]	1978–80 2001–02 09–11	
Netherlands[5]	1947–48 55–60 73–75 77–79 83–85 89–91 95–97 2001–03 07–09	2012
New Zealand[4]	1947–49 59–61 71–73 77–79 83–85 89–91 1998–2000 07–09	
Norway[7]	1946–47 54–56 69–71 75–77 81–83 87–89 93–95 1999–2001 08–11	
Portugal[4]	1976–78 82–84 88–90 94–96 2000–01 07–09	
Spain[8]	1959–61 73–75 79–81 85–87 91–93 97–99 2002–06 11	2012–14
Switzerland[7, 8]	2011	2012–13
Sweden[4]	1951–53 66–68 74 78–80 84–86 90–92 96–98 2002–04 08–09	
Turkey[4, 8]	1947–49 53–55 67–69 74–75 79–81 85–87 91–93 97–99 2003–06 09–10	2012–14
UK	1947–2004 05–07 08–10	2011–13
USA	1946–2009	2010–12

Countries that have never served on the Council are not listed.

Notes

1 The former Socialist Federal Republic of Yugoslavia served on ECOSOC for the following periods: 1946, 1962–64, 1969–71, 1974–78, 1980–82, 1984–86 and 1988–92. It was not automatically succeeded by any of the new states created following its dissolution.

2 Czechoslovakia served on ECOSOC from 1946–47, 1950–52, 1954–56, 1963–68, 1974–77 and 1989–91.

3 Hungary had a one-year term in 2011 and was replaced by Bulgaria.

4 On 26 October 2009, the General Assembly elected Australia, Finland, Malta and Turkey as ECOSOC members for the remaining terms of office of New Zealand, Sweden, Greece and Portugal, respectively. The terms for Australia and Finland were to end on 31 December 2010; Malta and Turkey on 31 December 2011.

5 Belgium had a two-year term and was replaced by Netherlands.

6 Liechtenstein had a one-year term in 2008 that replaced the final year of Germany's term.

7 Norway had a one-year term and was replaced by Switzerland.

8 On 25 October 2010, the General Assembly elected Spain and Switzerland to fill the un-expired terms of Turkey and Liechtenstein from 1 January to 31 December 2011.

The Economic and Social Council (ECOSOC) holds one substantive four-week session annually in July, alternating between New York and Geneva. The substantive session has a high-level segment open to all Member States, followed by coordination, operational activities, humanitarian affairs and general segments.

The high-level segment serves as a forum for ministers, international institution executive heads and high-ranking officials, as well as civil society and private sector representatives, to discuss key issues on the international agenda in the area of economic, social and environmental development. At the end of the high-level segment, a ministerial declaration is adopted, which provides policy guidance and recommendations for action.

The 2005 World Summit Outcome Document, paragraphs 155 and 156, mandated ECOSOC to hold Annual Ministerial Reviews to assess progress with implementing outcomes of the major UN conferences and summits of the past 15 years, including the internationally agreed development goals. It also asked ECOSOC to convene emergency meetings; serve as a quality platform of engagement on global policies and trends in the economic, social, environmental and humanitarian fields; and hold biennial Development Cooperation Forums to review trends in international development cooperation.

ECOSOC decisions are taken by a simple majority of members present and voting. An organisational session of not more than four days is held in late January/early February. Elections, appointments and nominations take place at a resumed organisational session, normally in late April/early May. GA res. 48/162 (1993) specifies issues to be addressed in the future regarding restructuring and revitalisation of the UN in the economic, social and related fields.

Prior to 1992, ECOSOC had usually held two sessions a year, as well as a brief organisational meeting. The high-level segment was followed by coordination, operational activities and committee segments, in which economic, social and related issues were considered in two separate committees meeting simultaneously. GA res. 45/264 (1991) changed this to one substantive session annually between May and July, alternating between New York and Geneva; GA res. 48/162 (1993) replaced the committee segment with a general segment; GA res. 50/227 (1996) limited the substantive session to four weeks in July; and GA res. 52/12 B established the humanitarian affairs segment.

In 2012, ECOSOC held an organisational session from 7 to 10 February. The resumed organisational session was held from 26 to 27 April for the purpose of elections. The substantive session of the Council took place from 2 to 27 July.

The Bureau is elected by ECOSOC at the beginning of each annual session. The following Bureau was elected in January 2012:

President
Miloš Koterec, Slovakia

Vice-Presidents
Fernando Arias, Spain
Luis Alfonso de Alba, Mexico
Mootaz Khalil, Egypt[1]
Desra Percaya, Indonesia

Note

1   In June 2012, ECOSOC elected Mootaz Khalil to replace Maged A Abdelaziz, Egypt, who had relinquished his post as Vice-President for 2012.

SUBSIDIARY BODIES OF ECOSOC

FUNCTIONAL COMMISSIONS

Commission on Narcotic Drugs (CND)

Vienna International Centre
PO Box 50
A–1400 Vienna
Austria
Telephone: (+43 1) 260 600
Fax: (+43 1) 260 605 866
Email: unodc@unodc.org
Internet: www.unodc.org (follow links from 'Commissions')
Secretary: Jo-Dedeyne-Amann, Belgium (since 2012)

Purpose

The Commission on Narcotic Drugs (CND) was established in 1946 (ECOSOC resolution 9 (I)) as the central UN policy-making body for addressing drug-related matters. Its main functions are to:

- Serve as the governing body of the Fund of the UN International Drug Control Programme (UNDCP), which is administered by the UN Office on Drugs and Crime (UNODC)
- Provide legislative overview and policy guidance on international drug control matters to UNODC
- Approve the budget of the UNDCP Fund and the administrative and programme support budget
- Analyse the world drug situation and develop proposals to strengthen international drug control
- Carry out functions assigned to it by international drug control treaties.

Evolution

At the Commission's high-level segment in 2009, Heads of State, ministers and government representatives from 132 states gathered to evaluate progress made since 1998 towards meeting the goals and targets established at the 20th special session of the General Assembly devoted to countering the world drug problem together. The high-level segment adopted the Political Declaration and Plan of Action on International Cooperation towards an Integrated and Balanced Strategy to Counter the World Drug Problem, which was subsequently adopted by the General Assembly (GA res. 64/182). The Assembly also strengthened the role of the Commission as the global forum for international cooperation in combating the world drug problem.

Meetings

The Commission meets annually, most recently in March 2012. Since 2010, the Commission has held its yearly one-day reconvened sessions in the second half of the year to consider budgetary matters (ECOSOC decision 2009/251). In 2011, the CND and the Commission on Crime Prevention and Criminal Justice (CCPCJ) for the first time held joint meetings during their reconvened sessions (ECOSOC decision 2011/259).

Membership

The Commission has 53 members, as follows: 11 from African states, 11 from Asia–Pacific states, six from Eastern European states, 10 from Latin American and Caribbean states, and 14 from Western European and Other states. One seat rotates between Asia–Pacific and Latin American and Caribbean states every four years.

Elections for 20 and then 33 members are held at two-year intervals. Members serve four-year terms and are elected from among UN Member States and States Parties to the international drug control treaties; with due regard to adequate representation of countries that are important producers of opium or coca leaves, of countries that are important in the manufacture of narcotic drugs, and of countries where drug addiction or illicit traffic in narcotic drugs is an important problem; and taking into account the principle of equitable geographical distribution. Memberships expire on 31 December of each term.

	Previous membership	Current membership
African states		
Algeria	1978–81 84–87 96–99 2004–07	2012–15
Angola	2000–03	
Benin	2000–03	
Botswana	2008–11	
Burkina Faso	2002–05	
Cameroon	2004–11	2012–15
Côte d'Ivoire	1984–85 88–91 1994–2001	2010–13
DR Congo	1982–85 2004–11	2012–15
Egypt	1946–77 1988–2003	2012–15
Ethiopia	2008–11	
Gabon	1992–95	
Gambia	1990–93 2002–05	
Ghana	1964–71 1990–2001	2010–13
Guinea	1994–97	
Kenya	1973–79	
Lesotho	1992–95	
Liberia	1994–97	
Libya	1990–93 2000–03	
Madagascar	1962 76–95 2004–07	
Malawi	1980–83	
Mali	1986–89	
Mauritius	1997–2001	
Morocco	1962–65 67–77 84–87 92–99 2008–11	
Mozambique	2000–03	
Namibia	2006–09	2012–15
Niger	2006–09	
Nigeria	1966–68 72–75 82–89 92–99 2002–09	
Senegal	1982–93 2006–09	
Sierra Leone	1997–2001	2010–13
South Africa	1996–99 2002–05	
Sudan	1996–2011	
Swaziland	2000–03	2010–13
Togo	1970–81	
Tunisia	1978–81 92–99	
Uganda	2004–11	
UR of Tanzania		2012–15
Zambia	1986–89 2004–07	
Zimbabwe		2012–15

	Previous membership	Current membership

Asia–Pacific states

Afghanistan		2012–15
China	1946–69 1986–2005 08–11	2012–15
India	1946–85 1988–2007	2010–13
Indonesia	1973–81 86–93 96–99 2002–05	
Iran	1946–72 74–81 84–87 1992–2011	2012–15
Japan	1962–2009	2012–15
Kazakhstan	2000–03 08–11	
Kyrgyzstan	2000–03	
Lao PDR	1997–2001 04–07	2010–13
Lebanon	1970–73 88–91 1994–2001 04–07	
Malaysia	1982–93 96–99 2004–07	
Myanmar	2004–07	2010–13
Pakistan	1969–99 2002–05 08–11	2012–15
Philippines	1992–95 2000–03	
ROK	1963–68 82–85 1992–2003 06–09	2012–15
Saudi Arabia	2006–09	2010–13
Sri Lanka	1984–87 94–97	
Syrian AR	1992–99	
Tajikistan	2006–09	
Thailand	1973–2011	2012–15
Turkmenistan		2012–15
UAE	2004–11	
Yemen	2008–11	

Eastern European states[1,2]

Belarus	2002–05	2010–13
Bosnia and Herzegovina	2004–07	
Bulgaria	1982–93 96–99	
Croatia	2004–07	
Czech Republic	1993–2003 08–11	
Hungary	1957–93 2004–07	2012–15
Lithuania	2008–11	
Macedonia	2000–03	
Poland	1946–56 62–63 88–99 2006–09	2012–15
Republic of Moldova	2008–11	
Romania	1973–77 1994–2001	2010–13
Russian Federation	1946–2009	2010–13
Slovakia	2000–03	
The former Yugoslav Republic of Macedonia		
Ukraine	1994–2009	2012–15

Latin American and Caribbean states

Argentina	1965–67 72–89 2000–11	
Bahamas	1982–85 90–97	
Bolivia	1988–2003 06–09	2010–13
Brazil	1962–64 67–81 84–91 1996–2007	2010–13
Chile	1973–77 92–95 1997–2001 04–07	2010–13
Colombia	1976–87 1990–2009	2010–13
Cuba	1996–2011	
Dominican Republic	1968–71	

	Previous membership	Current membership
Ecuador	1986–93 1996–2003	
El Salvador	2008–11	
Guatemala	2004–07	2012–15
Jamaica	1967–77 92–99 2002–09	
Mexico	1946–2009	2012–15
Nicaragua	1992–95 2002–05	
Panama	1978–85	
Paraguay	1994–97	
Peru	1946–75 84–95 2000–11	2012–15
Saint Vincent and the Grenadines		2012–15
Suriname		2012–15
Trinidad and Tobago	2008–11	
Uruguay	1992–95 1997–2001 08–11	2012–15
Venezuela	1986–89 1992–2003 08–11	

Western European and Other states

	Previous membership	Current membership
Australia	1973–2009	2010–13
Austria	1957–59 84–85 2000–11	2012–15
Belgium	1978–97 2006–09	2010–13
Canada	1946–79 1984–2003 06–09	2010–13
Denmark	1988–91 2000–03	2012–15
Finland	1984–87 94–97 2008–11	
France	1946–2007	2010–13
Germany	1963–2011	2012–15
Greece	1954–56 84–87 1996–2003	
Israel	2004–11	2012–15
Italy	1976–2011	2012–15
Netherlands	1946–53 60–62 84–99 2002–05 08–11	2012–15
Norway	1980–83 92–95 2004–07	
Portugal	1996–2003	
Spain	1980–83 1986–2005 08–11	2012–15
Sweden	1969–79 90–93 96–99 2004–07	
Switzerland	1961–75 88–95 1997–2001 04–11	
Turkey	1946–89 92–95 1997–2009	2012–15
UK	1946–2009	2010–13
USA	1946–2011	2012–15

Notes

1 The former Socialist Federal Republic of Yugoslavia served on the CND from 1946 to 1992. It was not automatically succeeded by any of the states created following its dissolution.

2 Czechoslovakia served on the CND in 1992.

Subcommission on Illicit Drug Traffic and Related Matters in the Near and Middle East

Internet: www.unodc.org/unodc/commissions/CND/06-subsidiarybodies.html

The Subcommission on Illicit Drug Traffic and Related Matters in the Near and Middle East was established as a subsidiary body of the Commission on Narcotic Drugs (CND) by ECOSOC res. 1776 (LIV) (1973) and CND res. 6 (XXV) (1973).

The Subcommission consists of representatives of:

Afghanistan	Kazakhstan	Syrian AR
Azerbaijan	Kuwait	Tajikistan
Bahrain	Kyrgyzstan	Turkey
Egypt	Lebanon	Turkmenistan
India	Oman	UAE
Iran	Pakistan	Uzbekistan
Iraq	Qatar	Yemen
Jordan	Saudi Arabia	

States from outside the region may attend as observers.

Regional meetings of Heads of National Drug Law Enforcement Agencies (HONLEA)

Internet: www.unodc.org/unodc/commissions/CND/06-subsidiarybodies.html

The Commission on Narcotic Drugs (CND) has four additional regional subsidiary bodies known as the meetings of Heads of National Drug Law Enforcement Agencies (HONLEA):
* Asia and the Pacific, established by ECOSOC res. 1845/LVI (1973)
* Africa, established by ECOSOC res. 1985/11
* Latin America and the Caribbean, established by ECOSOC res. 1987/34
* Europe, established by ECOSOC res. 1990/30.

HONLEA meetings are held annually except for HONLEA Europe, which meets every two years. The meetings are held to promote regional and sub-regional cooperation in drug law enforcement and to coordinate activities directed against illicit drug traffic in each region. Recommendations are conveyed to the CND. Membership is open to any state or territory that is a member of the relevant regional UN Economic Commission. Other states may attend as observers.

Commission on Population and Development (CPD)

2 United Nations Plaza, Room DC2–1950
New York, NY 10017
United States of America
Telephone: (+1 212) 963 3179
Fax: (+1 212) 963 2147
Internet: www.un.org/esa/population (follow links from 'Commission on Population and Development')
Secretary: Emer Herity

Purpose

The Population Commission (CPD), established by ECOSOC res. 3 (III) (1946), was tasked with studying and advising ECOSOC on population changes, including migration, and their effect on economic and social conditions.

Following the International Conference on Population and Development (ICPD) in 1994, the name of the Commission was changed to the Commission on Population and Development (GA res. 49/128 (1994)). GA res. 49/128 also decided that the Commission should meet annually from 1996 and be charged with monitoring and assessing implementation of the ICPD Programme of Action at the national, regional and international levels. In line with its new mandate, new terms of reference for the Commission were endorsed by ECOSOC res. 1995/55.

Under its terms of reference, the Commission assists ECOSOC by:

- Arranging for studies and advising the Council on:
  - Population issues and trends
  - Integrating population and development strategies
  - Population and related development policies and programmes
  - Population assistance, upon request, to developing countries and, on a temporary basis, to countries with economies in transition, and
  - Any other population and development questions referred to it by either the principal or subsidiary UN organs or specialised agencies.
- Monitoring, reviewing and assessing implementation of the Programme of Action of the ICPD
- Providing recommendations to ECOSOC on the basis of an integrated consideration of the reports and issues related to the implementation of the Programme of Action.

The CPD's current methods of work were the object of ECOSOC decision 2005/213 and CPD res. 2006/1.

The Population Division of the Department of Economic and Social Affairs acts as the CPD Secretariat. The Division Director was being recruited at the time of publication.

Meetings

The Commission meets annually in New York. The 46th session is scheduled for 22 to 26 April 2013, with the special theme "New trends in migration: demographic aspects".

Membership

Originally 12, membership has increased several times and now stands at 47 (GA res. 50/124 (1995)). Members are elected by ECOSOC for a four-year term on the following basis: 12 from African states, 11 from Asia–Pacific states, five from Eastern European states, nine from Latin American and Caribbean states, and 10 from Western European and Other states. Representatives of governments on the Commission are expected to have a relevant background in population and development.

ECOSOC decided (2005/213) that the term of office for members should run for four regular sessions of the Commission, beginning after the conclusion of the Commission's regular session. Memberships expire at the conclusion of the regular session held after 1 January.

	Previous membership	Current membership[1]
African states		
Algeria	1996–98 2000–03	2011–15
Angola		2010–14
Benin	2007–11	
Botswana	1990–93 2002–06	
Burkina Faso	1969–72	
Burundi	1986–89 1999–2002	
Cameroon	1966–69 85–88 1993–2009	
Central African Republic	1968–71	
Comoros	2005–09	
Congo	1996–98	

	Previous membership	Current membership[1]
Côte d'Ivoire	1997–2000	2009–13
DR Congo	1977–84 2003–07	2009–13
Egypt	1968–75 78–81 84–87 89–92 96–99 2001–04	2012–16
Equatorial Guinea	2007–11	
Ethiopia	1997–2000	
Gabon	1970–73	2011–15
Gambia	2002–06 07–10	
Ghana	1962–79 2001–04	2010–14
Guinea	1999–2002	
Kenya	1969–72 1996–2003 04–12	
Lesotho	1996–97	
Libya	2004–08	
Madagascar	1992–95 2004–08	
Malawi	1967–68 78–81 86–89 1998–2001	2010–14
Mauritania	1974–77 2003–07	
Mauritius	1985–88	
Morocco	1972–75 80–83 2005–09	
Niger	1967 73–76 1998–2001	
Nigeria	1967–68 80–91 1996–2006	
Rwanda	1967–69 73–84 88–95	2009–13
Senegal		2010–14
Sierra Leone	1976–83 2007–10	
South Africa	1998–2001 07–10	
Sudan	1982–85 92–99	
Togo	1984–91	
Tunisia	1964–67 70–77 94–97 2008–12	
Uganda	1976–79 89–92 96 2000–03 08–12	2012–16
UR of Tanzania	1993–96	2012–16
Zambia	1982–85 90–93 96–97 2002–06 07–10	

Asia–Pacific states[1]

	Previous membership	Current membership[1]
Bangladesh	1989–2009	2009–13
China	1947–67 1982–2006 07–10	2010–14
India	1965–72 74–81 84–87 1994–2006 07–10	2010–14
Indonesia	1952–54 68–69 76–83 96–99 2001–09	2009–13
Iran	1953–55 70–73 86–93 1996–2011	2011–15
Iraq	1988–91	
Japan	1958–85 1988–2012	2012–16
Kazakhstan	2008–12	
Lebanon	2002–06 07–10	
Malaysia	1984–87 1997–2009	2010–14
Nepal	1996	
Oman	2007–10	
Pakistan	1967–71 92–96 2008	2009–13
Philippines	1967–69 72–79 1996–2001 03–07	2010–14
ROK	1996–2001	
Sri Lanka	1961–64 80–83 2007–11	
Syria	1950–52 54–56 62–65 96–98	
Thailand	1973–88 1997–2000 02–06	
Turkmenistan		2011–15
Yemen	1999–2002	

	Previous membership	Current membership[1]

Eastern European states

Armenia	2004–08	
Belarus	2000–03	2009–13
Bulgaria	1984–87 96–99 2005–09	
Croatia	1999–2002 08–12	
Georgia		2011–15
Hungary	1977–84 1993–2000 03–07	2010–14
Lithuania	2001–04	
Poland	1988–95 2002–06 07–11	
Republic of Moldova		2012–16
Romania	1973–76	
Russian Federation	1947–2006 07–10	2010–14
The former Yugoslav Republic of Macedonia[2]	1996–98	
Ukraine	1947–83 85–92 1996–2001 07–10	

Latin American and Caribbean states[1]

Argentina	1954–60	
Barbados	1970–73 78–81	
Bolivia	1982–85 88–91 2003–07	
Brazil	1947–60 69–80 85–92 1996–2003 05–09	2009–13
Chile	1967–68 1999–2002	
Colombia	1985–96 2008–12	
Costa Rica	1954–57 73–76 84–87 1999–2000	
Cuba	1986–89 96	2009–13
Dominican Republic	1977–80	
Ecuador	1967–69 74–77 80–83	2011–15
El Salvador	1958–65 1996–2001 03–07	2011–15
Grenada	2007–11	
Guatemala		2010–14
Guyana	2002–09	
Haiti	1970–73 1999–2002 05–08	2009–13
Honduras	1981–84 92–95 2007–11	
Jamaica	1967–71 1994–2006 07–10	2010–14
Mexico	1961–64 76–79 1982–2006 07–10	
Nicaragua	1993–96 2002–06	
Panama	1965–68 74–81 90–93 1997–2000	
Paraguay	1999–2000	
Peru	1966–69 72–75 81–84 96–98 2001–09	
Saint Lucia		2010–14
Uruguay	1961–64 2007–10	
Venezuela	1969–72 96–97	

Western European and Other states

Australia	1947–49 52–53 65–68	
Austria	1965–68 2001–04	
Belgium	1951–64 1989–2009	2009–13
Canada	1947–49 54–60 1993–2000 05–09	
Denmark	1969–76	
Finland	1976–83 96 2008–12	
France	1947–2008	

	Previous membership	Current membership[1]
Germany	1985–2009	2009–13
Greece	1962–64 81–84	
Ireland	2002–06	
Israel	1956–59	2009–13
Italy	1960–63 96–97 1999–2002	
Luxembourg	2003–07	2010–14
Malta	1996–98	
Netherlands	1947–50 65–68 73–88 1992–2012	
New Zealand	1969–72	
Norway	1950–61 77–84 2002–06	2012–16
Portugal		2011–15
Spain	1969–72 77–80 2007–11	2012–16
Sweden	1950–55 64–75 84–91 1998–2006 07–10	
Switzerland	2005–09	2009–13
Turkey	1973–76 85–92 1997–2004	
UK	1947–2001 07–10	2010–14
USA	1947–2006 07–10	2011–14

Notes

1   Two positions are yet to be filled, one in the Asia–Pacific States Group and one in the Latin American and Caribbean States Group.

In April 2012, ECOSOC elected the following nine members to the CPD for four-year terms beginning at the first meeting of the Commission's 47th session in 2013 and expiring at the close of its 50th session in 2017: Chad and Madagascar (African states); Brazil, Mexico and Uruguay (Latin American and Caribbean states); and Belgium, Denmark, Netherlands and Switzerland (Western European and Other states). In the absence of other candidates for the remaining five slots on the Commission for the same terms, ECOSOC decided to postpone the election of one member from African states, three members from Asia–Pacific states and one member from Eastern European states.

2   The former Socialist Federal Republic of Yugoslavia served on the Commission from 1947–53 and 65–68. It was not automatically succeeded by any of the new states created following its dissolution.

Commission on Science and Technology for Development (CSTD)

Palais de Nations
8–14, Avenue de la Paix
1211 Geneva 10
Switzerland
Fax: (+41 22) 917 0052
Email: stdev@unctad.org
Internet: www.unctad.org/cstd
UNCTAD Secretary-General: Supachai Panitchpakdi, Thailand (since 2005; second four-year term confirmed by the General Assembly in 2009)

Purpose

ECOSOC res. 1992/218 established the Commission on Science and Technology for Development (CSTD) in accordance with GA res. 46/235 (1992) on the restructuring and revitalisation of the UN in the economic, social and related fields. It provides the General Assembly and ECOSOC with high-level advice on relevant issues through analysis and policy recommendations or options in order to enable those organs to guide the future work of the UN, develop common policies and agree on appropriate actions. The Commission replaced the Intergovernmental Committee on Science and Technology for Development and its subsidiary body, the Advisory Committee on Science and Technology for Development.

The Commission acts as a forum for:

- Examining science and technology questions and their implications for development
- Advancing understanding on science and technology policies, particularly in respect of developing countries
- Formulating recommendations and guidelines on science and technology matters within the UN system.

Since 2006, the Commission has been assisting ECOSOC in the system-wide follow up to the World Summit on the Information Society (WSIS).

The UN Conference on Trade and Development (UNCTAD) serves as the Secretariat for the Commission.

Evolution

ECOSOC res. 1992/62 reaffirmed the Commission's mandate as set forth in ECOSOC and General Assembly resolutions, including GA res. 34/218 (1979), 41/183 (1986), 42/192 (1987), 44/14 (1989) and 46/235 (1991). ECOSOC res. 2002/37 requested the Commission meet annually, starting from the sixth session held in May 2003. ECOSOC res. 1998/46 decided the Commission should work more closely with the Commission on Sustainable Development and UNCTAD.

Meetings

The Commission meets annually. The 15th regular session took place from 21 to 25 May 2012 in Geneva.

Membership

ECOSOC res. 2006/46 increased the Commission's membership from 33 to 43. Members are elected by ECOSOC for four-year terms on the basis of the following regional allocation of seats: 11 from African states, nine from Asia–Pacific states, five from Eastern European states, eight from Latin American and Caribbean states, and 10 from Western European and Other states.

Commission members and the year their term expires (on 31 December) are as follows. Terms that end in 2016 begin on 1 January 2013 and are marked with an asterisk.

Commission member	Expiry of term	Commission member	Expiry of term
African states			
Cameroon*	2016	Mauritius	2014
Central African Republic*	2016	Nigeria*	2016
DR Congo	2012	Rwanda	2014
Equatorial Guinea	2012	South Africa	2012
Ghana	2012	Tanzania	2014
Lesotho	2014	Togo	2014
Liberia*	2016	Tunisia	2014
Mali	2012	Zambia*	2016

Commission member	Expiry of term	Commission member	Expiry of term
Asia–Pacific states			
China	2014	Oman	2012
India	2014	Pakistan	2012
Iran	2014	Philippines	2014
Japan*	2016	Saudi Arabia	2014
Jordan	2012	Sri Lanka*	2012/16
Eastern European states			
Bulgaria	2014	Russian Federation*	2012/16
Hungary	2014	Slovakia	2012
Latvia	2014		
Latin American and Caribbean states			
Brazil*	2012/16	El Salvador	2014
Chile	2012	Jamaica	2012
Costa Rica	2012	Mexico*	2016
Cuba	2014	Peru	2014
Dominican Republic	2014		
Western European and Other states (plus Japan) (one seat vacant)			
Austria*	2012/16	Portugal*	2012/16
Finland*	2012/16	Sweden	2014
France	2014	Switzerland	2012
Israel	2012	Turkey	2014
Malta	2014	USA	2014

ECONOMIC AND SOCIAL COUNCIL

Commission on Sustainable Development (CSD)

Division for Sustainable Development (DSD)
Department of Economic and Social Affairs (UN-DESA)
2 United Nations Plaza, Room DC2–2220
New York, NY 10017
United States of America
Telephone: (+1 212) 963 8102
Fax: (+1 212) 963 4260
Internet: follow links from www.un.org/esa/dsd
Director, Division of Sustainable Development: Nikhil Seth (since 2011)

Purpose

The Commission on Sustainable Development (CSD) is the high-level forum for sustainable development within the UN system. It was established by ECOSOC res. 1993/207 in accordance with GA res. 47/191 (1992). Its task is to review progress in the implementation of Agenda 21 and the Rio Declaration, which were agreed at the 1992 UN Conference on Environment and Development in Rio de Janeiro, as well as to provide policy guidance to follow up with the Johannesburg Plan of Implementation (JPOI) adopted at the World Summit on Sustainable Development (WSSD) in 2002.

The Commission advances sustainable development through:

- Enhancing high-level policy dialogue among Member States, UN system organisations, regional and national institutions and major groups
- Encouraging technical cooperation and capacity building at international, regional and national levels
- Promoting multi-stakeholder partnerships to facilitate implementation.

The Commission also reviews implementation of the Barbados Programme of Action and the Mauritius Strategy for Implementation for Small Island Developing States (SIDS) in the context of its multi-year work programme.

Evolution

A Programme for the Further Implementation of Agenda 21 was agreed to by the UN General Assembly at its 19th Special Session in 1997. GA res. 55/199 (2000) decided the Commission's 10th session would be an open-ended preparatory committee for the WSSD, with full participation by all states and broad engagement of civil society. The WSSD, held in Johannesburg, South Africa, in 2002, reaffirmed the Commission's role as the high-level forum within the UN for discussion of sustainable development issues, and called for the Commission to be strengthened to facilitate implementation more effectively.

The Commission's 11th session, held in 2003, made specific recommendations on its work. These were adopted by ECOSOC res. 2003/61 and included organising the Commission's work on the basis of two-year implementation cycles, including review and policy sessions. The Commission also recommended that its multi-year programme of work after 2003 be organised on the basis of seven two-year thematic clusters of issues:

- 2010–11: Transport, chemicals, waste management, mining, sustainable consumption and production patterns (CSD 18 – CSD 19)
- Originally 2012–13 but on hold for one year: Forests, biodiversity, biotechnology, tourism and mountains (CSD 20 – CSD 21).

GA res. 64/236 (2009) agreed to hold the UN Conference on Sustainable Development (UNCSD) in 2012 in Brazil, also referred to as 'Rio+20' (see www.uncsd2012.org). In this context, the Commission's 2012–13 implementation cycle (CSD 20 – CSD 21) was put on hold for one year.

The Conference was held from 20 to 22 June 2012, with the aim of securing renewed political commitment to sustainable development, assessing the progress and implementation gaps in meeting already agreed commitments, and addressing new and emerging challenges.

Meetings

The Commission usually meets annually in May. There was no meeting in 2012 because of the Rio+20 conference.

Membership

ECOSOC res. 1993/207 decided the Commission should include 53 members elected from UN Member States and members of the specialised agencies for three-year terms. Members are elected according to the following allocation of seats: 13 from African states, 11 from Asia–Pacific states, six from Eastern European states, 10 from Latin American and Caribbean states, and 13 from Western European and Other states.

ECOSOC res. 1997/63 decided that at the end of each regular session, the first meeting of the subsequent regular session would be convened for the sole purpose of electing the new bureau. One-third of the members are elected annually and outgoing members are eligible for re-election. Membership terms expire on the last day of the regular session in the year listed.

Other Member States, UN organisations, accredited inter-governmental and non-governmental organisations can attend CSD sessions as observers.

	Previous membership	Current membership*
African states		
Algeria	1993–94 1998–2001 04–07	2010–13
Angola	1999–2002	2011–14
Benin	1993–94 96–99	2010–13
Botswana		2011–14
Burkina Faso	1993–95 2004–07	
Burundi	1995–98	
Cameroon	1999–2002 05–08	
Cape Verde	2007–10	
Central African Republic	1996–99	
Congo		2011–14
Côte d'Ivoire	1998–2001	2010–13
DR Congo	1999–2011	
Djibouti	1997–2000 06–09	
Egypt	1993–94 1997–2000 02–05	
Equatorial Guinea		2011–14
Eritrea	2009–12	
Ethiopia	1995–98 2003–06 09–12	
Gabon	1993–99 2002–05 08–11	
Gambia	2007–10	
Ghana	1995–98 2001–07	
Guinea	1993–96 2007–10	
Guinea-Bissau	2003–06	
Kenya		2012–15
Lesotho	2002–05	2011–14
Liberia		2012–15
Libya	2008–11	
Madagascar	2000–03	
Malawi	1993–95 2008–11	
Mali	2000–03	
Mauritania	1998–2001	
Mauritius	1998–2001 09–12	
Morocco	1993–96 2001–04	
Mozambique	1996–2002	
Namibia	1993–95 2008–11	
Niger	1997–2000	
Nigeria	1993–94 2001–04 09–12	
Senegal	1995–98 2001–04 06–09	
Sierra Leone	2004–07	
South Africa	2002–05 07–10	
Sudan	1997–2009	2012–15
Togo		2010–13
Tunisia	1993–95 1999–2002 05–08	
Uganda	1993–96 2003–06	2012–15

	Previous membership	Current membership*
UR of Tanzania	1994–96 2006–09	
Zambia	2005–08	
Zimbabwe	1996–99 2005–08	

Asia–Pacific states

	Previous membership	Current membership*
Bahrain	2007–10	
Bangladesh	1995–98 2008–11	
China	1993–2008 09–12	2012–15
DPRK	1998–2001 05–08	
Fiji	2003–06	
India	1993–2004 07–10	
Indonesia	1993–95 1997–2004 06–09	2011–14
Iran	1995–2010	2012–15
Japan	1993–2006 07–10	2011–14
Kazakhstan	1999–2002 04–07	2010–13
Kuwait	2006–09	
Kyrgyzstan	2009–12	
Lebanon	1999–2002	2011–14
Malaysia	1993–96	2010–13
Mongolia	2001–04	2010–13
Nepal	2002–05	
Pakistan	1993–2003 04–07 08–11	2012–15
Papua New Guinea	1995–98	
Philippines	1993–2001 09–12	
Qatar	2004–07	
ROK	1993–95 1999–2006 07–10	
Saudi Arabia	1996–99 2002–11	2011–14
Singapore	1993–94	
Sri Lanka	1993–94 1998–2001	
Thailand	1996–2003 05–08	2010–13
UAE	2008–11	
Uzbekistan	2002–05	
Vanuatu	1993–94	

Eastern European states

	Previous membership	Current membership*
Armenia		2011–14
Azerbaijan	2002–05	
Belarus	1993–96 2000–03 05–08	2010–13
Bulgaria	1993–2000	2012–15
Croatia	2002–05 07–10	
Czech Republic	1993–94 1998–2001 06–09	
Estonia	2008–11	
Georgia	2004–07	
Hungary	1993–2001 03–06	2012–15
Latvia		2010–13
Montenegro		2011–14
Poland	1993–2003 07–10	
Republic of Moldova	2001–04	
Romania	2008–11	
Russian Federation	1993–2012	
Serbia	2005–08	
Slovakia	1997–2004	

The former Yugoslav
  Republic of Macedonia............ 1999–2002 04–07

149

Ukraine... 1995–98 2009–12

Latin American and Caribbean states

	Previous membership	Current membership*
Antigua and Barbuda...................	1993–99 2002–05 06–12	
Argentina.......................................	2002–05 08–11	2012–15
Bahamas...	1995–98	2010–13
Barbados...	1993–96	
Belize..	2005–08	
Bolivia...	1993–2003 05–08	
Brazil..	1993–2007 08–11	2011–14
Chile...	1993–95 2006–09	
Colombia..	1993–94 1996–2002 04–07 09–12	
Costa Rica......................................	2002–05 07–10	
Cuba...	1993–94 1999–2002 05–08 09–12	2012–15
Ecuador..	2001–04	
El Salvador.....................................		2011–14
Guatemala.......................................	2000–03 07–10	
Guyana..	1996–2002	
Haiti..	2007–10	2012–15
Honduras...	2003–06	
Jamaica...	2003–06	
Mexico..	1993–2003 05–08	2011–14
Nicaragua..	1998–2001	2011–14
Panama..	1997–2000	2010–13
Paraguay...	1999–2002 04–07	
Peru..	1995–2005 06–09	2010–13
Saint Lucia.....................................	2003–06	
Uruguay..	1993–95 2008–11	
Venezuela..	1993–2004 08–11	

Western European and Other states (one seat vacant)

	Previous membership	Current membership*
Australia...	1993–98 2000–12	2012–15
Austria..	1993–94 2001–07	
Belgium...	1993–2011	2011–14
Canada..	1993–2000 02–11	
Denmark...	2000–02	2010–13
Finland..	1995–99 2004–07	
France...	1993–2010	2010–13
Germany..	1993–2011	2011–14
Greece...	2000–03	
Iceland..	1993–95 2001–04	
Israel...	2005–11	
Ireland..	1997–2000	2012–15
Italy..	1993–96 1999–2002 05–08	2011–14
Luxembourg....................................	2004–07 09–12	
Monaco...	2007–10	
Netherlands.....................................	1993–2006 07–10	2010–13
New Zealand...................................	1998–2001	
Norway..	1993–94 2002–05	2010–13
Portugal..	1998–2001	
Spain...	1995–2001 06–09	2011–14

ECONOMIC AND
SOCIAL COUNCIL

	Previous membership	Current membership*
Sweden	1996–98 2007–10	
Switzerland	1996–99 2001–04 08–11	
Turkey	1993–95 2002–05	
UK	1993–2006 06–12	2012–15
USA	1993–2012	2012–15

Note

* In April 2012, ECOSOC elected 15 members for three-year terms beginning at the organisational meeting of the Commission's 22nd session in 2013 and expiring at the close of its 24th session in 2016: Burkina Faso, Ghana, Mali, Mauritania (African states); India, Mongolia, Tajikistan and Viet Nam (Asia–Pacific states); Czech Republic and Russian Federation (Eastern European states); Antigua and Barbuda, Bolivia and Ecuador (Latin American and Caribbean states); and Iceland and Portugal (Western European and Other states). In the absence of other candidates, elections for the two remaining members from Western European and Other states were postponed.

Commission on the Status of Women (CSW)

UN Women
2 United Nations Plaza
Room DC2 – 12th Floor
New York, NY 10017
United States of America
Fax: (+1 212) 963 3463
Email: csw@unwomen.org
Internet: www.un.org/womenwatch/daw/csw
Under-Secretary-General and Executive Director: Michelle Bachelet, Chile (appointed by the UN Secretary-General in September 2010)

Purpose

The Commission on the Status of Women (CSW) was established by ECOSOC res. 11 (II) (1946) to prepare reports for ECOSOC on matters concerning the promotion of women's rights in the political, economic, social and educational fields, and to make recommendations to the Council on problems requiring immediate attention in the field of women's rights.

Evolution

The General Assembly (GA res. 50/203 (1995)) decided the Commission would have a central role in monitoring the implementation of the Platform for Action of the Fourth World Conference on Women (Beijing, 1995). This role was reaffirmed by GA res. 55/71 (2000), with the inclusion of monitoring implementation of the outcome of the 23rd Special Session of the General Assembly.

The Commission's principal output is the Agreed Conclusions on the priority theme for the year. In addition to the Agreed Conclusions, the Commission can adopt resolutions on women's rights issues.

The Working Group on Communications on the Status of Women, established by ECOSOC res. 1983/27, consists of five members selected from the membership of the Commission with regard to geographical representation. The Working Group holds closed meetings prior to each session of the Commission to consider communications received, including the replies of governments. This is done with a view to bringing to the Commission's attention to communications that appear to reveal a consistent pattern of reliably attested injustice and discriminatory practices against women.

The Secretariat for the substantive work of the Commission was the UN Division for the Advancement of Women. It is now the UN Entity for Gender Equality and Empowerment of Women (UN Women), which was created in 2010. UN Women is responsible for substantive servicing of the Commission, including preparation of analysis and reports for the sessions, supporting the work of the CSW Bureau, facilitating the participation of civil society representatives in the Commission's annual session, and coordinating parallel events held at the UN during the Commission's sessions.

Meetings

The Commission meets annually for 10 working days. The 56th session was held from 27 February to 9 March and 15 March 2012.

Membership

Originally 15, membership has been enlarged several times, most recently by ECOSOC res. 1989/45 (1989), and now stands at 45. Members are elected for four-year terms on the basis of: 13 from African states, 11 from Asia–Pacific states, four from Eastern European states, nine from Latin American and Caribbean states, and eight from Western Europe and Other states.

Until 2002, terms began on 1 January and ended on 31 December. ECOSOC decision 2002/234 provided that terms would begin immediately after the end of the Commission's regular session held after 1 January following their election, and finish at the end of the regular session held after 1 January following the election of the states that are to succeed them, unless they were re-elected.

	Previous membership	Current membership*
African states		
Algeria	1993–96 2003–07	
Angola	1995–98	
Benin	2000–04[2]	
Botswana	1968–70 2002–06	
Burkina Faso	1988–91 2002–06	
Burundi	1999–2003[1]	
Cameroon	2006–10	
Central African Republic	1971–74	2010–14
Comoros		2010–14
Congo	1995–98 2003–07	
Côte d'Ivoire	1987–94 1998–2001	
DR Congo	1971–78 81–84 87–94	2011–15
Djibouti	2006–10	
Egypt	1962–76 81–84 90–93 1999–2003[1]	
Eritrea	2008–12	
Ethiopia	1976–79 1997–2000	
Gabon	2002–06 07–11	
Gambia		2010–14
Ghana	1962–70 79–82 90–93 1997–2000 04–08	
Guinea	1964–69 73–76 94–97 2001–05[3]	2009–13
Guinea-Bissau	1993–96	
Kenya	1967 72–75 83–86 94–97	
Lesotho	1980–83 88–91 1998–2001 06–10	
Liberia (Chair)	1966–75 83–86	2011–15
Libya	1977–80 94–97	2010–14
Madagascar	1968–69 73–80 92–95	

	Previous membership	Current membership*
Malawi	2000–04[2]	2012–16
Mali	1996–99 2005–09	
Mauritania	1967–68 70–72	2009–13
Mauritius	1985–88 2004–08	
Morocco	1969–71 89–92 1997–2000 05–09	
Namibia	1994–97 2007–11	
Niger	1977–80 2007–11	2012–16
Nigeria	1971–74 80–83 90–93 2003–07	
Rwanda	1991–94 1998–2001	2009–13
Senegal	1975–78 79–82 1999–2003[1] 08–12	
Sierra Leone	1963–65 83–86	
South Africa	2002–06	
Sudan	1981–96 1998–2006	
Swaziland	1996–99	2010–14
Togo	1976–79 84–87 95–98 2006–10	
Tunisia	1967–72 85–88 94–97 2001–05[3]	
Uganda	1967 79–82 90–93 1998–2001	
UR of Tanzania	1989–92 2001–09[3]	
Zambia	1984–90 92–95 2006–10	
Zimbabwe	1990–93	2011–15

Asia–Pacific states

	Previous membership	Current membership*
Bangladesh	1987–94	2010–14
Cambodia	2007–11	
China	1947–63 65–67 73–76 1980–2004 04–12	2012–16
Cyprus	1968–70 90–97	
DPRK	1999–2003[1]	
India	1947–51 73–88 1990–2001 03–07 08–12	
Indonesia	1955–57 62–65 71–78 83–86 90–93 95–98 2002–10	2012–16
Iran	1952–54 62 64–72 76–79 1990–2001 02–10	2011–15
Iraq	1967–72 79–82	2009–13
Japan	1958–63 65–70 72–75 1977–2009[3]	2009–13
Kazakhstan	2004–08	
Kyrgyzstan	2000–04[2]	
Lebanon	1950–55 96–99	
Malaysia	1967–71 79–82 1990–2001 02–10	2010–14
Mongolia	1999–2003[1]	2010–14
Myanmar	1952–54	
Nepal	1964–66	
Pakistan	1952–60 76–95 2001–05[3] 07–11	
Philippines (Vice-Chair)	1961–75 83–98	2010–14
Qatar	2005–09	
ROK	1994–2001 02–10	2010–14
Sri Lanka	1998–2001	
Syrian AR	1947–49	
Thailand	1971–78 1989–2000 03–07	2011–15
UAE	2002–10	

Eastern European states[4]

	Previous membership	Current membership*
Armenia	2003–11	
Azerbaijan	2001–05[3] 07–11	
Belarus (Vice-Chair)	1952–57 67–78 85–88 93–96	2009–13
Bulgaria	1977–80 91–98	

	Previous membership	Current membership*
Croatia	2000–09[2]	
Estonia		2011–15
Georgia		2011–15
Hungary	1964–76 2004–08	
Lithuania	1999–2003[1]	
Poland	1951–68 89–92 1997–2000	
Romania	1969–75	
Russian Federation	1947–2007 08–12	2012–16
Slovakia	1993–99	
Ukraine	1981–84 91	

Latin American and Caribbean states

Argentina	1955–61 72–75 2001–05[3]	2010–14
Bahamas	1990–97	
Belize	2005–09	
Bolivia	1998–2001 03–07	
Brazil	1952–54 85–92 1996–2004[2] 06–10	2012–16
Chile	1952–54 66–75 1992–2004[2]	
Colombia	1960–65 70–76 89–96	2009–13
Costa Rica	1947–50 69–75 88–91 94–97	
Cuba	1952–62 76–79 80–91 93–96 1998–2001 02–06 08–12	2012–16
Dominican Republic	1951–59 64–66 68–78 1996–2008 1996–12	2012–16
Ecuador	1984–87 90–97 2006–10	
El Salvador (Vice-Chair)	2004–08	2010–14
Guatemala	1967–69 80–83 88–91 2002–06	
Haiti	1949–51 53–55 2008–12	
Honduras	1966–68 80–83	
Jamaica	1990–93	2011–15
Mexico	1947–52 57–68 76–79 1983–2003[1] 06–10	
Nicaragua	1969–71 73–76 84–87 2002–06	2009–13
Panama	1979–82	
Paraguay	1997–2000 07–11	
Peru	1963–65 67–69 77–80 92–95 1997–2009[3]	
Saint Lucia	1998–2001	
Suriname	2004–08	
Uruguay	1970–72	2010–14
Venezuela	1953–58 67 76–79 81–88 92–95	

Western European and Other states[5]

Australia	1955–57 61–63 67–69 83–90 93–96	
Austria	1965–67 70–72 89–96	
Belgium	1956–58 70–80 1995–2003 03–11	2011–15
Canada	1958–60 70–76 81–92 2003–07	
Denmark	1947–50 76–79 84–87 2000–04[2]	
Finland	1960–68 71–74 79–82 92–95	2012–16
France	1947–83 1985–2000	
Germany	1976–90 1997–2009[3]	2009–13
Greece	1949–51 59–61 73–76 85–88 95–98	
Iceland	2004–08	
Italy (Vice-Chair)	1981–84 87–94 1999–2003[1]	2009–13
Israel	1956–61	2009–13
Netherlands	1951–53 59–64 66–69 91–94 2001–09[3]	2011–15

	Previous membership	Current membership*
New Zealand	1952–53 77–80	
Norway	1969–75 80–83 96–99	
Portugal	1995–98	
Spain	1962–64 68–70 81–84 92–95 2007–11	2011–15
Sweden	1954–59 75–78 88–91 2008–12	
Turkey	1947–50 67–69 88–91 1999–2011[1]	
UK	1947–86 1997–2009[3]	
USA	1947–94 1996–2012	2012–16

Notes

* In April 2012, ECOSOC elected the following 11 members to the Commission for four-year terms beginning at the first meeting of its 58th session in 2013 and expiring at the close of its 61st session in 2017: Burkina Faso, Lesotho and Uganda (African states); Japan and Pakistan (Asia–Pacific states); Belarus (Eastern European states); Ecuador and Paraguay (Latin American and Caribbean states); and Germany, Israel and Switzerland (Western European and Other states).

1 ECOSOC decision 2002/234 extended the terms of office for members of the Commission whose terms were to expire on 31 December 2002 until the conclusion of the 47th session.

2 ECOSOC decision 2002/234 extended the terms of office for members of the Commission whose terms were to expire on 31 December 2003 until the conclusion of the 48th session.

3 ECOSOC decision 2002/234 extended the terms of office for members of the Commission whose terms were to expire on 31 December 2004 until the conclusion of the 49th session.

4 The former Socialist Federal Republic of Yugoslavia served on the Commission from 1954 to 56. It was not automatically succeeded by any of the new states created following its dissolution.

Statistical Commission

2 United Nations Plaza, Room DC2–1620
New York, NY 10017
United States of America
Telephone: (+1 212) 963 4849
Fax: (+1 212) 963 4569
Email: statcom@un.org
Internet: http://unstats.un.org/unsd/statcom/commission.htm

Purpose

The Statistical Commission helps ECOSOC:

- Promote the development of national statistics and improve their comparability
- Coordinate the statistical work of specialised agencies and the development of the central statistical services of the Secretariat
- Advise the organs of the UN on general questions relating to the collection, analysis and dissemination of statistical information
- Promote the improvement of statistics and statistical methods generally.

The Commission considers special issues of concern in international statistical development, methodological issues, coordination and integration of international statistical programmes, support of technical cooperation activities in statistics, and organisational matters. The Commission submits a report on each session to ECOSOC.

The Commission was established by ECOSOC res. 8 (I) (1946). Its terms of reference are set out in ECOSOC res. 8 (I), 8 (II) (1946) and 1566 (L) (1971).

Meetings

ECOSOC decision 1999/223 decided the Commission should meet annually in New York, beginning in 2000. The 43rd session was held from 28 February to 2 March 2012.

Membership

Originally 12, membership has been increased several times, most recently by ECOSOC res. 1147 (XLI) (1966). It now stands at 24. Members are elected by ECOSOC for four-year terms on the basis of five members from African states, four from Asia–Pacific states, four from Eastern European states, four from Latin American and Caribbean states, and seven from Western European and Other states. Terms expire on 31 December of the final year.

Elections for the new bureau were held in February 2012. The following officers were elected:

Chair	Vice-Chairs	Rapporteur
Gabriella Vukovich, Hungary	Jill Matheson, UK	Anna N Majelantle, Botswana
	Jiantang Ma, China	
	Eduardo Sojo Garza-Aldape, Mexico	

	Previous membership	Current membership*
African states		
Algeria	2002–05	
Botswana	1994–2001	2010–13
Cameroon		2010–13
Cape Verde	2004–07	
Côte d'Ivoire	1998–2001	
DR Congo	2006–09	
Egypt	1964–71 78–81 86–89	
Ethiopia	1978–81	
Gabon	1974–77	
Ghana	1967–95 2002–05	
Kenya	1972–87 90–97 2004–07	
Libya	1970–73 82–85	
Mali	1967–68	
Mauritania	2006–09	
Morocco	1966–73 88–95 2000–03	2010–13
Niger		2012–15
Nigeria	1982–85	
Sierra Leone	1974–77	
South Africa	2002–09	
Sudan	1962–63 96–99 2008–11	
Togo	1982–93 96–99 2008–11	
Tunisia	1967–69 74–81 1998–2001	
Uganda	1970–73 2000–03	
UR Tanzania		2012–15
Zambia	1986–97	
Asia–Pacific states		
China	1947–67 1984–2003 05–08	2009–12
India	1947–83 85–88 1993–2004	
Indonesia	1968–71	
Iran	1953–55 89–92 2004–07	

	Previous membership	Current membership*
Iraq	1976–83	
Japan	1962–69 1973–2008	2009–12
Lebanon	2008–11	
Malaysia	1972–75 77–84	
Mongolia		2012–15
Oman	2008–11	2012–15
Pakistan	1967–68 1984–2003	
Philippines	1951 69–72	
ROK	2004–07	
Sri Lanka	1973–76	
Thailand	1969–72	

Eastern European states[1]

	Previous membership	Current membership*
Armenia		2009–12
Belarus	2008–11	
Bulgaria	1984–91 96–99	
Croatia	2004–07	
Czech Republic	1993–95 1997–2004	2012–15
Hungary	1965–68 73–76 80–83 89–92 2000–03 05–08	2012–15
Lithuania	2008–11	
Poland	1969–72 92–95	
Romania	1957–64 77–80 1996–2003	
Russian Federation	1947–2009	2010–13
Ukraine	1947–79 81–88 93–96 2004–07	

Latin American and Caribbean states

	Previous membership	Current membership*
Argentina	1950–52 72–79 1982–2001	
Brazil	1960–67 69–96	
Colombia	1996–99 2005–08	2010–13
Costa Rica	2002–05	
Cuba	1957–64 67–71 84–87 2004–07	2012–15
Dominican Republic	1956–69	
Ecuador	1967–69 80–83	
Honduras	2008–11	
Jamaica	1978–81 92–95 1997–2004 06–09	
Mexico	1947–49 1981–2008	2009–12
Panama	1965–72 77–80 88–91	
Peru	2000–03	
Suriname		2009–12
Uruguay	1962–68 73–76	
Venezuela	1970–77	

Western European and Other states

	Previous membership	Current membership*
Australia	1952–57 60–71 81–84 93–96 1998–2001	2010–13
Austria	1980–83	
Belgium	1966–73	
Canada	1951–59 62–69 74–81 89–92 2006–09	
Denmark	1951–60 69–72 2002–05	
Finland	1981–88 2006–09	
France	1947–80 82–97 2001–04 06–09	
Germany	1986–2001 05–08	2009–12
Greece	2001–04	
Iceland	1974–76 1995–2001	
Ireland	1970–73 76–79 82–85	

	Previous membership	Current membership*
Italy		2010–13
Netherlands	1947–61 90–93 1997–2000 05–08	2009–12
New Zealand	1956–63 74–77 85–88 2002–05	
Norway	1947–50 61–68 89–92	2010–13
Portugal	1997–2000	
Spain	1972–75 78–89 94–97 2002–05	
Sweden	1973–80 93–96	
Turkey	1947–50	
UK	1947–2004 05–08	2009–12
USA	1947–81 1984–2003 04–11	2012–15

Notes

* In April 2012, ECOSOC elected the following five members to four-year terms beginning on 1 January 2013: China and Japan (Asia–Pacific states); Bulgaria (Eastern European states); and Germany and UK (Western European and Other states). It also elected Barbados and Dominican Republic (Latin American and Caribbean states) for the same term. In the absence of a third candidate from Western European and Other states, ECOSOC decided to postpone the election for the remaining slot for that region for the same term.

1 The former Socialist Federal Republic of Yugoslavia served on the Commission from 1954 to 1956. It was not automatically succeeded by any of the new states created following its dissolution.

Commission for Social Development (CSocD)

Division for Social Policy and Development
Department of Economic and Social Affairs
2 United Nations Plaza, Room DC2–1320
New York, NY 10017
United States of America
Telephone: (+1 212) 963 2569
Fax: (+1 212) 963 3062
Email: bas@un.org
Internet: http://social.un.org/index/CommissionforSocialDevelopment.aspx
Director: Daniela Bas

Purpose

Since the convening of the World Summit for Social Development in Copenhagen in 1995, the Commission for Social Development (CSocD) has been the key UN body in charge of the follow up and implementation of the Copenhagen Declaration and Programme of Action.

Evolution

Originally known as the Social Commission but renamed in 1966, CSocD was established by ECOSOC res. 10 (II) (1946). Its purpose was to advise ECOSOC on social policies of a general character and, in particular, on all matters in the social field not covered by the specialised inter-governmental agencies. The Commission's mandate was further developed by ECOSOC resolutions 830J (XXXII) (1961), 1139 (XLI) (1966) and 1996/7.

Since 2006, the Commission has taken up key social development themes as part of its follow up to the outcome of the Copenhagen Summit. The priority theme for 2011–12 was 'poverty eradication'.

Meetings

The Commission meets annually in New York. The 51st session is scheduled to be held in February 2013.

Membership

Originally 18, membership has been increased several times and now stands at 46. Members are elected by ECOSOC for four years on the following basis: 12 from African states, 10 from Asia–Pacific states, five from Eastern European states, nine from Latin American and Caribbean states, and 10 from Western European and Other states.

Until 2002, terms began on 1 January and ended on 31 December. ECOSOC decision 2002/210 decided that terms of office would begin immediately after the Commission's regular session and end at the conclusion of a regular session. Decision 2002/210 also decided that at the end of each regular session, the first meeting of the subsequent regular session would be convened for the sole purpose of electing the new bureau.

At its 50th session first meeting (10 February 2012), the Commission elected Jorge Valero, Venezuela, as Chair of the 51st session.

	Previous membership	Current membership*
African states		
Algeria	1999–2003[1]	
Angola	2005–09	
Benin	1995–98 2000–04[2] 07–11	
Botswana	1968–70	
Burkina Faso	1966–68	2011–15
Burundi	1989–92	
Cameroon	1968–74 1989–2000 07–11	2011–15
Central African Republic	1983–86 2003–07	
Chad	1979–82	
Comoros	2001–05[3]	
Congo	1969–71	
Côte d'Ivoire	1972–75 92–95 2004–08	
DR Congo	1975–78 2005–09	
Egypt	1956–78 95–98 2007–11	2011–15
Ethiopia	1995–98 2004–08	2009–13
Gabon	1963–65 69–71 75–78 96–99 2001–05[3]	2009–13
Gambia	1997–99	
Ghana	1983–94 2000–04 08–12	
Guinea	1977–80 91–94 1999–2003	
Kenya	1980–87	
Lesotho	1976–82	2009–13
Liberia	1983–90	2012–16
Libya	1987–90 2003–07	
Madagascar	1977–84 91–94	
Malawi	1997–2000	
Mali	1964–67 75–78 85–88 2004–08	
Mauritania	1964–76 97–99	2012–16
Mauritius		2009–13
Morocco	1967–69 80–87 1999–2003[1]	
Namibia	2007–11	
Nigeria	1972–75 91–94 2000–04[2] 08–12	2012–16
Senegal	1979–82 2003–07 08–12	
Sierra Leone	1970–72 76–79	
Somalia	1971–74	
South Africa	1947–51 1997–2009[3]	
Sudan	1973–76 81–84 1988–2004 08–12	2012–16
Swaziland	1999–2003[1]	

	Previous membership	Current membership*
Togo	1979–90 95–98	
Tunisia	1962–74 2004–08	
Uganda	1964–67 88–91 1997–2000	
UR of Tanzania	1967–68 2001–09[3]	
Zambia	2003–07	
Zimbabwe	1985–88 93–96	2011–15

Asia–Pacific states

Bangladesh	1987–90 2001–09[3]	2012–15
China	1947–64 66–68 1989–2005[3] 05–09	2009–13
Cyprus	1967–94	
DPRK	1999–2003 05–09	
India	1949–57 69–75 79–86 1997–2000 03–11	
Indonesia	1972–83 86–88 92–95 2000–08[2]	
Iran	1967–70 1991–2007	2009–13
Iraq	1962–65 73–80 88–91	
Israel	1951–56 61–64 66–68	
Japan	1971–78 1996–2012	2012–16
Jordan	1947–50 53–55	
Kazakhstan	2001–05[3]	
Lebanon	1969–71	
Malaysia	1962–65 84–87 97–98	
Mongolia	1976–87 95–98	2012–16
Myanmar	2005–09	
Nepal	1997–99 2007–11	2012–15
Pakistan	1967–69 88–95 1997–2000 03–07 08–12	
Philippines	1952–57 67–72 77–84 1989–2000	2009–13
Qatar		2009–13
ROK	1996–2012	2012–16
Sri Lanka	1962	
Thailand	1970–76 81–88 1999–2003[1]	
UAE	2007–11	
Viet Nam	2001–05[3]	2012–15

Eastern European states (one seat vacant)[4, 5]

Albania	1961–64	2009–13
Armenia	2008–12	
Belarus	1951–60 62–71 83–86 1992–2004	2012–16
Bulgaria	1964–67 2001–05[3]	
Croatia	1999–2003	
Czech Republic	2001–09[3]	
Hungary	1976–79	
Poland	1947–50 77–92 1997–2000	
Republic of Moldova	2004–08	
Romania	1968–70 75–82 84–91 1997–2000 03–07	
Russian Federation	1947–2012	2012–16
Slovakia	2007–11	
Ukraine	1972–75 80–83 91–98 2005–09	2012–15

Latin American and Caribbean states (one seat vacant)

Argentina	1964–66 68–70 1983–2007 08–12	
Bolivia	1950–52 79–82 93–96 2005–09	
Brazil	1950–55 60–63	2009–13[6]
Chile	1967–2000 04–08	
Colombia	1947–49 53–59 73–76	

	Previous membership	Current membership*
Costa Rica	1971–78 80–83	
Cuba	1964–67 69–71 1997–2000 07–11	2011–15
Dominican Republic	1956–59 72–79 1987–2007	2012–16
Ecuador	1957–64 77–80 83–86 89–92 1997–2004	2012–16
El Salvador	1980–87 2001–05[3] 08–12	
Grenada	1976–79	
Guatemala	1970–72 88–91 97–98 2000–04[2] 08–12	
Haiti	1984–95 1999–2008[1]	2009–13
Honduras	1964–67	
Jamaica	1971–74 1997–2005[3] 07–11	
Mexico	1968–70 75–78 92–95 2001–05[3] 07–11	2011–15
Nicaragua	1979–82	
Panama	1981–88	
Paraguay	2005–09	
Peru	1947–49 67–68 1996–2008	2011–15
Suriname	2003–07	
Uruguay	1954–56 60–69 72–75	
Venezuela	1967–71 96–99 2005–09	2009–13[6]

Western European and Other states (one seat vacant)

	Previous membership	Current membership*
Andorra	2007–11	2011–15
Australia	1950–52 54–56 58–61	
Austria	1962–65 73–76 83–98 2001–05[3]	
Belgium	1951–56 72–75	
Canada	1961–64 67–72 84–87 1997–2000	
Denmark	1964–66 77–80 85–88 93–96 2001–05[3]	2009–13[7]
Finland	1960–63 75–78 83–86 89–92 1997–2000 05–09	
France	1947–2012	
Germany	1987–2012	2012–16
Greece	1947–48 52–57 67–69	
Italy	1958–61 70–88 2001–09[3]	2009–13
Malta	1989–2000 03–07	
Monaco	2005–09	
Netherlands	1957–60 66–71 76–83 85–88 1995 93–2000 05–09	2009–13
New Zealand	1947–52 57–60 73–76	
Norway	1953–55 67–69 79–82 87–90 95–98	
Spain	1957–60 68–74 89–92 1997–2003 03–11	2011–15
Sweden	1956–59 70–72 81–84 91–94 1999–2003[1]	2009–13[7]
Switzerland	2001–05[3]	2009–13
Turkey	1949–51 77–84 1999–2011	
UK	1947–82	
USA	1947–2012	2012–16

Notes

*   In April 2012, ECOSOC elected the following 12 members to four-year terms beginning at the first meeting of the Commission's 52nd session in 2013 and expiring at the close of its 55th session in 2017: DR Congo, Madagascar, Malawi and Uganda (African states); China, Kuwait and Pakistan (Asia–Pacific states); Poland (Eastern European states); Argentina, Brazil and Chile (Latin American and Caribbean states); and Finland (Western European and Other states). It postponed, in the absence of more candidates, the election of one member from Asia–Pacific states, one from Eastern European states and three from Western European and Other states.

Filling outstanding vacancies from previously deferred elections, ECOSOC elected Ukraine (Eastern European states) for a term beginning immediately and expiring at the close of the Commission's 53rd session in 2015, as well as Dominican Republic (Latin American and Caribbean states) for a term beginning immediately until the close of the Commission's 54th session in 2016. Elections of four outstanding vacancies were postponed: including one from Eastern European states for a term expiring at the close of the 51st session in 2013; one from the Latin American and Caribbean states for a term expiring at the close of the 54th session in 2016; and two from Western European and Other states, one for a term expiring at the close of the 53rd session and the other expiring at the close of the 54th session.

1   ECOSOC decision 2002/210 decided to extend the terms of office for members of the Commission whose terms were to expire on 31 December 2002 until the conclusion of the 41st session.

2   ECOSOC decision 2002/210 decided to extend the terms of office for members of the Commission whose terms were to expire on 31 December 2003 until the conclusion of the 42nd session.

3   ECOSOC decision 2002/210 decided to extend the terms of office for members of the Commission whose terms were to expire on 31 December 2004 until the conclusion of the 43rd session.

4   Czechoslovakia served on the Commission from 1947–48, 1953–59 and 1964–76.

5   The former Socialist Federal Republic of Yugoslavia served on the Commission from 1947–52, 1960–63 and 1971–74. It was not automatically succeeded by any of the new states created following its dissolution.

6   ECOSOC, at its resumed organisational session for 2009, elected Brazil and Venezuela by acclamation to fill outstanding vacancies on the Commission for a term beginning on the date of election and expiring at the close of the Commission's 51st session in 2013.

7   ECOSOC was informed at its resumed organisational session for 2009 that Denmark had resigned its seat on the Commission effective at the conclusion of the Commission's 47th session. The Council then elected Sweden for a term beginning on the date of election to complete Denmark's term of office (expiring at the close of the Commission's 51st session in 2013).

Commission on Crime Prevention and Criminal Justice (CCPCJ)

Vienna International Centre
PO Box 500
A–1400 Vienna
Austria
Telephone: (+43 1) 260 600
Fax: (+43 1) 260 605 866
Email: unodc@unodc.org
Internet: www.unodc.org (follow links from 'Commissions')
Secretary: Jo Dedeyne-Amann, Belgium (since 2012)

Purpose

The main functions of the Commission on Crime Prevention and Criminal Justice (CCPCJ) are to:

- Provide policy guidance to UN Member States on crime prevention and criminal justice
- Develop, monitor and review implementation of the UN crime prevention programme
- Facilitate and help coordinate the activities of the inter-regional and regional institutes on the prevention of crime and the treatment of offenders
- Mobilise the support of Member States
- Prepare the UN Congresses on crime prevention and criminal justice.

The Commission's mandates are carried out by the UN Office on Drugs and Crime (UNODC) crime programme.

The CCPCJ was established by ECOSOC resolution 1992/1. This resolution dissolved the Committee on Crime Prevention and Control, the expert body of the Council, pursuant to GA res. 46/152 (1991).

Meetings

The Commission meets annually, most recently in April 2012. Since 2010, the Commission has also held annual one-day reconvened sessions in the second half of the year to consider budgetary matters (ECOSOC decision 2009/251). In 2011, the Commission on Narcotic Drugs (CND) and the CCPCJ for the first time held joint meetings during their reconvened sessions (ECOSOC decision 2011/259).

Membership

The Commission has 40 Member States. Members are elected by ECOSOC for a three-year term on the following basis: 12 from African states, nine from Asia–Pacific states, four from Eastern European states, eight from Latin American and Caribbean states, and seven from Western European and Other states. Terms begin on 1 January and end on 31 December of the years shown.

	Previous membership	Current membership*
African states		
Algeria	2003–05 09–11	2012–14
Angola		2010–12
Benin		2010–12
Botswana	2004–06	
Burundi	2004–06	
Cameroon	2007–09	2010–12
Central African Republic	2003–05	
Comoros	2004–05 06–11	
DR Congo	2002–03 06–11	2012–14
Egypt	2004–06	
Ethiopia	2003–05	
Gambia	2003–05	
Ghana	2009–11	
Kenya	2009–11	2012–14
Lesotho	2009–11	
Libya	2006–11	
Mauritania	2003–05	
Mauritius		2012–14
Namibia	2006–08	
Niger	2006–08	
Nigeria	2004–09	2010–12
Sierra Leone	2007–09	
Senegal	2006–08	
Sierra Leone		2012–14
South Africa	2007–09	2012–14
Sudan	2009–11	
Tunisia		2012–14
Uganda	2003–08	2012–14
UR of Tanzania	2006–08	
Zambia	2003–05	
Asia–Pacific states		
China	2003–11	2012–14
India	2004–09	2010–12
Indonesia	2004–09	
Iran	2004–09	2010–12
Japan	2003–11	2012–14

	Previous membership	Current membership*
Pakistan	2003–08	2010–12
Philippines		2010–12
ROK	2003–11	
Saudi Arabia	2004–09	2010–12
Thailand	2004–11	2012–14
UAE	2007–09	2012–14

Eastern European states

Armenia	2006–08	
Belarus		2010–12
Croatia	2003–05	2012–14
Czech Republic	2004–06	
Republic of Moldova	2007–09	
Romania	2009–11	
Russian Federation	2003–11	2012–14
Ukraine	2004–09	2010–12

Latin American and Caribbean states

Argentina	2007–09	2010–12
Bolivia	2006–08	
Brazil	2004–09	2010–12
Chile	2006–08	2010–12
Colombia	2007–09	2012–14
Costa Rica	2006–08	
Cuba	2004–06 09–11	2012–14
El Salvador	2004–06 09–11	
Guatemala	2007–09	
Jamaica	2004–09	
Mexico	2004–06	2010–12
Nicaragua	2003–05	
Paraguay	2004–06	
Peru	2003–05	
Saint Vincent and the Grenadines		2010–12
Uruguay	2009–11	2012–14

Western European and Other states

Austria	2003–05 06–11	2012–14
Belgium	2009–11	
Canada	2004–09	2010–12
Finland	2004–06	
Germany	2006–11	2012–14
Italy	2003–05 06–08	2012–14
Turkey	2003–05 07–09	2010–12
UK	2004–09	2010–12
USA	2004–09	2010–12

Note

*   In April 2012, ECOSOC elected 20 members to the Commission on Crime Prevention and Criminal Justice for three-year terms beginning on 1 January 2013: Cameroon, Ghana, Nigeria and Namibia (African states); Indonesia, Iran, Pakistan, ROK and Saudi Arabia (Asia–Pacific states); Belarus and Czech Republic (Eastern European states); Argentina, Bahamas, Brazil, Mexico and Peru (Latin American and Caribbean states); and Norway, Switzerland, UK and USA (Western European and Other states).

United Nations Forum on Forests (UNFF)

Secretariat of the United Nations Forum on Forests
Department of Economic and Social Affairs
1 United Nations Plaza, Room DC1–1245
New York, NY 10017
United States of America
Telephone: (+1 212) 963 3401 / (+1 917) 367 4244
Fax: (+1 917) 367 3186
Email: unff@un.org
Internet: www.un.org/esa/forests
Director: Jan McAlpine, USA (appointed by the UN Secretary-General in 2008)

Purpose

The United Nations Forum on Forests (UNFF) was established by ECOSOC in 2000. It provides a coherent, transparent and participatory global framework for policy development, implementation and coordination on sustainable forest management. It aims to promote the management, conservation and sustainable development of all types of forests in a holistic manner, and to strengthen long-term political commitment to this objective, thereby enhancing the contribution of forests to the achievement of internationally agreed development goals (IADGs), including the Millennium Development Goals (MDGs).

The UNFF operates as the only functional commission under ECOSOC with universal membership. Major legislative mandates are provided in ECOSOC resolutions 2000/35 and 2006/49, and GA res. 62/98.

Evolution

Adoption of the Non-Legally Binding Instrument on All Types of Forests (the Forest Instrument) in 2007 by the UNFF, and subsequently by the General Assembly, and the four Global Objectives on Forests (GOFs) were major achievements for forests and the international forest policy process. The purpose of the Forest Instrument is to strengthen political commitment and action at all levels to implement sustainable management of all types of forests and to achieve the shared GOFs; enhance the contribution of forests to the achievement of the internationally agreed development goals, including MDGs; and provide a framework for national actions and international cooperation. The GOFs adopted by the General Assembly are to:

- Reverse the loss of forest cover worldwide through sustainable forest management, including protection, restoration, afforestation and reforestation, and increase efforts to prevent forest degradation
- Enhance forest-based economic, social and environmental benefits, including by improving the livelihoods of forest-dependent people
- Increase significantly the area of protected forests worldwide and areas of sustainably managed forests, as well as the proportion of forest products from sustainably managed forests
- Reverse the decline in official development assistance for sustainable forest management and mobilise significantly increased, new and additional financial resources from all sources for the implementation of sustainable forest management.

Another major UNFF decision, in 2009, was to address the issue of forest financing. At its special session, the Forum established two major processes to make a lasting solution – the UNFF Facilitative Process and the open-ended inter-governmental ad hoc expert group on forest financing – in order to provide necessary input and recommendations to the UNFF's 10th session in 2013.

The Collaborative Partnership on Forests (CPF) was established in April 2001 following the recommendation by ECOSOC to support UNFF's work. CPF is a voluntary arrangement among 14 international organisations and secretariats with substantial programmes on forests, including the UNFF Secretariat. CPF is chaired by the Food and Agriculture Organization (FAO).

Meetings

The Forum meets every two years, as per its 2007–15 multi-year programme of work (MYPOW) adopted at its seventh session. The 10th session is scheduled to be held from 8 to 19 April 2013 in Istanbul, Turkey, and will focus on forests and economic development, and decide on forest financing. In 2015, UNFF11 will review the effectiveness of the international arrangement on forests and decide on options for the future of such an arrangement. UNFF11 will also review progress towards achieving the GOFs and implementation of the Forest Instrument, and the contribution of forests to the internationally agreed development goals.

Membership

Membership of the UNFF is open to all UN Member States and states members of the specialised agencies.

REGIONAL COMMISSIONS

Economic Commission for Africa (ECA)

Menelik II Avenue
PO Box 3001
Addis Ababa
Ethiopia
Telephone: (+251 11) 551 7200 (Addis Ababa) or (+1 212) 963 6905 (New York)
Fax: (+251 11) 551 0365 (Addis Ababa) or (+1 212) 963 4957 (New York)
Email: ecainfo@uneca.org
Internet: www.uneca.org
Executive Secretary: Carlos Lopes, Guinea Bissau (appointed by the UN Secretary-General in March 2012 to take up the role later in the year)

Purpose

The Economic Commission for Africa (ECA) is the regional arm of the UN in Africa. It is mandated to support the economic and social development of its 53 Member States, foster regional integration and promote international cooperation for Africa's development. Its work programme focuses on two areas:
- Promoting regional integration in support of the African Union vision and priorities
- Meeting Africa's special needs and emerging global challenges.

ECA was established in 1958 by ECOSOC res. 671A (XXV) (1958), and is one of five regional commissions under the administrative direction of UN Headquarters.

Structure

The Commission is organised around seven substantive programme clusters:
- African Centre for Statistics
- Food security and sustainable development
- Gender and social development
- Governance and public administration

- ICT and science and technology
- Economic development and the New Partnership for Africa's Development (NEPAD)
- Regional integration, infrastructure and trade division.

Five sub-regional offices contribute to the work programme and support outreach.

ECA has established the following subsidiary bodies:
- Committee on Women and Development
- Committee on Development Information
- Committee on Sustainable Development
- Committee on Human Development and Civil Society
- Committee on Industry and Private Sector Development
- Committee on Natural Resources and Science and Technology
- Committee on Regional Cooperation and Integration.

Membership

The geographical scope of the Commission's work is the whole continent of Africa, Madagascar and other African islands. Membership is open to members of the UN in this region and to any state in the area that may become a member of the UN in the future. Under its terms of reference, the Commission may invite UN Member States to participate in its work in a consultative capacity. Switzerland participates in a consultative capacity by virtue of ECOSOC res. 925 (XXXIV) (1962).

The 53 members of ECA are:

Algeria	Ethiopia	Niger
Angola	Gabon	Nigeria
Benin	Gambia	Rwanda
Botswana	Ghana	Sao Tome and Principe
Burkina Faso	Guinea	Senegal
Burundi	Guinea-Bissau	Seychelles
Cameroon	Kenya	Sierra Leone
Cape Verde	Lesotho	Somalia
Central African Republic	Liberia	South Africa
Chad	Libya	Sudan
Comoros	Madagascar	Swaziland
Congo	Malawi	Togo
Côte d'Ivoire	Mali	Tunisia
DR Congo	Mauritania	Uganda
Djibouti	Mauritius	UR of Tanzania
Egypt	Morocco	Zambia
Equatorial Guinea	Mozambique	Zimbabwe
Eritrea	Namibia	

UN Economic and Social Commission for Asia and the Pacific (ESCAP)

United Nations Building
Rajadamnern Nok Avenue
Bangkok 10200
Thailand
Telephone: (+66 2) 288 1234
Fax: (+66 2) 288 1000
Email: escap–registry@un.org
Internet: www.unescap.org
Executive Secretary: Noeleen Heyzer, Singapore (appointed by the UN Secretary-General in 2007)

Purpose

The UN Economic and Social Commission for Asia and the Pacific (ESCAP) serves as the regional arm of the UN in economic, social and related fields. Its work includes norm-setting, dissemination of information, analytical and operational functions, as well as providing an important forum for articulating regional perspectives on global issues and for building consensus within the Asia–Pacific region (GA res. 32/197 (1977) and ECOSOC res. 1998/46 (1998)).

The ESCAP programme promotes inclusive and sustainable economic and social development in Asia and the Pacific, with particular focus on reducing social and economic disparities within and among countries in the region. Under the programme structure endorsed by GA res. 63/263 (2008), ESCAP's work is implemented through eight inter-dependent and complementary sub-programmes:
- Macroeconomic policy and inclusive development
- Trade and investment
- Transport
- Environment and sustainable development
- Information and communications technology and disaster risk reduction
- Social development
- Statistics
- Sub-regional activities for development.

Evolution

The Economic Commission for Asia and the Far East (ECAFE) was established by ECOSOC res. 37 (IV) (1947). By res. 1895 (LVII) (1974), ECOSOC approved the change of name to ESCAP.

Structure

The main legislative organ of ESCAP is the Commission, which meets annually at the ministerial level and reports to ECOSOC. The Commission provides a forum for all Asia–Pacific region governments to review and discuss economic and social development issues, and to strengthen sub-regional and regional cooperation.

The Advisory Committee of Permanent Representatives and Other Representatives Designated by Members of the Commission (ACPR) was established in 1974. It is composed of ESCAP members and usually meets once every two months to advise and exchange views with the Executive Secretary on the Secretariat's work, and to maintain close cooperation and consultation between Member States and the Secretariat of the Commission.

The Commission is also responsible for the following regional institutions:
- Asian and Pacific Centre for Transfer of Technology (APCTT), New Delhi, India
- Asian and Pacific Training Centre for Information and Communications Technology for Development (APCICT), Incheon, ROK
- Centre for Alleviation of Poverty through Sustainable Agriculture (CAPSA), Bogor, Indonesia
- Statistical Institute for Asia and the Pacific (SIAP), Chiba, Japan
- UN Asian and Pacific Centre for Agricultural Engineering and Machinery (UNAPCAEM), Beijing, China.

Given the vast coverage and diversity of the Asia–Pacific region, ESCAP's programme of sub-regional activities for development strengthens the Commission's presence and interventions at that level in order to better target and deliver programmes that address specific key priorities, including poverty reduction and sustainable development, of Member States in the respective sub-regions.

ESCAP's work on sub-regional activities for development covers five sub-regions:
- The Pacific, with a sub-regional office in Suva, Fiji
- East and North-East Asia, with a sub-regional office in Incheon, ROK
- North and Central Asia, with a sub-regional office located in Almaty, Kazakhstan
- South and South-West Asia, with a sub-regional office located in New Delhi, India
- South-East Asia, coordinated by ESCAP's headquarters, in Bangkok, Thailand.

Meetings

The Commission meets annually, usually in April/May, and often in Bangkok, Thailand.

Membership

The majority of ESCAP members are states within the geographical scope of the Commission. This extends from the Russian Federation to Tonga. There are also four non-regional members: France, Netherlands, the UK and USA. Non-self-governing territories in the region may become associate members.

There are 53 Member States:

Afghanistan	Kiribati	Russian Federation
Armenia	Kyrgyzstan	Samoa
Australia	Lao PDR	Singapore
Azerbaijan	Malaysia	Solomon Islands
Bangladesh	Maldives	Sri Lanka
Bhutan	Marshall Islands	Tajikistan
Brunei Darussalam	Micronesia	Thailand
Cambodia	Mongolia	Timor-Leste
China	Myanmar	Tonga
DPRK	Nauru	Turkey
Fiji	Nepal	Turkmenistan
France	Netherlands	Tuvalu
Georgia	New Zealand	UK
India	Pakistan	USA
Indonesia	Palau	Uzbekistan
Iran	Papua New Guinea	Vanuatu
Japan	Philippines	Viet Nam
Kazakhstan	ROK	

There are nine associate members:

American Samoa	Guam	New Caledonia
Cook Islands	Hong Kong, China	Niue
French Polynesia	Macau, China	Northern Mariana Islands

UN Economic Commission for Europe (UNECE)

Palais des Nations
1211 Geneva 10
Switzerland
Telephone: (+41 22) 917 4444
Fax: (+41 22) 917 0505
Email: info.ece@unece.org
Internet: www.unece.org
Executive Secretary: Sven Alkalaj, Bosnia and Herzegovina (appointed by the UN Secretary-General in March 2012)

Purpose

The UN Economic Commission for Europe (UNECE) was created in 1947 by ECOSOC res. 36 (IV) (1947). Its major aim is to promote pan-European economic integration. To do so, UNECE brings together 56 countries from Europe, Central Asia and North America to work together on economic and sectoral issues.

The Commission provides analysis, policy advice and assistance to governments. In cooperation with other stakeholders, notably the business community, it gives focus to UN global economic mandates. It also sets out norms, standards and conventions to facilitate international cooperation within and outside the region.

UNECE expertise covers sectors including: economic cooperation and integration, sustainable energy, environment, housing and land management, population, statistics, timber, trade and transport.

Structure

The Commission is responsible for making strategic decisions on its work programme and provides a forum for policy dialogue on economic developments in the region.

Principal subsidiary bodies are:
- Committee on Economic Cooperation and Integration
- Committee on Environmental Policy
- Conference of European Statisticians
- Committee on Housing and Land Management
- Committee on Inland Transport
- Committee on Sustainable Energy
- Committee on Timber
- Committee on Trade.

Meetings

The Commission holds a public session every two years. The 55th session will be held in the northern hemisphere spring 2013. Meetings of its sectoral committees are held throughout the year.

ECONOMIC AND
SOCIAL COUNCIL

Membership

The Commission is composed of the European members of the UN, plus the USA, Canada, Israel and the Central Asian and Caucasian former USSR republics. The 56 members are:

Albania	Greece	Republic of Moldova
Andorra	Hungary	Romania
Armenia	Iceland	Russian Federation
Austria	Ireland	San Marino
Azerbaijan	Israel	Serbia
Belarus	Italy	Slovakia
Belgium	Kazakhstan	Slovenia
Bosnia and Herzegovina	Kyrgyzstan	Spain
Bulgaria	Latvia	Sweden
Canada	Liechtenstein	Switzerland
Croatia	Lithuania	Tajikistan
Cyprus	Luxembourg	The former Yugoslav
Czech Republic	Malta	Republic of Macedonia
Denmark	Monaco	Turkey
Estonia	Montenegro	Turkmenistan
Finland	Netherlands	Ukraine
France	Norway	UK
Georgia	Poland	USA
Germany	Portugal	Uzbekistan

Note

The Holy See, which is not a member of the UN, participates in UNECE activities in a consultative capacity. Provision is also made for participation by representatives of other Member States of the UN inter-governmental and non-governmental organisations in activities of concern to them.

Economic Commission for Latin America and the Caribbean (ECLAC)

United Nations Building
3477 Dag Hammarskjöld Ave
PO Box 179–D
Vitacura
Santiago
Chile
Telephone: (+56 2) 210 2000
Fax: (+56 2) 208 0252/1946
Email: dpisantiago@cepal.org
Internet: www.eclac.org
Executive Secretary: Alicia Bárcena, Mexico (appointed by the UN Secretary-General in 2008)

Purpose

The Economic Commission for Latin America and the Caribbean (ECLAC) was founded in 1948 by ECOSOC res. 106 (VI) to coordinate policies for the promotion of sustainable Latin American economic development and to foster regional and international trade. Later, its work was extended to the Caribbean countries and its programme of action expanded to promote sustainable social development.

In 1996, member governments updated ECLAC's mandate through res. 553 (XXVI). Under this provision, the Commission helps Member States analyse the development process by formulating, evaluating and following up on public policies, as well as by providing assistance in areas of specialised information.

ECLAC experts also offer advice, training and support on subjects such as:
- Agricultural development
- Economic and social planning
- Industrial, technological and entrepreneurial development
- International trade, regional integration and cooperation
- Investment and financing
- Social development and equity
- Integration of women in development
- Natural resources and infrastructure
- Environment and human settlements
- Statistics
- Administrative management
- Demography and population policies.

Structure

The work programme is carried out through the:
- Division of Economic Development
- Division of International Trade and Integration
- Division of Natural Resources and Infrastructure
- Division of Population
- Division of Production, Productivity and Management
- Division of Social Development
- Division of Statistics and Economic Projections
- Division of Sustainable Development and Human Settlements
- Division of Gender Affairs
- Latin American and Caribbean Institute for Economic and Social Planning (ILPES)
- Division of Programme Planning and Operations
- Division of Financing for Development
- Public Information and Web Services Section.

In addition to its headquarters in Santiago, Chile, the Commission has sub-regional headquarters in Mexico City for Mexico and Central America, and in Port of Spain, Trinidad and Tobago, for the Caribbean. It also maintains country offices in Buenos Aires, Argentina; Brasilia, Brazil; Montevideo, Uruguay; and Bogota, Colombia; and a liaison office in Washington DC.

ECLAC has a number of subsidiary organs:
- Committee of the Whole
- Regional Conference on Women in Latin America and the Caribbean
- Statistical Conference of the Americas of the ECLAC
- Committee of High-Level Government Experts (CEGAN)
- Regional Council for Planning
- Caribbean Development and Cooperation Committee (CDCC)
- Committee on Central American Economic Cooperation (CCE).

Meetings

Commission meetings are held every two years. The 2012 session was scheduled to be held in El Salvador in August. The Committee of the Whole meets between sessions.

ECONOMIC AND
SOCIAL COUNCIL

Membership

ECLAC membership is made up of the 33 countries of Latin America and the Caribbean, and 11 developed nations from North America, Europe and Asia that have strong economic, social and cultural linkages with the region. Additionally, eight non-independent territories in the Caribbean are associate members. The Member States are:

Antigua and Barbuda	El Salvador	Paraguay
Argentina	France	Peru
Bahamas	Germany	Portugal
Barbados	Grenada	ROK
Belize	Guatemala	Saint Kitts and Nevis
Bolivia	Guyana	Saint Lucia
Brazil	Haiti	Saint Vincent and the
Canada	Honduras	Grenadines
Chile	Italy	Spain
Colombia	Jamaica	Suriname
Costa Rica	Japan	Trinidad and Tobago
Cuba	Mexico	UK
Dominica	Netherlands	USA
Dominican Republic	Nicaragua	Uruguay
Ecuador	Panama	Venezuela

There are nine associate members:

Anguilla	Cayman Islands	Turks and Caicos Islands
Aruba	Montserrat	United States Virgin Islands
British Virgin Islands	Puerto Rico	

Economic and Social Commission for Western Asia (ESCWA)

PO Box 11–8575
Riad el-Solh Square, Beirut
Lebanon
Telephone: (+961 1) 981 301
Fax: (+961 1) 981 510
Email: webmaster–escwa@un.org
Internet: www.escwa.un.org
Under-Secretary-General and Executive Secretary: Rima Khalaf, Jordan (appointed by the UN Secretary-General in September 2010)

Purpose

The Economic and Social Commission for Western Asia (ESCWA) is mandated to initiate measures that promote economic and social development in Western Asia, and strengthen the economic and social relations of the countries in the region, both among themselves and with other countries.

The Commission's programme focuses on managing four region-specific priority areas central to the Millennium Declaration:
- Social policies
- Energy and water
- Globalisation
- Technology, with particular attention to information and communication technology.

Priority is given to the cross-cutting themes of gender mainstreaming, the special needs of Least Developed Countries and countries emerging from conflict.

Evolution

The Economic Commission for Western Asia (ECWA) was established under ECOSOC res. 1818 (LV) (1973). In 1985, the Commission was renamed the Economic and Social Commission for Western Asia to reflect its expanded mandate to cover the social development field.

Structure

The biennial Commission session is the highest inter-governmental source of recommendations on development issues to the member governments. It advises ECOSOC of the consolidated views of member governments on issues significant to economic and social development at the global level. The Commission sessions facilitate policy discussion among high-level government officials on the regional development agenda and emerging issues. The Commission sets mandates within the global development framework based on the expressed needs of the member countries.

The Commission has seven inter-governmental committees dealing with: statistics, water resources, energy, transport, social development, international trade, and women. It also has consultative committees on non-governmental organisations and science and technology.

Membership

ESCWA has 14 members:

Bahrain	Lebanon	Sudan
Egypt	Oman	Syrian AR
Iraq	Palestine	UAE
Jordan	Qatar	Yemen
Kuwait	Saudi Arabia	

STANDING COMMITTEES

Committee for Programme and Coordination (CPC)

Dag Hammarskjöld Library Building
L – 0321
New York, NY 10017
United States of America
Telephone: (+1 212) 963 2021
Fax: (+1 212) 963 0360
Email: FifthCommittee@un.org
Internet: www.un.org/en/ga/cpc

Purpose

The Committee for Programme and Coordination (CPC) is charged with:
- Reviewing UN programmes as defined in the strategic framework[1]
- Recommending priority programmes
- Guiding the Secretariat on translating legislation into programmes and making recommendations where duplication should be avoided
- Developing evaluation procedures
- Assisting ECOSOC in its coordination functions.

The CPC is required to consider the activities of UN agencies on a sectoral basis and recommend guidelines for them, taking into account the need for coherence and coordination. It must also carry out periodic reviews of the implementation of important legislative decisions. It is directed to cooperate with the Advisory Committee on Administrative and Budgetary Questions (ACABQ) and consult with the Joint Inspection Unit (JIU), whose members are free to participate in its meetings.

The Committee was established by ECOSOC res. 920 (XXXIV) (1962) and was given its present name by ECOSOC res. 1171 (XLI) (1966). Earlier legislation defining its terms of reference is consolidated in ECOSOC res. 2008 (LX) (1976), which provides that the Committee shall function as the main subsidiary organ of ECOSOC and the General Assembly for planning, programming and coordination.

Meetings

The CPC meets for six weeks in plan years and four weeks in budget years. The Committee's 52nd session was held from 4 June to 29 June 2012 in New York.

Membership

Originally 11, membership has been increased several times, most recently by GA res. 42/450 (1987), and now stands at 34. In accordance with GA res. 42/318 (1987) and ECOSOC res. 1987/94, members are elected by the General Assembly on the nomination of ECOSOC and on the basis of equitable geographical distribution. Allocation of seats is according to the formula: nine members from African states, seven from Asia–Pacific states, four from Eastern European states, seven from Latin American and Caribbean states, and seven from Western European and Other states. Members serve for terms of three years, expiring on 31 December.

	Previous membership	Current membership[2]
African states		
Algeria	1990–92 2005–07	2011–13
Benin	1986–91 95–97 1999–2001 03–08	2011–13
Botswana	2001–03	
Burkina Faso	1987–89	
Burundi	1978–80 91–93	
Cameroon	1981–92 1994–2002	2012–14
Central African Republic	2003–11	
Comoros	1994–96 1999–2001 04–09	2010–12
Congo	1991–99	
Côte d'Ivoire	1988–90	
DR Congo	1975–77 96–98	
Egypt	1984–86 1993–2001	
Eritrea		2011–13
Ethiopia	1983–85 2002–04	
Gabon	2000–05	
Ghana	1978–80 92–97 2005–07	
Guinea	2009–11	2012–14
Guinea-Bissau		2012–14
Kenya	1972–80 88–90 93–95 2005–10	
Liberia	1984–86	
Libya	2008–10	

	Previous membership	Current membership[2]
Mauritania	2000–02	
Morocco	1981–83 90–92	
Namibia		2010–12
Niger	2008–10	
Nigeria	1983–85 91–93 97–99 2002–04 09–11	
Rwanda	1988–90	
Senegal	1981–83 94–96 2006–08	
South Africa	2003–11	
Sudan	1977–82	
Togo	1974–76 93–98	
Tunisia	1987–89 2002–04	
Uganda	1972–79 88–93 1998–2000	
UR of Tanzania	1972–77 80–82 2001–03	
Zambia	1986–94 1998–2000	
Zimbabwe	1997–2002 04–09	2012–14

Asia–Pacific states

	Previous membership	Current membership[2]
Bahrain	1988–90	
Bangladesh	1985–90 2000–02 08–10	
China	1987–2010	2011–13
India	1975–86 88–96 2003–11	
Indonesia	1972–80 84–89 1991–2008	
Iran	1994–2011	2012–14
Iraq	1985–87 91–93	
Japan	1975–2007	2012–14
Kazakhstan	2009–11	2012–14
Malaysia		2012–14
Pakistan	1973–84 1988–2011	2012–14
Philippines	1981–83	
ROK	1993–2010	2011–13
Sri Lanka	1990–92	
Thailand	1997–99	

Eastern European states[3]

	Previous membership	Current membership[2]
Armenia	2003–11	
Belarus	1973–78 85–87 94–96 2006–11	2012–14
Bulgaria	1976–78 91–93 2006–08	2012–14
Hungary	1973–75	
Poland	1988–93 1997–2002	
Republic of Moldova	2000–05	2012–14
Romania	1979–84 88–90 94–99	
Russian Federation	1974–2009	2010–12
Ukraine	1991–2005 09–11	

Latin American and Caribbean states

	Previous membership	Current membership[2]
Antigua and Barbuda		2011–13
Argentina	1974–88 90–92 1994–2011	2012–14
Bahamas	1988–2006	
Brazil	1975–89 1991–2011	2012–14
Chile	1976–78 83–85 91–93	
Colombia	1977–79 88–93	
Costa Rica	1980–82	

	Previous membership	Current membership[2]
Cuba	1988–90 94–96 2008–11	2012–14
Guyana	1973–75	
Haiti	1974–76 2007–09	2010–12
Jamaica	2005–10	
Mexico	1988–90 1995–2006	
Nicaragua	1993–95 97–99 2003–05	
Peru	1986–88 2000–02	
Trinidad and Tobago	1979–99	
Uruguay	1992–94 1996–2004 06–11	2012–14
Venezuela	1989–91 2007–09	2010–12

Western European and Other states[4]

	Previous membership	Current membership[2]
Austria	1988–90 97–99	
Belgium	1973–81	
Canada	1988–90 94–96 2003–05	
Denmark	1973–78	
France	1974–2009	2010–12
Germany	1982–2005	
Israel	2006–08	2010–12
Italy	1991–93 1997–2002 06–11	2012–14
Luxembourg		
Monaco	2003–05	
Netherlands	1982–87 91–96	
Norway	1979–81 91–96	
Portugal	1999–2002 06–08	
San Marino	2000–02	
Spain	2009–11	
Sweden	1988–90	
Switzerland	2003–08	
UK	1973–2005	
USA	1974–2006	

Notes

1   In GA res. 58/269, the Assembly requested the Secretary-General to prepare, on a trial basis, a strategic framework to replace the medium-term plan. Pursuant to GA res. 62/224, the Assembly decided to maintain the strategic framework as the principal policy directive of the UN.

2   In April 2012, ECOSOC nominated Botswana and UR of Tanzania (African states), Russian Federation (Eastern European states) and Peru (Latin American and Caribbean states) for election by the General Assembly for a three-year term, beginning on 1 January 2013. In the absence of other candidates, it postponed nomination of one member from Latin American and Caribbean states and two from Western European and Other states. For outstanding vacancies, it nominated Japan and Kazakhstan (Asia–Pacific states) for terms beginning on the date of election and expiring on 31 December 2014, and postponed nominations for the four outstanding vacancies for members from Western European and Other states for the same term.

3   The former Socialist Federal Republic of Yugoslavia served on the Committee from 1979 to 1990. It was not automatically succeeded by any of the new states created following its dissolution.

4   As of 31 May 2012, there were four vacant seats in the Western European and Other States Group.

Committee on Non-Governmental Organizations (CNGO)

1 United Nations Plaza, Room DC1–1480
New York, NY 10017
United States of America
Telephone: (+1 212) 963 8652
Fax: (+1 212) 963 9248
Internet: www.un.org/ecosoc/ngo (follow link to Committee on NGOs)

Purpose

The Committee on Non-Governmental Organizations (CNGO) is an ECOSOC standing committee, established by ECOSOC res. 3 (II) (1946). It examines and reports on the consultative relationship that ECOSOC should accord to international non-governmental organisations (NGOs). It must also recommend what action should be taken on submissions that NGOs make to it. ECOSOC res. 1996/31 approved new criteria by which consultative arrangements between ECOSOC and NGOs may be established.

Meetings

The Committee meets annually for three weeks. If necessary, and with the approval of ECOSOC, the Committee holds a resumed session of up to two weeks annually. The 2012 regular session was held from 30 January to 8 February and 17 February, and the resumed session from 21 to 30 May and 8 June.

Membership

Originally five, membership was increased to seven in 1950, 13 in 1966 and 19 in 1981 (ECOSOC res. 1981/50). Membership is open to all states, with regard to equitable geographical representation: five members from African states, four from Asia–Pacific states, two from Eastern European states, four from Latin American and Caribbean states, and four from Western European and Other states. Under ECOSOC res. 70 (ORG–75) (1975) members are elected for four-year terms. Membership starts on 1 January and expires on 31 December of the years stated.

	Previous membership	Current membership
African states		
Angola	2007–10	
Burundi	2007–10	2011–14
Egypt	2007–10	
Guinea	2007–10	
Morocco		2011–14
Mozambique		2011–14
Senegal		2011–14
Sudan	2007–10	2011–14
Asia–Pacific states		
China	2007–10	2011–14
India	2007–10	2011–14
Kyrgyzstan		2011–14
Pakistan	2007–10	2011–14
Qatar	2007–10	

	Previous membership	Current membership

Eastern European states

Bulgaria		2011–14
Romania	2007–10	
Russian Federation	2007–10	2011–14

Latin American and Caribbean states

Colombia	2007–10	
Cuba	2007–10	2011–14
Dominica	2007–10	
Nicaragua		2011–14
Peru	2007–10	2011–14
Venezuela		2011–14

Western European and Other states

Belgium		2011–14
Israel	2007–10	2011–14
Turkey	2007–10	2011–14
UK	2007–10	
USA	2007–10	2011–14

EXPERT BODIES

Committee of Experts on International Cooperation in Tax Matters

Financing for Development Office
2 United Nations Plaza, Room DC2–2170
New York, NY 10017
United States of America
Telephone: (+1 212) 963 2587
Fax: (+1 212) 963 0443
Email: taxffdoffice@un.org
Internet: www.un.org/esa/ffd/tax

Purpose

The Committee of Experts on International Cooperation in Tax Matters is mandated to:

- Keep under review and update as necessary the UN Model Double Taxation Convention between Developed and Developing Countries, and the Manual for the Negotiation of Bilateral Tax Treaties between Developed and Developing Countries
- Provide a framework for dialogue with a view to enhancing and promoting international tax cooperation among national tax authorities
- Consider how new and emerging issues could affect international cooperation in tax matters and develop assessments, commentaries and appropriate recommendations
- Make recommendations on capacity-building and the provision of technical assistance to developing countries and countries with economies in transition
- Give special attention to developing countries and countries with economies in transition in dealing with all the above issues.

The Group's mandate is a broad one, and the Committee's current and recent focus has included matters such as:

- Tax treaties between developed and developing countries, including updating the UN Model and Manual
- Exchange of information
- Mutual assistance in collection of debts
- Dispute resolution
- Permanent establishments and attribution of profits to them
- Royalties and technical fees
- Transfer pricing
- Treaty shopping and treaty abuses
- Taxation of development projects
- A proposed UN Code of Conduct on Cooperation in Combating International Tax Evasion and Avoidance
- Capacity-building for national tax administrations.

Evolution

The Ad Hoc Group of Experts on Tax Treaties between Developed and Developing Countries was established in 1968 (ECOSOC res. 1273 (XLIII) (1967)). Its purpose was to promote the conclusion of treaties between developed and developing countries that were acceptable to all parties and that would fully safeguard their respective revenue interests. In 1980, the Group finalised the UN Model Double Taxation Convention between Developed and Developing Countries.

Also in 1980, the Group was given the title Ad Hoc Group of Experts on International Cooperation in Tax Matters, and its membership increased from 20 to 25 tax administrators drawn from 10 developed countries and 15 developing countries and economies in transition (ECOSOC res. 1980/13). In 2004, it was renamed the Committee of Experts on International Cooperation in Tax Matters (ECOSOC res. 2004/69).

In March 2012, the Committee launched the 2011 update of the UN Model Double Taxation Convention between Developed and Developing Countries, which had last been updated in 1999.

Meetings

The Committee meets annually. Its eighth session is scheduled to take place in Geneva from 15 to 19 October 2012.

Membership

ECOSOC res. 2004/69 determined the Committee should comprise 25 members nominated by governments and acting in their expert capacities. Nominees are required to be drawn from the fields of tax policy and tax administration, and are selected by the Secretary-General for a term of four years. The Secretary-General is required to take into account equitable geographic distribution and representation from different tax systems in making his or her selections. Members of the Committee of Experts are as follows. Terms expire 30 June 2013.

Kwame Adjei-Djan, Ghana	Keiji Aoyama, Japan	Claudine Devillet, Belgium
Sae Joon Ahn, ROK	Bernell L Arrindell, Barbados	El Hadj Ibrahima Diop, Senegal
Farida Amjad, Pakistan	Noureddine Bensouda, Morocco	Amr El Monayer, Egypt

continued next page

Juerg Giraudi, Switzerland

Mansor Hassan, Malaysia

Liselott Kana, Chile

Anita Kapur, India

Wolfgang Karl Lasars,
Germany

Tizhong Liao, China

Henry John Louie, USA

Julia Martínez Rico, Spain

Enrico Martino, Italy

Robin Oliver, New Zealand

Ifueko Omoigui Okauru,
Nigeria

Iskra Georgieva Slavcheva,
Bulgaria

Stig B Sollund, Norway

Marcos Aurélio Pereira
Valadão, Brazil

Ronald Peter van der Merwe,
South Africa

Armando Lara Yaffar, Mexico

Committee for Development Policy (CDP)

Secretariat of the United Nations Committee for Development Policy
2 United Nations Plaza, Room DC2–2014
New York, NY 10017
United States of America
Telephone: (+1 212) 963 4724
Fax: (+1 212) 963 1061
Email: cdp@un.org
Internet: www.un.org/en/development/desa/policy/cdp

Purpose

The Committee for Development Policy (CDP) provides input and independent advice to ECOSOC on emerging cross-sectoral development issues and on international cooperation for development, focusing on medium- and long-term aspects. It is responsible for setting the criteria for the designation of Least Developed Countries (LDCs), and reviewing the list of LDCs every three years.

The list of LDCs was first established in 1971. It now consists of the following 48 states:

Afghanistan	Gambia	Rwanda
Angola	Guinea	Samoa[1]
Bangladesh	Guinea-Bissau	Sao Tome and Principe
Benin	Haiti	Senegal
Bhutan	Kiribati	Sierra Leone
Burkina Faso	Lao PDR	Solomon Islands
Burundi	Lesotho	Somalia
Cambodia	Liberia	Sudan
Central African Republic	Madagascar	Timor-Leste
Chad	Malawi	Togo
Comoros	Mali	Tuvalu
DR Congo	Mauritania	Uganda
Djibouti	Mozambique	UR of Tanzania
Equatorial Guinea	Myanmar	Vanuatu
Eritrea	Nepal	Yemen
Ethiopia	Niger	Zambia

Note

1   In July 2007, ECOSOC endorsed the recommendation of the CDP that Samoa be graduated. Samoa was to graduate from the list in December 2010. GA res. 64/295 of 7 September 2010 deferred this to 1 January 2014 in view of the devastating consequences for the country caused by the Pacific Ocean tsunami of September 2009. The following countries have already graduated from the LDC category: Botswana (1994), Cape Verde (December 2007) and Maldives (January 2011).

Evolution

ECOSOC res. 1035 (XXXVII) (1964) requested the Secretary-General consider the establishment of a group of experts in development planning theory and practice to work as a consultative body within the UN. ECOSOC res. 1079 (XXXIX) (1965) set out the functions of this proposed group, which was appointed at the Council's 40th session and designated the Committee for Development Planning.

ECOSOC res. 1625 (LI) (1975) enlarged the membership of the Committee from 18 to 24, with effect from 1 January 1972. The Committee was suspended for one year in 1993, following a recommendation by the Secretary-General that it be replaced by a High-Level Advisory Board on Sustainable Development (A/47/598). Following an ECOSOC review of its subsidiary bodies, initiated by GA res. 50/227 (1996), the Committee was renamed in 1998 the Committee for Development Policy (ECOSOC res. 1998/46). The resolution also determined that ECOSOC should decide the work programme for the Committee, and that the Committee should continue three-yearly reviews of the status of LDCs and meet to discuss this issue once every three years.

ECOSOC res. 2004/66 and GA res. 59/209 re-emphasised the importance of a smooth transition for countries graduating from LDC status. It established a process under which the Committee considers a country for graduation once it has met the criteria at two consecutive triennial reviews. ECOSOC, in turn, takes action on the Committee's recommendation. Graduation becomes effective three years after the General Assembly takes note of the ECOSOC decision. During the three-year period, the graduating country, still an LDC, is invited to prepare a transition strategy in cooperation with its development and trading partners, which are invited to consider extending LDC benefits or to reduce them in a phased manner after the country graduates from the category.

Meetings

The Committee meets annually, usually in March or April, for five working days. The 14th session was held from 12 to 16 March 2012 in New York. The CDP expert group meeting on the triennial review of the LDC category was held in New York from 16 to 17 January 2012.

Membership

Members serve in their individual capacities as experts and not as representatives of states. They are nominated by the Secretary-General in consultation with interested governments and appointed by ECOSOC for three-year terms. The following members[1] were appointed for a term beginning on 1 January 2010 and ending on 31 December 2012:

Bina Agarwal, India	Norman Girvan, Jamaica	Hans Opschoor, Netherlands
Mary Helena Allegretti, Brazil	Philippe Hein, Mauritius	Pasuk Phongpaichit, Thailand
José Antonio Alonso, Spain	Mulu Ketsela, Ethiopia	Patrick Plane, France
Lourdes Arizpe, Mexico	Wahiduddin Mahmud, Bangladesh	Victor Polterovich, Russian Federation
Kwesi Botchwey, Ghana		
Giovanni Andrea Cornia, Italy	Amina Mama, South Africa	Fatima Sadiqi, Morocco
	Thandika Mkwandawire, Sweden	Frances Stewart, UK
Ricardo Ffrench-Davis, Chile		Milica Uvalic, Serbia
Sakiko Fukuda-Parr, Japan	Adil Najam, Pakistan	Yu Yongding, China

Note

1   Member Alice Amsden, USA, died in March 2012.

Committee of Experts on the Transport of Dangerous Goods and on the Globally Harmonized System of Classification and Labelling of Chemicals

Geneva Office
c/– UNECE
Transport Division
Palais des Nations
1211 Geneva 10
Switzerland
Telephone: (+41 22) 917 2456
Fax: (+41 22) 917 0039
Email: infotransport@unece.org
Internet: www.unece.org (follow 'Quick Links' to 'Dangerous Goods' then 'ECOSOC Bodies')
Director: Eva Molnar, Hungary (appointed by the UN Secretary-General in 2007)

Purpose

The main functions of the Committee are to:

- Approve work programmes for the sub-committees based on available resources
- Coordinate strategic and policy directions in areas of shared interests and overlap
- Give formal endorsement to the recommendations of the sub-committees and provide the mechanism for channelling these to ECOSOC
- Facilitate and coordinate the smooth running of the sub-committees.

The Committee is a subsidiary body of ECOSOC. It was previously known as the Committee of Experts on the Transport of Dangerous Goods, which was reconfigured by ECOSOC res. 1999/65 as the Committee of Experts on the Transport of Dangerous Goods and on the Globally Harmonized System of Classification and Labelling of Chemicals, with two specialised sub-committees:

- The Sub-Committee of Experts on the Transport of Dangerous Goods (TDG Sub-Committee)
- The Sub-Committee of Experts on the Globally Harmonized System of Classification and Labelling of Chemicals (GHS Sub-Committee).

Meetings

The Committee meets every two years in Geneva. Its next meeting will be held on 14 December 2012. Secretariat services are provided by the UN Economic Commission for Europe (UNECE).

Membership

The Committee comprises experts from the following 40 states:

Argentina	Iran	Qatar
Australia	Ireland	ROK
Austria	Italy	Russian Federation
Belgium	Japan	Senegal
Brazil	Kenya	Serbia
Canada	Mexico	South Africa
China	Morocco	Spain
Czech Republic	Netherlands	Sweden
Denmark	New Zealand	Switzerland
Finland	Nigeria	Ukraine
France	Norway	UK
Germany	Poland	USA
Greece	Portugal	Zambia
India		

Observers from the following countries also participate, in accordance with Rule 72 of the Rules of Procedure of ECOSOC:

Algeria	Indonesia	Slovakia
Bulgaria	Malaysia	Slovenia
Cambodia	Philippines	Thailand
Gambia	Romania	

Sub-Committee of Experts on the Transport of Dangerous Goods (TDG Sub-Committee)

Geneva Office
c/– UNECE
Transport Division
Palais des Nations
1211 Geneva 10
Switzerland
Telephone: (+41 22) 917 2456
Fax: (+41 22) 917 0039
Email: infotransport@unece.org
Internet: www.unece.org (follow links from 'Quick Links' to 'Dangerous Goods' then 'ECOSOC Bodies')

Purpose

The TDG Sub-Committee, established under ECOSOC res. 1989/104, develops recommendations on the transport of dangerous goods. These are updated every two years to take account of technical progress, the advent of new substances and materials, the requirements of modern transport systems and, above all, the requirement to ensure the safety of people, property and the environment.

The recommendations are addressed to governments and international organisations concerned with regulating the transport of dangerous goods, including hazardous wastes and environmentally hazardous substances. The aim is to achieve uniformity across different modes of transport (road, rail, inland waterways, sea and air) and ensure the safety of transport without impeding the movement of goods.

The recommendations form the basis of much national legislation and of international instruments such as:

- The International Maritime Organization (IMO) International Maritime Dangerous Goods Code
- The International Civil Aviation Organization (ICAO) Technical Instructions for the Safe Transport of Dangerous Goods by Air
- The European Agreement Concerning the International Carriage of Dangerous Goods by Road (ADR)
- The European Agreement Concerning the International Carriage of Dangerous Goods by Inland Waterways (ADN)
- Regulations concerning the International Carriage of Dangerous Goods by Rail (RID).

Evolution

The Sub-Committee initially replaced the Group of Experts on Explosives and Group of Rapporteurs, which were subsidiary bodies of the Committee of Experts on the Transport of Dangerous Goods. In 1999 (ECOSOC res. 1999/65), the Sub-Committee replaced the Committee of Experts on the Transport of Dangerous Goods, which had been established under ECOSOC res. 468G (XV) (1953) to recommend and define groupings or classification of dangerous goods based on the risk involved. The Committee of Experts was renamed the Committee of Experts on the Transport of Dangerous Goods and on the Globally Harmonized System of Classification and Labelling of Chemicals (ECOSOC res. 1999/65).

Since 2009, the Sub-Committee has developed a comprehensive set of recommendations covering not only listing, classification, marking and labelling, but also the use of packagings and tanks; their construction, testing and approval; training; consignment procedures including documentation; operational provisions; and security. They are grouped in the UN Model Regulations on the Transport of Dangerous Goods.

Meetings

The Sub-Committee meets twice a year, in June and November/December in Geneva (from 3 to 11 December 2012; 24 to 28 June and 25 November to 4 December 2013). Secretariat services are provided by the UN Economic Commission for Europe (UNECE).

Membership

The Sub-Committee comprises experts from 30 states:

Argentina	Germany	Poland
Australia	India	Portugal
Austria	Iran	ROK
Belgium	Italy	Russian Federation
Brazil	Japan	South Africa
Canada	Kenya	Spain
China	Mexico	Sweden
Czech Republic	Morocco	Switzerland
Finland	Netherlands	UK
France	Norway	USA

The following countries participate occasionally as observers in accordance with Rule 72 of the ECOSOC Rules of Procedure:

Algeria	Ireland	Slovakia
Bulgaria	Namibia	Thailand
Chile	New Zealand	Tunisia
Denmark	Nigeria	Ukraine
Fiji	Qatar	
Greece	Romania	

Sub-Committee of Experts on the Globally Harmonized System of Classification and Labelling of Chemicals (GHS Sub-Committee)

Geneva Office
c/– UNECE
Transport Division
Palais des Nations
1211 Geneva 10
Switzerland
Telephone: (+41 22) 917 2456
Fax: (+41 22) 917 0039
Email: infotransport@unece.org
Internet: www.unece.org (follow links from 'Quick Links' to 'Dangerous Goods' then 'ECOSOC Bodies')

Purpose

The GHS Sub-Committee was established under ECOSOC res. 1999/65 to give effect to a Globally Harmonized System of Classification and Labelling of Chemicals developed by several organisations in the follow up to the UN Conference on Environment and Development (Rio de Janeiro, June 1992) and Agenda 21, Chapter 19, Programme Area B.

The terms of reference of the Sub-Committee are to:
- Act as custodian of the Globally Harmonized System of Classification and Labelling of Chemicals (GHS), managing and giving direction to the harmonisation process
- Keep the GHS up to date as necessary, considering the need for changes to ensure its continued relevance and practical utility
- Determine the need for, and timing of, the updating of technical criteria while working with existing bodies as appropriate
- Promote understanding and use of the GHS and encourage feedback
- Make the GHS available for worldwide use and application
- Make guidance available on the application of the GHS, and on the interpretation and use of technical criteria to support consistency of application
- Prepare work programmes and submit recommendations to the Committee.

Meetings

The Sub-Committee meets twice a year, in June and December in Geneva (from 12 to 14 December 2012; 1 to 3 July and 4 to 6 December in 2013). Secretariat services are provided by the UN Economic Commission for Europe (UNECE).

Membership

The Sub-Committee comprises experts from the following 36 states:

Argentina	Greece	Qatar
Australia	Iran	ROK
Austria	Ireland	Russian Federation
Belgium	Italy	Senegal
Brazil	Japan	Serbia
Canada	Kenya	South Africa
China	Netherlands	Spain
Czech Republic	New Zealand	Sweden
Denmark	Nigeria	Ukraine
Finland	Norway	UK
France	Poland	USA
Germany	Portugal	Zambia

The following countries participate occasionally as observers in accordance with Rule 27 of the ECOSOC Rules of Procedure:

Bulgaria	Jamaica	Romania
Cambodia	Kenya	Slovenia
Chile	Lao PDR	Switzerland
Cyprus	Malaysia	Thailand
Gambia	Mexico	Uruguay
Indonesia	Philippines	Viet Nam

Committee on Economic, Social and Cultural Rights (CESCR)

The International Covenant on Economic, Social and Cultural Rights obliges States Parties to report to ECOSOC on its implementation.

ECOSOC has delegated consideration of such reports to the Committee on Economic, Social and Cultural Rights (CESCR), which was established as an expert subsidiary body of ECOSOC by its res. 1985/17. Its functions had previously been carried out by an inter-governmental working group established under decision 1978/10.

A full CESCR entry is on pages 283–284 of this book, in the section on human rights treaty bodies.

Committee of Experts on Public Administration (CEPA)

Division for Public Administration and Development Management
Department of Economic and Social Affairs
United Nations
2 United Nations Plaza, Room DC2-1714
New York, NY 10017
United States of America
Telephone: (+1 212) 963 2764
Fax: (+1 917) 367 0552
Email: unpan@un.org
Internet: www.unpan.org/cepa

Purpose

The Committee of Experts on Public Administration (CEPA) is responsible for supporting ECOSOC's work concerning the promotion and development of public administration and governance among Member States, in connection with the UN Millennium Development Goals. CEPA was established by ECOSOC res. 2001/45, and succeeded the Group of Experts on Public Administration, established in 1967 by ECOSOC res. 1199 (XLII).

Meetings

The Committee meets once a year (mostly recently in April 2012 in New York). It comprises 24 experts, serving in their personal capacities, who are nominated by the Secretary-General in consultation with Member States and approved by ECOSOC.

Members examine the implementation of GA res. 50/225 (1996) on the need for public administrations to be redesigned to meet the challenges of socio-economic development and change, and review actions to establish accountable, efficient and capable governance and public administration systems in all countries.

Membership

The CEPA members from 1 January 2010 to 31 December 2013 are:

Luis Aguilar Villanueva, Mexico

Peter Anyang' Nyong'O, Kenya

Rowena G Bethel, Bahamas

Vitoria Dias Diogo, Mozambique

Joseph Dion Ngute, Cameroon

Mikhail Dmitriev, Russian Federation

Meredith Edwards, Australia

Walter Fust, Switzerland

Bin Hao, China

Mushtaq Khan, Bangladesh

Pan Suk Kim, ROK

Francisco Longo Martinez, Spain

Hyam Nashash, Jordan

Paul Oquist, Nicaragua

Marta Oyhanarte, Argentina

Odette R Ramsingh,
South Africa

Siripurapu Kesava Rao, India

Margaret Saner, UK

Valeria Termini, Italy

Gwendoline A Williams,
Trinidad and Tobago

Susan L Woodward, USA

Philip Yeo Liat Kok,
Singapore

Najat Zarrouk, Morocco

Jan Ziekow, Germany

Permanent Forum on Indigenous Issues (UNPFII)

Secretariat of the Permanent Forum on Indigenous Issues
United Nations
2 United Nations Plaza, Room DC2–1454
New York, NY 10017
United States of America
Telephone: (+ 1 917) 367 5100
Fax: (+1 917) 367 5102
Email: indigenous_un@un.org
Internet: http://social.un.org/index/IndigenousPeoples.aspx

Purpose

The UN Permanent Forum on Indigenous Issues (UNPFII) serves as an advisory body to ECOSOC. It is mandated to provide expert advice and recommendations on indigenous issues relating to economic and social development, culture, the environment, education, health and human rights to the Council, as well as to programmes, funds and agencies of the UN, through the Council; raise awareness and promote the integration and coordination of activities related to indigenous issues within the UN system; and prepare and disseminate information on indigenous issues. The UN Declaration on the Rights of Indigenous Peoples (September 2007) provides the normative framework for implementing its mandate. The UNPFII was established by ECOSOC res. 2000/22.

Meetings

The Forum holds an annual session of 10 working days. The 11th session was held from 7 to 18 May 2012 in New York. States, UN bodies and organs, inter-governmental and non-governmental organisations, and organisations of indigenous peoples participate in the Forum as observers.

Membership

The Forum consists of 16 independent experts, functioning in their personal capacities, who serve three-year terms and may be re-elected or reappointed for one additional term.

Eight members are nominated by governments and eight directly by indigenous organisations in their regions. The government-nominated members are elected by ECOSOC based on the traditional UN regional groupings, with each group having one seat and the other three rotating. The indigenous organisation-nominated members are appointed by the ECOSOC President on the basis of selection processes undertaken by indigenous peoples in the different regions. They represent the seven socio-cultural regions determined to give broad representation to the world's indigenous peoples: Africa; Asia; Central and South America and the Caribbean; the Arctic; Central and Eastern Europe, Russian Federation, Central Asia and Transcaucasia; North America; and the Pacific. The one additional seat rotates among the three first listed here.

ECONOMIC AND
SOCIAL COUNCIL

Members elected to serve from 1 January 2011 until 31 December 2013 are:

Members nominated by states

Eva Biaudet, Finland

Andrey A Nikiforov, Russian Federation

Megan Davis, Australia

Alvaro Esteban Pop, Guatemala

Paimaneh Hasteh, Iran

Viktoria Tuula, Estonia[1]

Simon William M'Viboudoulou, Congo

Bertie Xavier, Guyana

Members nominated by indigenous non-governmental organisations

Mirna Cunningham Kain, Nicaragua

Raja Devasish Roy, Bangladesh

Dalee Sambo Dorough, USA

Paul Kanyinke Sena, Kenya

Edward John, Canada

Valmaine Toki, New Zealand

Anna Naikanchina, Russian Federation

Saúl Vicente Vásquez, Mexico

Note

1   In April 2012, ECOSOC elected Viktoria Tuula to replace Helen Kaljulate, Estonia, who had resigned.

OTHER SUBSIDIARY BODIES

UN Group of Experts on Geographical Names (UNGEGN)

UNGEGN Secretariat
United Nations Statistics Division
2 United Nations Plaza, Room DC2–1682
New York, NY 10017
United States of America
Telephone: (+1 212) 963 4297
Fax: (+1 212) 963 4569
Email: warschburger@un.org
Internet: http://unstats.un.org/unsd/geoinfo/UNGEGN

Purpose

The UN Group of Experts on Geographical Names (UNGEGN) collects and analyses the work of national and international bodies dealing with the standardisation of geographical names, and provides this information to interested bodies such as mapping organisations.

UNGEGN working groups help further worldwide communication by developing procedures for materials on geographical names, data files and gazetteers, training courses, terminology, romanisation systems, country names, and publicity and funding.

The Group was established by ECOSOC resolutions 715A (XXVII) (1959) and 1314 (XLIV) (1968), and a decision taken by ECOSOC on 4 May 1973 to further the standardisation of geographical names nationally and internationally.

Structure

To implement resolutions of UN Conferences on the Standardisation of Geographical Names, the Group's experts are from UN Member States and organised into 23 linguistic-geographical divisions. Governments may decide which division they belong to. Each division elects an expert to represent the division as a whole at group sessions.

Meetings

The 27th session was scheduled to be held in New York on 30 July and 10 August 2012.

UN System Chief Executives Board for Coordination (CEB)

New York Office
United Nations
2 United Nations Plaza, Room DC2–0610
New York, NY 10017
United States of America
Telephone: (+1 212) 963 8138
Fax: (+1 212) 963 4190

Geneva Office
Palais des Nations
Rooms A–503/C–553
CH–1211 Geneva 10
Switzerland
Telephone: (+41 22) 917 2740/917 1760
Fax: (+41 22) 917 0063/917 0308

Email: webmaster@unsystem.org
Internet: www.unsceb.org/ceb
Secretary: Thomas Stelzer, Austria (appointed by the UN Secretary-General in 2008)
Director, CEB Secretariat: Simona Petrova

Purpose

The UN System Chief Executives Board for Coordination (CEB) aims to advance cooperation and coherence through a coordinated approach for common objectives among UN system organisations (specialised agencies, funds and programmes, and other related organisations) in policy, programme, management and operational areas. It succeeded the Administrative Committee on Coordination (ACC) in 2001. The ACC had been established by ECOSOC res. 13 (III) (1946).

Structure

The CEB is composed of the Executive Heads of the 29 UN system organisations and is chaired by the UN Secretary-General. It is supported by three high-level committees – the High-Level Committee on Programmes (HLCP), High-Level Committee on Management (HLCM) and UN Development Group (UNDG). A number of thematic issues are the subject of inter-agency networks that are not formally subsidiary bodies of CEB but retain a relationship with it and its high-level committees. The CEB meets twice a year.

The members are the:

UN International Labour Organization (ILO)

UN Food and Agriculture Organization (FAO)

UN Educational, Scientific and Cultural Organization (UNESCO)

International Civil Aviation Organization (ICAO)

World Health Organization (WHO)

World Bank Group (WBG)

International Monetary Fund (IMF)

Universal Postal Union (UPU)

International Telecommunication Union (ITU)

World Meteorological Organization (WMO)

International Maritime Organization (IMO)

World Intellectual Property Organization (WIPO)

International Fund for Agricultural Development (IFAD)

Industrial Development Organization (UNIDO)

International Atomic Energy Agency (IAEA)

World Trade Organization (WTO)

World Tourism Organization (UNWTO)

UN Conference on Trade and Development (UNCTAD)

UN Development Programme (UNDP)

UN Environment Programme (UNEP)

UN High Commissioner for Refugees (UNHCR)

UN Relief and Works Agency for Palestine Refugees in the Near East (UNRWA)

UN Children's Fund (UNICEF)

UN Population Fund (UNFPA)

World Food Programme (WFP)

UN Office on Drugs and Crime (UNODC)

UN Human Settlements Programme (UN-HABITAT)

UN Entity for Gender Equality and the Empowerment of Women (UN Women)

High-Level Committee on Management (HLCM)

Palais des Nations
Rooms A–503/C–551
CH–1211 Geneva 10
Switzerland
Telephone: (+41 22) 917 2740
Fax: (+41 22) 917 0063
Email: webmaster@unsystem.org
Internet: www.unsceb.org/ceb (follow 'CEB High-level Committees' link)
Secretary: Remo Lalli

Purpose

The High-Level Committee on Management (HLCM) is the principal UN inter-agency body for coordination in the administration and management areas, particularly regarding financial and budgetary matters, human resources, information and communications technology (ICT), procurement and staff security issues within the UN system. It was established in October 2000, and is composed of senior representatives from member organisations with responsibilities in administration and management.

The main function of the Committee is to advise the UN System Chief Executives Board for Coordination (CEB) on administration and management issues that are of system-wide importance, and to promote inter-agency cooperation and coordination on these matters on behalf of the CEB.

Coordination work previously carried out by the Administrative Committee on Coordination (ACC) subsidiary bodies in the administration and management area is now undertaken through ICT, human resource management, finance and budget, and procurement networks. ACC was renamed CEB in 2001.

Priority items on the HLCM agenda include:
- Security and safety of UN staff
- Efficiency, harmonisation and simplification of business practices across the UN system
- Accountability and transparency
- Compilation and publication of UN system-wide statistics on staff, financial resources, management practices and so on
- Coordination of financial management practices and policies
- Harmonisation of ICT infrastructure and service delivery
- Accounting standards
- Representation of UN system organisations in coordinating with the International Civil Service Commission (ICSC) on issues related to the management of the common system of pay and benefits
- Enhancing efficiency and transparency of procurement processes.

The HLCM is also responsible for maintaining dialogue with staff representatives on concerns of a system-wide nature. It interacts, as appropriate, with Member States in the UN's Fifth Committee and Advisory Committee on Administrative and Budgetary Questions (ACABQ), as well as with other inter-governmental bodies, the ICSC and Joint Inspection Unit (JIU).

Meetings

The HLCM meets twice a year. It undertakes consultation and coordination on a continuing basis between sessions through electronic and other means of information and communications exchange.

Membership

The Chair is the World Intellectual Property Organization (WIPO) Director-General, Francis Gurry, Australia. The Vice-Chair is the Deputy Executive-Director of the Joint UN Programme on HIV/AIDS (UNAIDS), Jan Beagle, New Zealand.

High-Level Committee on Programmes (HLCP)

2 United Nations Plaza, Room DC2–0682
New York, NY 10017
United States of America
Telephone (+1 212) 963 4832
Fax: (+1 212) 963 4190
Email: webmaster@unsystem.org
Internet: www.unsceb.org/ceb (follow 'CEB High-level Committees' link)
Secretary: Phyllis Lee

Purpose

The High-Level Committee on Programmes (HLCP) is the principal mechanism for system-wide coordination in the programme area. Its main function is to advise the UN System Chief Executives Board for Coordination (CEB) on strategic planning, policy and programme matters of system-wide importance; and to foster inter-agency cooperation and coordination on these matters on behalf of the CEB. The HLCP's terms of reference are broadly to:

- Address issues of strategic planning, policy and programme development and implementation
- Foster and support the integrated and coordinated implementation and follow up of major UN conferences and summits
- Act as a forum for inter-agency dialogue on the development and launching of new programme initiatives
- Advise the CEB on matters that require its priority attention in responding to emerging issues and challenges facing the UN system
- Contribute to the translation of strategies and policies into broad guidance for elaboration of joint and related programmes and activities
- Share experience on policy development, programming and monitoring, and foster dialogue and propose ways in which collaboration and interaction with the private sector, non-governmental organisations and other parts of civil society can be enhanced.

Meetings

The HLCP meets twice a year and carries out consultation and coordination between sessions through electronic and other means.

Membership

The HLCP is composed of senior representatives of CEB member organisations who are responsible for programme matters and authorised to take decisions on behalf of their executive heads. The Chair is the Executive Director of the UN Environmental Programme, Achim Steiner. The Vice-Chair is Elliot Harris, Special Representative of the International Monetary Fund to the UN.

TRUSTEESHIP COUNCIL

TRUSTEESHIP COUNCIL

Internet: www.un.org/en/mainbodies/trusteeship

The Trusteeship Council was set up under chapters XII and XIII of the UN Charter to ensure that non-self-governing territories were administered in the best interests of their people and of international peace and security.

The Council's role was originally to consider reports submitted by the administering authority of the trust territory, accept petitions and examine them in consultation with the administering authority, provide for periodic visits to the territory, and take other actions in conformity with the trusteeship agreements.

The Trusteeship Council suspended operation on 1 November 1994, one month after the last remaining UN trust territory, Palau, became independent. With the Trusteeship Agreement for the Trust Territory of the Pacific Islands terminated by SC res. 956 (1994), and Palau's admission as the 185th member of the UN in December 1994, the Trusteeship Council completed the task entrusted to it under the Charter with respect to the last of the 11 territories that had been placed under the Trusteeship System. The Council amended its rules of procedure (res. 2200 (LXI) (1994)) to meet only as and where occasion might require.

The Secretary-General recommended in both his 1994 report on the work of the Organisation and his 2005 report *In Larger Freedom* that the General Assembly proceed with steps to eliminate the Trusteeship Council in accordance with article 108 of the Charter. World leaders endorsed this recommendation at the 2005 World Summit and recorded in the Outcome Document their agreement to delete chapter XIII of the Charter and references to the Council in chapter XII.

INTERNATIONAL
COURT OF JUSTICE

INTERNATIONAL COURT OF JUSTICE (ICJ)

Peace Palace
Carnegieplein 2
2517 KJ The Hague
The Netherlands
Telephone: (+31 70) 302 2323
Fax: (+31 70) 364 9928
Email: information@icj-cij.org
Internet: www.icj-cij.org
Registrar: Philippe Couvreur, Belgium (2000–14)

Purpose

The International Court of Justice (ICJ) is the UN's principal judicial organ, and its Statute is an integral part of the UN Charter and its Rules.

The Court's principal function is to decide, in accordance with international law, cases that are submitted to it by states. It is directed to apply:
- International conventions establishing rules expressly recognised by the contesting states
- International custom, as evidence of a general practice accepted as law
- The general principles of law recognised by civilised nations
- Judicial decisions and the teachings of the most highly qualified international law experts, as subsidiary means for the determination of rules of law.

The Court also gives advisory opinions to the General Assembly and Security Council on legal questions, and advisory opinions to other organs of the UN and specialised agencies that are authorised by the General Assembly to request them.

The Charter provisions concerning the Court are contained in chapter XIV (articles 92–96). Article 34, para. 1 of the Statute of the Court provides that only states may be parties in cases before the Court. States entitled to appear before the Court fall into three categories:
- States members of the UN (article 93, para. 1 of the Charter provides that all UN members are parties to the Statute)
- States not members of the UN that are parties to the Statute (article 93, para. 2 of the Charter). Conditions are to be determined in each case by the General Assembly on the recommendation of the Security Council
- States not parties to the Statute to which the Court is open (article 35, para. 2 of the Statute). The conditions upon which the Court is open to such states are to be laid down by the Security Council, but they must not place the parties in a position of inequality before the Court. These conditions were laid down in SC res. 9 (1946).

Structure

Under article 21, para. 2 of its Statute, the Court appoints its own officers. The Court elects its registrar by secret ballot from candidates proposed by members of the Court. The Registrar is elected for a term of seven years and is eligible for reappointment. The Registrar and all his or her staff are answerable to the Court itself and not to the UN Secretary-General.

The Registrar is Philippe Couvreur, Belgium, who was re-elected for a second seven-year term in February 2007. The Deputy Registrar, elected in the same way, is Thérèse de Saint Phalle, of American and French nationality, who was elected for a seven-year term from February 2008.

Membership

The Court comprises 15 members, no two of whom may be nationals of the same state.

Candidates for membership are nominated by the national groups in the Permanent Court of Arbitration or by national groups similarly appointed. The Permanent Court of Arbitration, established under conventions of 1899 and 1907, consists of a panel of members from which arbitrators may be chosen to hear any one case. Each State Party to the conventions may name no more than four people to be members of the panel. Those chosen constitute national groups.

UN members that are not members of the Permanent Court appoint national groups for nominating members of the ICJ, in the same way that the national groups of the Permanent Court of Arbitration are appointed. The UN Secretary-General draws up a list of candidates nominated. From this list, the General Assembly and the Security Council, voting independently, elect the members of the Court. An absolute majority in both the General Assembly and the Security Council is required for election.

The members of the Court are elected for nine years and may be re-elected. The terms of five (one-third) of the judges expire every three years.

The conditions under which a state that is a party to the Statute of the Court, but not a member of the UN, may participate in the election of judges were laid down on the recommendation of the Security Council by GA res. 264 (III) (1948).

The members of the Court, in official order of precedence and whose terms end on 5 February of the year shown, are as follows.

President		Vice-President	
Peter Tomka, Slovakia	2015	Bernardo Sepúlveda-Amor, Mexico	2015

Judges			
Hisashi Owada, Japan	2021	Abdulqawi Ahmed Yusuf, Somalia	2018
Ronny Abraham, France	2018	Christopher Greenwood, UK	2018
Kenneth Keith, New Zealand	2015	Xue Hanqin,[1] China	2021
Mohamed Bennouna, Morocco	2015	Joan E Donoghue,[2] USA	2015
Leonid Skotnikov, Russian Federation	2015	Giorgio Gaja, Italy	2021
Antônio Augusto Cançado Trindade, Brazil	2018	Julia Sebutinde, Uganda	2021
		Dalveer Bhandari,[3] India	2018

Notes

1   Judge Xue Hanqin replaced Judge Shi Jiuyong, who resigned as of 28 May 2010, to hold office for the remainder of Judge Shi's term, which expired on 5 February 2012. She was re-elected as from 6 February 2012.

2   Judge Thomas Buergenthal resigned as of 6 September 2010. Judge Joan E Donoghue was elected on 9 September 2010 to complete the term that expires on 5 February 2015.

3   Judge Awn Shawkat Al-Khasawneh resigned in December 2011. Judge Dalveer Bhandari was elected on 27 April 2012 to complete the term that expires on 5 February 2018.

SECRETARIAT

SECRETARIAT

United Nations Headquarters
United Nations Plaza
New York, NY 10017
United States of America
Internet: www.un.org/en/mainbodies/secretariat

Charter provisions

The Secretariat, which is headed by the UN Secretary-General, is one of the six principal organs of the UN. The main Charter provisions concerning the Secretariat are contained in chapter XV (articles 97–101). Other provisions are to be found in articles 7, 12, 20, 73, 102, 105 and 110.

Secretaries-General of the United Nations

Trygve Lie, Norway	Installed 2 February 1946
Dag Hammarskjöld, Sweden	Installed 10 April 1953 (died in office 18 September 1961)
U Thant, Burma (now Myanmar)	Installed 3 November 1961
Kurt Waldheim, Austria	Installed 22 December 1971
Javier Pérez de Cuéllar, Peru	Installed 15 December 1981
Boutros Boutros-Ghali, Egypt	Installed 1 January 1992
Kofi Annan, Ghana	Installed 1 January 1997
Ban Ki-moon, ROK	Installed 1 January 2007

Deputy Secretaries-General

Louise Fréchette, Canada, 1997

Mark Malloch Brown, UK, 2006

Asha-Rose Migiro, Tanzania, 2007

Jan Eliasson, Sweden, from July 2012

Under-Secretaries-General, Assistant Secretaries-General and Other Senior Officers

The Secretariat consists of the major organisational units listed as follows, each headed by an official accountable to the Secretary-General.

More information about the work of major individual units is included in the following pages.

Executive Office of the Secretary-General (EOSG)

Internet: www.un.org/sg

Chef de Cabinet	Susana Malcorra, Argentina (from 1 April 2012)
Deputy Chef de Cabinet	Kim Won-soo, ROK
Assistant Secretary-General for Policy Planning	Robert Orr, USA
Director Political Affairs	Nicholas Haysom, South Africa

Office of Internal Oversight Services (OIOS)
Internet: www.un.org/depts/oios

Under-Secretary-General................................ Carman Lapointe, Canada (appointed by the UN Secretary-General in July 2010 for a five-year term from September 2010)

Office of Legal Affairs (OLA)
Internet: http://untreaty.un.org/ola

Under-Secretary-General and Legal Counsel..... Patricia O'Brien, Ireland (appointed by the UN Secretary-General in August 2008)

Assistant Secretary-General............................ Stephen Mathias, USA (appointed by the UN Secretary-General in September 2010)

Department of Political Affairs (DPA)
Internet: www.un.org/depts/dpa

Under-Secretary-General................................ Jeffrey D Feltman, USA (appointed by the UN Secretary-General in June 2012)

Assistant Secretaries-General........................ Oscar Fernández-Taranco, Argentina (appointed by the UN Secretary-General in 2009)
Tayé-Brook Zerihoun, Ethiopia (appointed by the UN Secretary-General in April 2010)

Office for Disarmament Affairs (UNODA)
Internet: www.un.org/disarmament

High Representative...................................... Angela Kane, Germany (appointed by UN Secretary-General in March 2012)

Department of Peacekeeping Operations (DPKO)
Internet: www.un.org/en/peacekeeping/about

Under-Secretary-General................................ Hervé Ladsous, France (appointed by the UN Secretary-General in September 2011)

Assistant Secretary-General for Operations...... Edmond Mulet, Guatemala (appointed by the UN Secretary-General in 2007, reappointed June 2011 after 13 months as Head of the UN Stabilization Mission in Haiti (MINUSTAH))

Military Adviser.. Lieutenant-General Babacar Gaye, Senegal (appointed by the UN Secretary-General in August 2010)

Assistant Secretary-General for Office
of Rule of Law and Security Institutions........... Dmitry Titov, Russian Federation (appointed by the UN Secretary-General in 2007)

UN Mine Action Service (UNMAS)
Internet: www.un.org/en/peacekeeping/issues/mineaction

Director... Agnès Marcaillou, France (appointed March 2012)

Department of Field Support (DFS)
Internet: www.un.org/en/peacekeeping/about/dfs

Under Secretary-General................................ Ameerah Haq, Bangladesh (appointed by the UN Secretary-General in April 2012)

Assistant Secretary-General for Field Support.... Anthony Banbury, USA (appointed by the Secretary-General in 2009)

Office for the Coordination of Humanitarian Affairs (OCHA)

Internet: http://ochaonline.un.org

Under-Secretary-General:
Humanitarian Affairs
Emergency Relief Coordinator................Valerie Amos, UK (appointed by the UN Secretary-
General in September 2010)

Assistant Secretary-General:
Deputy Emergency Relief Coordinator............Catherine Bragg, Canada (appointed by the UN
Secretary-General in 2007)

The Under-Secretary-General for Humanitarian Affairs also serves as the Emergency Relief Coordinator and is responsible for the UN's system-wide response to humanitarian emergencies.

Inter-Agency Standing Committee (IASC)

Internet: www.humanitarianinfo.org/iasc

Under-Secretary-General................Valerie Amos, UK (appointed by the UN Secretary-
General in September 2010)

United Nations International Strategy for Disaster Reduction (UNISDR) Secretariat

Internet: www.unisdr.org and www.preventionweb.net

Special Representative for Disaster
Risk Reduction................Margareta Wahlström, Sweden (appointed by UN
Secretary-General in 2008)

Department of Economic and Social Affairs (DESA)

Internet: www.un.org/esa/desa

Under-Secretary-General................Wu Hongbo, China (appointed by the UN Secretary-
General in May 2012)

Assistant Secretary-General for Policy
Coordination and Inter-Agency Affairs............Thomas Stelzer, Austria (appointed by the UN
Secretary-General in 2008)

Assistant Secretary-General for
Economic Development................Shamshad Akhtar, Pakistan (appointed by the UN
Secretary-General in May 2012)

Department for General Assembly and Conference Management (DGACM)

Internet: www.un.org/depts/DGACM

Under-Secretary-General................Jean-Jacques Graisse, Belgium (appointed by the UN
Secretary-General in July 2012)

Assistant Secretary-General................Franz Baumann, Germany (appointed by the UN
Secretary-General in 2009)

Chief of Protocol................Desmond Parker, Trinidad and Tobago (appointed by
the UN Secretary-General in 2010)

Department of Public Information (DPI)

Internet: http://unic.un.org (follow 'Who we are' link)

Under-Secretary-General................Peter Launsky-Tieffenthal, Austria (appointment
announced by the UN Secretary-General in May 2012)

UN Department of Safety and Security (UNDSS)
Internet: http://dss.un.org/public

Under-Secretary General............................ Gregory B Starr, USA (appointed by the UN Secretary-General in 2009)

Department of Management (DM)
Internet: www.un.org/en/hq/dm

Under-Secretary-General............................ Yukio Takasu, Japan (appointed by the UN Secretary-General in April 2012)

Assistant Secretary-General: Programme
Planning, Budget and Accounts (Controller).... María Eugenia Casar, Mexico (appointed by the UN Secretary-General in 2011)

Assistant Secretary-General:
Human Resources Management.................. Catherine Pollard, Guyana (appointed by the UN Secretary-General in 2008)

Assistant Secretary-General:
Central Support Services........................... Warren Sach, UK (appointed by the UN Secretary-General in 2008)

Assistant Secretary-General:
Executive Director, Capital Master Plan......... Michael Adlerstein, USA (appointed by the UN Secretary-General in 2007)

Away from Headquarters

UN Office at Geneva (UNOG)
Internet: www.unog.ch

Under-Secretary-General:
Director-General..................................... Kassym-Jomart Tokayev, Kazakhstan (appointed by the UN Secretary-General in March 2011)

UN Office at Nairobi (UNON)
Internet: www.unon.org

Under-Secretary-General:
Director-General..................................... Sahle-Work Zewde, Ethiopia (appointed by the UN Secretary-General in March 2011)

UN Office at Vienna (UNOV)
Internet: www.unvienna.org

Under-Secretary-General:
Director-General..................................... Yuri Fedotov, Russian Federation (appointed by the UN Secretary-General in July 2010)

UN Office to the African Union (UNOAU)
Established by the General Assembly on 1 July 2010, in Addis Ababa.

Assistant Secretary-General:
Director-General..................................... Zachary Muburi-Muita, Kenya (appointed by the UN Secretary-General in August 2010)

Special Advisers, Representatives and Envoys

Office of the High Representative for the Least Developed Countries, Landlocked Developing Countries and Small Island Developing States (UN-OHRLLS)

Internet: www.unohrlls.org

Under-Secretary-General and
High Representative................................Cheick Sidi Diarra, Mali (appointed by the UN Secretary-General in January 2008)

Office of the Special Adviser on Africa (OSAA)

Internet: www.un.org/africa/osaa

Under-Secretary-General................................Maged Abdelaziz, Egypt (appointed by the UN Secretary-General in March 2012)

UN Office of the Special Adviser on the Prevention of Genocide

Internet: www.un.org/en/preventgenocide/adviser

Special Adviser/Under-Secretary-General.........Adama Dieng, Senegal (appointed by the UN Secretary-General in July 2012)

Special Adviser/Assistant-Secretary-General.....Edward Luck, USA (appointed by the UN Secretary-General in February 2008)

Office of the Special Representative of the Secretary-General for Children and Armed Conflict (OSRSG-CAAC)

Internet: www.un.org/children/conflict/english/theoffice

Under-Secretary-General and
Special Representative................................Leila Zerrougui, Algeria (appointed by the UN Secretary-General in July 2012)

UN Office on Sport for Development and Peace (UNOSDP)

Internet: www.un.org/sport

Special Adviser................................Wilfried Lemke, Germany (appointed by the UN Secretary-General in March 2008)

Special/Personal Representatives and Envoys of the Secretary-General

Internet: www.un.org/sg (follow links from 'The Team' and 'Special Representatives and envoys')

Country/region	Title	Name/Nationality	UN Mission	Date of appointment
Africa				
Africa	Special Adviser to the Secretary-General on Africa	Maged Abdelaziz, Eygpt		8 Mar 2012
	Special Adviser to the Secretary-General on Africa and High Representative for the Least Developed Countries, Landlocked Developing Countries and Small Island Developing States	Cheick Sidi Diarra, Mali	UN Office of the High Representative for the Least Developed Countries, Landlocked Developing Countries and the Small Island Developing States (UN-OHRLLS)	22 Jan 2008

Country/region	Title	Name/Nationality	UN Mission	Date of appointment
African Union	Special Representative of the Secretary-General to the African Union	Zachary Muburi Muita, Kenya	UN Office to the African Union (UNOAU)	18 Aug 2010
Burundi	Special Representative and Head of the UN Office in Burundi	Parfait Onanga-Anyanga, Gabon	UN Office in Burundi (BNUB)	7 Jun 2012
Central Africa	Special Representative and Head of the UN Regional Office for Central Africa	Abou Moussa, Chad	UN Regional Office for Central Africa (UNOCA)	14 Mar 2011
Central African Republic	Special Representative of the Secretary-General and Head of the UN Integrated Peacebuilding Office in the Central African Republic	Margaret Vogt, Nigeria	UN Integrated Peacebuilding Office in the Central African Republic (BINUCA)	19 May 2011
Côte d'Ivoire	Special Representative of the Secretary-General for Côte d'Ivoire	Albert Gerard Koenders, Netherlands	UN Operations in Côte d'Ivoire (UNOCI)	2 Aug 2011
DR Congo	Special Representative of the Secretary-General for the DR Congo	Roger Meece, USA	UN Organization Stabilization Mission in the Democratic Republic of the Congo (MONUSCO)	9 Jun 2010
Equatorial Guinea and Gabon	Special Adviser to the Secretary-General and Mediator in the border dispute between Equatorial Guinea and Gabon	Nicolas Michel, Switzerland		17 Sep 2008
Great Lakes Region	Special Representative of the Secretary-General for the Great Lakes Region	Olusegun Obasanjo, Nigeria	UN Integrated Peace-building Support Office in Guinea-Bissau (UNIOGBIS)	9 Dec 2008
Guinea-Bissau	Representative of the Secretary-General and Head of UNIOGBIS	Joseph Mutaboba, Rwanda		1 Jan 2010
Liberia	Special Representative of the Secretary-General for Liberia	Karin Landgren, Sweden	UN Mission in Liberia (UNMIL)	27 Apr 2012
Libya	Special Representative of the Secretary-General and Head of UNSMIL	Ian Martin, UK	United Nations Support Mission in Libya (UNSMIL)	19 Sep 2011
Sierra Leone	Executive Representative of the Secretary-General for the UN Integrated Peacebuilding Office in Sierra Leone	Jens Anders Toyberg-Frandzen, Denmark	UN Integrated Peacebuilding Office in Sierra Leone (UNIPSIL)	4 May 2012
Somalia	Special Representative of the Secretary-General for Somalia and Head of UNPOS	Augustine Mahiga, UR of Tanzania	UN Political Office for Somalia (UNPOS)	9 Jun 2010
South Sudan	Special Representative and Head of the UN Mission in the Republic of South Sudan	Hilde Johnson, Norway	UN Mission in the Republic of South Sudan (UNMISS)	8 Jul 2011
Sudan and South Sudan	Special Envoy of the Secretary-General for Sudan and South Sudan	Haile Menkerios, South Africa		29 Jul 2011

Country/region	Title	Name/Nationality	UN Mission	Date of appointment
Sudan/Abyei	Head of Mission and Force Commander of UNISFA	Lieutenant-General Tadesse Werede Tesfay, Ethiopia	UN Interim Security Force for Abyei (UNISFA)	27 Jul 2011
Sudan/Darfur	Joint African Union–UN Chief Mediator for Darfur

Joint Special Representative for the African Union and UNAMID | Ibrahim Gambari, Nigeria | AU–UN African Union Mission in Darfur (UNAMID) | 1 Jan 2010 |
West Africa	Special Representative of the Secretary-General and Head of the UN Office for West Africa	Said Djinnit, Algeria	UN Office for West Africa (UNOWA)	28 Feb 2008
Western Sahara	Special Representative of the Secretary-General for Western Sahara and Head of MINURSO	Wolfgang Weisbrod-Weber, Germany	UN Mission for the Referendum in Western Sahara (MINURSO)	15 Jun 2012
	Personal Envoy of the Secretary-General for Western Sahara	Christopher Ross, USA		6 Jan 2009

Americas

Guyana/Venezuela	Personal Representative of the Secretary-General on the Border Controversy between Guyana and Venezuela	Norman Girvan, Jamaica		20 Apr 2010
Haiti	Special Representative of the Secretary-General and Head of Mission	Mariano Fernández, Chile	UN Stabilization Mission in Haiti (MINUSTAH)	16 May 2011
	UN Special Envoy for Haiti	William J Clinton, USA		19 May 2009

Asia and the Pacific

Afghanistan	Special Representative of the Secretary-General for Afghanistan and Head of UNAMA	Ján Kubiš, Slovakia	UN Assistance Mission in Afghanistan (UNAMA)	1 Jan 2012
Central Asia	Special Representative and Head of the UN Regional Centre for Preventive Diplomacy for Central Asia	Miroslav Jenča, Slovakia	UN Regional Centre for Preventive Diplomacy for Central Asia (UNRCCA) in Ashgabat, Turkmenistan	1 May 2008
India–Pakistan	Chief Military Observer and Head of Mission	Major-General Young-Bum Choi, ROK	UN Military Observer Group in India and Pakistan (UNMOGIP)	11 Jun 2012
Myanmar	Special Adviser to the Secretary-General for Myanmar	Vijay Nambiar, India		26 Jan 2012
Pakistan	Special Envoy for Assistance to Pakistan	Rauf Engin Soysal, Turkey		27 Sep 2010
Timor-Leste	Acting Special Representative of the Secretary-General for Timor-Leste and Head of UNMIT	Finn Reske-Nielsen, Denmark	UN Mission in Timor-Leste (UNMIT)	Jun 2012

Country/region	Title	Name/Nationality	UN Mission	Date of appointment
Europe				
Cyprus	Special Representative of the Secretary-General and Head of Mission	Lisa Buttenheim, USA	UN Force in Cyprus (UNFICYP)	2 Jun 2010
	Special Adviser to the Secretary-General on Cyprus	Alexander Downer, Australia		17 Jul 2008
Former Yugoslav Republic of Macedonia (FYROM)–Greece	Personal Envoy of the Secretary-General for the Greece–FYROM talks	Matthew Nimetz, USA		21 Dec 1999
Georgia	UN Representative to the Joint Incident Prevention and Response Mechanism and the international discussions in Geneva on security and stability and the return of internally displaced persons and refugees	Antti Turunen, Finland		2 Mar 2010
Kosovo	Special Representative of the Secretary-General and Head of Mission	Farid Zarif, Afghanistan	UN Interim Administration Mission in Kosovo (UNMIK)	11 Oct 2011
Middle East				
Middle East	Special Coordinator for the Middle East Peace Process, Personal Representative of the Secretary-General to the Palestine Liberation Organization and the Palestinian Authority, and Secretary-General's Envoy to the Quartet	Robert H Serry, Netherlands		4 Nov 2007
	Special Envoy for the Implementation of Security Council Resolution 1559	Terje Roed-Larsen, Norway		3 Jan 2005
Iraq	Special Representative of the Secretary-General for Iraq	Martin Kobler, Germany	UN Assistance Mission for Iraq (UNAMI)	11 Aug 2011
Iraq (International Compact)	Special Advisor to the Secretary-General on the International Compact with Iraq and Other Issues	Ibrahim Gambari, Nigeria		5 Mar 2007
Iraq/Kuwait	Secretary-General's High-level Coordinator for compliance by Iraq with its obligations regarding the repatriation or return of all Kuwaiti and third country nationals or their remains, as well as the return of all Kuwaiti property, including archives seized by Iraq	Gennady P Tarasov, Russian Federation		11 Apr 2008
Lebanon	Special Coordinator of the Secretary-General for Lebanon	Derek Plumbly, UK	Office of the UN Special Coordinator for Lebanon (UNSCOL)	13 Jan 2012

Country/region	Title	Name/Nationality	UN Mission	Date of appointment
Syria	Joint Special Envoy of the United Nations and the League of Arab States on the Syrian crisis	Kofi Annan, Ghana		23 Feb 2012
Syrian Golan Heights	Head of Mission and Force Commander of UNDOF	Major-General Iqbal Singh Singha, India	UN Disengagement Observer Force (UNDOF)	6 Jul 2012
Yemen	Special Adviser to the Secretary-General for Yemen	Jamal Benomar, Morocco		

Other high-level appointments

Country/region	Title	Name/Nationality	UN Mission	Date of appointment
	Special Adviser to the Secretary-General	Joseph V Reed, USA		
	Special Adviser to the Secretary-General	Iqbal Riza, Pakistan		
	Special Adviser to the Secretary-General on the Responsibility to Protect	Edward Luck, USA	Office of the Special Adviser on the Prevention of Genocide	21 Feb 2008
Alliance of Civilizations	High Representative of the Secretary-General for the Alliance of Civilizations	Jorge Sampaio, Portugal		26 Apr 2006
Avian and Human Influenza (Bird flu)	Senior UN System Coordinator for Avian and Human Influenza	David Nabarro, UK		29 Sep 2005
Children and Armed Conflict	Special Representative of the Secretary-General for Children and Armed Conflict	Leila Zerrougui, Algeria		13 Jul 2012
Climate Change	Special Envoys of the Secretary-General on Climate Change	Gro Harlem Brundtland, Norway		1 May 2007
		Ricardo Lagos Escobar, Chile		1 May 2007
		Festus Mogae, Botswana		18 Sep 2008
		Srgjan Kerim, former Yugoslav Republic of Macedonia		18 Sep 2008
Disaster Reduction	Special Representative of the Secretary-General for the implementation of the International Strategy for Disaster Reduction	Vacant		
Financing for Development	Special Adviser on Innovative Financing for Development	Philippe Douste-Blazy, France		Feb 2008
Food Security and Nutrition	Special Representative of the Secretary-General on Food Security and Nutrition	David Nabarro, UK		29 Oct 2009

Country/region	Title	Name/Nationality	UN Mission	Date of appointment
Global Education	Special Envoy for Global Education	Gordon Brown, UK		13 Jul 2012
HIV/AIDS in Africa	Special Envoy of the Secretary-General for HIV/AIDS in Africa	Asha-Rose Migiro, Tanzania		13 Jul 2012
HIV/AIDS in Asia and in the Pacific	Special Envoy of the Secretary-General for HIV/AIDS in Asia and in the Pacific	Nafis Sadik, Pakistan		24 May 2002
HIV/AIDS in the Caribbean Region	Special Envoy of the Secretary-General for HIV/AIDS in the Caribbean Region	Edward Greene, Gyana		Nov 2011
HIV/AIDS in Eastern Europe and Central Asia	Special Envoy of the Secretary-General for HIV/AIDS in Eastern Europe and Central Asia	Michel Kazatchkine, France		Jul 2012
Human Rights and the Business Community	Special Representative of the Secretary-General on the Issue of Human Rights and Transnational Corporations and other Business Enterprises	John Ruggie, USA	Human Rights Council	28 Jul 2005
Human Rights for Internally Displaced Persons	Representative of the Secretary-General on the Human Rights for Internally Displaced Persons	Walter Kälin, Switzerland	Human Rights Council	21 Sep 2004
Human Security	Special Adviser to the Secretary-General on Human Security	Yukio Takasu, Japan		10 Dec 2010
Malaria	Special Envoy of the Secretary-General for Malaria	Ray Chambers, USA		14 Feb 2008
Migration	Special Representative of the Secretary-General for Migration	Peter Sutherland, Ireland		23 Jan 2006
Millennium Development Goals	Special Adviser to the Secretary-General on the Millennium Development Goals	Jeffrey D Sachs, USA		4 Feb 2002
Prevention of Genocide	Special Adviser to the Secretary-General on the Prevention of Genocide	Adama Dieng, Senegal	Office of the Special Adviser on the Prevention of Genocide	17 Jul 2012
Sexual Violence in Conflict	Special Representative of the Secretary-General on Sexual Violence in Conflict	Zainab Hawa Bangura, Sierra Leone		22 Jun 2012
Sport for Development and Peace	Special Adviser to the Secretary-General on Sport for Development and Peace	Wilfried Lemke, Germany	UN Office on Sport for Development and Peace (UNOSDP)	18 Mar 2008
Tuberculosis	Special Envoy of the Secretary-General to Stop Tuberculosis	Jorge Sampaio, Portugal		12 May 2006
UN International School (UNIS)	Special Representative of the Secretary-General for the UN International School	Michael Adlerstein, USA		

Country/region	Title	Name/Nationality	UN Mission	Date of appointment
Violence Against Children	Special Representative of the Secretary-General on Violence Against Children	Marta Santos Pais, Portugal		1 May 2009
World Summit on Information Society	Special Adviser of the Secretary-General for Internet Governance	Nitin Desai, India		21 Jul 2003

Executive Office of the Secretary-General (EOSG)

Internet: www.un.org/sg
Secretary-General: Ban Ki-moon, ROK (since 1 January 2007)
Deputy Secretary-General: Jan Eliasson, Sweden (since 1 July 2012)

Purpose

The Executive Office of the Secretary-General (EOSG) provides senior administrative leadership to the Secretariat and the wider UN.

The Secretary-General is the organisation's chief administrative officer. The UN Charter also requires the Secretary-General to perform other functions as are entrusted by the main UN organs, as well as to "bring to the attention of the Security Council any matter which in his opinion may threaten the maintenance of international peace and security". The Secretary-General may also use the 'good offices' of the position – the value of its independence, impartiality and integrity – to try to prevent or resolve international disputes.

The Secretary-General chairs the UN System Chief Executives Board for Coordination (CEB), which twice a year brings together the executive heads of all UN funds, programmes and specialised agencies.

The position of Deputy Secretary-General was established in 1997.

Structure

EOSG comprises:
- Secretary-General
- Deputy Secretary-General
- Senior Management Group
- Special Representatives and Envoys (listed on the previous pages)
- Messengers of Peace
- Spokesperson for the Secretary-General.

The Senior Management Group comprises senior UN managers. It serves as the Secretary-General's cabinet and the central policy planning body of the UN. Its objective is to ensure strategic coherence and direction in the work of the organisation. The cabinet was approved by the General Assembly in 1997 as part of the reform proposal submitted by the Secretary-General.

Messengers of Peace are people who possess widely recognised talents in the fields of arts, literature, music and sports, and who have agreed to help focus worldwide attention on the work of the UN.

The Spokesperson for the Secretary-General is Martin Nesirky.

Office of Internal Oversight Services (OIOS)

380 Madison Avenue, 10th Floor
New York, NY 10017
United States of America
Fax: (+1 212) 963 7010
Email: oios@un.org
Internet: www.un.org/depts/oios
Under-Secretary-General: Carman L Lapointe, Canada (appointed by the Secretary-General in July 2010 for a five-year term from September 2010)

Purpose

The Office of Internal Oversight Services (OIOS) is the UN's internal oversight body. Established in 1994 by the General Assembly, the Office assists the Secretary-General in fulfilling his oversight responsibilities in respect of the resources and staff of the organisation through the provision of audit, investigation, inspection and evaluation services.

The Office is mandated to provide oversight coverage of all UN activities under the Secretary-General's authority, including: the UN Secretariat in New York, Geneva, Nairobi and Vienna, and the newly opened UN Office to the African Union in Addis Ababa; five regional commissions; peacekeeping missions; special political missions, humanitarian operations; and assistance to funds and programmes administered separately under the authority of the Secretary-General (including the Office of the UN High Commissioner for Refugees, UN Environment Programme, UN Human Settlements Programme and Office of the UN High Commissioner for Human Rights).

In accordance with established memoranda of understanding, OIOS also provides oversight services to the UN Convention to Combat Desertification and the UN Framework Convention on Climate Change.

Each year, OIOS issues more than 300 reports and makes recommendations aimed at improving internal control and organisational efficiency and effectiveness. OIOS submits its reports to the Secretary-General, or delegated programme manager, and directly to the General Assembly. Member States' access to all OIOS reports was significantly expanded following the adoption of resolution 59/272 in December 2004.

Structure

The Office is organised into the following functional units:
- Internal Audit Division – assesses the adequacy and effectiveness of internal controls for the purpose of improving the organisation's risk management, control and governance processes
- Inspection and Evaluation Division – assesses the relevance, efficiency and effectiveness (including impact) of the organisation's programmes in relation to its objectives and mandates
- Investigations Division – establishes facts related to reports of possible misconduct to guide the Secretary-General on jurisdictional or disciplinary action to be taken.

The Office is headed by the Under-Secretary-General for Internal Oversight Services who is appointed by the Secretary-General, following consultations with Member States, and approved by the General Assembly for one five-year term without the possibility of renewal.

Office of Legal Affairs (OLA)

Internet: http://untreaty.un.org/ola
Telephone: (+1 212) 963 5338
Fax: (+1 212) 963 6430
Under-Secretary-General and Legal Counsel: Patricia O'Brien, Ireland (appointed by the UN Secretary-General in August 2008)

Purpose

The Office of Legal Affairs (OLA) was established by GA res. 13(l) (1946) to provide a unified central legal service for the Secretariat and organs of the UN. It provides secretariat functions to UN bodies, including the Sixth Committee of the General Assembly, the International Law Commission and the UN Commission on International Trade Law.

OLA also provides legal services for UN organs, offices, funds and programmes, and special political missions, peacekeeping operations and other field missions on issues, including respect for privileges and immunities and the legal status of the organisation. OLA provides legal advice on cooperation with international or internationalised judicial accountability mechanisms.

The Office discharges the Secretariat's responsibilities under article 102 of the UN Charter regarding the registration and publication of treaties, and the Secretary-General's responsibilities as the depository for multilateral conventions. It also contributes to the development and codification of international public and trade law, and assists in its teaching, study and dissemination. It prepares the Repertory of Practice of UN Organs (a record of the General Assembly procedural practice) and other legal publications.

Another OLA objective is to promote the strengthening, development and effective implementation of the international legal order for the seas and oceans. The Office:
*   Provides information and assistance to states on law of the sea and ocean affairs
*   Monitors and reviews reporting on related developments, services institutions and inter-governmental bodies as mandated by the UN Convention on the Law of the Sea and the General Assembly
*   Fulfils the Secretary-General's dispute settlement responsibilities.

Structure

OLA consists of six substantive units:
*   Office of the Legal Counsel
*   General Legal Division
*   Codification Division
*   Division for Ocean Affairs and the Law of the Sea
*   International Trade Law Division
*   Treaty Section.

The Office of the Under-Secretary-General coordinates the work of the substantive units.

OTHER BODIES SUBSIDIARY OR RELATED TO THE UN

OTHER BODIES SUBSIDIARY OR RELATED TO THE UN

FUNDS, PROGRAMMES AND BODIES OF THE UN

RECOGNISED FUNDS AND PROGRAMMES OF THE UN

UN Children's Fund (UNICEF)

UNICEF House
3 United Nations Plaza
New York, NY 10017
United States of America
Telephone: (+1 212) 326 7000
Fax: (+1 212) 887 7465/7454
Internet: www.unicef.org
Executive Director: Anthony Lake, USA (appointed by the UN Secretary-General in May 2010)

Purpose

The UN International Children's Emergency Fund (UNICEF) was established by the General Assembly to provide emergency assistance to children in war-ravaged countries following World War II (GA res. 57 (I) (1946)). By GA res. 417 (V) (1950), the General Assembly charged it with addressing the needs of children in developing countries. GA res. 802 (VIII) (1953) extended UNICEF'S mandate indefinitely, with an emphasis on programmes giving long-term benefits to children everywhere, particularly those in developing countries, and changed the organisation's name to the United Nations Children's Fund but retained the UNICEF acronym. The Fund also continued to provide relief and rehabilitation assistance in emergencies.

The priority areas for UNICEF's work are set out in its medium-term strategic plan for 2006 to 2013. They are:
- Young child survival and development
- Basic education and gender equality
- HIV/AIDS and children
- Child protection from violence, exploitation and abuse
- Policy advocacy and partnerships for children's rights.

Through its extensive field network, UNICEF undertakes programmes in health, nutrition, education, water and sanitation, the environment, child protection, gender issues and development, and other fields of importance to children. It works with governments, local communities and other aid organisations in developing countries and territories. UNICEF places emphasis on low-cost, community-based programmes, focusing on supporting children during critical periods of their lives, when intervention can make a lasting difference. Thirty-six National Committees for UNICEF, mostly in industrialised countries, support its work in raising funds and advocacy.

Structure

UNICEF reports through its Executive Board to the Economic and Social Council (ECOSOC), which in turn reports to the General Assembly. GA res. 48/162 (1993) decided the UNICEF Executive Board should be reconstituted to comprise 36 members (previously 41). The Board is responsible for providing inter-governmental support to, and monitoring of, UNICEF's activities, and for ensuring that UNICEF is responsive to the needs and priorities of recipient countries. It also approves UNICEF's policies, country programmes and budgets. The specific functions of the Board are set out in Annex I of that resolution. The Board's work is coordinated by a bureau comprising one representative from each of the five regional groups of Member States.

UNICEF's resources derive from voluntary contributions from governments, inter-governmental donors, non-governmental organisations and the private sector.

Meetings

The Board meets in one annual and two regular sessions a year, holding inter-sessional meetings as it deems necessary. In 2012, the Executive Board's first regular session was held in New York from 7 to 10 February and the annual session from 5 to 8 June. The second regular session is scheduled to take place from 11 to 14 September 2012. In conjunction with the First Regular Session meetings of the UN Development Programme (UNDP)/ UN Population Fund (UNFPA)/UN Office for Project Services (UNOPS) and UNICEF Executive Boards, a joint meeting is also held annually with the UNICEF, UNDP/UNFPA/ UNOPS, UN Women and World Food Programme (WFP) Executive Boards.

Membership

GA res. 48/162 (1993) specified that membership of the Executive Board should be based on equitable geographical representation and other relevant factors. Members come from each of the following UN regional groups: African states (eight), Asia–Pacific states (seven), Eastern European states (four), Latin American and Caribbean states (five), and Western European and Other states (12). Board membership is normally for three years and expires on 31 December. The following lists show the Executive Board Bureau members for 2012, and past and current board members.

President
Latin American and Caribbean group: John W Ashe, Antigua and Barbuda

Vice-Presidents
Africa group: Macharia Kamau, Kenya
Asia–Pacific group: Byrganym Aitimova, Kazakhstan
Eastern European group: Karin Kaup, Estonia
Western European and Other group: Nina Nordström, Finland

	Previous membership[1]	Current membership*

African states

	Previous membership[1]	Current membership*
Algeria	1971–74 82–85 2004–06	
Angola	1991–97	
Benin	1975–78 84–90	
Botswana	1980–83	

	Previous membership[1]	Current membership*
Burkina Faso	1982–85 93–96 2006–08	
Burundi	1979–82 95–97 2004–06	
Cameroon	1967–70 76–79 88–91 2007–09	
Cape Verde	1997 99	2010–12
Central African Republic	1973–76 82–85 91–94 2007–09	
Chad	1982–85	
Comoros	1998–2000	
Congo	1972–75 85–88 91–94 1998–2000	2010–12
Côte d'Ivoire	1981–84 2000–02	
DR Congo	2001–03	
Djibouti	1985–88 2004–06	
Egypt	1955–59 64–67 70–76 88–91	
Eritrea	2003–05	
Ethiopia	1966–69 85–88 91–94 2007–09	
Gabon	1970–73 85–88 2001–03	
Gambia	2001–03	2012–14
Ghana	1978–81 93–96 2003–05	
Guinea	1968–70 75–78 2000–02	
Kenya	1995–97	2012–14
Lesotho	1983–89 2002–04	
Liberia	1987–93 2009–11	
Libya	1979–82 1998–2000	
Madagascar	1982–85 2001–03	
Malawi	1970–73 2004–06	2010–12
Mali	1985–88 2007–09	
Mauritania	2007–09	
Morocco	1965–68 76–79 95–97 2001–03	
Mozambique	1992–95 2005–07	
Namibia	1996–98	2011–13
Niger	1984–87	
Nigeria	1961–64 70–75 88–91 97–99	
Rwanda	1973–76 2006–08	
Sao Tome and Principe	1988–91	
Senegal	1963–69 78–81 91–94 2004–06	
Sierra Leone	1969–71 90–93	
Somalia	1979–85	2010–12
South Africa	1946–51 1998–2000	
Sudan	1963–65 88–93 1998–2000 09–11	
Swaziland	1982–85	
Togo	1981–84	
Tunisia	1957–71 85–88	2010–12
Uganda	1967–70 74–77 88–91 95–97	
UR of Tanzania	1976–79 91–94	
Zambia	1977–80	
Zimbabwe	1989–92 1999–2001 08–10	

Asia–Pacific states

Afghanistan	1960–63 65–67 77–80	
Bahrain	1982–85	
Bangladesh	1982–91 1998–2000 04–06 09–11	
Bhutan	1984–87	
China	1946–56 58–73 1980–2010	2011–13
DPRK	2005–07	

3   The Western European and Other States Group has its own rotation scheme under which some of its members do not serve a full three-year term. The USA does not participate in this rotation scheme. The current terms listed, and the future terms noted here, reflect the rotation scheme correct as at 31 May 2012. Members for 2013 – Belgium, Canada, Denmark, Finland, France, Greece, Ireland, Israel, Norway, Sweden, Switzerland and USA; 2014 – Belgium, Denmark, France, Germany, Italy, Japan, New Zealand, Netherlands, Norway, Sweden, UK and USA.

*   In April 2012, ECOSOC elected 14 members for a three-year term beginning on 1 January 2013 as follows: Central African Republic, DR Congo, Djibouti, Egypt and Ghana (African states); Iran, Pakistan and Thailand (Asia–Pacific states); Bulgaria (Eastern European states); Guyana (Latin American and Caribbean states); and Canada, Denmark, France and Sweden (Western European and Other states). To replace members that had resigned effective 1 January 2013, and whose terms would expire on 31 December 2013, ECOSOC elected the following members: Switzerland (replacing Austria), Ireland (replacing Netherlands) and Israel (replacing UK). Replacements for members who had resigned effective 1 January 2013 and whose terms of office would expire on 31 December 2014 were: Greece (replacing Japan) and Belgium (replacing Spain).

UN Conference on Trade and Development (UNCTAD)

Palais des Nations
8–14, Avenue de la Paix
1211 Geneva 10
Switzerland
Telephone: (+41 22) 917 1234
Fax: (+41 22) 917 0051
Email: info@unctad.org
Internet: www.unctad.org
Secretary-General: Supachai Panitchpakdi, Thailand (appointed by the UN Secretary-General in 2005; reappointed September 2009 to August 2013)

Purpose

The UN Conference on Trade and Development (UNCTAD) promotes the integration of developing countries into the world economy. Its work aims to help shape policy debates and thinking on development, with a particular focus on ensuring that domestic policies and international action are mutually supportive in bringing about sustainable development. The organisation:

- Functions as a forum for inter-governmental deliberations, supported by discussions with experts and exchanges of experience, aimed at consensus building
- Undertakes research, policy analysis and data collection for informing government representative and expert discussions
- Provides technical assistance to developing countries, with special attention to the needs of the Least Developed Countries and of economies in transition. When appropriate, UNCTAD cooperates with other organisations and donor countries in the delivery of technical assistance.

The first UNCTAD session took place in Geneva in 1964 in accordance with ECOSOC res. 917 (XXXIV) (1962). GA res. 1995 (XIX) (1964) established UNCTAD as a UN organ and set its mandate.

Structure

The highest UNCTAD decision-making body is the quadrennial conference, at which Member States make assessments of current trade and development issues, discuss policy options and formulate global policy responses. The conference also sets the organisation's mandate and work priorities.

It adopted the Doha Mandate (TD/500/Add.1) at its session in Doha, Qatar, in April 2012 (UNCTAD XIII). The Doha Mandate reaffirms and builds upon the Accra Accord (TD/410) adopted in Accra, Ghana, in April 2008, and provides guidance for UNCTAD's work. The Doha theme was "Development-centred globalization: Towards inclusive and sustainable growth and development".

Between sessions of the Conference, the Trade and Development Board (TDB) functions as UNCTAD's executive body to take action in implementing Conference decisions and to ensure the overall consistency of UNCTAD's activities with agreed priorities.

Meetings

UNCTAD XIII was held in Doha, Qatar, in April 2012. The next conference will take place in 2016.

Membership

The 194 members are listed below. Members of the TDB are marked with an asterisk.

Afghanistan*
Albania*
Algeria*
Andorra
Angola*
Antigua and Barbuda
Argentina*
Armenia*
Australia*
Austria*
Azerbaijan*
Bahamas
Bahrain*
Bangladesh*
Barbados*
Belarus*
Belgium*
Belize
Benin*
Bhutan*
Bolivia*
Bosnia and Herzegovina
Botswana*
Brazil*
Brunei Darussalam
Bulgaria*
Burkina Faso*
Burundi*
Cambodia*
Cameroon*
Canada*
Cape Verde
Central African Republic*
Chad*
Chile*
China*
Colombia*
Comoros
Congo*
Costa Rica*

Côte d'Ivoire*
Croatia*
Cuba*
Cyprus*
Czech Republic*
DPRK*
DR Congo*
Denmark*
Djibouti*
Dominica*
Dominican Republic*
Ecuador*
Egypt*
El Salvador*
Equatorial Guinea*
Eritrea
Estonia*
Ethiopia*
Fiji
Finland*
France*
Gabon*
Gambia
Georgia*
Germany*
Ghana*
Greece*
Grenada*
Guatemala*
Guinea*
Guinea-Bissau
Guyana*
Haiti*
Holy See
Honduras*
Hungary*
Iceland*
India*
Indonesia*
Iran*

Iraq*
Ireland*
Israel*
Italy*
Jamaica*
Japan*
Jordan*
Kazakhstan*
Kenya*
Kiribati
Kuwait*
Kyrgyzstan*
Lao PDR
Latvia*
Lebanon*
Lesotho*
Liberia*
Libya*
Liechtenstein*
Lithuania*
Luxembourg*
Madagascar*
Malawi
Malaysia*
Maldives
Mali*
Malta*
Marshall Islands
Mauritania*
Mauritius*
Mexico*
Micronesia
Monaco
Mongolia*
Montenegro*
Morocco*
Mozambique*
Myanmar*
Namibia*
Nauru

continued next page

Nepal*
Netherlands*
New Zealand*
Nicaragua*
Niger
Nigeria*
Norway*
Oman*
Pakistan*
Palau
Panama*
Papua New Guinea*
Paraguay*
Peru*
Philippines*
Poland*
Portugal*
Qatar*
ROK*
Republic of Moldova*
Romania*
Russian Federation*
Rwanda*
Saint Kitts and Nevis
Saint Lucia
Saint Vincent and the
   Grenadines

Samoa
San Marino
Sao Tome and Principe*
Saudi Arabia*
Senegal*
Serbia*
Seychelles
Sierra Leone*
Singapore*
Slovakia*
Slovenia*
Solomon Islands
Somalia*
South Africa*
South Sudan
Spain*
Sri Lanka*
Sudan*
Suriname*
Swaziland
Sweden*
Switzerland*
Syrian AR*
Tajikistan
Thailand*
The former Yugoslav
   Republic of Macedonia*

Timor-Leste
Togo*
Tonga
Trinidad and Tobago*
Tunisia*
Turkey*
Turkmenistan
Tuvalu
Uganda*
Ukraine*
UAE*
UK*
UR of Tanzania*
USA*
Uruguay*
Uzbekistan
Vanuatu
Venezuela*
Viet Nam*
Yemen*
Zambia*
Zimbabwe*

Trade and Development Board (TDB)

Purpose

Between sessions of the UN Conference on Trade and Development (UNCTAD), the Trade and Development Board (TDB) functions under GA res. 1995 (XIX) (1964) as UNCTAD's executive body to take action in implementing Conference decisions and to ensure the overall consistency of UNCTAD's activities with agreed priorities. The TDB reports to the Conference and the General Assembly.

Structure

At the UNCTAD XII Conference in April 2008, it was agreed the TDB would have two subsidiary commissions that perform integrated policy work within specific terms of reference:
- Investment, Enterprise and Development Commission
- Trade and Development Commission.

Meetings

The TDB's regular session, which is held for 10 days in September, examines interdependence and global economic issues. It also examines international trade and investment issues from a trade and development perspective, and other issues relevant to UNCTAD's work. The 59th session is scheduled to be held from 17 to 28 September 2012 in Geneva.

The TDB can also meet in executive sessions up to three times a year to deal with urgent policy, management and institutional matters arising between its regular annual sessions; and for substantive discussions about, and analysis of, new challenges faced by developing countries. Such sessions are normally confined to one-day's duration but may last up to three days. The Board may also convene special TDB sessions. In recent years, such sessions have been used for mid-term reviews.

Membership

TDB membership is open to all UNCTAD Member States. There are 155 TDB members (listed in the UNCTAD section of this book).

UN Development Group (UNDG)

1 United Nations Plaza
DC1–16th floor
New York, NY 10017
United States of America
Telephone: (+1 212) 906 5500
Fax: (+1 212) 906 3609
Email: doco@undg.org
Internet: www.undg.org
Chair: Helen Clark, New Zealand (since 2009)

Purpose

The UN Development Group (UNDG) was established by the UN Secretary-General in 1997 to coordinate, harmonise and align UN development activities. The UNDG unites the 32 UN funds, programmes, agencies, departments and offices that play a role in development with a common objective to deliver more coherent, effective and efficient support to countries seeking to attain internationally agreed development goals, including the Millennium Development Goals (MDGs).

The UNDG develops policies, guidelines and procedures that allow agencies to work together to analyse country issues, plan support strategies, implement support programmes, monitor results and advocate for change. This is achieved through a combination of policy discussion, negotiations to reach agreement on detailed procedures, and guidance and support to members.

Evolution

Following a review of the UN System Chief Executives Board for Coordination (CEB), initiated at the request of the Secretary-General, the Board decided in 2008 to integrate the UNDG into the CEB framework. The UNDG now sits as a CEB third pillar alongside the two standing subsidiary bodies, the High-Level Committee on Management (HLCM) and the High-Level Committee on Programmes (HLCP).

Structure

The UNDG brings together all the operational agencies working on development. It is chaired by the UN Development Programme (UNDP) Administrator on behalf of the Secretary-General. The UNDG Chair reports to the Secretary-General and the CEB on progress in implementing the UNDG's workplan, and on the management of the Resident Coordinator system. The Vice-Chair is selected from a specialised agency on a one-year rotational basis.

A group of 13 UNDG members constitutes the UNDG Advisory Group, some of whom participate on a rotational basis. It convenes at the level of heads of agencies and at the Assistant Secretary-General/Assistant Director-General level. The Advisory Group provides guidance to the Chair on:

- Coherence of country-level development operations
- Management of the Resident Coordinator System
- Support to UN country teams experiencing particular challenges.

Policy decisions are taken as part of CEB proceedings, and operational decisions are taken by the full UNDG, which meets four times a year.

The UN Development Operations Coordination Office (DOCO) is the technical support unit for the UNDG. DOCO provides the link between UNDG discussions at headquarters and the work of the UN development system at the country level, and helps the group prepare system-wide agreements, policies and guidelines for country offices.

Membership

The full UNDG membership has grown to 32 UN entities, plus five observers. Follow 'About the UNDG' and 'UNDP Members' website links for the full membership list.

UN Development Programme (UNDP)

1 United Nations Plaza
New York, NY 10017
United States of America
Telephone: (+1 212) 906 5000
Fax: (+1 212) 906 5364
Email: hq@undp.org
Internet: www.undp.org
Administrator: Helen Clark, New Zealand (appointed by the UN Secretary-General in 2009)

Purpose

The UN Development Programme (UNDP) is the lead agency for the UN development system. It advocates for transformational change and connects countries to knowledge, experience and resources to help empower lives and build resilient nations. It has a presence in 177 countries and territories, and provides expert advice, training and financial support. Special attention is paid to the needs of Least Developed Countries (LDCs) and countries emerging from conflict. UNDP's focus is on working with developing countries to find solutions to the challenges of:

- Democratic governance
- Poverty reduction
- Crisis prevention and recovery
- Environment and energy.

UNDP coordinates global and national efforts to reach the Millennium Development Goals (MDGs), including the overarching goal of halving poverty by 2015. In all its activities, UNDP encourages the protection of human rights, capacity development and the empowerment of women.

UNDP administers special funds and programmes, including:
- UN Volunteers (UNV), see page 250.
- UN Capital Development Fund (UNCDF), see pages 245–246.

UNDP began operations in 1966 under GA res. 2029 (XX) (1965), which combined the UN Expanded Programme of Technical Assistance (EPTA) with the Special Fund.

Structure

The 36-member Executive Board is responsible for providing inter-governmental support to and supervision of the activities of UNDP, the UN Population Fund (UNFPA) and the UN Office for Project Services (UNOPS) in accordance with the overall policy guidance of the General Assembly and Economic and Social Council (ECOSOC), and the responsibilities set out in the UN Charter. It must also be responsive to the needs of programme countries. The Board is under ECOSOC's authority. Its functions are set out in GA res. 48/162 (1993). The Executive Board superseded the 48-member Governing Council on 1 January 1994.

The Executive Board Bureau comprises one president and four vice-presidents, elected from the members at the first regular session each year and taking into account the need for equitable geographical representation. The Bureau's primary functions are to prepare and organise Board meetings, facilitate transparent decision making and promote dialogue in decision making. The Bureau also agrees on the composition of the teams participating in Executive Board field visits.

UNDP's financial resources are derived primarily from voluntary contributions by participating Member States and multilateral partners. Contributions to regular (core) resources in 2011 increased slightly to $0.975 billion from $0.967 billion in 2010. Total contributions from all funding sources (including regular resources, co-financing from bilateral and multilateral donors, contributions from programme countries for local resources, and co-financing activities) in 2011 decreased by about 5 percent to $4.83 billion from $5.01 billion in 2010.

Meetings

The Board meets in one annual and two regular sessions each year. The annual session alternates between New York and Geneva. The regular sessions are held in New York. In 2012, the Board held its first regular session in February and annual session in June in Geneva. A second regular session was scheduled to be held from 4 to 10 September.

Membership

ECOSOC elects Executive Board members in May each year. Members are elected for three-year terms, with the exception of the Western European and Other States Group, which has determined its own internal rotation policy. GA res. 48/162 (1993) specifies that membership of the Executive Board should be based on equitable geographic representation and other relevant factors. It specifies there should be 36 members: eight from African states, seven from Asia–Pacific states, four from Eastern European states, five from Latin American and Caribbean states, and 12 from Western European and Other states.

Bureau members of the UNDP/UNFPA/UNOPS Executive Board for 2012 are:

President
Mårten Grunditz, Sweden

Vice-Presidents
Tarik Iziraren, Morocco
Yusra Khan, Indonesia
Candida Novák Hornakova, Czech Republic
Eduardo Porretti, Argentina

Members of the UNDP/UNFPA/UNOPS Board and their terms, expiring on 31 December of the year indicated, are:

	Previous membership	Current membership*
African states		
Algeria	2006–08	
Angola	2007–09	
Benin	2006–08	
Botswana	1998–2000 04–06	
Burkina Faso		2010–12
Burundi	1995–97	
Cameroon	1994 2004–06	2010–12
Cape Verde	2003–05	
Central African Republic	2007–09	
Comoros	2002–04	
Congo	1994 2004–06	
DR Congo	1995–2003	2010–12
Djibouti	2001–03	2011–13
Egypt	2000–02	
Eritrea	2004–06	
Ethiopia	1995–97 1999–2001	
Gabon	2001–03	
Gambia	1994–97 2004–06	
Ghana	1998–2000	
Guinea	1997–99	
Lesotho	1994	
Liberia		2012–14
Libya	1997–99	
Madagascar	1996–98	
Malawi	2007–09	
Mauritania	2001–03 09–11	
Morocco	1994–96	2012–14
Mozambique	2001–03	
Rwanda		2010–12
Senegal	2007–09	
Sierra Leone	1994–96 2009–11	
Somalia	1994 2007–09	
South Africa	1998–2000	2010–12
Sudan	1994–95	
Togo	2000–02	
Tunisia	2003–05	
Uganda	2005–07	
UR of Tanzania	1998–2000 08–10	
Zambia	1995–97	
Asia–Pacific states		
Bangladesh	1994–96 2006–08	2011–13
Bhutan	2007–09	
China	1994–2003 04–09	2011–13
DPRK	2005–07	
India	1994–2001 03–05 07–09	2010–12
Indonesia	1995–97 2000–02 04–06	2012–14
Iran	2001–03 04–06 09–11	

	Previous membership	Current membership*
Kazakhstan	2005–07	
Kyrgyzstan	1999–2001	
Lao PDR	2008–10	
Lebanon	1998–2000	
Malaysia	1996–98	
Nepal	2003–05	
Pakistan	1994–99 2002–04 06–08 10	2010–12
Papua New Guinea	1994	
Philippines	1994–97 2001–03	
Qatar		2010–12
ROK	1994–95 1998–2000 08–10	2012–14
Thailand	1997–99	
Viet Nam	2000–02	
Yemen	2002–04 09–11	

Eastern European states

Azerbaijan	2008–10	
Belarus	1999–2001 05–07	2011–13
Bulgaria	1994–95 2001–03	
Czech Republic	1998–2000 02–04	2011–13
Estonia		2011–12
Poland	1994–96 2004–06	
Romania	1996–98 2002–04	
Russian Federation	1994–95 1997–2005 06–11	2012–14
Serbia	2007–09	
Slovakia	1994–97 2008–10	
Slovenia	2010	
Ukraine	1996–2001 05–07	

Latin American and Caribbean states

Antigua and Barbuda	1997–99 2002–04 07–09	2010–12
Argentina	1994–98	2011–13
Belize	1996–98	
Brazil	1997–2002	2012–14
Colombia	2008–10	
Cuba	1994–97 1999–2001 04–06 09–11	
Ecuador	2001–03 06–08	
El Salvador	2003–05	2011–13
Guatemala	1999–2001 05–07	
Guyana	2005–07	
Haiti	2008–10	
Honduras	2000–02	
Jamaica	1998–2000 06–08	
Mexico	2009–11	
Nicaragua		2012–14
Peru	1994–96 2002–04	
Trinidad and Tobago	1994–96	
Uruguay	1994–95 2003–05	

Western European and Other states (plus Japan)[1]

Australia	1997–98 2003–05 08	2012
Austria	1997–99 2009–10	
Belgium	1994–96 2000–02 07 10	
Canada	1994–96 98–99 2001–04 07 10	2011–12

	Previous membership	Current membership*
Denmark	1994–96 98–99 2001–02 04–09	2011–12
Finland	1996–97 2001–03 09–11	
France	1994–95 97–98 2000–04 08–10	
Germany	1994–97 1999–2003 04–07 09 11	
Greece	2007	2012
Iceland	2008	
Ireland	1998–2000 08 11	
Israel		2012
Italy	1994–95 1999–2001 03–05 07–08	2011–12
Japan	1994–2005 06–08	2010–13
Luxembourg	2002	2011–12
Netherlands	1996–98 2000–02 04–06 08–09 10–11	
New Zealand	1994–95 2000–01 06 09	
Norway	1994–95 97–98 2000–01 03–09	2012–16
Portugal	1994–96 2005–07	
Spain	1996 98–99 2002 07 10	
Sweden	1995–97 1999–2003 04–06 08–11	2012–16
Switzerland	1996–97 1999–2000 02–04 08 10	2012
Turkey	2002 05–06 09	
UK	1994–95 97–99 2002–04 06–07 09–11	
USA	1994–2004 05–07 08–10	2011–13

Notes

* In April 2012, ECOSOC elected the following 14 members to the Executive Board for three-year terms beginning on 1 January 2013: Angola, Congo, Ethiopia, Lesotho and Niger (African states); Fiji, Iran and Pakistan (Asia–Pacific states); Bulgaria (Eastern European states); Guatemala (Latin American and Caribbean states); and France, Germany, Japan and Spain (Western European and Other states).

1 The Western European and Other States Group (WEOG), plus Japan, has had its own rotation scheme since 2006. As at 31 May 2012, terms in the chart reflect the rotation scheme. Future terms for this group (as at 31 May 2012), are: 2013 New Zealand, Portugal and Spain; 2013–14 France and Ireland; 2013–15 Germany and UK; 2013–16 Netherlands. The USA does not participate in this rotation scheme.

UN Population Fund (UNFPA)

605 Third Ave
New York, NY 10158
United States of America
Telephone: (+1 212) 297 5000
Fax: (+1 212) 370 0201
Email: hq@unfpa.org
Internet: www.unfpa.org
Executive Director: Babatunde Osotimehin, Nigeria (appointed by the UN Secretary-General in January 2011)

Purpose

The UN Population Fund (UNFPA) is an international development agency that promotes the right of every woman, man and child to enjoy a life of health and equal opportunity. UNFPA supports countries in using population data for policies and programmes to reduce poverty and to ensure that every pregnancy is wanted, every birth is safe, every young person is free of HIV, and every girl and woman is treated with dignity and respect.

Its work is guided by the Programme of Action, adopted at the 1994 International Conference on Population and Development, and the Millennium Development Goals (MDGs).

UNFPA places a strong emphasis on the human rights, including reproductive rights, of individual women and men. The three core areas of UNFPA's work are:

- Population and development strategies
- Sexual and reproductive health
- Gender equality and women's empowerment.

In all its work, UNFPA has three cross-cutting themes: mainstreaming young people's concerns; emergencies and humanitarian assistance; and special attention for marginalised and excluded populations. It works in partnership with governments, along with other UN agencies, communities, non-governmental organisations, foundations and the private sector to raise awareness and mobilise support and resources.

As part of the UN humanitarian system, UNFPA takes the lead in providing supplies and services to protect reproductive health, with an emphasis on the special needs and vulnerabilities of women and young people. The Fund supports various data collection activities, including censuses, to provide detailed information for planning, and rapid health assessments to allow for appropriate, effective and efficient relief. It also assists stricken communities as they move beyond the acute crisis and enter the reconstruction phase.

Evolution

UNFPA was set up by the Secretary-General in 1967 after GA res. 2211 (XXI) (1966) called on UN system organisations to provide assistance in the field of population. Originally called the UN Fund for Population Activities, it was then under the management of the UN Development Programme (UNDP) Administrator. In 1972, GA res. 3019 (XXVII) gave UNFPA a separate identity and designated the UNDP Governing Council to be its governing body, subject to conditions to be established by the Economic and Social Council (ECOSOC). ECOSOC res. 1763 (LIV) (1973) set down UNFPA's aims and purposes, and tasked the Fund with playing a leading UN role in promoting population programmes. ECOSOC res. 2025 (LXI) (1976) endorsed a set of general principles for the allocation of UNFPA resources.

GA res. 34/104 (1979) reaffirmed the 1972 resolution, including the Fund's status as a subsidiary organ of the General Assembly in terms of article 22 of the Charter. GA res. 42/430 (1987) renamed the Fund the UN Population Fund, but its official abbreviation, UNFPA, remained the same. GA res. 48/162 (1993) transformed the governing body of UNDP/UNFPA into the UNDP/UNFPA Executive Board, to provide inter-governmental support to, and supervision of, the Fund in accordance with the overall policy guidance of the General Assembly and ECOSOC.

UNDP/UNFPA Executive Board decision 95/15 (1995) determined that UNFPA's future programme of assistance should follow the principles in chapter II of the Programme of Action of the International Conference on Population and Development (ICPD), held in Cairo in 1994. Resolution S-21/2 of the General Assembly's 21st special session (1999) adopted key actions for the further implementation of the ICPD Programme of Action. Executive Board decision 2000/11 (2000), in line with res. S-21/2, encouraged UNFPA to fulfil its leadership role as an advocate for reproductive health, population and development issues.

In September 2011, the Executive Board adopted an extension of the 2008–11 Strategic Plan to guide the Fund's work through to 2013. By this plan, UNFPA's goal is to achieve universal access to sexual and reproductive health, including family planning; promote reproductive rights; reduce maternal mortality; and accelerate process on the ICPD agenda and Millennium Development Goal (MDG) 5 (a and b).

Structure

UNFPA is a subsidiary body of the UN General Assembly. The Fund is governed by decisions adopted by the UNDP Governing Council (1973–93) and the UNDP/UNFPA/UNOPS Executive Board (1994 to present). Since 2007, UNFPA has decentralised its operations as a way to become a more field-centred, efficient and strategic partner to the countries it serves. Toward this end, it established five regional and six sub-regional offices that help coordinate work in about 150 countries, areas and territories through a network of 129 country offices. In January 2013, the Africa regional office (in Johannesburg, South Africa) will split into two regional offices, one covering East and Southern Africa and the other covering West and Central Africa (in Dakar, Senegal). This change will bring the number of UNFPA regional offices to six.

UNFPA reports through the UNDP/UNFPA/UNOPS Executive Board to ECOSOC, which in turn reports to the General Assembly. See UNDP structure and membership sections for further information.

UNFPA's revenue in 2011 totalled $929.1 million, including $450.7 million in voluntary contributions from governments and private donors. This compared with a total of $876.7 million in 2010, including $498.1 million in voluntary contributions. Regular resource contribution revenue decreased by $47.4 million, or 9.5 percent, from 2010 to 2011, while total revenue to UNFPA increased by $52.4 million or 6 percent. Total expenses in 2011 were $824.5 million ($823.9 million in 2010). Of this amount, $685.4 million was spent on programme activities (compared with $679.2 million in 2010).

Committee for the UN Population Award

Internet: www.unfpa.org (follow link from 'About UNFPA')

Purpose

Each year, the Committee for the UN Population Award presents an award to an individual(s) and/or institution(s) in recognition of outstanding contributions to increasing the awareness of population questions and to their solutions.

The Award was established by the General Assembly in November 1981 (res. 36/201) and was first presented in 1983. It consists of a gold medal, diploma and monetary prize. Nominations for the award are accepted through to 31 December of each year.

An American reproductive health advocate, Adrienne Germain, and a Malaysian non-governmental organisation, the Federation of Reproductive Health Associations of Malaysia, won the Award in 2012.

Structure

The Committee comprises 10 UN Member States' representatives elected by the Economic and Social Council (ECOSOC) for three years, the Secretary-General and Executive Director of the UN Population Fund (UNFPA) (ex officio) and five eminent individuals. The UN Secretary-General selects the latter on the basis of their significant contributions to population-related activities. They serve in an advisory capacity for renewable terms of three years. The Executive Director of UNFPA is the designated Secretary.

Membership

ECOSOC elected the following Committee members for three-year terms beginning on 1 January 2010:

Bangladesh	Guatemala	Norway
Czech Republic	Jamaica	UR of Tanzania
Egypt	Malaysia	
Ghana	Nicaragua	

ECOSOC elected Czech Republic and Grenada for three-year terms beginning on 1 January 2013. Three members from African states, three from Asia–Pacific states, one from Latin American and Caribbean states, and one from Western European and Other states for three-year terms beginning on 1 January 2013 are to be elected by ECOSOC prior to that date.

UN Capital Development Fund (UNCDF)

2 United Nations Plaza
New York, NY 10017
United States of America
Telephone: (+1 212) 906 6565
Fax: (+1 212) 906 6479
Email: info@uncdf.org
Internet: www.uncdf.org
Executive Secretary: David Morrison, Canada (appointed 2008)

Purpose

UNCDF is the UN's capital investment agency for the world's 48 Least Developed Countries (LDCs). Its goals are to reduce poverty and advance the Millennium Development Goals (MDGs) by increasing access by poor people and small enterprises to microfinance, and improving delivery of pro-poor services and infrastructure at the local level.

The Fund focuses on Africa and the poorest countries of Asia, with a special commitment to countries emerging from conflict or crisis. It provides seed capital (grants and loans) and technical support to help microfinance institutions to reach more poor households and small businesses, and local governments to finance the capital investments (water systems, feeder roads, schools, irrigation schemes) that will improve poor people's lives. UNCDF programmes help to empower women and are designed to catalyse larger capital flows from the private sector, national governments and development partners, for maximum impact toward the MDGs.

Programmes supporting local development accounted for 60 percent of total delivery; programmes supporting financial services for the poor accounted for 40 percent. Sixty-three percent of UNCDF programme delivery was in Africa, 30 percent in Asia and the Pacific, and 7 percent in the Arab States and Haiti. Sixty-six percent of borrowers from CDF-supported financial service providers are women.

UNCDF was established by the General Assembly in its resolutions 2186 (XXI) (1966), 2321 (XXII) (1967) and 3122 (XXVIII) (1973).

Structure

UNCDF is a voluntarily funded UN organisation affiliated with UNDP. It is represented at country level by UNDP resident representatives. The UNCDF headquarters are in New York and there are regional offices in Bangkok, Dakar and Johannesburg as well as a presence in 40 LDCs.

The UNDP Administrator serves simultaneously as the UNCDF Managing Director. UNCDF reports through its managing director to the UNDP Executive Board.

Total income in 2011 was $52 million, including $3 million allocated by UNDP to UNCDF programme funding. The number of donors reached 33 in 2011. The top five donors to UNCDF in 2011 were the MasterCard Foundation, Sweden, Belgium, the Australian Agency for International Development and the Canadian International Development Agency.

UN Entity for Gender Equality and the Empowerment of Women (UN Women)

Street address:
220 East 42nd Street
New York, NY 10017
United States of America

Mailing address:
405 East 42nd Street
New York, NY 10017
United States of America

Telephone: (+1 646) 781 4400
Fax: (+1 646) 781 4444
Internet: www.unwomen.org
Under-Secretary-General and Executive Director: Michelle Bachelet, Chile (appointed by the UN Secretary-General in September 2010)

Purpose

UN Women was established in July 2010 by the General Assembly (res. 64/289) to improve the coordination and coherence of gender equality and empowerment of women, and promote more effective gender mainstreaming across the UN system. It also has the role of leading, coordinating and promoting the accountability of the UN system in its work on gender equality and the empowerment of women.

UN Women merges and builds on the work of four previously distinct parts of the UN system that focused exclusively on gender equality and women's empowerment:
• UN Development Fund for Women (UNIFEM)
• Division for the Advancement of Women (DAW)
• Office of the Special Adviser on Gender Issues (OSAGI)
• UN International Research and Training Institute for the Advancement of Women (UN-INSTRAW).

The main roles of UN Women are to:
• Support inter-governmental bodies, such as the Commission on the Status of Women, in their formulation of policies, global standards and norms
• Help Member States to implement these standards, standing ready to provide suitable technical and financial support to those countries that request it, and to forge effective partnerships with civil society
• Hold the UN system accountable for its own commitments on gender equality, including regular monitoring of system-wide progress.

UN Women's five thematic priorities are: expanding women's voice, leadership and participation; ending violence against women; strengthening implementation of women's peace and security agenda; enhancing women's economic empowerment; and making gender equality priorities central to national, local and sectoral planning, budgeting and statistics.

Several international agreements guide the work of UN Women: the Universal Declaration of Human Rights; the Convention on the Elimination of All Forms of Discrimination against Women (CEDAW); Beijing Declaration and Platform for Action (PFA); UN Security Council Resolution 1325 on Women, Peace and Security (2000) and subsequent resolutions 1820 (2008), 1888 (2009), 1889 (2009) and 1960 (2010); and the Millennium Declaration and Millennium Development Goals.

Evolution

The establishment of UN Women was part of efforts to improve UN system-wide coherence that came from the World Summit of global leaders in 2005 when the UN Secretary-General was asked to undertake reforms within the UN to reduce waste and improve results in several areas. The goal was to have a stronger focus on operational outcomes 'on the ground' and more efficient operational practices. Streamlining the UN's gender architecture was part of this.

Structure

UN Women functions as a secretariat, providing support to inter-governmental policy and normative processes, and also carries out programmes of operational activities at the country level to support Member States, at their request. It is headed by an Under-Secretary-General and governed by a multi-tiered structure comprising the General Assembly, Economic and Social Council, Commission on the Status of Women and an executive board. The Board engages with the executive boards of other UN development agencies to coordinate work on gender equality and women's empowerment across the UN system. The Board is responsible for providing inter-governmental support to, and monitoring of, UN Women's activities, and for ensuring that UN Women is responsive to national priorities and needs. It also approves UN Women's strategic plan and budget. The specific functions of the Board are set out in GA res. 64/289 (2010). The Bureau, comprising one representative from each of the five Member States regional groups, coordinates the Board's work.

Meetings

The Board meets in one annual and two regular sessions a year, holding inter-sessional meetings as it deems necessary. In 2012, the Executive Board's first regular session was held in New York from 24 to 25 January, and the annual session from 29 May to 1 June. The second regular session is scheduled to take place from 28 to 30 November 2012. In addition to the scheduled Board meetings, joint meetings are held with the UN Children's Fund (UNICEF), UN Development Programme (UNDP), UN Population Fund (UNFPA), UN Office for Project Services (UNOPS) and World Food Programme (WFP) boards.

Membership

GA res. 64/289 (2010) specified there should be 41 members on the Executive Board, made up of 35 representatives from the five UN regional groups of Member States and six from contributing countries (including non-Organisation for Economic Co-operation and Development (OECD) countries). The numbers from each regional group are: African states 10, Asia–Pacific states 10, Eastern European states four, Latin America and the Caribbean states six, Western European and Other states five, and six from contributing countries (four for the top 10 largest providers of voluntary core contributions and two seats for top 10 non-OECD Development Assistance Committee (DAC) developing countries providing voluntary core contributions, giving due consideration to geographical balance).

Board terms began from the day of election in 2010 and run until 31 December of the year in which the term ends (the Western European and Other States Group has its own rotation system). In subsequent elections, members will be elected for three years, beginning on 1 January and running until 31 December of the year in which their term ends.

The Executive Board Bureau is composed of one president and four vice-presidents elected from the members at the first regular session each year, taking into account the need for equitable geographical representation. The primary functions of the Bureau are to prepare and organise board meetings, facilitate transparent decision making and promote dialogue in decision making.

Bureau members for 2012 are:

President	Vice-Presidents
Kim Sook, ROK	Carmen Arias, Peru
	Fernando Fernández Arias, Spain
	John Alhassan Gana, Nigeria
	Ketlin Viimsalu, Estonia

Executive Board members are:

	Previous membership	Current membership[1]
African states		
Angola		2010–13
Cape Verde		2010–13
Congo		2010–13
Côte d'Ivoire		2010–12
DR Congo		2010–12
Ethiopia		2010–13
Lesotho		2010–12
Libya		2010–12
Nigeria		2010–13
Tanzania		2010–12
Asia–Pacific states		
Bangladesh		2010–12
China		2010–13
India		2010–12
Indonesia		2010–13
Japan		2010–13

	Previous membership	Current membership[1]
Kazakhstan		2010–13
Malaysia		2010–12
Pakistan		2010–12
ROK		2010–13
Timor-Leste		2010–12

Eastern European states

Estonia		2010–12
Hungary		2010–13
Russian Federation		2010–12
Ukraine		2010–13

Latin America and the Caribbean states

Argentina		2010–12
Brazil		2010–12
Dominican Republic		2010–13
El Salvador		2010–12
Grenada		2010–13
Peru		2010–13

Western Europe and Other states[2]

Canada		2012
Denmark	2010–11	
Finland		2012
France	2010–11	
Italy	2010–11	
Luxembourg	2010–11	
Netherlands		2012
New Zealand		2012
Sweden	2010–11	
USA		2012

Contributing countries

Mexico		2010–13
Norway		2010–13
Saudi Arabia		2010–13
Spain		2010–13
Sweden		2012
UK		2010–13
USA	2010–11	

Notes

1 In April 2012, ECOSOC elected the following 17 members to the Executive Board for three-year terms beginning on 1 January 2013: Algeria, Djibouti, Gabon, Gambia and Malawi (African states); Maldives, Philippines, Solomon Islands, Thailand and UAE (Asia–Pacific states); Latvia and Russian Federation (Eastern European states); Brazil, Uruguay and Venezuela (Latin American and Caribbean states); and Ireland and Switzerland (Western European and Other states).

2 The Western European and Other States Group has its own rotation scheme under which some of its members do not serve a full three-year term. The terms above, and the 2013 term noted here, reflect the rotation scheme correct as at 31 May 2012. Members for 2013 – Australia, Switzerland, Ireland, Belgium and Austria; the USA is scheduled to replace Sweden as a contributing country.

United Nations Volunteers (UNV)

PO Box 260111
D–53153 Bonn
Germany
Telephone: (+49 228) 815 2000
Fax: (+49 228) 815 2001
Email: information@unvolunteers.org
Internet: www.unvolunteers.org, www.facebook.com/unvolunteers, www.youtube.com/unv
Executive Coordinator: Flavia Pansieri, Italy (appointed by the UNDP Administrator in 2008)

Purpose

The United Nations Volunteers (UNV) programme was created as an operational partner in international development (GA res. 2659 (XXV) (1970)). Administered by the UN Development Programme (UNDP), UNV contributes to peace and development through volunteerism worldwide. It advocates for recognition of volunteers, works with partners to integrate volunteerism into development programming and helps to mobilise volunteers throughout the world.

UNV supports sustainable human development globally in key areas such as poverty reduction, democratic governance, crisis prevention and recovery, energy, the environment and health. It helps set up national volunteer schemes, starts creative and pioneering volunteer activities, and develops research capacity on volunteerism in developing countries.

Since 1971, UNV has mobilised more than 50,000 professionals. In 2011, 7303 UN Volunteers (in 7708 UNV assignments) from 162 countries supported UN partners in their peace and development activities in the field. Reaffirming the programme's commitment to promoting south–south cooperation, the majority of volunteers (83 percent) were nationals of developing countries.

UNV has run the Online Volunteering service (www.onlinevolunteering.org) since 2000. In total, more than 47,071 people have engaged in online assignments with some of the 1723 registered organisations working for peace and development. UNV's Online Volunteering service continued to experience growth in 2011, with 10,910 online volunteers undertaking 16,982 assignments. Sixty percent of the volunteers were from developing countries, 56 percent women and 2 percent people with disabilities. UNV also manages the World Volunteer Web (www.worldvolunteerweb.org), a global clearinghouse for information and resources about volunteerism.

In 2011, UNV took the lead in promoting the 10th anniversary of the International Year of Volunteers. On 5 December 2011, International Volunteer Day, the UN General Assembly adopted resolution A/Res/66/67, which calls for global action on volunteering. During the General Assembly's special meeting on volunteerism, UNDP Administrator Helen Clark launched the UN's first State of the World's Volunteerism Report, produced by UNV.

In February 2012, UN Secretary-General Ban Ki-moon announced the expansion of UNV to open the doors for youth who are "still marginalized and underprivileged" and his plan to appoint, under the aegis of UNV, the first UN Special Adviser on Youth.

UN Environment Programme (UNEP)

PO Box 30552
Gigiri, Nairobi 00100
Kenya
Telephone: (+254 20) 762 1234
Fax: (+254 20) 762 3 927/3692
Email: unepinfo@unep.org
Internet: www.unep.org
Telex: 22068, 22173
Executive Director: Achim Steiner, Germany (elected by the UN General Assembly in 2006 for a four-year term; re-elected in 2010 for a further four-year term)

Purpose

The UN Environment Programme (UNEP) aims to provide leadership and encourage partnerships in caring for the environment by inspiring, informing and enabling nations and people to improve their quality of life, without compromising that of future generations. It was established by GA res. 2997 (XXVII) (1972) following the Stockholm Conference on the Human Environment.

In 1997, the Governing Council adopted the Nairobi Declaration on the Role and Mandate of the UN Environment Programme, which established the following core mandate for UNEP:

- Analyse the state of the global environment and assess global and regional environmental trends, provide policy advice and early warning information on environmental threats, and promote international cooperation and action, based on the best scientific and technical capabilities available
- Further the development of international environmental law aimed at sustainable development, including the links between existing international environmental conventions
- Advance agreed international norms and policies, monitor and foster compliance with environmental principles and international agreements, and stimulate cooperation on emerging environmental challenges
- Strengthen its role in coordinating environmental activities in the UN system, and its role as an implementing agency of the Global Environment Facility
- Promote greater awareness of and facilitate effective cooperation in implementing the international environmental agenda, and serve as an effective link between the scientific community and policy-makers at national and international levels
- Provide policy and advisory services in key areas of institution-building to governments and other relevant institutions.

Evolution

In 2005, the Governing Council/Global Ministerial Environment Forum adopted the Bali Strategic Plan for Technology Support and Capacity-building. This was developed to meet the urgent need from within developing countries, and countries with economies in transition, for technology support and capacity-building.

In 2010, the Council/Forum adopted the Nusa Dua Declaration, in preparation for the UN Conference on Sustainable Development, or Rio+20 Conference, from 20 to 22 June 2012. The Declaration articulated the determination and commitments by ministers responsible for the environment to address major issues, namely climate change, international environmental governance and sustainable development, green economy, biodiversity and ecosystems.

In 2012, UNEP's 40th anniversary year, the Council/Forum, among other things, welcomed the Rio+20 Conference as a unique opportunity to tackle economic, social and environmental challenges in the context of sustainable development, and committed to making the Conference a success.

Structure

- Governing Council
- Secretariat
- Environment Fund (voluntary)
- Committee of Permanent Representatives

The Governing Council reports to the General Assembly through ECOSOC. The Committee of Permanent Representatives is a subsidiary organ of the Governing Council.

Meetings

The Governing Council meets in regular session biennially and in special session in alternate years, usually in February. In addition, GA res. 53/242 (1999) instituted an annual ministerial-level global environmental forum (the Global Ministerial Environment Forum), which meets as part of the Governing Council's regular or special sessions. The 27th regular session of the Council/Forum is scheduled to be held from 18 to 22 February 2013 in Nairobi.

Membership

The Governing Council comprises 58 members elected by the General Assembly for four-year terms on the basis of 16 seats for African states, 13 for Asia–Pacific states, six for Eastern European states, 10 for Latin American and Caribbean states, and 13 for Western European and Other states. Terms expire on 31 December of the year stated.

	Previous membership	Current membership
African states		
Algeria	1978–80 84–86 96–99 2006–09	
Angola	2006–09	
Benin	1996–2003 06–11	
Botswana	1979–95 1998–2001 06–09	
Burkina Faso	1996–2007	
Burundi	1973–75 79–84 1987–2001 06–09	
Cameroon	1973–74 83–85 92–95 1998–2001 04–07	
Cape Verde	2004–07	
Central African Republic	1973–78 96–99	2010–13
Chad	1977–79 2002–05	
Comoros	1998–2001	
Congo	1986–88 92–95 2002–05 08–11	2012–15
Côte d'Ivoire	1974–79 83–85 89–95	
DR Congo	1975–97 2006–09	
Egypt	1975–77 81–83 2000–03	2012–15
Equatorial Guinea	2000–03	
Ethiopia	1980–82	
Gabon	1973–76 80–82 87–97	2010–13
Gambia	1990–97 2000–03	
Ghana	1973–79 81–83 85–88 2004–07	
Guinea	1979–84 2008–11	

Guinea-Bissau	1994–97	
Kenya	1973–83 85–99 2002–09	2010–13
Lesotho	1983–85 89–93	2010–13
Liberia	1976–81	2012–15
Libya	1975–83 85–91 2000–03	
Madagascar	1973–75	
Malawi	1973–74 79–81 1998–2001	
Mali	2008–11	
Mauritania	1980–82 87–89 96–99	2010–13
Mauritius	1989–93 2008–11	2012–15
Morocco	1973–76 82–84 96–99 2004–07	
Mozambique		2010–13
Namibia	2002–05	
Niger	1985–88 2008–11	
Nigeria	1973–75 83–88 92–95 1998–2005	2012–15
Rwanda	1976–78 84–86 89–95	
Senegal	1973–75 77–79 82–84 87–89 92–95 2000–07	2012–15
Sierra Leone	1973–76 80–82	
Somalia	1973–74 76–78 2004–11	
South Africa	2006–09	
Sudan	1973 75–77 80–82 84–86 89–91 1994–2005	2012–15
Swaziland	1986–88	
Togo	1976–78 84–86 89–91	2012–15
Tunisia	1973–74 78–80 85–88 90–93 96–99 2008–11	
Uganda	1976–81 83–91 2000–03 06–09	
UR of Tanzania	1973–75 77–79 82–84 2004–07	2010–13
Zambia	1986–88 94–97 2002–05	2010–13
Zimbabwe	1989–2005	

Asia–Pacific states (one seat vacant)

Afghanistan	1982–84	
Bangladesh	1977–82 89–95 2004–11	2012–15
Bhutan	1992–95	
China	1973–2009	2010–13
Cyprus	1976–78	
DPRK	1994–97	
Fiji	2008–11	2012–15
India	1973–77 1979–2011	2012–15
Indonesia	1973–2009	2010–13
Iran	1973–80 87–89 1992–2011	2012–15
Iraq	1973–81 87–89	
Japan	1973–2009	2010–13
Jordan	1973–75 85–91	
Kazakhstan	1998–2001 04–11	
Kuwait	1973–74 76–81 84–86 90–93	
Kyrgyzstan	2004–07	
Lebanon	1973–76	
Malaysia	1975–86 92–95	2010–13
Marshall Islands	1996–2003	
Myanmar	2002–05	
Nepal	1984–86	
Oman	1982–91	
Pakistan	1973–75 78–83 1989–2003 06–09	2010–13

	Previous membership	Current membership
Papua New Guinea	1983–88	
Philippines	1973–79 83–85 90–93 96–99	
ROK	1987–89 1994–2009	2010–13
Samoa	1996–2003	
Saudi Arabia	1980–85 89–91 2000–11	2012–15
Sri Lanka	1973–75 81–83 85–95	
Syrian AR	1973–79 86–88 1994–2005	
Thailand	1976–84 86–88 90–93 1996–2003 06–09	2012–15
Tuvalu	2004–11	
UAE	1980–82	

Eastern European states

	Previous membership	Current membership
Albania		2012–15
Belarus[1,2]	1979–84 1998–2001 08–09 11	
Bulgaria	1977–82 85–91 94–97 2004–07	
Croatia[2]	2008–10	
Czech Republic[3]	1996–99 2002–09	2010–13
Georgia		2012–15
Hungary[1,4]	1976–78 83–85 1994–2001 04–08 10–11	
Poland	1973–78 1982–2007	2012–15
Republic of Moldova	2000–03	
Romania	1973–80 92–95 2002–09	2010–13
Russian Federation	1973–2009	2010–13
Serbia and Montenegro	1973–93	
Serbia[2,4]	2009–11	
Slovakia[3]	1993–2003	
Ukraine	1981–93	

Latin American and Caribbean states

	Previous membership	Current membership
Antigua and Barbuda	1998–2009	2010–13
Argentina	1973–2009	2010–13
Bahamas	2000–11	
Barbados	1986–93	
Brazil	1973–97 2000–07	2010–13
Chile	1973–75 80–99 2006–09	2012–15
Colombia	1975–80 1982–2011	2012–15
Costa Rica	1989–91 94–97 2004–11	
Cuba	1998–2005 08–11	2012–15
Dominican Republic	1987–89	
Ecuador		2012–15
Grenada	1976–78	
Guatemala	1973–79	
Guyana	1989–95	
Haiti	1981–86 2006–09	
Jamaica	1973–79 82–88 1998–2001	
Mexico	1973–2011	2012–15
Nicaragua	1973–75 94–97 2002–05	
Panama	1973–75 79–81 85–88 96–99	
Peru	1973–74 76–78 80–85 90–93 96–99	
Suriname	2000–03	
Trinidad and Tobago	1979–81	2010–13
Uruguay	1976–84 92–95 2002–09	2010–13
Venezuela	1973–2001	

Western European and Other states

	Previous membership	Current membership
Australia	1973–75 79–81 83–89 92–99 2006–09	2010–13
Austria	1973–74 78–80 84–86 90–93 1998–2001 06–09	
Belgium	1976–78 80–82 84–86 1998–2009	2010–13
Canada	1973–79 82–91 1994–2009	2010–13
Denmark	1978–80 86–88 92–95 2000–03	
Finland	1975–77 83–85 89–91 96–99 2008–11	
France	1973–2009	2010–13
Germany	1973–2009	2010–13
Greece	1976–78 82–84 87–89 2002–05	
Iceland	1973–74 81–83	
Israel	2004–11	2012–15
Italy	1973–77 79–81 83–85 1996–2003 08–11	2012–15
Malta	1985–91	
Monaco	2004–11	
Netherlands	1973–75 78–83 1986–2011	2012–15
New Zealand	1976–78 80–82 90–93 2000–03	
Norway	1977–79 84–86 90–93 1998–2001	2012–15
Portugal	1992–95	
Spain	1973–79 82–84 90–97 2008–11	2012–15
Sweden	1973–76 80–82 87–89 94–97 2004–07	
Switzerland	1975–77 81–83 87–89 94–97 2002–05	2010–13
Turkey	1973–75 79–81 85–91 1996–2007	
UK	1973–2007	2012–15
USA	1973–2009	2010–13

Notes

1 On 3 November 2009, the General Assembly, acting on a request from the representative of Belarus to the UN (A/64/297) contained in a letter of 12 August 2009 announcing that his country would relinquish its seat on the Governing Council for the remainder of its term in favour of Hungary, elected Hungary, as endorsed by the Eastern European states to the Governing Council, for a two-year term beginning on 1 January 2010 and expiring on 31 December 2011.

2 On 28 July 2010, the General Assembly, acting on a request from the representative of Croatia to the UN (A/64/869) contained in a letter of 22 July 2010 informing that his country would relinquish its seat on the Governing Council for the remainder of its term in favour of Belarus, elected Belarus, as endorsed by the Eastern European states to the Governing Council, for a one-year term beginning on 1 January 2011 and expiring on 31 December 2011.

3 Insofar as they formed part of Czechoslovakia until 31 December 1992, the Czech Republic and Slovakia were members of the Governing Council 1973–76 and 1986–92.

4 On 23 July 2008 at the 115th plenary meeting of the General Assembly, Hungary announced its intention to relinquish its seat on the Governing Council as from 31 December 2008, in favour of Serbia, in accordance with the rotation agreement within the Eastern European group. An election was conducted at that same meeting, as a result of which Serbia was declared to have been elected a member of the Governing Council for a term of office beginning on 1 January 2009 and expiring on 31 December 2011.

Office of the UN High Commissioner for Refugees (UNHCR)

94 rue de Montbrillant
Geneva
Switzerland
Telephone: (+41 22) 739 8111
Fax: (+41 22) 731 9546
Email: hqpi00@unhcr.org
Internet: www.unhcr.org
High Commissioner: António Guterres, Portugal (elected by the UN General Assembly on the nomination of the Secretary-General in June 2005; re-elected in April 2010 for a second five-year term)

Purpose

The work of the Office of the UN High Commissioner for Refugees (UNHCR) is humanitarian and non-political. UNHCR's principal functions are to provide international protection to refugees and other persons of concern, including stateless people, and to seek durable solutions for them. Protection includes preventing *refoulement* (the involuntary return of a refugee or a person of concern to a country where he or she may have a well-founded fear of persecution) and ensuring that host countries follow international norms in the treatment of refugees.

UNHCR helps refugees who wish to go home to do so once circumstances permit, assisting them to reintegrate into their home communities. Where this is not feasible, UNHCR seeks other solutions, whether in the countries where they have already found asylum or in third countries. Emergency and other material assistance is provided in collaboration with governmental, inter-governmental and non-governmental partners in the form of food, shelter, medical aid, education and other social services.

While its mandate specifically covers refugees, UNHCR has also frequently been asked by the UN Secretary-General to protect and assist internally displaced persons (IDPs) in conflict-generated emergencies. A comprehensive inter-agency agreement in 2005 reinforced and made more explicit the role of the UN and other humanitarian agencies involved in helping IDPs. Under this mechanism, UNHCR has assumed leadership for the protection, emergency shelter and camp coordination and management aspects of conflict-related, internal displacement situations.

Evolution

The Office emerged in the wake of World War II to help Europeans displaced by conflict. In 1949, the UN General Assembly decided to appoint a High Commissioner for Refugees (GA res. 319 (IV) (1949)). The Statute of the Office of the UN High Commissioner for Refugees, detailing its functions and responsibilities, was embodied in GA res. 428 (V) (1950), and the Office came into being on 1 January 1951. It was initially given a three-year mandate to complete its work and then disband. Following regular five-year extensions, in 2003, the General Assembly removed the time limitation on the organisation's mandate "until the refugee problem is solved" (GA res. 58/153).

Structure

UNHCR's governing body, the Executive Committee of the Programme of the UN High Commissioner for Refugees (ExCom), determines the general policies under which the Office plans, develops and administers refugee projects and programmes around the world, and advises the High Commissioner, on request, on the discharge of his or her duties under the Statute of the Office.

Meetings

ExCom holds an annual plenary session in Geneva, Switzerland, usually in October to discuss programmes, budgets and other key issues, and approves the use of funds to carry out its activities. The 63rd plenary session is scheduled to be held from 1 to 5 October 2012. The Executive Committee's subsidiary body, the Standing Committee, meets three times each year to carry on its work between plenary sessions.

Membership

With wide geographical representation, ExCom is made up of states and others that have demonstrated interest in, and devotion to, solving refugee problems. New members requesting admission may be admitted by the UN's Economic and Social Council (ECOSOC) upon approval by the General Assembly to enlarge the Executive Committee's membership. As of May 2012, the Executive Committee is composed of the following 87 members:

Algeria	Ghana	Poland
Argentina	Greece	Portugal
Australia	Guinea	ROK
Austria	Holy See	Republic of Moldova
Azerbaijan*	Hungary	Romania
Bangladesh	India	Russian Federation
Belgium	Iran	Rwanda*
Benin	Ireland	Serbia
Brazil	Israel	Slovenia
Bulgaria	Italy	Somalia
Cameroon	Japan	South Africa
Canada	Jordan	Spain
Chile	Kenya	Sudan
China	Lebanon	Sweden
Colombia	Lesotho	Switzerland
Congo	Luxembourg	Thailand
Costa Rica	Madagascar	The former Yugoslav
Côte d'Ivoire	Mexico	Republic of Macedonia
Croatia	Montenegro	Togo
Cyprus	Morocco	Tunisia
DR Congo	Mozambique	Turkey
Denmark	Namibia	Turkmenistan
Djibouti	Netherlands	Uganda
Ecuador	New Zealand	UK
Egypt	Nicaragua	UR of Tanzania
Estonia	Nigeria	USA
Ethiopia	Norway	Venezuela
Finland	Pakistan	Yemen
France	Philippines	Zambia
Germany		

Note

* In accordance with GA res. A/66/134 (2011), ECOSOC elected Azerbaijan and Rwanda to the Executive Committee on 26 April 2012.

UN Relief and Works Agency for Palestine Refugees in the Near East (UNRWA)

UNRWA Headquarters
PO Box 140157
Amman 11814
Jordan
Telephone: (+962 6) 580 8100
Fax: (+962 6) 580 8335
Email: unrwanewyork@un.org
Internet: www.unrwa.org
Commissioner-General: Filippo Grandi, Italy (appointed by the UN Secretary-General in consultation with members of UNRWA's Advisory Commission in January 2010)

Purpose

The UN Relief and Works Agency for Palestine Refugees in the Near East (UNRWA) is the main provider of basic services to about 5 million registered Palestine refugees in the Middle East.

UNRWA was established by the General Assembly (res. 302 (IV)) on 8 December 1949, following the 1948 Arab–Israeli conflict, to carry out direct relief and works programmes for Palestine refugees. The Agency began operations on 1 May 1950. In the absence of a solution to the Palestine refugee situation, the General Assembly has repeatedly renewed UNRWA's mandate, most recently extending it until 30 June 2014.

UNRWA provides essential services to eligible registered Palestine refugees in its fields of operation: Jordan, Lebanon, the Syrian Arab Republic and the occupied Palestinian territory. The Agency defines eligible Palestine refugees as persons whose normal place of residence was Palestine between June 1946 and May 1948, who lost both their homes and means of livelihood as a result of the 1948 Arab–Israeli conflict. Their descendants are registered as refugees through the male line.

UNRWA's services are available to those living in its area of operations who meet this definition, who are registered with the Agency and need assistance.

In line with its mandate to promote the human development and well-being of Palestine refugees, UNRWA's principal areas of activity are education, health, relief, social services, micro-credit and camp improvement programmes. UNRWA also provides emergency assistance to refugees affected by conflict in its area of operations. It has been conducting emergency operations in the West Bank and Gaza since the outbreak of the Intifada (uprising) in September 2000 and in northern Lebanon since June 2007.

UNRWA is by far the largest UN operation in the Middle East. It has around 29,000 staff (almost all of whom are refugees themselves) working directly to benefit their communities as teachers, doctors, nurses, social workers or in other practical capacities. UNRWA's operations are financed almost entirely by voluntary contributions from donors. The Agency's budget for 2012–13 was $1.3 billion, which covered the recurrent costs of the Agency's education, health and relief, and social services activities.

Structure

- Office of the Commissioner-General (headquarters)
- Field Offices
- Representative Offices
- Advisory Commission

The Commissioner-General is appointed by the UN Secretary-General after consultation with UNRWA's Advisory Commission for a three-year renewable term. He or she is the only head of a UN body to report directly to the General Assembly. The Office of the Commissioner-General is the focal point for coordination between UNRWA and host authorities, donor governments, other UN organs and organisations, and inter-governmental bodies.

UNRWA maintains headquarters in the Gaza Strip and Amman. Some headquarter functions are being temporarily carried out from Jerusalem as well. There are five UNRWA field offices, located in the West Bank, the Gaza Strip, Jordan, Lebanon and the Syrian Arab Republic. Each office is headed by a director, who is accountable to the Commissioner-General. The responsibilities and functions of each field office include the implementation of UNRWA programmes and services, advising and making recommendations to the Commissioner-General on matters affecting UNRWA operations in the field, and providing advice and assistance to the Commissioner-General on relations with host authorities, government and non-governmental organisations. UNRWA also maintains representative offices in New York, Washington, Brussels and Geneva, and a liaison office in Cairo.

The Advisory Commission was established under the same General Assembly resolution as UNRWA itself. It advises and assists the UNRWA Commissioner-General in the execution of the Agency's programmes.

Membership

There are now 25 Advisory Commission members. Membership expanded following the General Assembly's decision on 9 December 2005 to include countries whose contributions to the Agency had exceeded an annual average of $5 million over the previous three years (*). Two further countries meeting the criteria joined in December 2008 (**) and two in 2011 (***). The Commission members are:

Australia*	Italy*	Spain*
Belgium	Japan	Sweden
Canada*	Jordan	Switzerland*
Denmark*	Kuwait***	Syrian AR
Egypt	Lebanon	Turkey
Finland**	Luxembourg***	UK
France	Netherlands*	USA
Germany*	Norway*	
Ireland**	Saudi Arabia*	

The European Union, League of Arab States and Palestine Liberation Organization attend Advisory Commission meetings as observers. The Chair rotates among members annually. Spain is the Chair from 1 July 2012 to 30 June 2013.

UN Human Settlements Programme (UN-HABITAT) Secretariat

PO Box 30030
Nairobi 00100
Kenya
Telephone: (+254 20) 762 1234
Fax: (+254 20) 762 4266/4267
Email: infohabitat@unhabitat.org

New York Office
2 United Nations Plaza, Room DC2–0943
New York, NY 10017
United States of America
Telephone: (+1 212) 963 4200
Fax: (+1 212) 963 8721
Email: habitatny@un.org

Internet: www.unhabitat.org
Executive Director: Joan Clos, Spain (appointed by the General Assembly in October 2010)

Purpose

The UN Human Settlements Programme (UN-HABITAT) is charged with coordinating human settlement activities within the UN system and facilitating the global exchange of information on shelter and sustainable urban development. It also assists countries with policy and technical advice in solving their human settlement problems.

GA res. 32/162 (1977) established UN-HABITAT, which was previously known as the UN Centre for Human Settlements, its Secretariat and Governing Council. Headquarters are in Nairobi, Kenya.

UN-HABITAT has four main objectives, to:
* Promote the development of socially and environmentally sustainable human settlements and the achievement of adequate shelter for all
* Research and conduct monitoring to coordinate global efforts both within and outside the UN
* Promote technical cooperation and provide technical support to national and local governments and other partners
* Promote greater international cooperation in order to increase financing for human settlements.

Working mainly in developing countries and in countries recovering from conflict and disaster, UN-HABITAT helps governments create policies and strategies aimed at strengthening management capacity at both national and local levels. It focuses on promoting shelter for all, including slum prevention and slum upgrading, improving urban governance, reducing urban poverty, improving the living environment, helping cities deal with climate change problems and threats, and managing disaster mitigation and post-conflict rehabilitation.

Evolution

The Second UN Conference on Human Settlements (Habitat II) was held in Istanbul, Turkey, in 1996. The Conference adopted the Habitat Agenda and the Istanbul Declaration, through which governments committed themselves to the goals of adequate shelter for all and sustainable human settlements development in an urbanising world.

The 25th special session of the General Assembly for an Overall Review and Appraisal of the Implementation of the Habitat Agenda, known as Istanbul+5, was held in New York in 2001. The special session adopted the Declaration on Cities and Other Human Settlements in the New Millennium (res. S-25/2, annex, of 9 June 2001).

GA res. 56/206 (2001) transformed the Commission on Human Settlements and its Secretariat into the Governing Council of the UN Human Settlements Programme, to be known as UN-HABITAT, a subsidiary organ of the General Assembly.

UN-HABITAT continues its predecessor's role as the focal point for the implementation of the Habitat Agenda. It is guided in its work by the Declaration on Cities and Other Human Settlements in the New Millennium. GA res. 56/206 (2001) reaffirmed that the Governing Council's objectives, functions and responsibilities would remain as mandated by GA res. 32/162 (1977) and paragraph 222 of the Habitat Agenda.

Structure

Every two years, the Governing Council examines UN-HABITAT's work and partner relationships. This is a ministerial-level forum at which the organisation's policy guidelines and budget are established for the next two-year period. The Council approves UN-HABITAT's work programme (the medium-term plan and the two-year work programme) and the budget. It also provides overall policy guidance, direction and supervision to UN-HABITAT.

The Governing Council reports to the General Assembly through the Economic and Social Council (ECOSOC), which coordinates the work of the General Assembly's subsidiary bodies. A Committee of Permanent Representatives to UN-HABITAT serves as the Governing Council's inter-sessional subsidiary body.

The programme's resources come from the UN regular budget and voluntary contributions from governments and the private sector. The 2012–13 budget approved by the Governing Council was $393 million.

Meetings

The Governing Council meets once every two years. The 24th session is scheduled to be held from 15 to 19 April 2013 in Nairobi, Kenya.

Membership

The Governing Council's 58 members are elected by ECOSOC for four-year terms, expiring on 31 December. The Council is made up of 16 members from African states, 13 from Asia–Pacific states, six from Eastern European states, 10 from Latin American and Caribbean states, and 13 from Western European and Other states, as listed on the following pages.

Bureau President (23rd session)	Vice-Presidents	Rapporteur
Albert Nsengiyumva, Rwanda	Guangyuan Liu, China	Sofie From-Emmersberger, Finland
	Konrad Paulsen, Chile	
	Sergey Trepelkov, Russian Federation	

OTHER BODIES

	Previous membership	Current membership

African states

	Previous membership	Current membership
Algeria	1983–85 1996–2003	2011–14
Benin	1978–80 1996–2003	
Botswana	1985–95	
Burkina Faso	2003–06 08–11	2012–15
Burundi	1978–83 85–91 2003–10	
Cameroon	1979–81 1987–2002	
Central African Republic	1978–80 84–86	2011–14
Congo	2004–11	2012–15
Côte d'Ivoire		2009–12
DR Congo	1986–88 1999–2006	
Egypt	1977–82 88–94 2001–04	
Equatorial Guinea	2007–10	
Ethiopia	1997–2004	2009–12
Gabon	1984–90 1995–2002	2011–14
Gambia	1995–2002	
Ghana	1984–86 92–95 2005–08	
Guinea	1981–86 2001–04	
Kenya	1979–2003 04–11	
Lesotho	1980–82 85–87 89–96	2012–15
Liberia	1982–84 1997–2000	
Libya	1983–85 93–96 2005–08	
Madagascar	1987–90 93–96 2001–04	
Malawi	1979–81 1986–2000 03–06	
Mali	1999–2002	2011–14
Mauritania	2007–10	
Morocco	1982–84 86–88 2000–03	
Mozambique		2011–14
Namibia	1997–2000	
Niger	2007–10	
Nigeria	1977–88 91–98 2004–07	2011–14
Rwanda	1978–80 84–86 2005–08	2009–12
Senegal	1979–81 1999–2010	
Sierra Leone	1977–85 87–94 2003–06	
Somalia	1981–83 89–96	
South Africa	2004–07	2012–15
Sudan	1978–80 82–84 92–99	2009–12
Swaziland	1981–83 86–92 2004–11	
Togo	1979–81 87–90	
Tunisia	1977–79 85–87 89–92 96–99	2009–12
Uganda	1977–85 87–98 2000–03 05–08	
UR of Tanzania	1978–86 88–95 2001–04 05–08	2012–15
Zambia	1981–83 1997–2000 08–11	
Zimbabwe	1982–84 91–98 2007–10	

Asia–Pacific states

	Previous membership	Current membership
Afghanistan[1]		2009–12
Bahrain	2008–11	2012–15
Bangladesh	1979–94 1997–2004 05–08	2009–12
China	1989–2004 05–08	2009–12
Cyprus	1982–91	
India	1979–2011	2012–15

	Previous membership	Current membership
Indonesia	1980–2000 03–10	2011–14
Iran	1978–80 1988–2010	2011–14
Iraq	1977–81 84–86 89–92 2001–04 08–11	
Japan	1978–2010	2011–14
Jordan	1979–2007	2012–15
Kazakhstan	1995–98	
Lebanon	1983–85	
Malaysia	1977–88 92–95 2000–03	
Nepal	1988	
Pakistan	1978–2010	2011–14
Papua New Guinea	1977–85 93–96	
Philippines	1978–90 1992–2007	
ROK	1997–2000	2009–12
Saudi Arabia	2004–11	2012–15
Sri Lanka	1979–2011	
Syrian AR	1977–79 81–83 89–92	
Thailand		2012–15
UAE	1993–99 2001–04 05–08	
Viet Nam	1979–81 1999–2000	

Eastern European states[2, 3, *]

	Previous membership	Current membership
Albania		2011–14
Armenia		2009–12
Azerbaijan	1993–96	
Belarus	1982–84 88–95 1997–2000 04–07	
Bulgaria	1977–79 81–90 92–99 2004–07	
Croatia	2000–03	
Czech Republic	1996–2003 05–08	2009–12
Hungary	1980–96	
Lithuania	1999–2002	
Poland	1979–81 86–88 90–91 1997–2000 03–10	
Republic of Moldova	2001–04	
Romania	1982–84 91–98 2008–11	
Russian Federation	1978–2010	2011–14
Serbia	2008–11	
Slovakia	2005–08	
The former Yugoslav Republic of Macedonia	2001–04	
Ukraine	1985–87	

Latin American and Caribbean states

	Previous membership	Current membership
Antigua and Barbuda	1991–94 2005–08	2009–12
Argentina	1978–83 87–90 1999–2010	2011–14
Bahamas	1993–96	
Barbados	1981–83 1992–2003	
Bolivia	1982–84 86–92 1999–2002	
Brazil	1987–2006 08–11	2012–15
Chile	1979–87 1991–2010	2011–14
Colombia	1977–85 1987–2003	
Costa Rica	1995–98 2004–07	
Cuba	1977–85	2009–12
Dominican Republic	1986–88 95–98	
Ecuador	1978–80 87–90 1997–2000 03–06	

	Previous membership	Current membership
El Salvador	1982–84	
Grenada	2007–10	2011–14
Guatemala	1979–81 89–92	2009–12
Haiti	1984–86 92–95 2001–04 05–08	2012–15
Honduras	1984–86 2008–11	
Jamaica	1978–83 85–91 1993–2004 08–11	
Mexico	1978–83 1985–2007	2012–15
Nicaragua	1984–86	
Panama	1986–88	
Paraguay	1989–92 2004–07	
Peru	1977–85 88–91	
Trinidad and Tobago	2001–07 05–08	
Venezuela	1979–81 84–86 1993–2000 07–10	2011–14

Western European and Other states*

	Previous membership	Current membership
Australia	1979–81	
Austria	1977–79 92–95 2001–04	
Belgium	1980–82 1997–2004 05–08	
Canada	1977–96 2005–08	
Denmark	1981–83 86–91 96–99	
Finland	1977–79 1981–2002 07–10	2011–14
France	1977–2004 05–08	2009–12
Germany	1979–2007 08–11	2012–15
Greece	1979–2007	
Israel	2004–11	2012–15
Italy	1979–84 1986–2004 07–10	2012–15
Netherlands	1977–2000 03–10	
New Zealand	1982–84	
Norway	1980–2003 05–08	2009–12
Portugal	1978–80	
Spain	1981–86 1996–2007	2009–12
Sweden	1978–80 1983–2004 05–08	2011–14
Turkey	1984–2006	2011–14
UK	1978–80 1987–2006	
USA	1978–2010	2011–14

Notes

* Two seats vacant in the Eastern European States Group, and three seats vacant in the Western European and Other States Group.

1 Afghanistan's term began 15 December 2009.

2 The former Socialist Federal Republic of Yugoslavia served on the Governing Council from 1978 to 1980 and from 1989 to 1992. It was not automatically succeeded by any of the new states created following its dissolution.

3 Czechoslovakia served on the Governing Council from 1979 to 1981.

World Food Programme (WFP)

Via Cesare Giulio Viola 68/70
Parco de Medici
00148 Rome
Italy
Telephone: (+39 06) 65131
Fax: (+39 06) 6513 2840
Email: wfpinfo@wfp.org
Internet: www.wfp.org
Executive Director: Ertharin Cousin, USA (appointed jointly by the UN Secretary-General and FAO Director-General in April 2012 for a five-year term)

Purpose

The World Food Programme (WFP) is the world's largest humanitarian agency fighting hunger worldwide. It was established in 1961 by the General Assembly and UN Food and Agriculture Organization (FAO) Conference as the UN system's food aid organisation.

In 2008, WFP was transformed from a food aid organisation to a food assistance organisation. WFP's five goals are to:

- Save lives and protect livelihoods in emergencies
- Prevent acute hunger and invest in disaster preparedness and mitigation
- Restore and rebuild lives and livelihoods after wars and disasters
- Reduce chronic hunger and undernutrition
- Strengthen the ability of nations to curb hunger.

The Programme also administers the International Emergency Food Reserve (IEFR), established by the General Assembly with a minimum target of 500,000 tonnes of cereals.

In 2011, donors contributed $3.65 billion. All contributions to the Programme are on a voluntary basis. WFP helped feed 99.1 million people in 75 countries and provided 3.6 million metric tons of food.

Evolution

By GA res. 50/227 (1995), the FAO and the WFP absorbed the functions of the World Food Council, which was discontinued.

Structure

Supervision of the Programme is vested in the Executive Board, which meets four times a year in Rome. The Executive Board became effective on 1 January 1996. It replaced the Committee on Food Aid Policies and Programmes (CFA), which had been established in 1975 by General Assembly resolutions and the FAO Conference on the recommendation of the 1974 World Food Conference. The CFA had replaced the Inter-government Committee (IGC) of the World Food Programme.

Membership of the WFP Executive Board has been reduced from 42 to 36. Eighteen members are elected by the Economic and Social Council (ECOSOC) and 18 by the FAO Council.

Each member serves a three-year term and is eligible for re-election. The Board:

- Provides a forum for inter-governmental consultations on national and international food aid programmes and policies
- Reviews general trends in food aid requirements and availability
- Formulates proposals for effective coordination of multilateral, bilateral and non-governmental food aid programmes, including emergency food aid
- Examines and approves projects and programmes submitted to it by the Executive Director
- Examines and approves the Programme's administrative and project budget.

The Board reports to ECOSOC and the FAO Council on its yearly activities.

Membership*

Term of office expiring 31 December 2012

Elected by the FAO Council

Finland[1] (List D)	Kenya (List A)	Philippines (List B)
Jordan (List B)	Mexico (List C)	USA (List D)

Elected by ECOSOC

Burkina Faso (List A)	India (List B)	Russian Federation (List E)
France (List D)	Iran (List B)	Spain[2] (List D)

Term of office expiring 31 December 2013

Elected by the FAO Council

Cameroon (List A)	Germany (List D)	Saudi Arabia (List B)
Canada (List D)	Haiti (List C)	South Africa (List A)

Elected by ECOSOC

Australia (List D)	Morocco (List A)	ROK (List B)
Cuba (List C)	Norway (List D)	Sudan (List A)

Term of office expiring 31 December 2014

Elected by the FAO Council

Belgium (List D)	Ghana[3] (List A)	Sweden (List D)
Brazil (List C)	Slovak Republic (List E)	Tunisia (List A)

Elected by ECOSOC

China (List B)	Guatemala (List C)	UK (List D)
Czech Republic (List E)	Japan (List D)	Zambia (List A)

Notes

1   The Netherlands, elected for the term 2010–12, resigned effective 1 January 2012 in favour of Finland, which will occupy the seat for the remainder of the term.

2   Luxembourg, elected for the term 2010–12, resigned effective 1 January 2011 in favour of Spain, which will occupy the seat for the remainder of the term.

3   Ghana is occupying a rotating seat, which is occupied by a country according to the following: List A, first term 2012/2013/2014; List B, second term 2015/2016/2017; List A, third term 2018/2019/2020; and List C, fourth term 2021/2022/2023.

*   In April 2012, ECOSOC elected Sierra Leone (List A); Iraq (List B); Netherlands and Switzerland (List D); and Russian Federation (List E) for three-year terms beginning on 1 January 2013, and postponed the election of one member from List B due to the absence of other candidates. To replace members that had resigned effective 1 January 2013 and whose terms would expire on 31 December 2013, ECOSOC elected Spain (replacing Norway) and Pakistan (replacing ROK).

OTHER UN ENTITIES

Office of the UN High Commissioner for Human Rights (OHCHR)

Palais des Nations
1211 Geneva 10
Switzerland
Telephone: (+41 22) 917 9000
Fax: (+41 22) 917 9012
Email: InfoDesk@ohchr.org
Internet: www.ohchr.org
High Commissioner: Navanethem Pillay, South Africa (appointed by the UN Secretary-General in July 2008, took up the post on 1 September 2008; mandate renewed for two years from 1 September 2012)

Purpose

GA res. 48/141 (1993) established the post of High Commissioner for Human Rights to promote and protect the effective enjoyment by all people of all civil, cultural, economic, political and social rights, including the right to development. It further held that the High Commissioner should function as the UN official with principal responsibility for global human rights efforts. The High Commissioner acts under the direction and authority of the Secretary-General. GA res. 48/141 (1993) lists the activities that comprise the High Commissioner's mandate.

The Office represents the world's commitment to universal human rights and is the principal UN office mandated to promote and protect the human rights of all people. OHCHR also serves as the Secretariat to the Human Rights Council in accordance with GA res. 60/251 (2006) and provides assistance to the system of Special Procedures, the Universal Periodic Review and the core human rights treaty bodies.

The High Commissioner is appointed by the Secretary-General and approved by the General Assembly, with regard to geographical rotation. Appointments are for a fixed term of four years, with the possibility of one renewal.

Joint United Nations Programme on HIV/AIDS (UNAIDS)

20 Avenue Appia
1211 Geneva 27
Switzerland
Telephone: (+41 22) 791 3666
Fax: (+41 22) 791 4187
Email: unaids@unaids.org
Internet: www.unaids.org
Executive Director: Michel Sidibé, Mali (appointed by the UN Secretary-General on the recommendation of the Committee of Co-sponsoring Organisations in 2009)

Purpose

The Joint UN Programme on HIV/AIDS (UNAIDS) brings together the efforts and resources of 10 UN system organisations to help prevent new HIV infections, care for people living with HIV and mitigate the impact of the epidemic. UNAIDS helps mount and support an expanded response to the AIDS virus that engages the efforts of many sectors and partners from government and civil society. The Programme's number one priority is contributing to achieving global commitments to universal access to comprehensive interventions for HIV prevention, treatment, care and support.

The UNAIDS Secretariat supports a more effective global response to AIDS through:
- Leadership and advocacy for effective action on the epidemic
- Strategic information to guide the efforts of partners
- Tracking, monitoring and evaluating the epidemic and responses to it
- Civil society engagement and partnership development
- Mobilisation of resources.

Evolution

The need for a programme to take collective action against AIDS was outlined by a World Health Assembly resolution in 1993 and further endorsed by Economic and Social Council (ECOSOC) res. 1994/24.

UNAIDS began operation on 1 January 1996. Early that year, a Memorandum of Understanding was signed by the six original co-sponsors of UNAIDS: the UN Children's Fund (UNICEF), UN Development Programme (UNDP), UN Population Fund (UNFPA), UN Educational, Scientific and Cultural Organization (UNESCO), World Health Organization (WHO) and the World Bank. These agencies were joined in 1999 by the UN International Drug Control Programme (UNDCP), which is now an integral part of the UN Office on Drugs and Crime (UNODC); in 2001 by the International Labour Organization (ILO); in 2003 by the World Food Programme (WFP); and in 2004 by the Office of the UN High Commissioner for Refugees (UNHCR).

Structure

UNAIDS has a secretariat with headquarters in Geneva and offices in more than 80 countries. The organisation is guided by a Programme Coordination Board (PCB), which serves as its governing body. This comprises 22 Member States elected by ECOSOC with a regional distribution (five African states, five Asia–Pacific, two Eastern European, three Latin American and Caribbean, and seven Western European and Other), as well as the 10 co-sponsors and five non-governmental organisations, including associations of people living with HIV/AIDS. The following list shows current PCB members. Terms are usually three years, beginning on 1 January and ending 31 December of the years shown.

African states*

Botswana	2010–12	Egypt	2011–13
Congo	2012–14	Togo	2010–12
Djibouti	2011–13		

Asia–Pacific states*

Bangladesh	2011–13	Iran	2012–14
China	2010–12	Japan	2010–12
India	2011–13		

Eastern European states*

Poland	2010–12	Russian Federation	2011–13

Latin American and Caribbean states*

Brazil	2012–14	Mexico	2011–13
El Salvador	2010–12		

Western European and Other states*

Canada	2012–14	Sweden	2010–12
Germany[1]	2012–13	UK	2010–12
Norway	2012–14	USA	2011–13
Portugal[2]	2012		

Non-governmental organisations

Africa: Association de Lutte Contre le Sida (ALCS)/African Sex Worker Alliance

Asia–Pacific: Asia Pacific Network of People Living with HIV/AIDS (APN+)/International Treatment Preparedness Coalition (ITPC)

Europe: International Network of People who Use Drugs (INPUD)/International AIDS Vaccine Initiative (IAVI)

Latin America/Caribbean: Fundación para Estudio e Investigación de la Mujer (FEIM)/Gestos – HIV+, Communication and Gender

North America: The Global Forum on MSM & HIV (MSMGF)/International Community of Women Living with HIV/AIDS (ICW)

Notes

* In April 2012, ECOSOC elected the following nine members for three-year terms beginning on 1 January 2013: Sierra Leone and Zimbabwe (African states); China and Japan (Asia–Pacific states); Poland (Eastern European states); Guyana (Latin American and Caribbean states); and Belgium, Switzerland and UK (Western European and Other states).

1 Monaco relinquished its seat effective 1 January 2012. Germany was elected to complete the term.

2 Netherlands relinquished its seat effective 1 January 2012. Portugal was elected to complete the term.

Committee of Cosponsoring Organizations (CCO)

The Committee of Cosponsoring Organizations (CCO) comprises representatives from the 10 Joint UN Programme on HIV/AIDS (UNAIDS) co-sponsors and the UNAIDS Secretariat. It serves as the forum for the co-sponsoring organisations to meet on a regular basis to consider matters concerning UNAIDS, provides input from the co-sponsoring organisations into the policies and strategies of UNAIDS, and serves as a standing committee of the Programme Coordination Board (PCB).

The UNAIDS Executive Director is the Secretary of the CCO. Each co-sponsor rotates as chair annually. The UNAIDS PCB membership (six seats) also rotates among co-sponsors. The Chair for 1 January to 31 December 2012 is the World Bank.

UN Office on Drugs and Crime (UNODC)

Vienna International Centre
PO Box 500
A–1400 Vienna
Austria
Telephone: (+43 1) 260 600
Fax: (+43 1) 26 060 5866
Email: unodc@unodc.org
Internet: www.unodc.org
Under-Secretary-General and Executive Director: Yury Fedotov, Russian Federation (took office in September 2010; also Director-General of the UN Office in Vienna)

Purpose

The UN Office on Drugs and Crime (UNODC) is a global leader in the struggle against illicit drugs and transnational organised crime. The Office is also the Secretariat of the:
• Conference of the Parties to the UN Convention against Transnational Organized Crime and its three supplementary protocols on: Trafficking in Persons, especially Women and Children; Smuggling of Migrants; and Illicit Manufacturing of and Trafficking in Firearms
• Conference of the States Parties to the UN Convention against Corruption.

UNODC promotes the ratification and implementation of these conventions and protocols through capacity building, training and technical assistance.

The UNODC Terrorism Prevention Branch provides, through its Global Programme against Terrorism, technical and legal assistance to Member States seeking to ratify and implement all of the international legal instruments relating to the prevention and suppression of terrorism.

The Office's mandate is to support Member States in the prevention of illicit drugs, crime and terrorism. The three pillars of its work programme are:

- Research and analytical work to increase knowledge and understanding of drugs and crime issues through the production of authoritative reports and crop surveys
- Assistance for states in the ratification and implementation of relevant international treaties; the development of domestic legislation on drugs, crime and terrorism; training judicial officials; and the provision of secretariat and other services to the treaty-based and governing bodies
- Field-based technical cooperation projects to enhance the capacity of Member States to prevent and counteract illicit drugs, crime and terrorism.

The drug programme works to inform the world on the dangers of drug abuse and to strengthen international action against production and trafficking of illicit drugs. The crime programme works to strengthen the rule of law and to promote stable criminal justice systems. It pays special attention to trafficking in human beings, the smuggling of migrants and firearms, and combating corruption.

Evolution

The UN International Drug Control Programme (UNDCP), the predecessor of UNODC, was established under GA res. 45/179 (1990) as the body responsible for coordinated international action in the field of drug abuse control. The Crime Prevention and Criminal Justice Programme was established under GA res. 46/152 (1991) and was, from 1992, implemented under ECOSOC res. 1992/1 by the Commission on Crime Prevention and Criminal Justice (CCPCJ). The authority for the Programme's Fund was conferred on the Executive Director by GA res. 46/185C (1991). Former Secretary-General Kofi Annan (ST/SGB/2004/6) established UNODC on 15 March 2004 to implement the two programmes in an integrated manner.

Structure

UNODC has more than 50 regional, country and programme offices around the world, with about 1500 staff. They represent the operational arm of the organisation and work directly with institutions, civil society organisations and local communities to develop and implement drug control and crime prevention programmes that are tailored to the needs of assisted countries. UNODC also maintains liaison offices in New York and Brussels.

UNODC has regional offices for: Brazil and the Southern Cone; Central Asia; Eastern Africa; the Middle East and North Africa; Mexico, Central America and the Caribbean; Peru, South Asia; Southern Africa; West and Central Africa (Senegal); and East Asia and the Pacific.

UN Office for Project Services (UNOPS)

UNOPS HQ
PO Box 2695
2100 Copenhagen
Denmark
Telephone: (+45) 3546 7000
Fax: (+45) 3546 7501
Email: info@unops.org
Internet: www.unops.org
Executive Director: Jan Mattsson, Sweden (appointed by the UN Secretary-General in 2006)

Purpose

The UN Office for Project Services' (UNOPS') mission is to expand the capacity of the UN system and its partners to implement peacebuilding, humanitarian and development operations that matter for people in need. Working in some of the world's most challenging environments, UNOPS' core services include project management, procurement, human resources management, fund management and UN common services.

UNOPS offers implementation support services to partners who have political, policy or substantive mandates. Its focus areas are demand-driven and reviewed annually. The current focus is to provide implementation support services to partners in the following areas: census and elections, environment, health, physical infrastructure and justice, and security reform.

UNOPS' services contribute to four high-level goals: rebuilding peace and stability after conflict; early recovery of communities affected by natural disasters; the ability of people to develop local economies and obtain social services; and environmental sustainability and adaption to climate change.

Evolution

Established as part of the UN Development Programme (UNDP) in 1974, UNOPS became an independent self-financing organisation in 1995 under GA res. 48/501 (1994).

An updated governance structure for UNOPS was endorsed by the General Assembly in December 2010, confirming a series of decisions and policies developed by the Executive Board during the previous four years that have made UNOPS more accountable and transparent.

The General Assembly also decided to rename the Executive Board to include UNOPS in its title, making it the Executive Board of the UN Development Programme, UN Population Fund and UN Office for Project Services. It also endorsed an earlier decision whereby the Executive Director reports directly to the UN Secretary-General and the Executive Board, and has the authority to sign host country agreements and appoint UNOPS representatives in the field. For more information about the Executive Board, see the UN Development Programme entry on pages 238–242.

Other key decisions by the Executive Board that have helped transform the organisation include the Financial Regulations and Rules, which govern the financial management of UNOPS, and the Strategic Plan 2010–13, which defines UNOPS' position in the UN and its goals.

The full text of the legislative documents can be found in GA res. A/RES/65/176 (December 2010), ECOSOC res. 2010/23 (July 2010) and Executive Board decisions 2008/35 (September 2008), 2009/25 (September 2009), 2010/7 (January 2010) and 2010/21 (June 2010).

UNOPS is a self-financing organisation, operating on a full cost-recovery basis from fees earned for services rendered, with no assessed or voluntary budget funding. The management fees are determined on a case-by-case basis and take into account the level of effort, complexity and risk of the services delivered.

United Nations University (UNU)

53–70, Jingumae 5-chome
Shibuya-ku, Tokyo 150–8925
Japan
Telephone: (+81 3) 5467 1212
Fax: (+81 3) 3499 2828
Email: mbox@unu.edu
Internet: www.unu.edu
Rector: Konrad Osterwalder, Switzerland (appointed by the UN Secretary-General, with the concurrence of the Director-General of UNESCO, from 2007 to 31 August 2012)

Purpose

The UN University (UNU) is the academic arm of the UN system and implements research and educational programmes in the area of sustainable development, with the particular aim of assisting developing countries. It was established by GA res. 2951 (XXVII) (1972) as an autonomous organ of the General Assembly. The resolution provided that the University:
* Be a system of academic institutions, rather than an inter-governmental organisation
* Comprise a central programming and coordinating body along with a decentralised network of affiliated research, teaching and training institutions
* Be integrated into the world university community, and devoted to research into "pressing global problems of human survival, development and welfare" and to post-graduate training and teaching of young scholars and researchers (particularly those from developing countries)
* Have a special mandate to alleviate the intellectual isolation of academics in developing countries by organising worldwide networks of collaborating scholars and research institutions
* Be funded by voluntary contributions (from governments, international organisations, foundations, universities and others).

The UNU mission is to contribute – through collaborative research, education and capacity development, and advisory services – to efforts to resolve the pressing global problems of human survival, development and welfare.

UNU undertakes a wide range of activities focused on knowledge generation (basic and applied research, and foresight and policy studies), education and capacity development (developing human and organisational capabilities), and knowledge transfer and sharing (communications, dissemination and outreach).

Structure

The University's academic activities are coordinated and carried out by the UNU Centre in Tokyo and a network of UNU Research and Training Centres and Programmes (RTC/Ps) located in 13 UN Member States around the world. This core UNU system is assisted by a global network of UNU Associated Institutions, cooperating institutions and scholars.

Membership

The UNU Council has 28 members: 24 appointed members who serve in their individual capacities for six-year terms; the UNU Rector; and three ex officio members, the UN Secretary-General, Director-General of the UN Educational, Scientific and Cultural Organization (UNESCO) and Executive Director of the UN Institute for Training and Research (UNITAR). The appointed members of the UNU Council, with terms expiring in the year indicated, are:

Nobuyasu Abe,
Japan (2016)

Gajaraj Dhanarajan,
Malaysia (2016)

Lily Kong,
Singapore (2016)

J Michael Adams,
USA (2016)

Juan Ramón de la Fuente,
Mexico (2013) (Chair)

Goolam Mohamedbhai,
Mauritius (2013)

Paolo Blasi,
Italy (2013)

Louise Fresco,
Netherlands (2013)

Francisco Komlavi Seddoh,
Togo (2013)

Jean-Pierre Bourguignon,
France (2016)

Mohamed H A Hassan,
Sudan (2016)

Gita Sen,
India (2013)

Rahma Bourqia,
Morocco (2016)

Zellynne Doloris Jennings-
Craig, Jamaica (2016)

Lydia Shouleva,
Bulgaria (2016)

Christovam Buarque,
Brazil (2016)

Jin Xiaoming,
China (2016)

Mala Singh,
South Africa (2016)

Fiona Caldicott,
UK (2016)

Konstantin Khudoley,
Russian Federation (2016)

Ivan Wilhelm,
Czech Republic (2013)

Angela Cropper,
Trinidad and Tobago (2013)

Fadia Kiwan,
Lebanon (2013)

Margret Wintermantel,
Germany (2013)

RESEARCH AND TRAINING INSTITUTES

UN Institute for Disarmament Research (UNIDIR)

Palais des Nations
1211 Geneva 10
Switzerland
Telephone: (+41 22) 917 3186
Fax: (+41 22) 917 0176
Email: unidir@unog.ch
Internet: www.unidir.org
Director: Theresa Hitchens, USA (appointed by the UN Secretary-General in consultation with the Advisory Board on Disarmament Matters in 2009)

Purpose

The UN Institute for Disarmament Research (UNIDIR) is an autonomous body of the UN, established by the General Assembly to carry out independent research on disarmament and related international security issues. It was established in 1980 and its Statute approved by the General Assembly in res. 39/148H (1984). The Statute stipulates that UNIDIR should aim to:

- Provide the international community with more diversified and complete data on problems relating to international security, the armaments race and disarmament in all fields, particularly nuclear, and to facilitate progress through negotiations towards greater security for all states, and the economic and social development of all peoples
- Promote informed participation by all states in disarmament efforts
- Assist with negotiations on disarmament and continued efforts to ensure greater international security at a progressively lower level of armaments, particularly nuclear, by means of objective, factual studies and analyses

- Carry out more in-depth, forward-looking and long-term research on disarmament, to provide general insight into the problems involved and stimulate initiatives for new negotiations.

UNIDIR develops practical ideas for building peace and security through analysis of disarmament and security issues.

The Institute's work encompasses diverse themes, from small arms to weapons of mass destruction, and from the reintegration of former combatants to preventing an arms race in outer space. Through its research projects, publications, conferences and expert networks, UNIDIR serves as a bridge between decision-makers, researchers, practitioners, Member States and UN agencies to promote creative thinking and dialogue about current and emerging security challenges.

UNIDIR is one of the three founding partners of the Geneva Forum, a process for information exchange and informal discussion among the diplomatic and research communities in Geneva.

Structure

The UNIDIR Director reports annually to the General Assembly on the Institute's activities. The UN Secretary-General's Advisory Board on Disarmament Matters functions as UNIDIR's Board of Trustees.

The Institute is funded by voluntary contributions from UN Member States and foundations, and receives a small contribution from the UN budget.

United Nations System Staff College (UNSSC)

Viale Maestri del Lavoro 10
I–10127 Turin
Italy
Telephone: (+39 011) 653 5911
Fax: (+39 011) 653 5901
Email: info@unssc.org
Internet: www.unssc.org
Director: Carlos Lopes, Guinea-Bissau (appointed by the UN Secretary-General in 2007)

Purpose

Since 1 January 2002, the UN System Staff College (UNSSC) has operated as a knowledge-management and learning institution to serve UN organisations without duplicating their learning and training activities (GA A/RES/55/278).

The Staff College's main goal is to be a centre of excellence in inter-agency learning and training for UN staff and an agent for change, carrying out its programmes on the basis of needs expressed by the UN system. The College's services include: residential workshops, seminars and training courses; e-learning; advisory services; coaching and mentoring services; tailor-made projects and technical support for UN organisations and publications. Its main areas of focus include: UN leadership, development and human rights, UN coherence, knowledge management and learning skills, and peace and security.

Structure

The College's governing body is the Board of Governors, appointed by the UN Secretary-General in consultation with the UN System Chief Executives Board for Coordination (CEB). The UNSSC Board is chaired by the UN Deputy Secretary-General. It meets once a year and receives technical advice on the College's activities by an Expert Technical Review Panel.

Membership

As established in the new UNSSC Statute, approved by ECOSOC in July 2009 (res. 2009/10), the UNSSC Board is composed of a maximum of nine individuals and two ex officio members nominated by the UN Secretary-General and selected from staff of the member organisations of the CEB. Board members serve for two-year terms, which may be renewed for an additional year.

The technical review panel is composed of experts selected by the Board to serve for periods not exceeding three years.

United Nations Institute for Training and Research (UNITAR)

Palais des Nations
1211 Geneva 10
Switzerland
Telephone: (+41 22) 917 8400
Fax: (+41 22) 917 8047
Email: info@unitar.org
Internet: www.unitar.org
Executive Director: Carlos Lopes, Guinea-Bissau (appointed by the UN Secretary-General in March 2007)

Purpose

The United Nations Institute for Training and Research (UNITAR) provides short-term executive training to Member States' national and local government officials, and representatives of civil society and the private sector. It is an autonomous body within the UN system, founded in 1963 (GA res. 1934 (XVIII)).

Aiming to become a centre of excellence for adult learning, UNITAR strives to respond to the growing demand from Member States, especially the least-developed and other developing countries, for capacity development in the fields of the environment; governance; peace, security and diplomacy; and research. UNITAR advances its learning objectives through briefings and seminars, workshops and specialised regional training, and often collaborates with other UN agencies on its senior-level management training.

Technology-enhanced learning continues to grow, with about a third of the Institute's 435 annual events now delivered in the form of e-learning. UNITAR has also increased its satellite mapping and analysis technical capability through its satellite operational application programme (UNOSAT), which has supported the UN system in responding to natural disasters and overseeing elections and humanitarian operations.

Evolution

The Institute began operating in 1965, with activities primarily supporting the training of diplomats accredited to the UN in New York. UNITAR has since grown considerably and undergone restructuring measures, including shifting its headquarters from New York to Geneva in 1993, reopening its New York office in 1994 and opening a new office in Hiroshima, Japan, in 2002. UNITAR also has a project office in Nigeria (Niger Delta Local Development Office in Port Harcourt) and local authority training centres in Atlanta, USA; Curitiba, Brazil; Durban, South Africa; Findhorn, Scotland; Jeju, ROK; Kuala Lumpur, Malaysia; Ouagadougou, Burkina Faso; Plock, Poland; and Shanghai, China.

Since 2007, UNITAR has rationalised and upgraded its institutional structure with a view to increasing its capacity. It is working to further enhance the quality and diversity of its training and increase its autonomy, particularly through the diversification of funding sources.

Meetings

The UNITAR Board of Trustees meets in session at least once a year, and has been rotating the venue between Geneva and other cities. The next meeting is scheduled to be held in October 2012 in Geneva, Switzerland.

Board of Trustees

The Board is the Institute's governing body. It approves the work programme and budget, and formulates principles and policies that govern the Institute's activities and operations. Board members are appointed by the UN Secretary-General, in consultation with the Presidents of the General Assembly and ECOSOC. The 12 trustees and four ex officio members are:

Lakhdar Brahimi, Algeria

Simon Compaore, Burkina Faso

Shirin Ebadi, Iran

Shirley Franklin, USA

Geraldine Joslyn Fraser-Moleketi, South Africa

Radha Kumar, India

Henri Lopes, Congo (Chair)

U Joy Ogwu, Nigeria

Alfonso Quiñónez, Guatemala

Portia Simpson Miller, Jamaica

Anne Kristin Sydnes, Norway

Alfredo G A Valladão, Brazil

Ex officio members

UN Secretary-General

President of the UN General Assembly

President of the Economic and Social Council

Executive Director of UN Institute for Training and Research

UN Interregional Crime and Justice Research Institute (UNICRI)

Viale Maestri del Lavoro 10
10127 Turin
Italy
Telephone: (+39 011) 653 7111
Fax: (+39 011) 631 3368
Email: information@unicri.it
Internet: www.unicri.it
Director: Jonathan Lucas, Seychelles (appointed by the UN Secretary-General in April 2011)

Purpose

The UN Interregional Crime and Justice Research Institute (UNICRI) is one of five UN research and training institutes. It was created to help inter-governmental, governmental and non-governmental organisations in formulating and implementing improved policies in crime prevention and criminal justice. It does this through applied research, training, technical cooperation, field activities, and the collection, exchange and dissemination of information.

The Institute's major goals are to:
- Advance understanding of crime-related problems
- Foster just and efficient criminal justice systems
- Support respect for international instruments and other standards
- Facilitate international law enforcement cooperation and judicial assistance.

Evolution

UNICRI was established as the UN Social Defense Research Institute (UNSDRI) in 1967 following ECOSOC res. 1086 B (XXXIX) (1965), which requested the Secretary-General to strengthen UN action in the prevention and control of both juvenile delinquency and adult criminality.

On 24 May 1989, through its resolution 1989/56, ECOSOC renamed the Institute the UN Interregional Crime and Justice Research Institute and adopted its present Statute, which reconfirms and enlarges the previous mandate.

Structure

The Institute has an Applied Research Programme that is organised in the following work areas: security governance and counter-terrorism; emerging crimes; and post-graduate and specialised training within crime prevention and criminal justice.

The UNICRI Documentation Centre supports the Institute's research, training and field activities, and enables it to serve the needs of international organisations, national institutions, non-governmental organisations, experts and professionals.

Membership

UNICRI is governed by a Board of Trustees with 11 members. Seven members are selected by the Commission on Crime Prevention and Criminal Justice on the principle of equitable geographical distribution. They are nominated by the Secretary-General and endorsed by ECOSOC. Members retire by rotation – when the members are first appointed, three serve for five years, two for four years and two for three years. The four ex officio members include a representative of the UN Secretary-General, UN Development Programme Administrator, host country (Italy) and the Director of UNICRI.

Board members (other than ex officio members) and the year of membership expiry are:

Pedro David,
Argentina (2013)

Eduardo Fungairiño,
Spain (2013)

Stuart Page,
Australia (2014)

Elizabeth Verville,
USA (2014)

Alexander Vladimirovic
Zmeyevskiy,
Russian Federation (2014)

Feroukhi Taous,
Algeria (2017)

Jayantilal M Karia,
Uganda (2017)

UN Research Institute for Social Development (UNRISD)

Palais des Nations
1211 Geneva 10
Switzerland
Telephone: (+41 22) 917 3020
Fax: (+41 22) 917 0650
Email: info@unrisd.org
Internet: www.unrisd.org
Director: Sarah Cook, UK (appointed by the UN Secretary-General in 2009)

Purpose

The UN Research Institute for Social Development (UNRISD) is an autonomous body of the UN that was established in 1963 by a decision of the Secretary-General (ST/SGB/126). Its mandate is to conduct policy-relevant research on pressing issues of social development.

UNRISD's mission is to generate knowledge and articulate policy alternatives on contemporary social development issues, thereby contributing to the UN system's broader goals of reducing poverty and inequality, advancing well-being and rights, and creating more democratic and just societies.

UNRISD undertakes independent, multi-disciplinary research in collaboration with an extensive network of research partners in developed and developing countries. The Institute sits at the interface of the UN system, civil society and the academic community. It aims to use this position to create spaces for reflection, debate and dialogue, and to encourage sharing of knowledge and ideas across the international development community.

A hallmark of UNRISD's work is its integration of the economic and social dimensions of development with analysis of the political factors and institutional arrangements that underpin processes of social change. The Institute's research programme spans a range of themes, including social policy, governance, social movements and gender. Recent priority areas include social policy in a development context, combating poverty and inequality, gender and the care economy, green economy and corporate accountability. UNRISD's 2010–14 research agenda is framed around two main themes: Social Policies for Inclusive and Sustainable Development, and Political and Institutional Dynamics of Social Development.

Structure

As an autonomous body of the UN, UNRISD is not associated with any particular specialised agency. It is funded entirely by voluntary contributions. Its work is coordinated with specialised agencies, and it is supervised by an independent board.

Membership

The Board is composed of a chair appointed by the Secretary-General, 10 members nominated by the Commission for Social Development and confirmed by the Economic and Social Council (ECOSOC), who serve in their personal capacity, and eight ex officio members.

Board membership is for four years, with the possibility of extension for a further two years. The members, with year of term expiry, are:

Maureen O'Neil, Canada (Chair)	2015	Huang Ping, China	2015
Bina Agarwal, India	2013	Patricia Schultz, Switzerland	2015
Yesim Arat, Turkey	2013	Annika Sundén, Sweden	2013
Evelina Dagnino, Brazil	2013	Julia Szalai, Hungary	2013
Peter Evans, USA	2013	Zenebeworke Tadesse, Ethiopia	2013
Rosalind Eyben, UK	2013		

Ex officio members

A representative of the Secretary-General

Director, Latin American and Caribbean Institute for Economic and Social Planning

Director, African Institute for Economic Development and Planning

Director, Asian and Pacific Development Centre

Executive Secretary, UN Economic and Social Commission for Western Asia (ESCWA)

Representatives of two of the following agencies appointed in rotation: UN Food and Agriculture Organization (FAO), International Labour Organization (ILO), UN Educational, Scientific and Cultural Organization (UNESCO), World Health Organization (WHO)

Director of the Institute

HUMAN RIGHTS TREATY BODIES

Committee Against Torture (CAT)

Office of the UN High Commissioner for Human Rights
United Nations Office at Geneva
1211 Geneva 10
Switzerland
Telephone: (+41 22) 917 9000
Fax: (+41 22) 917 9022
Email: InfoDesk@ohchr.org or registry@ohchr.org
Internet: www2.ohchr.org (follow links from 'Human rights bodies')
Chair: Claudio Grossman, Chile

Purpose

The Committee Against Torture (CAT) is the body of independent experts that monitors implementation by States Parties of the Convention against Torture and other Cruel, Inhuman or Degrading Treatment or Punishment. The Convention was adopted by GA res. 39/46 (1984) and entered into force on 26 June 1987. As at 31 May 2012, there were 150 parties to the Convention.

The Committee considers States Parties' reports on the measures adopted and progress made in observance of the Convention. States Parties are obliged to submit a report within one year, then every four years (article 19). In certain circumstances, the Committee may conduct an inquiry if it receives reliable evidence of grave and systematic violations of the Convention being carried out by a State Party to the Convention (article 20).

A State Party may declare that it recognises the Committee's competence to receive and consider communications from a State Party claiming that another State Party is not fulfilling its obligations under the Convention (article 21). A State Party may declare that it recognises the Committee's competence to receive and consider communications from, or on behalf of, individuals subject to its jurisdiction who claim to be victims of a violation of the provisions of the Convention by a State Party (article 22).

The Optional Protocol to the Convention, which entered into force in June 2006, created the Subcommittee on Prevention of Torture (SPT – see next entry).

Meetings

The Committee normally meets twice a year for four weeks, in May and November, in Geneva. The 49th session is scheduled to be held from 20 October to 23 November 2012.

Membership

CAT consists of 10 experts in the field of human rights, serving in their personal capacity (article 17), as listed on the next page. Consideration is given to equitable geographical distribution and the legal experience of candidates. Members are elected by States Parties, generally for staggered four-year terms and may be re-elected.

Term ending 31 Dec 2013	Term ending 31 Dec 2015
Essadia Belmir, Morocco (Vice-Chair)	Satyabhoosun Gupt Domah, Mauritius
Alessio Bruni, Italy	Felice Gaer, USA (Vice-Chair)
Fernando Mariño Menendez, Spain	Abdoulaye Gaye, Senegal
Nora Sveaass, Norway (Rapporteur)	Claudio Grossman, Chile (Chair)
Xuexian Wang, China (Vice-Chair)	George Tugushi, Georgia

Subcommittee on Prevention of Torture (SPT)

Office of the UN High Commissioner for Human Rights
United Nations Office at Geneva
1211 Geneva 10
Switzerland
Telephone: (+41 22) 917 9000
Fax: (+41 22) 917 9022
Email: opcat@ohchr.org
Internet: www2.ohchr.org (follow links from 'Human rights bodies')
Chair: Malcolm Evans, UK (since 2011)

Purpose

The Subcommittee on Prevention of Torture (SPT) was created under the Optional Protocol to the Convention against Torture and other Cruel, Inhuman or Degrading Treatment or Punishment. Its mandate is to establish a system of regular visits by independent experts to places where people are or may be deprived of their liberty, in order to prevent torture and other cruel, inhuman or degrading treatment or punishment.

The Optional Protocol establishes the SPT as the international preventive mechanism with a global remit. It requires each State Party to set up, designate or maintain at the domestic level one or several visiting bodies for the prevention of torture and other cruel, inhuman or degrading treatment or punishment. The SPT assists and advises the national preventive mechanisms about ways to strengthen safeguards relating to detention and reinforce their powers and independence.

The Optional Protocol was adopted by GA res. 57/199 (2002) and entered into force on 22 June 2006. As at 31 May 2012, there were 63 parties to the Optional Protocol.

Meetings

The SPT convenes three times a year in Geneva for one week. The 18th session is scheduled to be held from 12 to 16 November 2012.

Membership

The SPT originally had 10 members, increasing to 25 in 2011 following the 50th ratification of or accession to the Optional Protocol. Members are experts in the field and serve in their personal capacity. Consideration is given to equitable geographic distribution, representation of different social and legal systems, and gender balance. Members are elected by States Parties, generally serve for staggered four-year terms and can be re-elected once.

Term ending 31 December 2012	Term ending 31 December 2014
Mario Luis Coriolano, Argentina (Vice-Chair)	Mari Amos, Estonia
Marija Definis-Gojanovic, Croatia	Arman Danielyan, Armenia
Malcolm Evans, UK* (Chair)	Emilio Ginés Santidrián, Spain
Lowell Patria Goddard, New Zealand	Petros Michaelides, Cyprus
Zdenek Hajek, Czech Republic (Vice-Chair)	Aisha Shujune Muhammad, Maldives (Vice-Chair)
Suzanne Jabbour, Lebanon (Vice-Chair)	
Goran Klemencic, Slovenia	Olivier Obrecht, France
Paul Lam Shang Leen, Mauritius	Hans Draminsky Petersen, Denmark
Zbigniew Lasocik, Poland	Judith Salgado, Ecuador
Maria Margarida E Pressburger, Brazil	Miguel Sarre Iguíniz, Mexico
Christian Pross, Germany	Aneta Stancevska, the former Yugoslav Republic of Macedonia
Victor Manuel Rodriguez-Rescia, Costa Rica	
	Wilder Tayler-Souto, Uruguay
	Felipe Villavicencio Terreros, Peru
	Fortuné Gaétan Zongo, Burkina Faso

Note

* Replaced Silvia Casale, who resigned in June 2009.

Committee on the Elimination of Discrimination against Women (CEDAW)

Office of the UN High Commissioner for Human Rights
Palais Wilson
52 Rue des Pâquis
CH-1201 Geneva
Switzerland
Telephone: (+41 22) 917 9000
Fax: (+41 22) 917 9008
Email: cedaw@ohchr.org
Internet: www2.ohchr.org (follow links from 'Human rights bodies')
Chair: Silvia Pimentel, Brazil

Purpose

CEDAW is the body of independent experts that monitors implementation by States Parties to the Convention on the Elimination of All Forms of Discrimination against Women. The Convention is often described as an international bill of rights for women. It defines discrimination against women and outlines a comprehensive range of measures to end it. The Convention was adopted by GA res. 34/180 (1979) and entered into force on 3 September 1981.

The Committee considers States Parties' reports on the measures adopted and progress made in observance of the Convention. States Parties are obliged to submit a report within one year of the Convention's entry into force for the state concerned, then at least every four years (article 18).

As of 31 May 2012, there were 187 parties to the Convention.

Evolution

In January 2008, responsibility for servicing CEDAW was transferred from the Division for the Advancement of Women to the Office of the UN High Commissioner for Human Rights (OHCHR).

An Optional Protocol to the Convention was adopted by GA res. A/54/4 (1999) and entered into force on 22 December 2000. The Protocol contains two procedures:

- A communication procedure allows individuals or groups of individuals to submit claims of violations of rights protected under the Convention to CEDAW
- An inquiry procedure enables CEDAW to initiate inquiries into grave or systematic violations of the rights of women.

As of 31 May 2012, there were 104 parties to the Optional Protocol.

Meetings

The 53rd session is scheduled to be held from 1 to 19 October 2012 in Geneva; 54th in February 2013 in Geneva; and 55th in July 2013 in New York.

Membership

CEDAW consists of 23 experts in the fields covered by the Convention serving in their personal capacity (article 17). Consideration is given to equitable geographical distribution and the representation of different cultures, as well as the principal legal systems. Experts are elected by States Parties. Members usually serve staggered and renewable four-year terms.

Term ending 31 Dec 2012*	Term 1 Jan 2011 to 31 Dec 2014
Nicole Ameline, France (Vice-Chair)	Ayse Feride Acar, Turkey
Magalys Arocha Dominguez, Cuba	Olinda Bareiro-Bobadilla, Paraguay
Violet Tsisiga Awori, Kenya (Rapporteur)	Meriem Belmihoub-Zerdani, Algeria
Barbara Evelyn Bailey, Jamaica	Naela Mohamed Gabr, Egypt
Niklas Bruun, Finland	Ruth Halperin-Kaddari, Israel
Indira Jaising, India	Yoko Hayashi, Japan
Soledad Murillo de la Vega, Spain	Ismat Jahan, Bangladesh
Silvia Pimentel, Brazil (Chair)	Violeta Neubauer, Slovenia
Victoria Popescu, Romania (Vice-Chair)	Pramila Patten, Mauritius
Zohra Rasekh, Afghanistan (Vice-Chair)	Maria Helena Lopes de Jesus Pires, Timor-Leste
Zou Xiaoqiao, China	Patricia Schulz, Switzerland
	Dubravka Šimonović, Croatia

Note

* On 26 June 2012, States Parties to the Convention on the Elimination of all Forms of Discrimination against Women elected the following experts to serve on the Committee for the term 1 January 2013 to 31 December 2016: Noor Al Malki Al-Jehani, Qatar; Nicole Ameline, France; Barbara Bailey, Jamaica; Niklas Bruun, Finland; Hilary Gbedemah, Ghana; Nahla Haidar, Lebanon; Dalia Leinarte, Lithuania; Theodora Oby Nwankwo, Nigeria; Silvia Pimentel, Brazil; Bianca Pomeranzi, Italy; and Xiaoqiao Zou, China.

Committee on Economic, Social and Cultural Rights (CESCR)

Office of the UN High Commissioner for Human Rights
United Nations Office at Geneva
1211 Geneva 10
Switzerland
Telephone: (+41 22) 917 9000
Fax: (+41 22) 917 9008
Email: InfoDesk@ohchr.org or cescr@ohchr.org
Internet: www2.ohchr.org (follow links from 'Human rights bodies')
Secretariat: Maja Andrijasevic-Boko

Purpose

CESCR is the body of independent experts that monitors the implementation of the International Covenant on Economic, Social and Cultural Rights by its States Parties. The Covenant was adopted by GA res. 2200 A (1966) and entered into force on 3 January 1976. As at 31 May 2012, there were 160 parties to the Covenant.

The Committee considers States Parties' reports on the measures adopted and progress made in observance of the Covenant. States Parties are obliged to submit a report within two years of accepting the Covenant, then every five years.

While other core international human rights instruments have treaty bodies to examine States Parties' reports, the Covenant obliges States Parties to report to the Economic and Social Council (ECOSOC) on its implementation. ECOSOC res. 1988 (LX) (1976) laid down the procedures for this. The Committee's reports to ECOSOC include observations on each State Party's report, with a view to helping ECOSOC fulfil its responsibilities under articles 21 and 22 of the Covenant.

Evolution

The Committee was originally named the Sessional Working Group of Governmental Experts on the Implementation of the International Covenant on Economic, Social and Cultural Rights (ECOSOC decision 1978/10). ECOSOC res. 1985/17 renamed it CESCR.

Meetings

CESCR normally meets twice a year in Geneva. Its 49th session is scheduled to be held from 12 to 30 November 2012.

Membership

CESCR comprises 18 experts of recognised competence in human rights serving in their personal capacity, as listed on the next page. Consideration is given to equitable geographical distribution and representation of different social and legal systems. Committee members are elected by ECOSOC secret ballot from a list of people nominated by States Parties to the Covenant. Members generally serve staggered four-year terms and may be re-elected.

OTHER BODIES

Term ending 31 Dec 2012	Term ending 31 Dec 2014	Term beginning 1 Jan 2013 and ending 31 Dec 2016
Mohamed Ezzeldin Abdel-Moneim, Egypt	Aslan Khuseinovich Abashidze, Russian Federation	Egypt and Mauritius (African states)
Maria del Rocío Barahona Riera, Costa Rica	Clement Atangana, Cameroon	China and Jordan (Asia–Pacific states)
Jun Cong, China		
Zdzislaw Kedzia, Poland (Vice-Chair)	Chandrashekhar Dasgupta, India	Poland and Belarus (Eastern European states)
Sergei Martynov, Belarus	Azzouz Kerdoun, Algeria	Spain and Netherlands (Western European and Other states)
Ariranga Govindasamy Pillay, Mauritius (Chair)	Jaime Marchan Romero, Ecuador	
Waleed Sadi, Jordan (Rapporteur)	Renato Zerbini Ribeiro Leão, Brazil	Suriname (Latin American and Caribbean states)
Nikolaas Jan Schrijver, Netherlands (Vice-Chair)	Eibe Riedel, Germany	
	Heisoo Shin, ROK	
Philippe Texier, France	Alvaro Tirado Mejia, Colombia (Vice-Chair)	

Committee on the Elimination of Racial Discrimination (CERD)

Office of the UN High Commissioner for Human Rights
United Nations Office at Geneva
1211 Geneva 10
Switzerland
Telephone: (+41 22) 917 9193
Fax: (+41 22) 917 9008
Email: cerd@ohchr.org
Internet: www2.ohchr.org (follow links from 'Human rights bodies')
Chair: Alexei S Avtonomov, Russian Federation

Purpose

CERD is the body of independent experts that monitors implementation of the International Convention on the Elimination of All Forms of Racial Discrimination by its States Parties. The Convention entered into force on 4 January 1969 (GA res. 2106A (1965)). As of 31 May 2012, there were 175 parties to the Convention.

The Committee considers States Parties' reports on the measures adopted and progress made in observance of the Convention. States Parties are obliged to submit a report within one year of acceding to the Convention, then every two years.

Under article 14, a State Party may declare that it recognises the competence of the Committee to consider communications from individuals or groups of individuals within its jurisdiction who claim to be victims of a violation by that State Party of any of the rights set forth in the Convention. As of 31 May 2012, 54 States Parties had made a declaration under article 14.

The Committee reports annually to the General Assembly and may make suggestions and recommendations based on its examination of the reports and information provided by States Parties.

Evolution

GA res. 47/111 (1992) made an amendment to the Convention's fund provisions that will enter into force when it is accepted by two-thirds of States Parties to the Convention. As of 31 May 2012, 43 States Parties had accepted the amendment.

Meetings

The Committee normally meets twice a year in Geneva. The 81st session was scheduled for August 2012.

Membership

The Committee consists of 18 experts elected by States Parties, who serve in their personal capacity (article 8). Consideration is given to equitable geographical distribution and the representation of different cultures, as well as of the principal legal systems. Members generally serve staggered four-year terms and may be re-elected.

Term ending 19 Jan 2014

Noureddine Amir, Algeria (Vice-Chair)

Anastasia Crickley, Ireland (Rapporteur)

Kokou Mawuena Ika Kana (Dieudonnè) Ewomsan, Togo

Régis de Gouttes, France

Anwar Kemal, Pakistan

Gün Kut, Turkey

José Augusto Lindgren Alves, Brazil

Waliakoye Saidou, Niger

Patrick Thornberry, UK

Term ending 19 Jan 2016

Alexei S Avtonomov, Russian Federation (Chair)

José Francisco Cali Tzay, Guatemala (Vice-Chair)

Fatimata Binta Victoire Dah, Burkina Faso

Ion Diaconu, Romania

Yong'an Huang, China

Patricia Nozipho January-Bardill, South Africa

Dilip Lahiri, India (Vice-Chair)

Elias Murillo Martinez, Colombia

Carlos Manuel Vázquez, USA

Committee on the Protection of the Rights of All Migrant Workers and Members of Their Families (CMW)

Office of the UN High Commissioner for Human Rights
1211 Geneva 10
Switzerland
Telephone: (+41 22) 917 9301
Fax: (+41 22) 917 9008
Email: cmw@ohchr.org
Internet: www2.ohchr.org (follow links from 'Human rights bodies')
Chair: Abdelhamid El Jamri, Morocco (since 2008)

Purpose

CMW is the body of independent experts that monitors implementation of the International Convention on the Protection of the Rights of All Migrant Workers and Members of Their Families. The Convention was adopted by the General Assembly (GA res. 45/158) on 18 December 1990 and entered into force on 1 July 2003. As at 31 May 2012, there were 45 parties to the Convention.

The Committee considers States Parties' reports on the measures adopted and progress made in observance of the Convention. States Parties are obliged to submit a report within one year of acceding to the Convention, then every five years (article 74).

A State Party may declare that it recognises the competence of the Committee to receive and consider communications from or on behalf of individuals subject to its jurisdiction who claim their rights under the Convention have been violated by that State Party (article 77).

Meetings

The Committee meets three weeks a year: two weeks in spring and one week in autumn. The 16th session was held from 16 to 27 April 2012.

Membership

The CMW originally consisted of 10 experts, increasing to 14 on 1 January 2010, once the number of parties to the Convention had reached 40 (article 72). Members are experts in the field and serve in their personal capacity. Consideration is given to equitable geographical distribution, as well as representation of the principal legal systems. Members are usually elected for staggered four-year terms and may be re-elected.

Term ending 31 Dec 2013	Term ending 31 Dec 2015
José Serrano Brillantes, Philippines	Francisco Carrión Mena, Ecuador (Vice-Chair)
Fatoumata Abdourhamana Dicko, Mali	Ahmed Hassan El-Borai, Egypt
Miguel Ángel Ibarra Gonzalez, Guatemala	Abdelhamid El Jamri, Morocco (Chair)
Prasad Kariyawasam, Sri Lanka	Khedidja Ladjel, Algeria
Andrea Miller-Stennett, Jamaica	Marco Nuñez-Melgar Maguiña, Peru
Mehmet Sevim, Turkey	Myriam Poussi, Burkina Faso (Vice-Chair)
Ahmadou Tall, Senegal (Rapporteur)	Azad Taghizade, Azerbaijan (Vice-Chair)

Committee on the Rights of the Child (CRC)

Office of the UN High Commissioner for Human Rights
1211 Geneva 10
Switzerland
Telephone: (+41 22) 917 9141
Fax: (+41 22) 917 9008
Email: crc@ohchr.org
Internet: www2.ohchr.org (follow links from 'Human rights bodies')
Chair: Jean Zermatten, Switzerland (elected by the Committee in May 2011)

Purpose

The CRC is the body of independent experts that monitors implementation of the Convention on the Rights of the Child. It also monitors implementation of two optional protocols to the Convention – on the involvement of children in armed conflict, and on the sale of children, child prostitution and child pornography.

The Convention was adopted by the General Assembly (GA res. 44/25) on 20 November 1989 and entered into force on 2 September 1990. As at 31 May 2012, there were 193 parties to the Convention.

The CRC considers States Parties' reports on the measures adopted and progress made in observance of the Convention. States Parties are obliged to submit a report within two years of acceding to the Convention, then every five years (article 44).

Evolution

The Optional Protocol to the Convention on the involvement of children in armed conflict (OPAC) and the Optional Protocol to the Convention on the sale of children, child prostitution and child pornography (OPSC) were adopted by GA res. 54/263 (2000) and opened for signature and ratification or accession in New York on 5 June 2000. They entered into force on 12 February and 18 January 2002 respectively. As at 31 May 2012, there were 157 parties to the Optional Protocol on the sale of children and 147 parties to the Optional Protocol on children in armed conflict.

The Optional Protocol to the Convention on the Rights of the Child on a communications procedure (OPIC) was adopted by the UN General Assembly on 19 December 2011 (res. 66/138) and opened for signature on 28 February 2012. It establishes a communications procedure that would allow the CRC to receive and examine individual complaints from children and to organise country visits to investigate cases of grave and systematic violations of children's rights. This Optional Protocol will enter into force three months after the deposit of the 10th instrument of ratification or accession. As of 31 May 2012, there were 22 signatures but no parties.

Meetings

The Committee normally meets three times a year in Geneva. The 61st session is scheduled to be held from 17 September to 5 October 2012 and the 62nd from 14 January to 1 February 2013.

Membership

The CRC originally had 10 experts, increasing to 18 in 2002 (article 43 and GA res. 50/55 (1995)). Members are experts in the field and serve in their personal capacity. Consideration is given to equitable geographic distribution, as well as representation of the principal legal systems. Members generally serve staggered four-year terms and may be re-elected.

Term ending Feb 2013	Term ending Feb 2015
Hadeel Al-Asmar, Syrian AR	Agnes Akosua Aidoo, Ghana (Rapporteur)
Peter Guran, Slovakia	Aseil Al-Shehail, Saudi Arabia
Sanphasit Koompraphant, Thailand	Jorge Cardona Llorens, Spain
Yanghee Lee, ROK (Vice-Chair)	Bernard Gastaud, Monaco
Marta Mauras Perez, Chile (Vice-Chair)	Maria Herczog, Hungary
Pilar Nores, Peru	Hatem Kotrane, Tunisia (Vice-Chair)
Awich Pollar, Uganda	Gehad Madi, Egypt
Kamla Devi Varmah, Mauritius (Vice-Chair)	Kirsten Sandberg, Norway
Jean Zermatten, Switzerland (Chair)	Hiranthi Wijemanne, Sri Lanka

Committee on the Rights of Persons with Disabilities (CRPD)

Office of the UN High Commissioner for Human Rights
United Nations Office at Geneva
1211 Geneva 10
Switzerland
Telephone: (+41 22) 917 9000
Fax: (+41 22) 917 9022
Email: crpd@ohchr.org
Internet: www2.ohchr.org (follow links from 'Human rights bodies')
Chair: Ronald McCallum, Australia

Purpose

The CRPD is the body of independent experts that monitors implementation by States Parties to the Convention on the Rights of Persons with Disabilities. The Convention was adopted on 13 December 2006 (GA res. A/RES/61/106) and received its 20th ratification on 3 April 2008, triggering its entry into force on 3 May 2008. Its Optional Protocol entered into force on the same day, having received the necessary 10 ratifications.

The Committee considers States Parties' reports on the measures adopted and progress made in observance of the Convention. States Parties are obliged to submit a report within two years of accepting the Convention, then every four years (article 35).

The Committee is also mandated to receive and examine individual communications alleging violations of the Convention by States Parties that have become party to the Optional Protocol. In certain circumstances, the Committee may conduct an inquiry if it receives reliable evidence of grave and systematic violations of the Convention being carried out by a State Party to the Optional Protocol.

As of 31 May 2012, there were 112 parties to the Convention and 67 to the Optional Protocol.

Meetings

The Committee convenes for ordinary sessions twice a year in Geneva. Its eighth is scheduled to be held from 17 to 28 September 2012.

Membership

The CRPD originally had 12 members, increasing to 18 in 2010 following an additional 60 ratifications or accessions to the Convention (article 34). Members are experts in the field and serve in their personal capacity. Consideration is given to equitable geographic distribution, representation of different social and legal systems, gender balance and participation of experts with disabilities. Members generally serve staggered four-year terms and can be re-elected once.

Term ending 31 Dec 2012	Term ending 31 Dec 2014
Amna Ali Al Suweidi, Qatar	Theresia Degener, Germany
Mohammed Al-Tarawneh, Jordan	Hyung Shik Kim, ROK
Monsur Ahmed Choudhuri, Bangladesh	Lofti Ben Lallahom, Tunisia[2]
Maria Soledad Cisternas Reyes, Chile	Stig Langvad, Denmark
Gábor Gombos, Hungary[1]	Edah Wangechi Maina, Kenya[2]
Fatiha Hadj-Salah, Algeria[1]	Ronald McCallum, Australia[2]
Ana Peláez Narváez, Spain	Carlos Rios Espinosa, Mexico
Silvia Judith Quang-Chang, Guatemala[1]	Damjan Tatic, Serbia
Jia Yang, China	Germán Xavier Torres Correa, Ecuador[2]

Notes

1   Two-year term.

2   Re-elected for a four-year term.

Conference of States Parties to the Convention on the Rights of Persons with Disabilities

2 United Nations Plaza, Room DC2–1382
New York, NY 10017
United States of America
Telephone: (+1 212) 967 9587
Fax: (+1 917) 367 9587
Email: enable@un.org
Internet: www.un.org/disabilities (follow link from 'Convention')

Purpose

Under article 40 of the Convention on the Rights of Persons with Disabilities, the States Parties meet regularly to consider any matter with regard to implementation of the Convention. The Conference of States Parties was established when the Convention entered into force in 2008, and its first meeting took place in New York in the same year.

Structure

The Conference is made up of States Parties to the Convention. Other states and non-governmental organisations may also participate. The Bureau consists of one chair and four vice-chairs, and is elected for two years.

Meetings

Meetings can be convened by the Secretary-General biennially or by the Conference. The fifth session is scheduled to take place in New York from 12 to 14 September 2012.

Human Rights Committee

Office of the UN High Commissioner for Human Rights
1211 Geneva 10
Switzerland
Telephone: (+41 22) 917 9309
Fax: (+41 22) 917 9008
Email: ccpr@ohchr.org
Internet: www2.ohchr.org (follow links from 'Human rights bodies')
Chair: Zonke Zanele Majodina, South Africa

Purpose

The Human Rights Committee is the body of independent experts that monitors implementation by its States Parties of the International Covenant on Civil and Political Rights. The Covenant came into force on 23 March 1976 (GA res. 2200 A (1966)). As at 31 May 2012, there were 167 parties to the Covenant.

The Committee considers States Parties' reports on the measures adopted and progress made in observance of the Covenant. All States Parties are obliged to submit regular reports to the Committee on how the rights are being implemented. States Parties are obliged to submit a report within one year of acceding to the Convenant, then when the Committee requests (usually every four years).

The (First) Optional Protocol of the Covenant, which also came into effect on 23 March 1976, established the competence of the Committee to consider communications from individuals regarding alleged violations of their rights under the Covenant. As at 31 May 2012, there were 114 parties to the First Optional Protocol. The Second Optional Protocol, aimed at the abolition of the death penalty, entered into force on 11 July 1991 and, as at 31 May 2012, had 74 parties.

Meetings

The Committee normally meets three times a year. Usually there are two sessions in Geneva and one in New York. The 106th session is scheduled to be held from 15 October to 2 November 2012; 107th from 11 to 28 March 2013; and 108th in July 2013.

Membership

The Committee has 18 members who have recognised competence in human rights and serve in their personal capacity (article 28), as listed on the next page. Given the legal nature of the Committee's work, many of its members are lawyers, judges or professors of law. Consideration is given to equitable geographical distribution and representation of different social and legal systems. Members are elected by States Parties, generally serve staggered four-year terms and may be re-elected.

Term ending Dec 2012*	Term ending Dec 2014
Lazhari Bouzid, Algeria	Christine Chanet, France
Ahmed Amin Fathalla, Egypt	Cornelis Flinterman, Netherlands
Michael O'Flaherty, Ireland (Vice-Chair)	Yuji Iwasawa, Japan (Vice-Chair)
Rafael Rivas Posada, Colombia	Walter Kalin, Switzerland[3]
Nigel Rodley, UK	Zonke Zanele Majodina, South Africa (Chair)
Fabián Omar Salvioli, Argentina (Vice-Chair)	Iulia Antoanella Motoc, Romania
Marat Sarsembayev, Kazakhstan[1]	Gerald L Neuman, USA
Krister Thelin, Sweden	Margo Waterval, Suriname
Vacant[2]	Ben Achour Yadh, Tunisia[4]

Notes

1   Replaced Mahjoub El-Haiba, Morocco, who resigned.

2   Rajsoomer Lallah, Mauritius, died in June 2012.

3   Replaced Hellen Keller, Switzerland (Rapporteur), who resigned.

4   Replaced Abdelfattah Amor, Tunisia, who died in January 2012.

*   Elections were scheduled to be held on 6 September 2012 for the nine members whose terms expire on 31 December 2012 (including the late Rajsoomer Lallah).

UN Committee on Enforced Disappearances (CED)

Palais Wilson 52
Rue des Pâquis
CH-1201 Geneva
Switzerland
Telephone: (+41 22) 917 9395
Fax: (+41 22) 917 9008
Email: ced@ohchr.org
Internet: www2.ohchr.org (follow link 'Human rights bodies')
Chair: Emmanuel Decaux, France

Purpose

CED is the body of independent experts that monitors implementation by States Parties of the International Convention for the Protection of All Persons from Enforced Disappearance. All States Parties are obliged to submit an initial report to the Committee within two years of accepting the Convention. The Committee may request additional information.

In some circumstances, the Committee can consider requests that a disappeared person be sought as a matter of urgency (article 30) and request to visit a State Party (article 33). If the Committee receives well-founded information that a State Party practises enforced disappearance in a widespread or systematic basis, it may urgently bring the matter to the attention of the General Assembly (article 34).

A State Party may declare that it recognises the competence of the Committee to receive and consider communications from or on behalf of individuals subject to its jurisdiction claiming to be victims of a violation under the Convention (article 31).

The Convention was adopted on 20 December 2006 during the General Assembly's 61st session (res. A/RES/61/177). It opened for signature on 6 February 2007. The Convention entered into force on 23 December 2010, 30 days after 20 states had ratified or acceded to it (article 39(1)). As at 31 May 2012, there were 91 signatories and 32 parties.

Meetings

The first meeting of State Parties to the Convention was held on 31 May 2011 in New York to elect committee members. The Committee meets in Geneva, Switzerland, and holds two sessions a year. The third session is scheduled to be held from 29 October to 9 November 2012.

Members

CED consists of 10 experts of recognised competence in the field of human rights, serving in their personal capacity (article 26). Consideration is given to equitable geographical distribution, relevant legal experience and gender balance. Members are elected for four-year terms, except for the first election when half the terms expire after two years, and are eligible for re-election once.

Term ending 30 June 2013*	Term ending 30 June 2015
Mohammed Al-Obaidi, Iraq	Mamadou Badio Camara, Senegal
Luciano Hazan, Argentina	Emmanuel Decaux, France
Juan José López Ortega, Spain	Alvaro Garcé García Y Santos, Uruguay
Enoch Mulembe, Zambia	Rainer Huhle, Germany
Kimio Yakushiji, Japan	Suela Janina, Albania

Note

*   In accordance with article 26, paragraph 4, these members serve for two years, while the others serve for four years.

LAW OF THE SEA TREATY BODIES

Commission on the Limits of the Continental Shelf

Division for Ocean Affairs and the Law of the Sea
Office of Legal Affairs
United Nations
2 United Nations Plaza, Room DC2–0450
New York, NY 10017
United States of America
Telephone: (+1 212) 963 3194
Fax: (+1 212) 963 5847
Email: doalos@un.org
Internet: www.un.org/Depts/los/clcs_new/clcs_home.htm
Chair: Galo Carrera Hurtado, Mexico (since 2012)

Purpose

The Commission's purpose is to facilitate implementation of the UN Convention on the Law of the Sea (UNCLOS). It was established in accordance with UNCLOS Part VI and Annex II of 10 December 1982. The Commission's functions are to:

*   Consider data and other material submitted by coastal states concerning the outer limits of the continental shelf in areas where those limits extend beyond 200 nautical miles, and to make recommendations to coastal states on matters related to the establishment of the outer limits of their continental shelf, in accordance with article 76 and the Statement of Understanding adopted on 29 August 1980 by the Third UN Conference on the Law of the Sea

*   Provide scientific and technical advice if requested by coastal states during preparation of data concerning the outer limits of the continental shelf in areas where those limits extend beyond 200 nautical miles.

Meetings

The Commission ordinarily holds two sessions a year, in the northern hemisphere spring and autumn, in New York. Often these sessions are resumed to allow the subcommissions to continue examination of submissions. The 30th session was scheduled to be held from 30 July to 10 August 2012.

In June 2011, States Parties requested the Commission to consider that from June 2012 it, and its subcommissions meeting simultaneously as far as possible, meet in New York for up to 26 weeks but not less than an intended minimum of 21 weeks a year for a period of five years, and that no two sessions be sequential.

Membership

The Commission consists of 21 members who are experts in the field of geology, geophysics or hydrography. They are elected by States Parties to UNCLOS from among their nationals and serve in their personal capacities. No fewer than three members are elected from each geographical region. Members are elected for a term of five years, from June to June, and may be re-elected.

The following 20 members were elected in June 2012 for the 2012–17 term. One seat remained vacant.

African states

Lawrence Folajimi Awosika, Nigeria
Emmanuel Kalngui, Cameroon
Estevao Stefane Mahanjane, Mozambique
Simon Njuguna, Kenya
Isaac Owusu Oduro, Ghana

Asia–Pacific states

Muhammad Arshad, Pakistan
Lu Wenzheng, China
Mazlan Bin Madon, Malaysia
Yong Ahn Park, ROK
Sivaramakrishnan Rajan, India
Tetsuro Urabe, Japan

Eastern European states

Ivan F Glumov, Russian Federation
George Jaoshvili, Georgia

Latin American and Caribbean states

Galo Carrera, Mexico
Francis L Charles, Trinidad and Tobago
Jair Alberto Ribas Marques, Brazil
Carlos Marcelo Paterlini, Argentina

Western European and Other states

Richard Thomas Haworth, Canada/UK
Martin Vang Heinesen, Denmark
Walter R Roest, France

International Seabed Authority (ISA)

14–20 Port Royal Street
Kingston
Jamaica
Telephone: (+1876) 922 9105
Fax: (+1876) 922 0195
Email: postmaster@isa.org.jm
Internet: www.isa.org.jm
Secretary-General: Nii Allotey Odunton, Ghana (elected by the Assembly of the International Seabed Authority for 2009–12)

Purpose

The International Seabed Authority (ISA) is the organisation through which States Parties to UN Convention on the Law of the Sea (UNCLOS) organise and control activities in 'the Area' – the seabed and ocean floor beyond the limits of national jurisdiction.

It was established under Part XI of UNCLOS of 10 December 1982 and the Agreement relating to the Implementation of Part XI adopted by GA res. 48/263 (1994).

Structure

The Authority's principal organs are the Assembly, Council and Secretariat. The Authority has 161 members (160 states and the European Union), all parties to the Convention.

The Council comprises 36 Member States selected from five categories, ensuring representation of countries with the greatest global consumption; those that have made significant investment in seabed activities; those that produce and export minerals sourced from the seabed; those with special interests; and others, with due regard to equitable geographical distribution.

Meetings

Annual sessions are held in in Kingston, Jamaica. The 18th session was scheduled to be held from 9 to 27 July 2012.

Membership[1]

The members of the Council are listed below. Expiry dates for the four-year terms are shown in brackets, ending 31 December of the year shown.

Group A (4 members[2])

China (2012)	Japan (2012)	Russian Federation (2014)
Italy (2014)		

Group B (4 members[2])

France (2014)	India (2012)	ROK (2014)
Germany (2014)		

Group C (4 members)

Australia (2014)	Indonesia (2014)	South Africa (2012)
Canada (2012)		

Group D (6 members)

Bangladesh (2012)	Egypt (2014)	Jamaica (2014)
Brazil (2012)	Fiji (2014)	Sudan (2012)

Group E (18 members[1])

Angola (2012)	Kenya (2012)	Qatar (2014)
Argentina (2012)	Mexico (2014)	Senegal (2012)
Cameroon (2014)	Namibia (2012)	Spain (2012)
Chile (2014)	Netherlands (2012)	Trinidad and Tobago (2012)
Côte d'Ivoire (2014)	Nigeria (2014)	UK (2012)
Czech Republic (2012)	Poland (2012)	Viet Nam (2014)

Notes

1   The agreed allocation of seats on the Council is 10 seats to the African group, nine seats to the Asia–Pacific group, eight seats to the Western European and Others group, seven seats to the Latin American and Caribbean group and three seats to the Eastern European group. Since the total number of seats allocated according to that formula is 37, it is understood that each regional group other than the Eastern European group will relinquish in rotation one seat for one year during the first four-year period in order to conform to the requirement of 36 members of the Council under the Convention. The member whose seat is relinquished by its regional group will participate in the meetings of the Council but will not be entitled to vote on any matters.

2   The arrangements for Groups A and B are without prejudice to future elections for the two groups and any interim arrangements for the substitutions in those groups.

The 15 members of the Finance Committee, elected by the Assembly in 2011 for a five-year term that began on 1 January 2012 and ends on 31 December 2016, are:

Frida María Armas-Pfirter, Argentina

Zaw Minn Aung, Myanmar

Aleksey P Bakanov, Russian Federation

Pradip K Choudhary, India

Trecia Elliott, Jamaica

Francesca Graziani, Italy

Pavel Kavina, Czech Republic

Duncan M Laki, Uganda

Olav Myklebust, Norway

Serge Segura, France

Reinaldo Storani, Brazil

Chris Whomersley, UK

David C M Wilkens, Germany

Shinichi Yamanaka, Japan

Jinsong Yao, China

The 25 members of the Legal and Technical Commission, elected by the Council in 2011 for a five-year term that began on 1 January 2012 and ends on 31 December 2016, are:

Adesina Thompson Adegbie, Nigeria

Farhan M S Al-Farhan, Saudi Arabia

David Billet, UK

Harald Brekke, Norway

Winifred M Broadbelt, Netherlands

Aleksander Čičerov, Slovenia

Domenico Da Empoli, Italy

Laleta Davis-Mattis, Jamaica

Kaiser De Souza, Brazil

Elva Escobar, Mexico

Russell Howorth, Fiji

Kiseong Hyeong, ROK

Elie Jarmache, France

Emmanuel Kalngui, Cameroon

Denis Gennadyevich Khramov, Russian Federation

Eusebio Lopera, Spain

Pedro Madureira, Portugal

Hussein Mubarak, Egypt

Nobuyuki Okamoto, Japan

Mario Oyarzábal, Argentina

Andrzej Przybycin, Poland

Christian Reichert, Germany

Cristian Rodrigo, Chile

Maruthadu Sudhakar, India

Haiqi Zhang, China

International Tribunal for the Law of the Sea (ITLOS)

Am Internationalen Seegerichtshof 1
22609 Hamburg
Germany
Telephone: (+49 40) 35 607 0
Fax: (+49 40) 35 607 275
Email: itlos@itlos.org
Internet: www.itlos.org
Registrar: Philippe Gautier, Belgium (elected by the Tribunal for 2006–11; re-elected March 2011 for a further five-year term)

Purpose

The International Tribunal for the Law of the Sea (ITLOS) is an international court that deals with the peaceful settlement of disputes relating to use of the seas and oceans, and their resources. It was constituted in 1996 and functions in accordance with the relevant provisions of Part XV and Part XI, section 5, of the UN Convention on the Law of the Sea (UNCLOS) and its Statute, contained in Annex VI to the Convention.

The Tribunal deals with cases submitted to it in accordance with the Convention and all matters specifically provided for in any other international agreement that confers jurisdiction on the Tribunal. Cases may be submitted by or against States Parties to the Convention, and (in relation to cases concerning 'the Area' – the seabed and ocean floor beyond the limits of national jurisdiction – or submitted pursuant to other agreements) by other states, international organisations and entities other than states, including natural or juridical persons.

The Tribunal's budget, as well as contributions by States Parties and the International Seabed Authority, is decided by the Meeting of States Parties to UNCLOS.

Structure

The Tribunal has compulsory jurisdiction to deal with requests for the prompt release of vessels and crew submitted by or on behalf of a vessel's flag state. It may prescribe provisional measures (interim injunction) to preserve the rights of the parties to a dispute or to prevent serious harm to the marine environment in the relevant circumstances.

The Tribunal's Seabed Disputes Chamber, composed of 11 elected members of the Tribunal, has certain compulsory jurisdiction with respect to disputes arising out of the exploitation and exploration of the Area. The Chamber gives advisory opinions on legal questions arising within the scope of its activities, at the request of the Assembly or the International Seabed Authority Council.

Membership

The Tribunal comprises 21 independent members (judges), elected from among persons enjoying the highest reputation for fairness and integrity, and of recognised competence in the law of the sea. The Tribunal Statute requires equitable geographical distribution and representation of the world's principal legal systems. There must be no fewer than three members from each geographical group and no two judges may be of the same nationality.

The members are elected for nine years and may be re-elected. Every three years the terms of office of one-third of the 21 members expire. Elections to replace seven of the Tribunal's members were most recently held during the 21st Meeting of States Parties to UNCLOS in June 2011, with terms beginning on 1 October 2011. Members of the Tribunal, whose terms end on 30 September of the year shown, are:

Shunji Yanai, Japan (President[1])	2014
Albert Hoffmann, South Africa (Vice-President[1])	2014
Vicente Marotta Rangel, Brazil	2017
L Dolliver M Nelson, Grenada	2014
P Chandrasekhara Rao, India	2017
Joseph Akl, Lebanon	2017
Rüdiger Wolfrum, Germany	2017
Tafsir Malick Ndiaye, Senegal	2020
José Luis Jesus, Cape Verde	2017
Jean-Pierre Cot, France	2020
Anthony Amos Lucky, Trinidad and Tobago	2020
Stanislaw Pawlak, Poland	2014
Helmut Tüerk, Austria	2014
James L Kateka, UR of Tanzania	2014
Zhiguo Gao, China	2020
Boualem Bouguetaia, Algeria	2017
Vladimir Vladimirovich Golitsyn, Russian Federation (President of the Seabed Disputes Chamber[1])	2017

continued next page

Notes

1 On 11 October 2011, Judge Yanai was elected President; Judge Hoffmann Vice-President; and Judge Golitsyn President of the Seabed Disputes Chamber.

2 Judge Paik was elected on 6 March 2009 by a special meeting of States Parties to fill the vacancy created by the death of Judge Choon-Ho Park (ROK).

ENVIRONMENTAL BODIES

Intergovernmental Panel on Climate Change (IPCC)

C/O World Meteorological Organization
7 bis Avenue de la Paix
Case Postale 2300
1211 Geneva 2
Switzerland
Telephone: (+41 22) 730 8208/54/84
Fax: (+41 22) 730 8025
Email: ipcc-sec@wmo.int
Internet: www.ipcc.ch
Secretary: Renate Christ, Austria (appointed by the WMO Secretary-General, in consultation with the Executive Director of UNEP, in 2004)

Purpose

The Intergovernmental Panel on Climate Change (IPCC) is a scientific body that was established in 1988 by the UN Environment Programme (UNEP) and the World Meteorological Organization (WMO) to:

- Assess available information on the science, impacts and economics of climate change, and on the response options available to address it
- Assess, and develop as needed, methodologies such as the IPCC Guidelines for National Greenhouse Gas Inventories
- Provide, on request, scientific, technical and socio-economic advice to the Conference of the Parties to the UN Framework Convention on Climate Change (UNFCCC) and its bodies.

The IPCC does not conduct research nor does it monitor climate-related data or parameters. Thousands of scientists from all over the world contribute voluntarily to the IPCC's work.

Evolution

Since its inception, the IPCC has produced four multi-volume Assessment Reports. The First, in 1990, confirmed the scientific basis for concern about climate change. The Second, in 1995, concluded that the balance of evidence suggested a discernible human influence on the global climate. The Third, in 2001, concluded that there was new evidence that most of the warming observed over the previous 50 years was attributable to human activities. The Fourth Assessment Report (AR4), in 2007, led to the IPCC, jointly with former USA Vice-President Al Gore, being awarded the 2007 Nobel Peace Prize. The IPCC is currently working on its Fifth Assessment Report (AR5), which is scheduled to be finalised in 2013–14.

The IPCC also publishes Special Reports and Methodology Reports, often in response to a request from parties to the UNFCCC. Two Special Reports were released in 2011, 'Renewable Energy Sources and Climate Change Mitigation' (SRREN) and 'Managing the Risks of Extreme Events and Disasters to Advance Climate Change Adaptation' (SREX).

Structure

The IPCC has 195 member countries. All UN and WMO Member States are members. The Panel has three working groups:
- Working Group I (WG I) assesses the physical scientific aspects of the climate system and climate change
- Working Group II (WG II) assesses the vulnerability of natural and socio-economic systems to climate change and its observed and projected effects on them, along with adaptation options
- Working Group III (WG III) assesses options for mitigating climate change through limiting or preventing greenhouse gas emissions and enhancing activities that remove them from the atmosphere.

The Task Force on National Greenhouse Gas Inventories (TFI) develops methodology and software for the calculation and reporting of national greenhouse gas (GHG) emissions and removals.

The Panel makes decisions at its plenary sessions and is assisted by the Bureau.

Meetings

The 35th session was held from 6 to 9 June 2012 in Geneva, Switzerland.

Membership

Bureau members are elected for the duration of the preparation of an IPCC assessment report (five to six years). The 31 members are (as of May 2012):

Chair
Rajendra Pachauri, India

Vice-Chairs

Ismail A R El Gizouli, Sudan	Hoesung Lee, ROK	Jean Pascal Van Ypersele, Belgium

Working Group Co-Chairs

Vicente Barros, Argentina	Taka Hiraishi, Japan[1]	Dahe Qin, China
Ottmar Edenhofer, Germany	Thelma Krug, Brazil[1]	Youba Sokona, Mali
Christopher Field, USA	Ramon Pichs-Madruga, Cuba	Thomas Stocker, Switzerland

Working Group Vice-Chairs

Amjad Abdulla, Maldives	Abdalah Mokssit, Morocco	Jim Skea, UK
Eduardo Calvo Buendia, Peru	Jose M Moreno, Spain	Neville Smith, Australia
Carlo Carraro, Italy	Fatemeh Rahimzadeh, Iran	Fredolin T Tangang, Malaysia
Antonina Ivanova Boncheva, Mexico	Nirivololona Raholijao, Madagascar	David Wratt, New Zealand
Jean Jouzel, France	Sergey Semenov, Russian Federation	Francis D Yamba, Zambia
Suzana Kahn Ribeiro, Brazil		Taha Zatari, Saudi Arabia
		Francis Zwiers, Canada

Bureau of the Task Force on National Greenhouse Gas Inventories

Co-Chairs

Taka Hiraishi, Japan[1]   Thelma Krug, Brazil[1]

Members

Rizaldi Boer, Indonesia

Leonidas O Girardin, Argentina

William N Irving, USA

Art Jaques, Canada

Sergio Gonzalez Martineaux, Chile

Enmanuel Mpeta, UR of Tanzania

Jim Penman, UK

Detelina Petrova, Bulgaria/ Sadeddin Kherfan, Syrian AR[2]

Robert Sturgiss, Australia/ Leonard J Brown, New Zealand[3]

Sirintornthep Towprayoon, Thailand

Washington Zhakata, Zimbabwe

Zhou Lingxi, China

Notes

1   The Task Force on National Greenhouse Gas Inventories Co-Chairs are members of the IPCC Bureau.

2   There is agreement between Bulgaria and the Syrian Arab Republic to split the term to allow each Task Force Bureau member to serve three consecutive years.

3   There is agreement between Australia and New Zealand to split the term to allow each Task Force Bureau member to serve three consecutive years.

Secretariat for the Vienna Convention for the Protection of the Ozone Layer and the Montreal Protocol on Substances that Deplete the Ozone Layer (the Ozone Secretariat)

PO Box 30552
United Nations Avenue, Gigiri
Nairobi 00100
Kenya
Telephone: (+254 20) 762 3851/3611
Email: ozoneinfo@unep.org
Internet: http://ozone.unep.org
Executive Secretary: Marco González, Costa Rica (appointed by the UN Secretary-General, in consultation with the UNEP Executive Director, in 2002)

Purpose

The Ozone Secretariat services the Vienna Convention for the Protection of the Ozone Layer (the Vienna Convention) and the Montreal Protocol on Substances that Deplete the Ozone Layer (the Montreal Protocol), and their subsidiary bodies. The Secretariat was formally established on a permanent basis in 1991. Its duties are defined under article 7 of the Vienna Convention and article 12 of the Montreal Protocol.

The objective of the Convention and Protocol is the total elimination of all substances that deplete the ozone layer, as listed under the Protocol, on the basis of developments in scientific knowledge, taking into account technical and economic considerations and bearing in mind the developmental needs of developing countries.

Over the past 20 years, implementation of the Convention and Protocol has led to the phasing out of the production and consumption of about 98 percent of historic levels of ozone-depleting substances (ODSs). The remaining 2 percent is scheduled to be phased out by 2030. Because most ozone depleting substances are potent global warming gasses, the Montreal Protocol has achieved important climate co-benefits.

From 1990–2010, implementation of the Montreal Protocol has avoided greenhouse gas emissions by an estimated carbon dioxide-equivalent of a net 135 gigatons.

Evolution

In 2009, the Convention and Protocol became the first treaties in the history of the UN to achieve universal ratification, with 197 parties including the European Union. The Montreal Protocol has been amended four times, in London (1990), Copenhagen (1992), Montreal (1997) and Beijing (1999), with each amendment requiring separate ratification by parties. The Secretariat is striving to achieve universal ratification of all amendments to the Protocol. As of 31 May 2012, 177 parties had ratified all the amendments.

Meetings

The Conference of the Parties to the Vienna Convention usually meets every three years (most recently in November 2011). Parties to the Montreal Protocol usually meet annually. The 24th meeting is scheduled to be held in Geneva in November 2012.

Secretariat of the Basel Convention on the Control of Transboundary Movements of Hazardous Wastes and their Disposal (SBC)

International Environment House
13–15 Chemin des Anémones
1219 Châtelaine, Geneva
Switzerland
Telephone: (+41 22) 917 8218
Fax: (+41 22) 797 3454
Email: sbc@unep.org
Internet: www.basel.int; http://synergies.pops.int
Executive Secretary of the Basel, Rotterdam and Stockholm Conventions: Jim Willis, USA (appointed by the UN Secretary-General in April 2011)

Purpose

The Secretariat services the Basel Convention on the Control of Transboundary Movements of Hazardous Wastes and their Disposal, which was adopted at Basel in March 1989 and entered into force in May 1992. As at 31 May 2012, there were 179 parties (178 States Parties and the European Union) to the Convention.

The main goal of the Convention is to protect human health and the environment from the adverse effects that may result from handling, transporting and disposing of hazardous and other wastes. To achieve this, the Convention pursues four objectives:
- Reducing transboundary movements of hazardous wastes to a minimum consistent with their environmentally sound management (ESM)
- Treating and disposing of such wastes as close as possible to their source of generation
- Promoting the environmentally sound management of hazardous wastes
- Minimising the generation of hazardous wastes.

Evolution

A decision containing an Amendment to the Basel Convention (Ban Amendment) was adopted during the third meeting of the Conference of the Parties (COP3) in Geneva in September 1995. The objective of this Amendment, which will enter into force when it has been ratified by three-quarters of the parties that have accepted it, is to prohibit all transboundary movements of hazardous wastes from State Parties and other states that are

Evolution

The Convention was amended at the first meeting of the Conference of the Parties (COP) to add a new Annex G on arbitration and conciliation procedures.

The Convention text has also been amended on two occasions to add new POPs to the original 12. In 2009, the COP decided to add nine new POPs and, in 2011, added a further one, endosulfan. Countries that become parties to the Stockholm Convention following the adoption of these amendments are bound to the whole of the Convention as amended.

Structure

The Convention provides for a Conference of the Parties, the Convention's governing body, and a secretariat administered by the UN Environment Programme (UNEP). A subsidiary body to the COP is the Persistent Organic Pollutants Review Committee, which is responsible for assessing whether additional POPs should be made subject to the Convention.

A single integrated secretariat to serve the Basel, Rotterdam and Stockholm Conventions was proposed in 2011. Joint managerial functions will be reviewed by each COP in 2013 (see http://synergies.pops.int).

Meetings

COP meetings take place every two years. The sixth COP meeting is tentatively scheduled to be held between 29 April and 10 May 2013 in Geneva, Switzerland.

Secretariat of the Convention on Biological Diversity (CBD)

World Trade Centre
413 Saint Jacques Street, Suite 800
Montreal, Quebec
Canada H2Y 1N9
Telephone: (+1 514) 288 2220
Fax: (+1 514) 288 6588
Email: secretariat@cbd.int
Internet: www.cbd.int
Executive Secretary: Braulio Ferreira de Souza Dias, Brazil (appointed by the UN Secretary-General on 20 January 2012)

Purpose

The Secretariat services the Convention on Biological Diversity, which provides a global legal framework for action on biodiversity. The Convention opened for signature at the Earth Summit in Rio de Janeiro in June 1992 and entered into force on 29 December 1993. As at 31 May 2012, there were 193 parties to the Convention.

The Convention has three objectives:
- Conserving biological diversity
- Ensuring the sustainable use of the components of biological diversity
- Ensuring the fair and equitable sharing of the benefits arising from the utilisation of genetic resources.

Evolution

In January 2000, the Conference of the Parties (COP) adopted the Cartagena Protocol on Biosafety to the Convention on Biological Diversity. The Protocol seeks to protect biological diversity from the potential risks posed by living modified organisms resulting from modern biotechnology. As at 31 May 2012, there were 163 parties to the Cartagena Protocol.

In October 2010, the COP adopted the Nagoya Protocol on Access to Genetic Resources and the Fair and Equitable Sharing of Benefits Arising from their Utilization to the Convention on Biological Diversity. It will enter into force on the 90th day after deposit of the 50th instrument of ratification, acceptance, approval or accession by states or regional economic integration organisations that are parties to the Convention. As at 31 May 2012, five parties to the Convention had deposited their instrument of ratification (Gabon, Jordan, Mexico, Rwanda and Seychelles).

Also in October 2010, at the fifth meeting of the COP, serving as the Meeting of the Parties to the Cartagena Protocol on Biosafety (COP-MOP 5), the parties to the Cartagena Protocol adopted the Nagoya – Kuala Lumpur Supplementary Protocol on Liability and Redress to the Cartagena Protocol on Biosafety. It will enter into force on the 90th day after the date of deposit of the 40th instrument of ratification, acceptance, approval or accession by states or regional economic integration organisations that are parties to the Protocol. As at 31 May 2012, two parties had deposited their instrument of ratification (Czech Republic and Latvia).

Structure

The Secretariat was established by article 24 of the Convention and is administered by UNEP. It also serves as the Secretariat to the Cartagena Protocol on Biosafety (and supplementary Protocol on Liability and Redress) and the Nagoya Protocol on Access and Benefit Sharing.

The Convention's governing body is the COP. It is assisted by the Subsidiary Body on Scientific, Technical, and Technological Advice (SBSTTA), which is made up of government representatives with expertise in relevant fields, as well as observers from non-party governments, the scientific community and relevant organisations.

Ad hoc open-ended working groups, which are open to all parties and observers, have been established to make recommendations to the COP on specific issues. Current groups are:
- Working Group on Access and Benefit-Sharing (ABS) – currently the forum for negotiating an international regime on access and benefit sharing
- Working Group on Article 8(j) – addresses issues related to protection of traditional knowledge
- Working Group on the Review of Implementation of the Convention (WGRI) – examines the implementation of the Convention, including national biodiversity strategies and action plans.

The COP and SBSTTA may also establish expert groups or call for the Secretariat to organise liaison groups, workshops and other meetings.

A clearing-house mechanism was established under article 18.3 of the Convention to promote and facilitate technical and scientific cooperation.

Article 21 established a mechanism for providing financial resources to developing countries for the purposes of the Convention. The Global Environment Facility (GEF) acts as that financial mechanism.

The COP to the Convention serves as the meeting of the parties and governing body for the Cartagena Protocol (COP-MOP).

Meetings

The COP meets every two years or as needed. The 11th meeting is scheduled to be held in Hyderabad, India, from 8 to 19 October 2012. The sixth meeting of the COP serving as the meeting of the parties to the Cartagena Protocol (COP-MOP) is scheduled to be held in Hyderabad, India, from 1 to 5 October 2012.

Secretariat of the UN Convention to Combat Desertification in Countries Experiencing Serious Drought and/or Desertification, particularly in Africa (UNCCD)

UNCCD Secretariat
Hermann-Ehlers-Strasse 10
53113 Bonn
Germany
Telephone: (+49 228) 815 2800
Fax: (+49 228) 815 2898/99
Email: secretariat@unccd.int
Internet: www.unccd.int
Executive Secretary: Luc Gnacadja, Benin (appointed by the UN Secretary-General in 2007)

Purpose

The UN Convention to Combat Desertification in Countries Experiencing Serious Drought and/or Desertification, particularly in Africa (UNCCD) pursues long-term, integrated strategies that focus on improving land productivity and rehabilitation, conservation, and sustainable management of land and water resources, with a view to achieving sustainable development in affected areas. As recognised by the World Summit on Sustainable Development, the Convention plays a key role in efforts to reach the Millennium Development Goals (MDGs), particularly with regard to the eradication of extreme poverty and hunger.

The Convention was established by GA res. 47/188 (1992), adopted in June 1994 and entered into force in December 1996. The UNCCD Permanent Secretariat was established in article 23 of the Convention.

Under a 10-year Strategic Plan and Framework to enhance the implementation of the Convention for 2008–18, adopted at the eighth Conference of the Parties (COP) in Madrid, Spain (2007), the UNCCD aims to forge a global partnership to reverse and prevent desertification/land degradation and to mitigate the effects of drought in order to support poverty reduction and environmental sustainability. The Strategic Plan and Framework supports the development and implementation of national and regional policies, programmes and measures to prevent, control and reverse desertification/land degradation; and to mitigate the effects of drought through scientific and technological excellence, raising public awareness, standard-setting, advocacy and resource mobilisation.

As of May 2012, there were 195 parties to the Convention.

Structure

- Permanent Secretariat
- Conference of the Parties (COP)
- Committee for the Review of the Implementation of the Convention (CRIC)
- Committee on Science and Technology (CST)
- Global Mechanism (GM)

The Permanent Secretariat was established in 1999 and, in conformity with decision five of the first COP, was relocated to headquarters in Bonn. The Secretariat services the COP and subsidiary bodies such as the CST and CRIC, and facilitates the implementation of national, regional and sub-regional programmes.

The COP is the supreme governing body of the UNCCD and the Permanent Secretariat is accountable to it.

The following bodies established by the UNCCD are accountable to the COP:
- The GM promotes actions leading to the mobilisation and channelling of substantial financial resources, including for the transfer of technology, on a grant basis, and/or on concessional or other terms, to affected developing country parties.
- The CST provides the COP with information and advice on scientific and technological matters relating to combating desertification and mitigating the effects of drought
- The CRIC, established by COP5, reviews and analyses national reports submitted to the COP that describe the status of the Convention's implementation by parties.

Since 2003, the Global Environment Facility (GEF) has served as a financial mechanism to the Convention. To strengthen the implementation of the Convention, an Operational Programme on Sustainable Land Management is being implemented by the GEF and its implementing agencies. Since May 2010, all eligible countries have had access to GEF resources to enable implementation of activities under the UNCCD.

Meetings
The COP has met every two years since 2001. The 11th COP is scheduled to be held in the 2013 northern hemisphere autumn.

Secretariat of the Convention on International Trade in Endangered Species of Wild Fauna and Flora (CITES)

International Environment House
15 Chemin des Anémones
1219 Châtelaine, Geneva
Switzerland
Telephone: (+41 0) 22 917 8139/40
Fax: (+41 0) 22 797 3417
Email: info@cites.org
Internet: www.cites.org
Secretary-General: John Scanlon, Australia (appointed by the Executive Director of UNEP in May 2010)

Purpose
The Secretariat services the Convention on International Trade in Endangered Species of Wild Fauna and Flora (CITES), which is an international agreement between governments that seeks to ensure international trade in specimens of wild animals and plants does not threaten their survival.

CITES provides a three-tier licensing framework to control the trade in specimens of selected species covered by the Convention and to which Member States voluntarily adhere. Members must adopt their own domestic legislation to ensure that CITES is implemented at the national level. The species covered by CITES are listed in three appendices according to the degree of protection they need. Appendix I includes species threatened with extinction. Trade in specimens of these species is permitted only in exceptional circumstances. Appendix II includes species not necessarily threatened with extinction but in which trade must be controlled in order to avoid utilisation incompatible with their survival. Appendix III contains species that are protected in at least one country that has asked other CITES parties for assistance in controlling the trade.

Evolution

The Convention was adopted in March 1973 and entered into force in July 1975. As of May 2012, 175 countries had joined the Convention, which covers more than 30,000 animal and plant species.

Structure

The Convention is governed by the Conference of the Parties (COP) and serviced by a standing committee and secretariat. Two further committees, the Animals and Plants Committees, comprise scientists and provide technical support to decision making about species that are, or might become, subject to CITES trade controls.

Meetings

The 15th meeting of the COP was held in Doha, Qatar, from 13 to 25 March 2010. COP16 is scheduled to be held in Thailand in 2013.

Secretariat of the UN Framework Convention on Climate Change (UNFCCC)

UNFCCC Secretariat
PO Box 260124
53153 Bonn
Germany
Telephone: (+49 228) 815 1000
Fax: (+49 228) 815 1999
Email: secretariat@unfccc.int
Internet: www.unfccc.int
Executive Secretary: Christiana Figueres, Costa Rica (appointed by the UN Secretary-General in May 2010)

Purpose

The UN Framework Convention on Climate Change (UNFCCC) opened for signature at the Earth Summit (UN Conference on Environment and Development) in Rio de Janeiro in June 1992. It entered into force in March 1994. As at 31 May 2012, there were 195 parties to the Convention.

The ultimate objectives of the Convention and related legal instruments are to:
- Stabilise greenhouse gas concentrations in the atmosphere at a level that will prevent dangerous human interference with the climate system, and within a timeframe sufficient to allow ecosystems to adapt naturally to climate change
- Ensure that food production is not threatened
- Enable economic development to proceed in a sustainable manner.

The Secretariat supports all institutions involved in international climate change negotiations, particularly the Conference of the Parties (COP), the COP serving as the Meeting of the Parties to the Kyoto Protocol (CMP), the subsidiary bodies (which advise the COP and the CMP) and the Bureau (which deals mainly with procedural and organisational issues arising from the COP, the CMP and the subsidiary bodies, and also has technical functions).

Structure

The UNFCCC COP is the supreme body of the Convention and serves as the CMP. The CMP is the supreme body of the Kyoto Protocol.

There are subsidiary bodies for implementation and for scientific and technological advice, and two ad hoc working groups on further commitments for Annex I parties under the Kyoto Protocol and long-term cooperative action under the Convention. At the first Conference of the Parties (COP1) session, held in Berlin in April 1995, it was decided that the Secretariat to service all bodies established by the COP would be based in Bonn and institutionally linked to the UN, but not fully integrated in any department or programme.

Evolution and meetings

COP1 agreed that the Convention commitments were inadequate for meeting its objectives. In a decision known as the Berlin Mandate, the parties agreed to establish a process to negotiate strengthened commitments for developed countries. The result of these negotiations, the Kyoto Protocol, was adopted by consensus at COP3 in Kyoto in December 1997.

The Protocol includes legally binding emission targets for developed country (Annex I) parties for the six major greenhouse gases. It entered into force on 16 February 2005, after it had been adhered to by 55 parties to the Convention. Its first commitment period was scheduled to end in December 2012. As at 31 May 2012, there were 192 parties[1] to the Kyoto Protocol.

COP13 was held in conjunction with the third Meeting of the Parties to the Kyoto Protocol in Bali in December 2007. Parties agreed to launch negotiations towards an agreed outcome that would strengthen the international climate change regime. These negotiations remain ongoing.

COP17 was held from 28 November to 9 December 2011, in Durban, South Africa. The outcomes included a decision by parties to adopt a universal legal agreement on climate change as soon as possible, and no later than 2015.

COP18 is scheduled to be held from 26 November to 7 December 2012 in Qatar.

Note

1   In accordance with article 27 (2) of the Kyoto Protocol to the UN Framework Convention on Climate Change, the Government of Canada notified the Secretary-General that it had decided to withdraw from the Kyoto Protocol as from 15 December 2012.

UNEP/CMS Secretariat of the Convention on the Conservation of Migratory Species of Wild Animals (CMS or Bonn Convention)

UNEP/CMS Secretariat
Hermann-Ehlers-Strasse 10
53113 Bonn
Germany
Telephone: (+49 228) 815 2426
Fax: (+49 228) 815 2449
Email: cms@cms.int
Internet: www.cms.int
Officer in Charge: Lambertus Lenten, Netherlands (a new Executive Secretary was being recruited in 2012)

Purpose

The CMS or Bonn Convention originated in Recommendation 32 of the 1972 UN Conference on the Human Environment. The Convention was concluded in 1979 and entered into force on 1 November 1983. As of 1 June 2012, there were 117 parties to the Convention.

The objective of the Convention is to conserve migratory species and their habitat by:
- Providing strict protection measures for migratory species listed as endangered in Appendix I
- Concluding multilateral agreements for the conservation and management of migratory species listed in Appendix II (such as water birds, terrestrial and marine mammals, reptiles and bats) that have an unfavourable conservation status or would benefit significantly from international cooperation
- Undertaking joint research and monitoring activities.

The Secretariat, under the auspices of the UN Environment Programme (UNEP), provides administrative support to the Convention.

Structure

The Convention is governed by the Conference of the Parties (COP). A standing committee provides policy and administrative guidance between regular meetings of the COP. A scientific council gives advice on scientific matters.

Meetings

The COP meets every three years. COP11 is scheduled to be held in 2014. The Standing Committee meets at least annually and the Scientific Council meets at least once and normally twice every three years.

Secretariat of the Convention on Wetlands (Ramsar Convention)

Rue Mauverney 28
1196 Gland
Switzerland
Telephone: (+41 22) 999 0170
Fax: (+41 22) 999 0169
Email: ramsar@ramsar.org
Internet: www.ramsar.org
Secretary General: Anada Tiéga, Niger (appointed by the Ramsar Convention Standing Committee in 2007)

Purpose

The Secretariat services the Convention on Wetlands, often referred to as the Ramsar Convention, which was adopted in Ramsar, Iran, in February 1971 and entered into force on 21 December 1975.

The Convention provides a framework for national action and international cooperation for the conservation and sustainable use of wetlands and their resources. To accede to the Convention, potential contracting parties (or Member States) must designate at least one wetland for inclusion in the Ramsar List of Wetlands of International Importance. Contracting parties are also expected to manage all wetlands within their territories, in accordance with the principles of sustainable use, and to engage in international cooperation to further the Convention's objectives.

Structure

The Convention is governed by the Conference of the Parties (COP). The Secretariat carries out the day-to-day coordination of the Convention's activities, including preparing for and servicing meetings of the COP, Standing Committee and relevant subsidiary bodies.

The Standing Committee runs for a three-year term and is the inter-sessional executive body that represents the COP between meetings. A new committee was to be elected at COP11 in July 2012, with the term running from 2012 to 2015. The Committee consists of 16 elected contracting parties as regional representatives, as well as the host countries of the previous and forthcoming COPs. It meets annually (most recently in Romania in July 2012) to supervise the implementation of the Convention and work of the Secretariat.

A subsidiary body, the Scientific and Technical Review Panel (STRP), advises the Standing Committee and COP on technical issues. The STRP comprises six independent experts from each of the Convention's regions, as well as experts in thematic areas of work and representatives of the Convention's five International Organisation Partners (IOPs) – BirdLife International, International Union for Conservation of Nature (IUCN), International Water Management Institute (IWMI), Wetlands International, and WWF International (World Wide Fund for Nature).

As of May 2012, the Convention's 160 contracting parties have designated more than 2000 Ramsar Sites onto the Ramsar List of Wetlands of International Importance. These cover almost 200 million hectares.

Meetings

The Conference of the Parties meets every three years. COP11 was held in Bucharest, Romania, in July 2012.

Global Environment Facility (GEF)

1818 H Street NW
Washington DC 20433
United States of America
Telephone: (+1 202) 473 0508
Fax: (+1 202) 522 3240
Email: gef@thegef.org
Internet: www.thegef.org
Chief Executive Officer: Naoko Ishii of Japan (appointed by the GEF Council, on the recommendation of the Implementing Agencies, in June 2012 to take up the position on 1 August 2012)

Purpose

The Global Environment Facility (GEF) provides grants and concessional funding to eligible countries for projects and programmes that protect the global environment and promote sustainable development. It is the designated financial mechanism for the UN Framework Convention on Climate Change, the Convention on Biological Diversity, the Stockholm Convention on Persistent Organic Pollutants and the Convention to Combat Desertification.

The GEF funds the agreed incremental costs of activities that benefit the global environment in six focal areas:
- Biological diversity
- Climate change
- International waters
- The ozone layer
- Persistent organic pollutants
- Land degradation.

OTHER BODIES

Originally set up as a pilot programme in 1991, the GEF has been restructured and undergone several replenishment rounds. The GEF-5 replenishment is expected to fund operations and activities from 1 July 2010 to 30 June 2014.

GEF funds come from participant countries. Co-financing for particular projects comes from bilaterals, governments hosting projects, non-governmental organisations and the private sector.

Structure
- Council
- Assembly
- Scientific and Technical Advisory Panel (STAP)

The Council, the main governing body, comprises 32 members, of which 16 represent developing countries, 14 developed countries and two economies in transition. The Assembly, which meets every four years, consists of representatives of all participating countries. The STAP provides expert advice to the GEF.

GEF projects and programmes are managed through three implementing agencies: the UN Development Programme (UNDP), the UN Environment Programme (UNEP) and the World Bank. Seven other specialised UN agencies and regional development banks also administer GEF projects:
- Food and Agriculture Organization (FAO)
- UN Industrial Development Organization (UNIDO)
- International Fund for Agricultural Development (IFAD)
- African Development Bank (AfDB)
- Asian Development Bank (ADB)
- European Bank for Reconstruction and Development (EBRD)
- Inter-American Development Bank (IDB).

The GEF Secretariat, which is independent of the three implementing agencies, reports to and serves the GEF Council and Assembly.

Meetings
The GEF Assembly meets every three or four years. The fourth meeting was in Punta del Este, Uruguay, in May 2010. The fifth is likely to be held in 2014.

Membership
As of May 2012, the GEF had 182 participating countries. Countries may be eligible for GEF funds if:
- They are eligible for financial assistance through the Climate Change Convention, the Convention on Biological Diversity or the Stockholm Convention on Persistent Organic Pollutants
- They are eligible to borrow from the World Bank (International Bank for Reconstruction and Development and/or International Development Association) or receive technical assistance grants from UNDP through a country programme.

A country must be a party to the Climate Change Convention, the Convention on Biological Diversity, the Stockholm Convention on Persistent Organic Pollutants or the Convention to Combat Desertification to receive funds from the GEF in the relevant focal area.

Member countries and date of entry into the GEF:

Afghanistan	7 Apr 1994	Djibouti	24 May 1994
Albania	6 May 1994	Dominica	8 Jun 1994
Algeria	13 May 1994	Dominican Republic	21 Apr 1994
Angola	29 Oct 2009	Ecuador	23 Jun 1994
Antigua and Barbuda	29 Mar 1994	Egypt	8 Jun 1994
Argentina	12 May 1994	El Salvador	20 May 1994
Armenia	16 Jun 1994	Equatorial Guinea	20 Jun 2003
Australia	27 Jun 1994	Eritrea	27 Dec 1995
Austria	21 Jun 1994	Estonia	12 May 1994
Azerbaijan	24 Jul 1995	Ethiopia	27 Oct 1994
Bahamas	19 Apr 1994	Fiji	10 May 1994
Bangladesh	22 Jun 1994	Finland	9 Jun 1994
Barbados	13 May 1994	France	20 Jun 1994
Belarus	30 Mar 1994	Gabon	20 Mar 1998
Belgium	30 Jan 1995	Gambia	16 Aug 1994
Belize	29 Apr 1994	Georgia	8 Jul 1994
Benin	29 Jun 1994	Germany	23 Jun 1994
Bhutan	12 Dec 1995	Ghana	16 Jan 1997
Bolivia	17 Jun 1994	Greece	11 May 1994
Bosnia and Herzegovina	29 Oct 2001	Grenada	20 Apr 1994
Botswana	12 Jul 1994	Guatemala	20 May 1994
Brazil	13 Jun 1994	Guinea	17 Oct 1994
Bulgaria	22 Mar 1994	Guinea-Bissau	2 May 1995
Burkina Faso	24 Aug 1994	Guyana	12 May 1994
Burundi	30 Mar 1998	Haiti	10 May 1994
Cambodia	31 Jan 1995	Honduras	6 Sep 1994
Cameroon	31 Oct 1994	Hungary	22 Jun 1994
Canada	6 Jul 1994	India	12 May 1994
Cape Verde	18 Jul 1994	Indonesia	29 Jun 1994
Central African Republic	23 Mar 1995	Iran	25 May 1994
Chad	27 Jul 1994	Iraq	3 Feb 2010
Chile	1 Jul 1994	Ireland	14 Jun 1994
China	16 May 1994	Israel	19 Mar 1995
Colombia	28 Jun 1994	Italy	28 Jun 1994
Comoros	5 Sep 1995	Jamaica	29 Jun 1994
Congo	22 Sep 1995	Japan	27 Jun 1994
Cook Islands	6 May 1994	Jordan	10 May 1994
Costa Rica	19 May 1994	Kazakhstan	30 Mar 1998
Côte d'Ivoire	24 Jun 1994	Kenya	25 May 1994
Croatia	4 Mar 1994	Kiribati	10 May 1994
Cuba	4 Apr 1994	Kosovo	11 Mar 2010
Czech Republic	30 Jun 1994	Kuwait	5 Jun 2010
DPRK	6 May 1994	Kyrgyzstan	9 Jan 1997
DR Congo	6 Feb 1997	Lao PDR	2 Aug 1994
Denmark	9 Jun 1994	Latvia	27 Jun 1994

Lebanon	21 Jul 1994
Lesotho	29 Jun 1994
Liberia	5 Dec 2000
Libya	13 Dec 1994
Lithuania	13 May 1994
Luxembourg	28 Apr 1995
Madagascar	14 Jul 1994
Malawi	23 Feb 1996
Malaysia	4 May 1994
Maldives	25 Aug 1994
Mali	4 Jul 1994
Malta	27 Jul 1994
Marshall Islands	15 Apr 1994
Mauritania	8 May 1994
Mauritius	4 Jul 1994
Mexico	17 May 1994
Micronesia	26 Apr 1994
Mongolia	14 Apr 1994
Montenegro	25 Aug 2006
Morocco	29 Jun 1994
Mozambique	27 Dec 1995
Myanmar	13 May 1994
Namibia	30 Apr 2001
Nauru	5 May 1994
Nepal	10 Aug 1994
Netherlands	20 Jun 1994
New Zealand	18 May 1994
Nicaragua	19 May 1994
Niger	23 Aug 1994
Nigeria	12 Jul 1994
Niue	4 May 1994
Norway	1 Jul 1994
Pakistan	8 Apr 1994
Palau	12 Oct 1998
Panama	7 Apr 1994
Papua New Guinea	6 May 1994
Paraguay	15 Feb 1995
Peru	14 Jun 1994
Philippines	16 Jun 1994
Poland	18 Apr 1994
Portugal	17 Jun 1994
ROK	3 May 1994
Republic of Moldova	27 Oct 1995
Romania	29 Jul 1994
Russian Federation	23 Jun 1994
Rwanda	11 Jun 2002
Saint Kitts and Nevis	25 Jul 1994

Saint Lucia	31 Mar 1994
Saint Vincent and the Grenadines	4 May 1994
Samoa	28 Mar 1994
Sao Tome and Principe	7 Jun 2002
Senegal	7 Apr 1994
Serbia	16 Sep 2001
Seychelles	20 Sep 2001
Sierra Leone	6 Sep 1994
Slovakia	1 Nov 1994
Slovenia	12 Jul 1994
Solomon Islands	16 Apr 1994
Somalia	11 Apr 2007
South Africa	6 Jul 1994
Spain	9 Jun 1994
Sri Lanka	26 May 1994
Sudan	14 Jun 1994
Suriname	12 May 1994
Swaziland	16 May 1994
Sweden	28 Jun 1994
Switzerland	1 Jul 1994
Syrian AR	15 Apr 1996
Tajikistan	1 Oct 1999
Thailand	30 Jun 1994
The former Yugoslav Republic of Macedonia	7 Jul 1994
Timor-Leste	6 Oct 2003
Togo	21 Jul 1994
Tonga	4 May 1994
Trinidad and Tobago	19 May 1994
Tunisia	13 May 1994
Turkey	6 Jul 1994
Turkmenistan	29 May 1997
Tuvalu	3 May 1994
Uganda	28 Jun 1994
Ukraine	15 Jun 1994
UK	13 Jun 1994
UR of Tanzania	26 Mar 1996
USA	24 Jun 1994
Uruguay	22 Apr 1994
Uzbekistan	5 Apr 1995
Vanuatu	19 May 1994
Venezuela	1 Jul 1994
Viet Nam	12 May 1994
Yemen	30 Mar 1994
Zambia	13 Jun 1994
Zimbabwe	7 Jul 1994

SPECIALISED AGENCIES AND OTHER RELATED BODIES

SPECIALISED AGENCIES

International Labour Organization (ILO)

4 Route des Morillons
1211 Geneva 22
Switzerland
Telephone: (+41 22) 799 6111
Fax: (+41 22) 798 8685
Email: ilo@ilo.org
Internet: www.ilo.org
Director-General: Guy Ryder, UK (elected by the Governing Body for a five-year term beginning October 2012)

Purpose

The International Labour Organization (ILO) is responsible for drawing up and overseeing international labour standards. It was founded in 1919, its Constitution forming part of the Treaty of Versailles. In 1946, it became the first specialised agency of the UN.

The ILO is the only 'tripartite' UN agency. It brings together representatives of governments, employers and workers to jointly shape policies and programmes about employment and work. The Organization is devoted to advancing opportunities for women and men to obtain decent and productive work in conditions of freedom, equity, security and human dignity. Its main aims are to:

- Promote rights at work
- Encourage decent employment opportunities
- Enhance social protection
- Strengthen dialogue in handling work-related issues.

In promoting social justice and internationally recognised human and labour rights, the Organization continues to pursue its founding mission that labour peace is essential to prosperity. Today, the ILO helps advance the creation of decent jobs and the kinds of economic and working conditions that give working and business people a stake in lasting peace, prosperity and progress.

Structure

- International Labour Conference
- Governing Body
- International Labour Office

The International Labour Conference meets each year to adopt and oversee compliance with international labour standards, establish the Organization's budget and elect Governing Body members. Since 1919, the Conference has served as a major international forum for debate on social and labour questions of worldwide importance.

The Governing Body is the executive body of the International Labour Office (the ILO's Permanent Secretariat). It meets three times a year (March, June and November) and takes decisions on ILO policy, the International Labour Conference agenda and the Organization's draft programme and budget for submission to the Conference, and elects the Director-General.

The International Labour Office is the focal point of ILO activities, which are carried out under the scrutiny of the Governing Body and leadership of the Director-General. The Office employs more than 2500 people in Geneva and 40 field offices around the world.

Meetings

The International Labour Conference is held in Geneva, Switzerland, in June each year.

Membership

Each of the ILO's 183 Member States has the right to send four delegates to the Conference: two from government and one each representing workers and employers, each of whom may speak and vote independently.

The ILO Governing Body has 56 titular members (28 governments, 14 employers and 14 workers) and 66 deputy members (28 governments, 19 employers and 19 workers). Ten of the titular government seats are permanently held by states of chief industrial importance (Brazil, China, France, Germany, India, Italy, Japan, the Russian Federation, UK and USA). The other government members are elected by the Conference every three years (most recently on 6 June 2011). The employer and worker members are elected in their individual capacity.

The following list of ILO members includes their previous and current terms of office on the Governing Body.

	Previous membership[1]	Current membership[1]
Afghanistan		
Albania		
Algeria[2]	1969–72 81–87 1996–2002	2011–14
Angola[2]	1978–87	2011–14
Antigua and Barbuda	1987–90	
Argentina	1969–99 2002–11	2011–14
Armenia		
Australia	1972–96 2005–11	2011–14
Austria	1975–78 84–87 96–99 2008–11	
Azerbaijan		
Bahamas	2002–05	
Bahrain	1981–84	
Bangladesh	1978–84 87–93 1996–2011	
Barbados	1981–84 2002–11	
Belarus	1987–93 2002–08	
Belgium	1969–72 81–84 90–93 2002–11	
Belize		
Benin	1972–75 84–90 1999–2011	
Bolivia	1972–75 84–87 90–93	
Bosnia and Herzegovina		
Botswana[2]	1984–90	2011–14
Brazil[3]		2011–14
Brunei Darussalam		
Bulgaria[2]	1969–75 81–84 90–93 1999–2005 08–11	2011–14
Burkina Faso	1969–72 84–87 1999–2002	
Burundi	1975–78 84–90 2002–11	
Cambodia[2]	2005–11	2011–14
Cameroon	1975–81 87–93 2002–08	
Canada	1969–81 1984–2011	2011–14

	Previous membership[1]	Current membership[1]
Cape Verde		
Central African Republic	1969–72 96–99	
Chad	1999–2002	
Chile	1969–72 1993–2002 05–08	
China[3]		2011–14
Colombia	1969–84 87–90 1996–2002	2011–14
Comoros		
Congo	1969–72 90–99 2008–11	2011–14
Costa Rica[2]	1990–93 96–99	2011–14
Côte d'Ivoire	1978–81 96–99 2005–08	
Croatia	1996–2002	
Cuba[2]	1975–78 81–90 1993–2002 05–11	2011–14
Cyprus[2]	1984–87 1999–2002	2011–14
Czech Republic	1993–96 2005–11	
DR Congo	1975–78	
Denmark	1969–72 82–84 90–93 1999–2002	2011–14
Djibouti	1984–87	
Dominica		
Dominican Republic	1999–2002 02–05	
Ecuador	1969–75 81–84 87–90 2002–05	
Egypt	1978–84 93–99 2008–11	2011–14
El Salvador	1999–2011	2011–14
Equatorial Guinea		
Eritrea		
Estonia		
Ethiopia	1981–87 1996–2008	
Fiji		
Finland	1972–75 84–87 96–99 2005–08	
France[3]		2011–14
Gabon	1972–75 78–81 93–96 1999–2005	
Gambia		
Georgia		
Germany[3]		2011–14
Ghana[2]	1972–75 81–87 93–96 1999–2005 08–11	2011–14
Greece	1975–78 87–90 2005–08	
Grenada		
Guatemala	1999–2002	
Guinea	1975–78 87–90 96–99 2008–11	
Guinea-Bissau		
Guyana	1978–81	
Haiti		
Honduras	1975–81 90–93 2005–08	
Hungary	1975–78 81–87 93–99 2005–11	2011–14
Iceland		
India[3]		2011–14
Indonesia[2]	1969–78 81–87 1990–2005	2011–14
Iran	1969–81 84–90 1993–2011	2011–14
Iraq	1984–87	
Ireland	1972–75 90–93 2005–08	
Israel		
Italy[3]		2011–14
Jamaica	1972–75 84–87	
Japan[3]		2011–14

	Previous membership[1]	Current membership[1]
Jordan	1972–75 96–99 2002–11	
Kazakhstan[2]		2011–14
Kenya[2]	1969–72 78–84 90–96 2002–11	2011–14
Kiribati		
Kuwait	1975–78 87–90 2005–08	
Kyrgyzstan		
Lao PDR		
Latvia		
Lebanon[2]	1978–81 2008–11	2011–14
Lesotho	1988–93	
Liberia	1975–78	
Libya	1984–90 1999–2005	
Lithuania	1999–2005 08–11	2011–14
Luxembourg	2002–05	
Madagascar	1972–75 81–84 90–93	
Malawi	1990–93 2002–08	
Malaysia	1987–90 1996–2002	
Mali	1981–84 93–96 2002–05	
Maldives		
Malta[2]	1978–81 90–93	2011–14
Marshall Islands		
Mauritania	1972–75	
Mauritius	1975–78 93–99	
Mexico[2]	1972–87 1990–2011	2011–14
Mongolia	1981–87 96–99	
Montenegro		
Morocco	1972–75 87–93 2002–08	
Mozambique	1978–84 2005–11	
Myanmar	1981–84	
Namibia	1996–2002	
Nepal		
Netherlands[2]	1981–84 93–96 1999–2002 05–08	2011–14
New Zealand	1990–96 1999–2005	
Nicaragua	1978–81 84–90 93–96	
Niger	1978–81 90–96 2002–05	2011–14
Nigeria	1969–72 78–84 90–93 1996–2011	
Norway	1975–78 84–87 93–96 2002–05	
Oman	2002–05	
Pakistan[2]	1969–72 75–81 84–87 1990–2011	2011–14
Panama[2]	1972–78 81–84 93–99 2008–11	2011–14
Papua New Guinea		
Paraguay		
Peru	1978–81 90–93 1996–2002 05–11	
Philippines	1978–84 1990–2008	
Poland	1972–78 93–99 2005–11	
Portugal	1981–84 93–96 1999–2002 08–11	
Qatar	1993–96 2008–11	2011–14
ROK[2]	1996–2011	2011–14
Republic of Moldova		
Romania[2]	1969–72 75–81 90–96 2002–08	2011–14
Russian Federation[3]		2011–14
Rwanda	1972–75	
Saint Kitts and Nevis		

	Previous membership[1]	Current membership[1]
Saint Lucia		
Saint Vincent and the Grenadines		
Samoa		
San Marino		
Sao Tome and Principe	1984–87	
Saudi Arabia	1996–2008	
Senegal	1981–84 96–99 2005–08	
Serbia		
Seychelles		
Sierra Leone	1975–81	
Singapore	2002–11	
Slovakia	1996–2002	
Slovenia	2002–05	
Solomon Islands		
Somalia	1969–72 75–78 87–90	
South Africa	1996–2011	
Spain	1972–75 78–81 84–87 93–99 2008–11	
Sri Lanka[2]	1972–78 87–90 2005–08	2011–14
Sudan[2]	1969–72 75–78 93–96 1999–2005 08–11	2011–14
Suriname	1996–99	
Swaziland	1993–99	
Sweden	1978–81 87–90 96–99 2008–11	
Switzerland[2]	1978–81 87–90 1999–2002	2011–14
Syrian AR	1969–72 96–99	
Tajikistan		
Thailand[2]	1975–81 84–90 1996–2002 08–11	2011–14
The former Yugoslav Republic of Macedonia	1975–81 84–90	
Timor-Leste		
Togo	1975–78 90–93	2011–14
Trinidad and Tobago	1975–78 1999–2002 05–08	2011–14
Tunisia	1975–81 90–96 2005–11	
Turkey	1975–78 87–90 96–99 2002–05	
Turkmenistan		
Tuvalu		
Uganda	1969–75 87–90 96–99 2005–08	
Ukraine	1972–75 81–87 1996–2002	
UAE[2]	1990–93 1999–2002	2011–14
UK[3]		2011–14
UR of Tanzania	1975–78 87–90 1999–2002 08–11	2011–14
USA[3]		2011–14
Uruguay[2]	1969–72 78–84 87–96 2002–05 08–11	2011–14
Uzbekistan		
Vanuatu		
Venezuela[2]	1969–72 75–96 1999–2011	2011–14
Viet Nam	1969–72 2002–11	2011–14
Yemen	1999–2002	
Zambia	1972–75 78–81 2008–11	2011–14
Zimbabwe[2]	1981–87 93–96	2011–14

Notes

1   Includes elected regular and deputy members.

2   Elected deputy members.

continued next page

OTHER BODIES

3   Members holding non-elective seats as 'states of chief industrial importance'.

Czechoslovakia served on the Governing Body 1969–72, 1978–81 and 1984–92.

The former Socialist Federal Republic of Yugoslavia served on the ILO Governing Body from 1975–81 and 1984–90. It was not automatically succeeded by any of the new states created following its dissolution.

Workers' Group members for 2011–14

Regular members

N Adyanthaya, India	S Fox, USA	H Kelly, New Zealand
K Asamoah, Ghana	J Gómez Esguerra, Colombia	T Sakurada, Japan
B Byers, Canada	S Gurney, UK	M Shmakov, Russian Federation
L Cortebeeck, Belgium	G Jiang, China	
R Diallo, Guinea	H Kaddous, Algeria	M Sommer, Germany

Deputy members

F Atwoli, Kenya	B Hossu, Romania	R Silaban, Indonesia
I Carcamo, Honduras	A Hussain, Bahrain	S Siwela, Zimbabwe
R de Leeuw, Belgium	G Martinez, Argentina	N Souza da Silva, Brazil
C Del Rio, Italy	M Nizamani, Pakistan	T L Sundnes, Norway
F Djondang, Chad	B Ntshalintshali, South Africa	Y Veyrier, France
E Familia, Dominican Republic	B Pandey, Nepal	A Wolanska, Poland
M Francisco, Angola		

Employers' Group members for 2011–14

Regular members

S Allam, Egypt	E Julien, France	J Mugo, Kenya
P Anderson, Australia	D Lima-Godoy, Brazil	J Rønnest, Denmark
D Funes de Rioja, Argentina	H Matsui, Japan	C Syder, UK
R Goldberg, USA	K Mattar, UAE	L Traore, Mali
R Hornung-Draus, Germany	Y Modi, India	

Deputy members

O M S Alrayes, Bahrain	A Jeetun, Mauritius	K Rahman, Bangladesh
K de Meester, Belgium	J Lacasa Aso, Spain	A Savané, Guinea
J A de Regil, Mexico	H Liu, China	A Urtecho Lopez, Honduras
D Djimanto, Indonesia	M Mdwaba, South Africa	F Welzijn, Suriname
A Echavarría Saldarriaga, Colombia	M Megateli, Algeria	P Woolford, Canada
A Frimpong, Ghana	M Moskvina, Russian Federation	A Yuma, DR Congo
L Horvatic, Croatia		

Food and Agriculture Organization (FAO)

Viale delle Terme di Caracalla
00153 Rome
Italy
Telephone: (+39 06) 57051
Fax: (+39 06) 570 53152
Email: FAO-HQ@fao.org
Internet: www.fao.org
Director-General: José Graziano da Silva, Brazil (elected in June 2011 to serve from 1 January 2012 to 31 July 2015, renewable for one four-year term)

Purpose

The Food and Agriculture Organization's (FAO's) mandate is to raise levels of nutrition, improve agricultural productivity, better the lives of rural populations and contribute to the growth of the world economy.

Evolution

The FAO was established in 1945, when 44 governments accepted the Constitution as drafted by an interim commission. The functions and assets of the former International Institute of Agriculture in Rome were transferred to the new body. By GA res. 50/227 (1996), the FAO and the World Food Programme absorbed the functions of the World Food Council, which was discontinued.

Structure

- Governing bodies: Conference, Council, Programme Committee, Finance Committee, Committee on Constitutional and Legal Matters, and Regional Conferences
- Technical Committees: Committee on Commodity Problems, Committee on Fisheries, Committee on Forestry, Committee on Agriculture, Committee on World Food Security
- Other inter-governmental bodies
- Secretariat

The Conference is the Organization's sovereign governing body and comprises all members and associate members. Representatives of members meet at the biennial FAO Conference to review global governance policy issues and international frameworks, as well as to evaluate work carried out and approve the budget for the next biennium. The Conference elects 49 Council members to serve three-year staggered terms to carry out executive oversight of programme and budgetary activities. The Director-General is elected at the Conference, for a four-year term, renewable once. The next Director-General election will take place in June 2015. The Independent Chair of the Council is also appointed by the Conference, for a two-year term, renewable once. As of May 2012, the Chair is Luc Guyau, France (appointed November 2009 and reappointed mid-2011).

Meetings

The Conference meets in regular session every two years. The 38th Conference session is scheduled to be held in Rome from 15 to 22 June 2013. The Council normally meets at least five times between the two-yearly Conference sessions. All sessions are held in Rome.

Membership

FAO has 191 member nations, two associate members (the Faroe Islands and Tokelau) and one member organisation (the European Union).

The following list shows members and their terms of office on the FAO Council. For the purpose of Council elections, FAO membership is divided into seven regional groups, each with a fixed number of seats. The 2011–13 terms run from 1 January 2011 to the end of the 38th session of the Conference in June 2013 (except for Côte d'Ivoire, for which the term began 1 July 2011); 2011–14 from 1 December 2011 to 30 June 2014; 2012–15 from 1 July 2012 to 30 June 2015.

For membership details about the Council's three elected committees concerned with particular aspects of management (Programme Committee, Finance Committee, and Committee on Constitutional and Legal Matters), see www.fao.org/unfao/govbodies/gsbhome/gsb-home/en/ (or follow the 'FAO Governance' link on the FAO home page www.fao.org).

	Previous membership	Current membership*
Africa (48 members, 12 seats)		
Algeria	1978–80 87–89 95–98 2005–07	2011–14
Angola	1981–83 89–94 2003–06	
Benin	1973–75 83–85	
Botswana	1979–81	
Burkina Faso	1969–72 81–84 93–96 1999–2004	
Burundi	1975–77 85–92	
Cameroon	1961–63 79–82 85–92 1995–2003 05–07	2011–14
Cape Verde	1981–84 91–96 2005–07	2011–13
Central African Republic	1967–70	
Chad	1965–67 77–80	
Comoros		
Congo	1973–76 81–86 89–98 2003–06 07–10	2012–15
Côte d'Ivoire	1979–82 91–93 2003–08	2011–13
DR Congo	1971–73 77–80 87–89 93–95	
Equatorial Guinea		2011–13
Eritrea	1997–2000 05–07	2012–15
Ethiopia	1965–70 73–75 81–84 89–91 1999–2002 07–09	
Gabon	1973–77 1987–2004 07–12	2012–15
Gambia	1975–77 83–89	
Ghana	1959–62 77–81 89–92 95–98 2001–04 09–11	
Guinea	1973–76 87–90	2011–14
Guinea-Bissau	1977–79	
Kenya	1965–68 71–74 81–83 87–93 2001–03 07–10	
Lesotho	1973–75 81–84 87–90 1999–2002	
Liberia	1953–56 77–80 85–90	
Madagascar	1961–64 79–81 87–95 1999–2001 05–08	
Malawi	1975–78 83–85	
Mali	1967–69 2005–07	
Mauritania	1997–2002 09–11	
Mauritius	1975–78 95–98 2003–05 09–12	
Morocco	1959–65 71–74 81–83 89–92 1999–2001 07–10	
Mozambique	2009–12	
Namibia	1997–2000	
Niger	1975–78 85–88 2007–10	
Nigeria	1963–65 69–71 81–83 87–90 93–95 1999–2001 03–08	
Rwanda	1977–79 83–85 92–94	
Sao Tome and Principe	1983–86	
Senegal	1963–66 79–81 85–87 1997–2002 07–10	
Seychelles		
Sierra Leone	1983–86	

	Previous membership	Current membership*
South Africa	1947–59 97–99 2007–09	
Swaziland	1993–96 2003–05	
Togo	1971–73	2011–14
Tunisia	1965–68 75–77 83–86 93–95 2001–04	2011–13
Uganda	1967–68 83–86 93–99 2003–06	2011–13
UR of Tanzania	1969–72 77–80 85–87 91–97 2001–04 09–11	
Zambia	1969–71 79–82 85–88 91–93 2005–08	
Zimbabwe	1985–87 95–97 2001–03 09–11	

Asia (23 members, 9 seats)

	Previous membership	Current membership*
Bangladesh	1977–88 1991–2000 03–09	2012–15
Bhutan		
Cambodia		
China	1947–48 1973–2012	2012–15
DPRK		
India	1947–2008 09–11	2011–14
Indonesia	1955–64 1967–2000 03–08 09–11	2011–14
Japan	1953–61 1965–2012	2012–15
Kazakhstan		
Lao PDR		
Malaysia	1965–67 79–91 93–97 1999–2002 07–09	
Maldives		
Mongolia		
Myanmar	1949–52	
Nepal	1967–70	
Pakistan	1949–55 57–93 1997–2008 09–11	2011–14
Philippines	1947–49 53–58 61–64 67–79 81–93 2001–06 09–12	2012–15
ROK	1965–67 1989–2012	2012–15
Sri Lanka	1961–64 71–81 93–96 2001–03 09–12	
Thailand	1973–2012	2012–15
Timor-Leste		
Uzbekistan		
Viet Nam		

Europe (48 members, 10 seats)

	Previous membership	Current membership*
Albania		
Andorra		
Armenia	2003–06	
Austria	1961–64 83–86 1999–2001	
Azerbaijan		
Belarus		
Belgium	1949–52 55–58 61–64 69–71 77–80 93–95 2007–10	
Bosnia and Herzegovina		
Bulgaria	1973–80 83–86 2001–04	
Croatia		
Cyprus	1983–85 91–94 2001–03	
Czech Republic	2001–03	
Denmark	1947–51 61–63 73–75 85–87 97–99	2011–14
Estonia	1995–97	
European Union (member organisation)[1]		
Faroe Islands (associate member)[2]		
Finland	1951–54 63–66 75–78 87–90 2003–05	
France	1947–2008 09–11	2011–14

	Previous membership	Current membership*
Georgia		
Germany	1959–61 1965–2012	2012–15
Greece	1965–67 77–79 89–91 1997–2000	2011–13
Hungary	1971–74 77–80 87–89 91–94 1999–2001	
Iceland	1999–2002	
Ireland	1961–64 81–83 1995–2002	2011–13
Israel	1967–68	
Italy	1947–65 1971–2008 09–11	2011–14
Latvia		
Lithuania		
Luxembourg		
Malta	1977–80 2005–07	
Monaco		
Montenegro		
Netherlands	1947–49 53–55 59–61 75–77 89–92 2005–07	
Norway	1957–60 69–72 81–84 93–96 2009–11	
Poland	1965–67 69–71 81–83 89–92 1997–2000	2011–14
Portugal	1979–82 89–92 95–98 2001–04	2012–15
Republic of Moldova	2007–09	
Romania	1967–73 81–83 95–98 2003–06	
Russian Federation	2007–10	2011–13
San Marino		
Serbia		
Slovakia	1993–95 2009–12	
Slovenia	2005–07	
Spain	1953–58 75–77 83–85 87–89 93–95 1999–2001 09–12	
Sweden	1953–57 67–69 79–81 91–93 2005–08	
Switzerland	1953–57 71–74 87–89 2001–04	
The former Yugoslav Republic of Macedonia		
Turkey	1955–58 67–70 85–88 95–97 2007–10	
Ukraine	2007–09	
UK	1947–55 1957–2008 09–11	2012–15

Latin America and Caribbean (33 members, 9 seats)

	Previous membership	Current membership*
Antigua and Barbuda		
Argentina	1953–58 61–67 1971–2000	2011–13
Bahamas		
Barbados	1981–83 1995–2004	
Belize		
Bolivia	2001–10	
Brazil	1947–53 1957–2010	2011–13
Chile	1947–56 59–64 67–75 1995–2012	2012–15
Colombia	1953–61 65–95	
Costa Rica	1955–57 63–71 91–93	
Cuba	1947–49 51–54 57–63 1977–2010	2011–13
Dominica		
Dominican Republic		
Ecuador	1975–78 81–87	2011–14
El Salvador	1979–81 2005–08 09–11	2012–15
Grenada		
Guatemala	1999–2005	
Guyana		
Haiti		

	Previous membership	Current membership*
Honduras	1993–99	
Jamaica	1977–80	
Mexico	1947–51 57–62 1973–2010	2011–13
Nicaragua	1985–91	
Panama	1963–65 73–85 2003–09	
Paraguay	1999–2001	
Peru	1965–76 87–90 2001–06	
Saint Kitts and Nevis		
Saint Lucia		
Saint Vincent and the Grenadines		
Suriname		
Trinidad and Tobago	1975–77 83–95 2005–10	2011–13
Uruguay	1953–56 67–70 95–97 2007–12	
Venezuela	1949–52 63–66 71–75 1977–2000 09–12	2012–15

Near East (21 members, 6 seats)

Afghanistan	1965–71 77–83 85–87 2009–11	2011–14
Bahrain		
Djibouti		
Egypt	1947–63 1967–2008 09–11	2011–14
Iran	1957–65 71–74 87–90 1995–2009	2011–13
Iraq	1953–56 69–71 77–91	
Jordan	1963–66 75–77 2009–12	2012–15
Kuwait	1973–75 79–81 1995–2001 07–10	
Kyrgyzstan		
Lebanon	1953–56 59–65 75–79 81–98 2005–08	
Libya	1975–78 87–95 2001–04	
Oman	2005–07	
Qatar	1999–2004	
Saudi Arabia	1969–72 1979–2008 09–11	2011–14
Somalia	1967–69	
Sudan	1965–68 73–78 81–84 91–93 2007–10	
Syrian AR	1957–58 71–74 79–82 1993–2005	2011–13
Tajikistan		
Turkmenistan		
UAE	2005–07	
Yemen	1983–86	

North America (2 members, 2 seats)

Canada	1947–2010	2011–13
USA	1947–2010	2011–13

South-West Pacific (16 members, 1 seat)

Australia	1947–57 61–63 67–69 73–75 79–81 1985–2008 09–11	2011–14
Cook Islands		
Fiji		
Kiribati		
Marshall Islands		
Micronesia		
Nauru		
New Zealand	1957–60 63–66 69–72 75–78 81–84	
Niue		
Palau		

324

Papua New Guinea
Samoa
Solomon Islands
Tokelau (associate member)[2]
Tonga
Tuvalu
Vanuatu

Notes

1   The European Union (EU) has the right to participate in matters within its competence in any meeting of the
     Organization, other than those bodies with restricted membership, in which any of its Member States are
     entitled to participate. It exercises membership rights in those meetings on an alternative basis with those of
     its Member States that are members of the Council, or other bodies concerned in the areas of their respective
     competencies. The EU is not eligible for election or designation to any such body in its own right, nor is it
     entitled to participate in voting for elective places or to hold office itself. The EU is not entitled to participate in
     the Programme Committee, Finance Committee or Committee on Constitutional and Legal Matters.

2   Article III.l of the FAO Constitution and GRO Rules XIII.3, XIV.1, XV.1 and XXV.8(c) provide that associate
     members have the right to participate in the deliberations of the FAO Conference, commissions of the
     Conference, committees of such commissions and other committees established by the Conference for the
     duration of the Conference and in any discussions at meetings of the Council, but shall not hold office nor
     have the right to vote. They cannot participate in the Credentials Committee, Nominations Committee and
     General Committee.

*   On 1 July 2011, the following Member States were elected to serve for the terms shown. Africa: Côte d'Ivoire
     (1 July 2011 to 30 June 2013); Algeria, Cameroon, Guinea and Togo (1 December 2011 to 30 June
     2014); and Congo, Eritrea and Gabon (1 July 2012 to 30 June 2015). Asia: India, Indonesia and Pakistan
     (1 December 2011 to 30 June 2014); and Bangladesh, China, Japan, Philippines, ROK and Thailand (1 July
     2012 to 30 June 2015). Europe: Denmark, France, Italy and Poland (1 December 2011 to 30 June 2014);
     and Germany, Portugal and UK (1 July 2012 to 30 June 2015). Latin America and the Caribbean: Ecuador
     (1 December 2011 to 30 June 2014); and Chile, El Salvador and Venezuela (1 July 2012 to 30 June 2015).
     Near East: Afghanistan, Egypt and Saudi Arabia (1 December 2011 to 30 June 2014); and Jordan (1 July
     2012 to 30 June 2015). South-West Pacific: Australia (1 December 2011 to 30 June 2014).

FAO/WHO Codex Alimentarius Commission

Secretariat
Nutrition and Consumer Protection Division (AGN)
Viale delle Terme di Caracalla
00153 Rome
Italy
Telephone: (+39 06) 57051
Fax: (+39 06) 5705 4593
Email: Codex@fao.org
Internet: www.codexalimentarius.org

Purpose

The Codex Alimentarius Commission was established jointly by the Food and Agriculture
Organization (FAO) and World Health Organization (WHO) in 1963 in the framework of
the Joint FAO/WHO Food Standards Programme. The Commission's mandate is to protect
the health of consumers and ensure fair practices in the food trade by preparing, publishing
and revising international food standards and by promoting the coordination of all food
standards work undertaken by international organisations.

To date, the Commission has adopted hundreds of standards (for single commodities, groups of commodities or horizontal subjects such as labelling or hygiene), codes of practice and guidelines. It has adopted thousands of maximum limits for food additives and contaminants, as well as pesticide and veterinary drug residues in foods. Together, these texts form the Codex Alimentarius. All information on the Commission's work and its results are public and available on the internet and in selected thematic paper compilations.

The Codex Alimentarius promotes the harmonisation of food standards at the international level. Codex food safety related standards, guidelines and codes of practice serve as a reference in the World Trade Organization (WTO) Agreement on the Application of Sanitary and Phytosanitary Measures. The Agreement recognises the Commission as one of three international standard-setting organisations known as 'the three sisters', the other two being the World Organisation for Animal Health (OIE) and the International Plant Protection Convention (IPPC). Codex texts also have relevance as international standards in the Agreement on Technical Barriers to Trade.

Structure

The Executive Committee provides advice to the Commission on general orientation, strategic planning and work programming. The technical work is done by some 20 Codex specialist committees and task forces, which prepare draft standards and related texts for adoption by the Commission. The committees rely on independent scientific advice provided by FAO and WHO expert groups – the Joint FAO/WHO Expert Committee on Food Additives (JECFA), Joint FAO/WHO Expert Meetings on Microbiological Risk Assessment (JEMRA), Joint FAO/WHO Meetings on Pesticide Residues (JMPR) and ad hoc consultations. Six regional coordinating committees collect information on regional implementation of Codex standards and other regional issues, and also prepare standards of regional relevance. The Secretariat is based in the FAO (Nutrition and Consumer Protection Division).

Membership

Membership of the Commission is open to FAO and WHO members and associate members. As of May 2012, there were 184 countries and the European Union, covering more than 99 percent of the world's population. About 200 international observer organisations are accredited to participate in meetings of the Commission and its subsidiary bodies.

United Nations Educational, Scientific and Cultural Organization (UNESCO)

7 Place de Fontenoy
75352 Paris 07–SP
France
Telephone: (+33 1) 4568 1000
Fax: (+33 1) 4567 1690
Email: info@unesco.org
Internet: www.unesco.org
Director-General: Irina Bokova, Bulgaria (elected by the General Conference, on the recommendation of the Executive Board, for 2009–13)

Purpose

The UN Educational, Scientific and Cultural Organization (UNESCO) was established in 1945 to promote the aims set out in article 1, para. 3 of the UN Charter. Its purpose, as stated in article 1 of its Constitution, is to contribute to peace and security by promoting collaboration among nations through education, science and culture.

Structure
- General Conference
- Executive Board
- Secretariat

The General Conference is UNESCO's supreme body. On the proposal of the Executive Board, the General Conference, during its ordinary session, sets the next session's venue. The Executive Board is elected by the General Conference and consists of 58 Member States that serve four-year terms (membership is renewed by half at each General Conference). Each Member State appoints a representative with competence in fields related to UNESCO and qualified to fulfil the administrative and executive duties of the Board. Alternates may also be appointed. The Board Chair for 2011–13 is Alissandra Cummins, Barbados (elected 11 November 2011 for a two-year term).

The following are some of the inter-governmental bodies that are sub-organs of the UNESCO General Conference:
- Intergovernmental Council of the International Hydrological Programme (IHP)
- International Coordinating Council of the Programme on Man and the Biosphere (MAB)
- International Geoscience Programme (IGCP)
- Intergovernmental Oceanographic Commission (IOC)
- Intergovernmental Council for the Information for All Programmes (IFAP)
- Intergovernmental Council of the International Programme for the Development of Communication (IPDC)
- Intergovernmental Committee for Physical Education and Sport (CIGEPS)
- Intergovernmental Committee for Promoting the Return of Cultural Property to its Countries of Origin or its Restitution in the Case of Illicit Appropriation
- Intergovernmental Council of the Management of Social Transformations Programme (MOST)
- Intergovernmental Bioethics Committee (IGBC).

Meetings

UNESCO's General Conference meets every two years. The 37th session is scheduled to be held from 4 to 19 November 2013 (tentative dates) in Paris, France.

The Board meets in regular sessions at least four times in any two-year period. As a general rule, there are at least two regular sessions a year, normally in April and October.

Membership

UNESCO has 195 Member States and eight associate members (as of March 2012), one of the highest memberships in the UN system. The electoral grouping system allocates each region a specific number of Executive Board seats: Group I (Western European and North American countries), nine seats; Group II (Eastern European countries), seven seats; Group III (Latin America and the Caribbean countries or GRULAC), 10 seats; Group IV (Asia and the Pacific countries or ASPAC), 12 seats; Group V(a) (Africa), 13 seats; Group V(b) (Arab States), seven seats.

The following list shows the members of UNESCO and their terms of office on the Executive Board. Members serve from the close of the General Conference session that elected them until the close of the second ordinary General Conference session following their election.

Group I

	Previous terms	Current terms
Andorra		
Austria	1972–76 95–99	2011–15
Belgium	1946–51 56–64 74–78 80–89 95–99	2009–13
Canada	1946–51 68–74 83–87 89–93 1997–2001 03–07	
Cyprus	1987–91	
Denmark	1952–58 78–83 91–95	2009–13
Finland	1966–74 87–91 1997–2001	
France	1948–2011	2011–15
Germany	1954–68 1970–2005 07–11	
Greece	1946–51 56–64 83–87 1999–2003 07–11	
Iceland	1983–87 2001–05	
Ireland		
Israel	1962–70	
Italy	1948–58 62–70 72–89 93–97 1999–2011	2011–15
Luxembourg	2005–09	
Malta	1995–99	
Monaco		2009–13
Netherlands	1946–47 51–56 66–74 91–95 1999–2003	
Norway	1946–52 74–78 89–93 2005–09	
Portugal	1976–80 91–95 2005–09	
San Marino		
Spain	1954–60 70–76 80–85 87–91 93–97 1999–2003 07–11	2011–15
Sweden	1958–66 85–89 95–99	
Switzerland	1950–54 64–72 76–80 87–91 93–97 2003–07	
Turkey	1946–52 58–66 78–83 91–95 2001–05	
UK	1946–85 1997–2005 05–07	2011–15
USA	2003–11	2011–15

Group II[1]

	Previous terms	Current terms
Albania[2]	2007–09	
Armenia		
Azerbaijan	2005–09	
Belarus	1989–93 1999–2005	2009–13
Bosnia and Herzegovina		
Bulgaria[2]	1972–76 85–89 93–97 2007–09	
Croatia		
Czech Republic	1995–99 2003–07	2011–15
Estonia		
Georgia	1999–2003	
Hungary[2]	1964–72 78–83 95–99 2003–07 07–09	
Latvia	2009–11	
Lithuania	1997–2001 05–09	
Montenegro		2011–15
Poland	1946–50 56–64 76–80 87–91 93–97 1999–2003 09–11	
Republic of Moldova		
Romania	1962–68 76–80 91–95 1999–2003 09–11	
Russian Federation	1954–2011	2011–15
Serbia	2005–09	

	Previous terms	Current terms
Slovakia	1995–99 2001–05	2009–13
Slovenia	2003–07	
Tajikistan		
The former Yugoslav Republic of Macedonia		2011–15
Ukraine	1980–85 95–99 2001–05	
Uzbekistan		2009–13

Group III

	Previous terms	Current terms
Antigua and Barbuda	1985–89	
Argentina	1962–70 72–76 78–83 85–93 95–99 2007–11	
Bahamas	2001–05	
Barbados	1976–80 1997–2001	2009–13
Belize		
Bolivia	1995–99	
Brazil	1946–52 54–62 64–72 74–78 80–89 91–95 2001–09	2011–15
Chile	1962–70 72–76 93–97 1999–2003 07–11	
Colombia	1948–54 70–76 80–89 91–95 1997–2001 05–09	
Costa Rica	1966–74 80–85 89–97	
Cuba	1974–78 80–85 87–91 95–99 2001–05 07–11	2011–15
Dominica	2001–05	
Dominican Republic	1999–2003	
Ecuador	1947–48 54–62 76–80 2003–07	2011–15
El Salvador	1956–64 93–97 2007–11	
Grenada		2009–13
Guatemala	1978–83 89–93 2003–07	
Guyana	1983–87 93–97	
Haiti	1980–85 1997–2001	2009–13
Honduras	1997–2001	
Jamaica[2]	1970–76 80–85 91–95 2001–05 07–09	
Mexico	1946–54 58–66 68–74 76–80 83–87 89–97 1999–2003 05–09	2011–15
Nicaragua	1989–93	
Panama	1962–68 76–80	
Paraguay		
Peru	1952–54 64–72 76–80 85–89 1999–2003	2009–13
Saint Kitts and Nevis	2005–09	
Saint Lucia	1997–2001	2009–13
Saint Vincent and the Grenadines	2005–09	
Suriname	1987–91 2001–05	
Trinidad and Tobago	1985–89 93–97	
Uruguay	1952–58 72–76 89–93 1997–2001 03–07	
Venezuela	1946–52 56–64 76–80 83–91 2003–07	2009–13

Group IV

	Previous terms	Current terms
Afghanistan	1968–74 2003–07	2011–15
Australia	1946–50 56–60 74–78 85–89 91–95 1999–2005	
Bangladesh	1983–87 1995–2007	2009–13
Bhutan		
Brunei Darussalam		
Cambodia	2003–07	
China	1946–50 1972–2009	2009–13
Cook Islands		

	Previous terms	Current terms
DPRK		
Fiji	2005–09	
India	1946–2009	2009–13
Indonesia	1954–62 76–80 85–89 95–99 2003–07	2011–15
Iran	1952–58 64–68 74–78 1999–2003	
Japan	1952–95 1997–2009	2009–13
Kazakhstan	1997–2001	2009–13
Kiribati		
Kyrgyzstan		
Lao PDR		
Malaysia	1978–83 87–91 93–97 1999–2003 07–11	
Maldives		
Marshall Islands		
Micronesia		
Mongolia	1983–87 2007–11	
Myanmar		
Nauru		
Nepal	1974–78 95–99 2005–09	
New Zealand	1960–64 78–83 95–99	
Niue		
Palestine*		
Pakistan	1951–66 68–74 1978–2011	2011–15
Palau		
Papua New Guinea	1989–93	2011–15
Philippines	1950–54 58–62 74–78 83–87 91–95 1999–2003 07–11	
ROK	1987–2003 07–11	2011–15
Samoa	1997–2001	
Singapore[3]		
Solomon Islands		
Sri Lanka	1968–74 87–91 2003–11	
Thailand	1952–56 80–85 89–93 95–99 2005–09	2011–15
Timor-Leste		
Tonga	1993–97	
Turkmenistan		
Tuvalu		
Vanuatu	2001–05	
Viet Nam	1978–83 2001–05	2009–13

Group V

Algeria	1968–74 80–89 91–95 2001–09	2009–13
Angola	1993–97	2011–15
Bahrain	1991–95 2003–07	
Benin	1972–76 85–89 93–97 1999–2003 05–09	
Botswana	1991–95	
Burkina Faso	1974–78 89–93 2001–05	2009–13
Burundi	1978–83 89–93	
Cameroon	1962–68 80–89 95–99 2003–07	
Cape Verde	1989–93 2003–07	
Central African Republic	1983–87	
Chad	1962–70 76–80 89–93 1999–2003	
Comoros		
Congo	1968–74 85–89 2003–07	2009–13

	Previous terms	Current terms
Côte d'Ivoire	1964–72 76–80 85–89 91–95 1997–2001 07–11	
DR Congo	1970–76 80–85 2005–11	
Djibouti		2009–13
Egypt	1946–51 54–80 1985–2009	2009–13
Equatorial Guinea	1987–91	
Eritrea		
Ethiopia	1968–74 85–89 93–97 1999–2003 05–09	2011–15
Gabon	1974–78 83–87 1997–2001	2011–15
Gambia	1989–93	2011–15
Ghana	1970–76 80–85 91–95 1997–2001 03–07	2009–13
Guinea	1980–85 89–93 1997–2001	
Guinea-Bissau	1980–85	
Iraq	1978–83 89–93	
Jordan	1976–80 85–89 93–97 2001–05	
Kenya	1972–76 87–91 95–99 2001–05	2009–13
Kuwait	1983–87 1999–2003 07–11	
Lebanon	1950–58 66–74 83–87 1997–2001 05–09	
Lesotho	1978–83 95–99	
Liberia	1953–56 76–80	
Libya	1976–80 1997–2001	
Madagascar	1960–64 83–87 91–95 1999–2003 07–11	
Malawi	1987–91 1999–2003	2011–15
Mali	1962–70 85–89 93–97 2003–07	2011–15
Mauritania	1974–78 87–91	
Mauritius	1976–80 95–99 2003–07	
Morocco	1958–66 78–83 93–97 1999–2011	
Mozambique	1987–91 2001–05	
Namibia	1993–97 2003–07	2011–15
Niger	1983–87 93–97 2007–11	
Nigeria	1962–70 76–85 87–91 93–97 1999–2003 05–09	2011–15
Oman	1991–95 1999–2003	
Qatar	1987–91	
Rwanda	1976–80 2001–05	
Sao Tome and Principe		
Saudi Arabia	1972–76 95–99 2007–11	2011–15
Senegal	1966–74 78–83 85–89 95–99 2001–05 07–11	
Seychelles	1991–95	
Sierra Leone	1976–80	
Somalia	1987–91	
South Africa	1997–2001 05–09	
South Sudan		
Sudan	1962–66 78–87	
Swaziland	1983–87 2001–05	
Syrian AR	1951–54 74–78 83–87	2009–13
Togo	1972–76 87–91 1997–2001 05–09	
Tunisia	1974–78 80–85 91–95 1999–2003 07–11	2011–15
Uganda	1974–78 87–91 1997–2001 05–09	
UAE	1980–85 95–99	2011–15
UR of Tanzania	1964–72 80–85 89–93 95–99 2001–05 07–11	
Yemen	1989–93 95–99 2003–07	
Zambia	1966–74 91–95 2007–11	
Zimbabwe	1983–87 95–99	2009–13

Associate members[4]

Aruba	Curaçao	Saint Maarten
British Virgin Islands	Faroe Islands	Tokelau
Cayman Islands	Macau, China	

Observer status*

Holy See

Notes

1 The former Socialist Federal Republic of Yugoslavia occupied a seat on the Executive Board as a member of Group II from 1951–53, 1972–76, 1983–87, 1989–91 and 1991–92.

2 Four members, Albania, Bulgaria, Hungary and Jamaica – whose mandate was to expire in 2011 – volunteered to leave the Executive Board in 2009 to facilitate the rotation among countries.

3 Singapore moved from observer status to full Member State on 8 October 2007.

4 Netherlands Antilles was previously an associate member. On 10 October 2010, the five-island Dutch Caribbean dependency ceased to exist. Curaçao and Saint Maarten now have internal self-government within the Netherlands, joining Aruba, which gained similar status in 1986. Bonaire, Saint Eustatius and Saba have become part of the Netherlands. The Netherlands retains responsibility for defence and foreign policy, and remains the subject of international law with which agreements are concluded. Curaçao and Saint Maarten became UNESCO associate members in October 2011.

* The UNESCO General Conference voted in October 2011 to admit Palestine as a Member State of the Organization. Palestine had previously been an observer.

World Heritage Committee (WHC)

World Heritage Centre
UNESCO
7, Place de Fontenoy
75352 Paris 07 SP
France
Telephone: (+33 1) 4568 2496
Fax: (+33 1) 4568 5570
Email: wh-info@unesco.org
Internet: http://whc.unesco.org
Director: Kishore Rao, India (appointed by the UNESCO Director-General in March 2011)

Purpose

The World Heritage Committee (WHC) is an inter-governmental body established in 1972 by the Convention concerning the Protection of the World's Cultural and Natural Heritage, which was adopted by the UN Educational, Scientific and Cultural Organization (UNESCO) General Conference of the same year.

The Committee is responsible for implementation of the World Heritage Convention, defines the use of the World Heritage Fund and allocates financial assistance upon requests from States Parties. It inscribes properties on the World Heritage List and the List of World Heritage in Danger. It examines reports on the state of conservation of inscribed properties on both lists and asks States Parties to take action when properties are not being properly managed. It also decides on deletion of properties from the lists.

As of July 2012, 962 properties in 157 countries were inscribed on the World Heritage List – 745 cultural, 188 natural and 29 mixed properties.

The Convention has 189 States Parties (as of April 2012). The year 2012 is the Convention's 40th anniversary.

Structure

The WHC consists of representatives from 21 of the States Parties to the Convention, elected by the Convention General Assembly.

The WHC Bureau consists of seven States Parties elected annually at the end of each ordinary session of the Committee. It is composed of a chair, five vice-chairs and a rapporteur. The Bureau coordinates the Committee's work and fixes the dates, hours and order of business of meetings.

The UNESCO World Heritage Centre is the WHC's Secretariat. It was established in 1992 to develop an integrated, multi-disciplinary approach to the conservation of both cultural and natural heritage of outstanding universal value.

Meetings

The WHC meets annually. The 36th session was held in Saint-Petersburg, Russian Federation, in July 2012. The 37th session will be held in Cambodia in 2013. The Bureau meets only during WHC sessions.

The General Assembly of States Parties to the Convention meets every two years during the ordinary session of the UNESCO General Conference to elect WHC members. The 19th session is scheduled to be held in Paris, France, in November 2013 during the 37th session of the UNESCO General Conference.

Membership

According to the World Heritage Convention, a committee member's term of office is for six years. In practice, most States Parties choose to serve four years to give others an opportunity to be on the Committee. The WHC Chair until the end of the 36th session in July 2012 was Eleonora Mitrofanova, Russian Federation.

WHC members, all elected for four-year terms, are as follows. Terms end in the year shown (at the end of the ordinary session of the UNESCO General Conference).

Algeria	2015	Mali	2013
Cambodia	2013	Mexico	2013
Colombia	2015	Qatar	2015
Estonia	2013	Russian Federation	2013
Ethiopia	2013	Senegal	2015
France	2013	Serbia	2015
Germany	2015	South Africa	2013
India	2015	Switzerland	2013
Iraq	2013	Thailand	2013
Japan	2015	UAE	2013
Malaysia	2015		

World Health Organization (WHO)

20 Avenue Appia
1211 Geneva 27
Switzerland
Telephone: (+41 22) 791 2111
Fax: (+41 22) 791 3111
Email: info@who.int
Internet: www.who.int
Director-General: Margaret Chan, China (reappointed in May 2012 by the World Health Assembly for a second five-year term, beginning July 2012)

Purpose

Representatives of 61 states adopted the World Health Organization (WHO) Constitution in 1946. The Organization formally came into existence on 7 April 1948 and became a UN specialised agency on 10 July 1948. Article 1 of the Constitution defines the WHO's objective as "the attainment by all peoples of the highest possible level of health". The detailed functions are set out in article 2 of the Constitution.

Structure

- World Health Assembly
- Executive Board
- Secretariat

The Executive Board is composed of 34 individuals technically qualified in the health field, each one designated by a Member State elected to do so by the World Health Assembly. The Chair from May 2012 to May 2013 is Joy St John, Barbados.

Meetings

The World Health Assembly takes place annually, usually in Geneva, Switzerland. The 65th session was held from 21 to 26 May 2012 in Geneva. The Board meets at least twice a year in Geneva.

Membership

As of May 2012, there were 194 Member States. The following is a list of WHO members showing their three-year terms on the Executive Board. Terms end with the election of new board members at the World Health Assembly.

	Previous terms	Current terms
Africa (46 members)		
Algeria	1969–72 95–98	
Angola	1977–80 96–99	
Benin	1966–69 96–99	
Botswana	1977–80 96–99	
Burkina Faso	1969–72 96–99	
Burundi	1978–81 1997–2000 09–12	
Cameroon	1964–67 92–95	2011–14
Cape Verde	1978–81 1998–2001	
Central African Republic	1969–72 1998–2001	
Chad	1978–81 1999–2002	2012–15
Comoros	1978–81 1999–2002	

	Previous terms	Current terms
Congo	1979–82 1999–2002	
Côte d'Ivoire	1967–70 84–87 1999–2002	
DR Congo	1972–75 93–96	
Equatorial Guinea	1984–87 2000–03	
Eritrea	1983–86 2001–04	
Ethiopia	1969–73 2001–04	
Gabon	1980–83 2002–05	
Gambia	1980–83 2002–05	
Ghana	1960–63 83–86 2002–05	
Guinea	1965–68 84–87 2002–05	
Guinea-Bissau	1981–84 2003–06	
Kenya	1970–73 84–87 2004–07	
Lesotho	1971–74 85–88 2004–07	
Liberia	1951–54 57–60 86–89 2005–08	
Madagascar	1961–64 86–89 2005–08	
Malawi	1973–76 87–90 2007–10	
Mali	1963–66 87–90 2006–09	
Mauritania	1975–78 87–90 2008–11	
Mauritius	1974–77 87–90 2008–11	
Mozambique	1981–84 88–91	2010–13
Namibia	2005–08	
Niger	1972–75 89–92 2008–11	
Nigeria	1961–62 66–69 89–92	2011–14
Rwanda	1975–78 90–93 2005–08	
Sao Tome and Principe	1981–84 90–93 2007–10	
Senegal	1961–64 90–93	2011–14
Seychelles	1981–84 90–93	2010–13
Sierra Leone	1963–66 91–94	2011–14
South Africa	1948–51 54–57	
Swaziland	1975–78 92–95	
Togo	1975–77 93–96	
Uganda	1968–71 93–96 2008–11	
UR of Tanzania	1975–78 93–96	
Zambia	1976–79 94–97	
Zimbabwe	1982–85 95–98	

The Americas (35 members)

	Previous terms	Current terms
Antigua and Barbuda		
Argentina	1955–58 60–62 66–69 74–77 83–86 88–91 95–98	
Bahamas	1989–92 2007–10	
Barbados	1995–98	2010–13
Belize		
Bolivia	1977–80 91–94 2004–07	
Brazil	1948–51 52–55 58–61 63–66 80–83 87–90 95–98 2004–07 08–11	
Canada	1952–59 62–65 68–71 75–78 80–83 85–88 92–95 1997–2000 03–06 09–12	
Chile	1950–53 54–57 61–62 68–72 82–85 89–92 1998–2001 09–12	
Colombia	1962–65 72–75 79–82 89–92 2001–04	
Costa Rica	1953–56 93–96	
Cuba	1951–54 77–80 85–88 94–97 2001–04	2012–15

	Previous terms	Current terms
Dominica		
Dominican Republic		
Ecuador	1955–58 71–74 85–87 2003–06	2010–13
El Salvador	1950–53 2006–09	
Grenada	2001–04	
Guatemala	1958–61 74–77 80–83 1999–2002	
Guyana	1975–76 86–89	
Haiti	1962–65	
Honduras	1976–79 96–99	
Jamaica	1968–71 79–82 92–95 2004–07	
Mexico	1948–50 56–59 65–68 78–81 86–89 92–95 2005–08	2011–14
Nicaragua	1970–73 88–91	
Panama	1967–70 83–86	2012–15
Paraguay	1964–67 2007–10	
Peru	1959–62 65–68 76–79 1997–2000 07–10	
Saint Kitts and Nevis		
Saint Lucia		
Saint Vincent and the Grenadines		
Suriname		
Trinidad and Tobago	1971–74 82–85 1998–2001	
USA	1949–52 54–56 58–60 62–64 66–68 70–72 74–76 78–80 82–85 87–89 91–93 95–97 1999–2001 03–09	2010–13
Uruguay	1971–74 91–94	
Venezuela	1949–52 59–62 74–77 83–86 2000–03	

Eastern Mediterranean (22 members)

	Previous terms	Current terms
Afghanistan	1972–75 91–94 2006–09	
Bahrain	1978–81 95–98 2004–07	
Djibouti	1983–86 2006–09	
Egypt	1949–51 57–60 67–70 84–87 95–98 2001–04	
Iran	1948–49 52–55 58–61 63–66 73–76 79–82 88–91 2000–03	2012–15
Iraq	1953–56 61–64 82–85 87–93 2005–08	
Jordan	1960–63 74–77 87–90 2000–03	
Kuwait	1964–67 80–83 94–97 2002–05	
Lebanon	1951–54 68–71 86–89 1999–2002	2012–15
Libya	1964–67 77–80 88–91 2004–07	
Morocco	1965–68 82–85 93–96	2010–13
Oman	1979–82 1997–2000 08–11	
Pakistan	1950–53 55–58 61–63 67–70 76–79 82–85 94–97 2003–06	
Qatar	1976–79 92–95 1998–2001	2011–14
Saudi Arabia	1954–57 70–73 86–89 2001–04	
Somalia	1966–69 75–78 2009–12	
South Sudan		
Sudan	1959–62 75–77 89–92 2003–06	
Syrian AR	1956–58 71–74 83–86 92–95 2009–12	
Tunisia	1958–59 62–65 77–80 91–94 2007–10	
UAE	1981–84 96–99 2007–10	
Yemen	1965–68 73–76 80–83 85–88 90–92 1998–2001	2010–13

	Previous terms	Current terms
Europe (53 members)[1, 2]		
Albania		
Andorra		
Armenia		2010–13
Austria	1953–56 70–73 88–91	
Azerbaijan	2005–08	2012–15
Belarus	1948–50	
Belgium	1951–54 68–71 83–86 1999–2002	2012–15
Bosnia and Herzegovina		
Bulgaria	1969–72 81–84 91–94	
Croatia	1995–98	2012–15
Cyprus	1969–72 85–88 1997–2000	
Czech Republic	2003–06	
Denmark	1952–55 71–74 91–94 2006–09	
Estonia	2009–12	
Finland	1955–58 75–78 94–97	
France	1948–2001 03–06 09–12	
Georgia		
Germany	1957–60 67–70 73–80 85–88 1997–2000 09–12	
Greece	1951–54 76–79 91–94	
Hungary	1972–75 84–87 2008–11	
Iceland	1961–63 83–86 2003–06	
Ireland	1959–62 95–98	
Israel	1961–64 93–96	
Italy	1950–53 56–59 61–64 71–74 2000–03	
Kazakhstan	2001–04	
Kyrgyzstan		
Latvia	2006–09	
Lithuania	2000–03	2012–15
Luxembourg	1959–62 2004–07	
Malta	1985–88	
Monaco		
Montenegro		
Netherlands	1948–51 63–66 79–82 1997–2000	
Norway	1948–49 63–66 79–82 1997–2000	2010–13
Poland	1948–51 61–64 73–76 85–88 1996–2000	
Portugal	1955–58 77–80 92–95 2005–08	
Republic of Moldova	2007–10	
Romania	1967–70 80–83 2004–07	
Russian Federation	1948–50 1958–2005 08–11	
San Marino		
Serbia	1948–51 64–67 75–78 89–92 2009–12	
Slovakia		
Slovenia	2006–09	
Spain	1961–64 81–84 89–92 2002–05	
Sweden	1949–52 67–70 87–90 2000–03	
Switzerland	1953–56 73–76 1999–2002	2011–14
Tajikistan		
The former Yugoslav Republic of Macedonia		
Turkey	1949–52 64–67 79–82 93–96 2006–09	
Turkmenistan		
Ukraine		
UK	1948–99 2001–04 07–10	
Uzbekistan		2011–14

South-East Asia (11 members)

	Previous terms	Current terms
Bangladesh	1975–78 87–90 1998–2001 08–11	
Bhutan	1995–98 2005–08	
DPRK	1990–93 2000–03	
India	1948–51 56–59 65–68 77–80 88–91 1999–2002 09–12	
Indonesia	1953–56 63–66 72–75 84–88 96–99 2007–10	
Maldives	1981–84 91–94 2002–05	2012–15
Myanmar	1954–57 66–69 78–81 90–93 2001–04	2011–14
Nepal	1959–62 69–72 83–86 93–96 2003–06	
Sri Lanka	1948–49 51–54 62–65 74–77 86–89 1997–2000 06–09	
Thailand	1950–53 60–63 71–74 84–87 94–97 2004–07	
Timor-Leste		2010–13

Western Pacific (27 members)

	Previous terms	Current terms
Australia	1948–49 57–60 67–70 75–78 85–88 95–98 2004–07	2012–15
Brunei Darussalam	2009–12	
Cambodia		
China	1948–50 73–76 78–85 1990–2009	2010–13
Cook Islands	1997–2000	
Fiji	1976–79	
Japan	1954–57 61–64 69–72 75–76 81–84 87–90 1992–2003 05–08 09–12	
Kiribati		
Lao PDR	1970–73 1998–2001	
Malaysia	1964–67 82–85	2012–15
Marshall Islands		
Micronesia		
Mongolia	1968–71 80–83 92–95	2010–13
Nauru		
New Zealand	1952–55 63–66 72–75 79–82 2007–10	
Niue		
Palau		
Papua New Guinea	1989–92	2011–14
Philippines	1949–52 55–58 66–69 76–79 91–94 2001–04	
ROK	1960–63 84–87 95–98 2001–04 07–10	
Samoa	1979–82 2008–11	
Singapore	2006–09	
Solomon Islands		
Tonga	1985–86 88–91 2004–07	
Tuvalu		
Vanuatu	1999–2002	
Viet Nam	1958–61 93–96 2003–06	

Associate members

Puerto Rico

Tokelau

OTHER BODIES

Notes

1   The former Socialist Federal Republic of Yugoslavia served on the Executive Board from 1948–51, 1964–67, 1975–78 and 1989–92.

2   Czechoslovakia served on the Executive Board from 1965–68, 1976–79 and 1988–91.

International Civil Aviation Organization (ICAO)

999 University Street
Montréal, Quebec
Canada H3C 5H7
Telephone: (+1 514) 954 8219
Fax: (+1 514) 954 6077
Email: icaohq@icao.int
Internet: www.icao.int
Secretary-General: Raymond Benjamin, France (appointed by the ICAO Council for a second three-year term from 1 August 2012 to 31 July 2015)

Purpose

The Convention on International Civil Aviation, which provided for the establishment of the International Civil Aviation Organization (ICAO), was signed in Chicago in 1944. The Organization came into existence on 4 April 1947 after 26 states had ratified the Convention.

Under article 44 of the Convention, the ICAO is charged with developing the principles and techniques of international air navigation, and fostering the planning and development of international air transport to ensure the safe and orderly growth of international civil aviation throughout the world.

Structure

- Assembly
- Council
- Committees of the Council
- Air Navigation Commission
- Secretariat

The Assembly is the Organization's sovereign body. It meets at least every three years to review its work and establish guidelines for future activities.

The Council is the ICAO's executive body. It comprises 36 contracting states elected by the ordinary session of the Assembly for a three-year term. The President is Roberto Kobeh González, Mexico (elected in November 2006, re-elected November 2007 and November 2010 for second and third three-year terms). In electing Council members, the Assembly gives adequate representation to states of chief importance to air transport, states not otherwise included that make the largest contribution to the provision of facilities for international civil air navigation, and states whose designation will ensure that all major geographical areas of the world are represented.

The ICAO's committees are: the Air Transport Committee, Legal Committee, Committee on Joint Support of Air Navigation Services, Finance Committee, Committee on Unlawful Interference, Technical Cooperation Committee and the Committee on Aviation Environmental Protection. All committee members, except those of the Legal Committee, are appointed by the Council. Membership of the Legal Committee is open to all Member States.

The Air Navigation Commission is the principal body concerned with the development of Standards and Recommended Practices (SARPs). It comprises 19 people qualified and experienced in the science and practice of aeronautics. Its members are nominated by contracting states and are appointed by the Council.

Meetings

The ICAO Assembly's 38th session is expected to be held in the northern hemisphere autumn of 2013.

Membership

The ICAO has 191 members. The following is a list of the ICAO members' terms on the Council. Terms expire at the end of session in the year stated.

	Previous terms	Current terms
Afghanistan		
Albania		
Algeria	1980–86 1998–2004	
Andorra		
Angola	1995–98	
Antigua and Barbuda		
Argentina	1947–2010	2010–13
Armenia		
Australia	1947–2010	2010–13
Austria	2004–07	
Azerbaijan		
Bahamas		
Bahrain		
Bangladesh		
Barbados		
Belarus		
Belgium	1983–86 92–95	2010–13
Belize		
Benin		
Bhutan		
Bolivia	1995–98	
Bosnia and Herzegovina		
Botswana	1998–2001	
Brazil	1947–2010	2010–13
Brunei Darussalam		
Bulgaria		
Burkina Faso		2010–13
Burundi		
Cambodia		
Cameroon	1980–83 1992–2010	2010–13
Canada	1947–2010	2010–13
Cape Verde		
Central African Republic		
Chad		
Chile	1947–50 89–92 2002–07	
China	1974–2010	2010–13
Colombia	1962–86 1992–2001 04–07	2010–13
Comoros		
Congo	1962–74	
Cook Islands		
Costa Rica	1974–77 2001–04	
Côte d'Ivoire		
Croatia		

	Previous terms	Current terms
Cuba	1986–89 1998–2004	2010–13
Cyprus		
Czech Republic	1993–95 2001–04	
DPRK		
DR Congo		
Denmark	1980–83 95–98	2010–13
Djibouti		
Dominican Republic	2007–10	
Ecuador	1992–95 2007–10	
Egypt	1947–2010	2010–13
El Salvador	1980–83 95–98 2007–10	
Equatorial Guinea		
Eritrea		
Estonia		
Ethiopia	2001–07	
Fiji		
Finland	1977–80 89–92 2004–07	
France	1948–2010	2010–13
Gabon		
Gambia		
Georgia		
Germany	1959–2010	2010–13
Ghana	1986–92 2004–10	
Greece		
Grenada		
Guatemala		2010–13
Guinea		
Guinea-Bissau		
Guyana		
Haiti		
Honduras	1977–80 89–92 2004–07	
Hungary	2004–07	
Iceland	1992–2001 07–10	
India	1947–2010	2010–13
Indonesia	1968–2001	
Iran		
Iraq	1980–92	
Ireland	1947–59 2001–04	
Israel		
Italy	1950–2010	2010–13
Jamaica	1977–86	
Japan	1956–2010	2010–13
Jordan		
Kazakhstan		
Kenya	1983–89 1992–2001	
Kiribati		
Kuwait		
Kyrgyzstan		
Lao PDR		
Latvia		
Lebanon	1953–86 1992–2007	
Lesotho		
Liberia		

	Previous terms	Current terms
Libya		
Lithuania		
Luxembourg		
Madagascar	1974–86	
Malawi		
Malaysia	2007–10	2010–13
Maldives		
Mali		
Malta		
Marshall Islands		
Mauritania		
Mauritius	2001–04	
Mexico	1962–2010	2010–13
Micronesia		
Monaco		
Mongolia		
Montenegro		
Morocco	1974–80 92–98	2010–13
Mozambique	2004–07	
Myanmar		
Namibia	2007–10	
Nauru		
Nepal		
Netherlands	1980–83 89–92 1998–2001	
New Zealand		
Nicaragua	1971–74 92–95	
Niger		
Nigeria	1962–2010	2010–13
Norway	1983–86 1998–2001	
Oman		
Pakistan	1973–2007	
Palau		
Panama	1986–2001	
Papua New Guinea		
Paraguay	2001–04	2010–13
Peru	1986–89 2004–07	2010–13
Philippines	1959–68	
Poland		
Portugal	1947–62	
Qatar		
ROK	2001–10	2010–13
Republic of Moldova		
Romania	1995–98 2005–10	
Russian Federation	1972–2010	2010–13
Rwanda		
Saint Kitts and Nevis		
Saint Lucia	2004–07	
Saint Vincent and the Grenadines		
Samoa		
San Marino		
Sao Tome and Principe		
Saudi Arabia	1986–2010	2010–13
Senegal	1968–2004	

OTHER BODIES

	Previous terms	Current terms
Serbia		
Seychelles		
Sierra Leone		
Singapore	2002–10	2010–13
Slovakia	1998–2001	
Slovenia		2010–13
Solomon Islands		
Somalia		
South Africa	1950–65 2002–10	2010–13
South Sudan		
Spain	1951–2010	2010–13
Sri Lanka		
Sudan		
Suriname		
Swaziland		2010–13
Sweden	1986–89 2001–04	
Switzerland	1986–89 95–98 2002–10	
Syrian AR		
Tajikistan		
Thailand		
The former Yugoslav Republic of Macedonia		
Timor-Leste		
Togo		
Tonga		
Trinidad and Tobago	1972–77 89–98	
Tunisia	1986–92 2004–10	
Turkey	1947–50	
Turkmenistan		
Uganda	1980–83 2007–10	2010–13
Ukraine		
UAE	2007–10	2010–13
UK	1947–2010	2010–13
UR of Tanzania	1977–80 83–95	
USA	1947–2010	2010–13
Uruguay	1998–2001 07–10	
Uzbekistan		
Vanuatu		
Venezuela	1980–92 95–98 2001–04 07–10	
Viet Nam		
Yemen		
Zambia		
Zimbabwe		

Universal Postal Union (UPU)

International Bureau
Case Postale
3000 Berne 15
Switzerland
Telephone: (+41 31) 350 3111
Fax: (+41 31) 350 3110
Email: info@upu.int
Internet: www.upu.int
Director-General: Edouard Dayan, France (elected by the UPU Congress in 2004; re-elected in 2008; the next election was scheduled to take place at the October 2012 Congress)

Purpose

The Universal Postal Union (UPU) was established by the Berne Treaty of 1874 and became a specialised agency of the UN in 1948. Article 1 of the Vienna Constitution 1964 states that the aim of the Union is to secure the organisation and improvement of postal services, promote the development of international collaboration and undertake, as far as possible, technical assistance in postal matters requested by member countries. To this end, the countries that have adopted the Constitution comprise a single postal territory.

Structure

* Universal Postal Congress
* Council of Administration (CA)
* Postal Operations Council (POC)
* Consultative Committee (CC)
* International Bureau

The Universal Postal Congress is the four-yearly conference at which the general legislation, except the Constitution, is revised, and members of the Council of Administration and Postal Operations Council are elected. An extraordinary congress may be held at the request of two-thirds of the members. The provisions in force are those approved by the 24th Universal Postal Congress in Geneva in 2008, which came into effect on 1 January 2010.

The Council of Administration carries on the work of the Union between Congresses. Forty members are elected by the Congress on the basis of equitable geographical distribution, and may not hold office for more than two consecutive terms. The 41st member is the representative of the Congress host country, which automatically becomes the Chair. Although the 2008 Congress was hosted in Geneva, Switzerland, Kenya was given the Chair.

The Postal Operations Council is responsible for operational, commercial, technical and economic postal matters. The Congress elects the 40 Council members on a geographical basis. The POC members elect the Chair during the Congress. The Chair for 2008–12 is Greece.

The Consultative Committee was created by the 2004 Bucharest Congress. It gives postal stakeholders other than public postal operators and regulators a voice in the organisation's deliberations. It consists of non-governmental organisations, delivery service providers, workers' organisations, suppliers of goods and services to the postal sector, and other organisations that have an interest in international postal services. The Chair is from the Global Envelope Alliance.

OTHER BODIES

The International Bureau is the Permanent Secretariat of the Union and the UPU's headquarters. Located in Berne, Switzerland, it provides logistical and technical support for the UPU's bodies. It also serves as an office of liaison, information and consultation, and promotes technical cooperation among Union members.

Meetings

The Congress meets every four years. The 25th Congress is scheduled to be held from 24 September to 15 October 2012 in Doha, Qatar.

Membership

The UPU has 192 members.

Members	Membership of UPU bodies
Zone 1 – Western Hemisphere	
Antigua and Barbuda	
Argentina	Postal Operations Council
	Council of Administration
Aruba, Curaçao and Saint Maarten[1]	
Bahamas	
Barbados	
Belize	
Bolivia	
Brazil	Postal Operations Council
Canada	Postal Operations Council
	Council of Administration
Chile	
Colombia	Council of Administration
Costa Rica	Postal Operations Council
	Consultative Committee
Cuba	Council of Administration
	Postal Operations Council
Dominica	
Dominican Republic	
Ecuador	
El Salvador	
Grenada	
Guatemala	
Guyana	
Haiti	
Honduras	
Jamaica	
Mexico	Postal Operations Council
Nicaragua	
Panama	Council of Administration
Paraguay	
Peru	
Saint Kitts and Nevis	
Saint Lucia	
Saint Vincent and the Grenadines	
Suriname	
Trinidad and Tobago	Council of Administration
USA	Postal Operations Council
	Council of Administration
Uruguay	Postal Operations Council
	Council of Administration
Venezuela	
Zone 2 – Eastern Europe and Northern Asia	
Armenia	
Azerbaijan	Council of Administration
	Postal Operations Council
Belarus	
Bosnia and Herzegovina	
Bulgaria	
Czech Republic	
Estonia	
Georgia	
Hungary	
Kazakhstan	Council of Administration
Kyrgyzstan	
Latvia	
Lithuania	Council of Administration
Montenegro	
Poland	Postal Operations Council
Republic of Moldova	
Romania	

Members	Membership of UPU bodies	Members	Membership of UPU bodies
Russian Federation	Postal Operations Council of Administration	The former Yugoslav Republic of Macedonia	
		Turkmenistan	
Serbia		Ukraine	Council of Administration
Slovakia		Uzbekistan	
Tajikistan			

Zone 3 – Western Europe

Albania		Malta	
Austria		Monaco	
Belgium	Council of Administration Postal Operations Council	Netherlands	Postal Operations Council Consultative Committee
Croatia		Norway	
Cyprus		Portugal	Postal Operations Council
Denmark	Postal Operations Council	San Marino	
Finland		Slovenia	
France	Postal Operations Council Council of Administration	Spain	Postal Operations Council Consultative Committee
Germany	Council of Administration Postal Operations Council	Sweden	Council of Administration Consultative Committee
Greece	Chair of the Postal Operations Council	Switzerland	Postal Operations Council
		Turkey	Postal Operations Council Council of Administration
Iceland			
Ireland		UK	Council of Administration Postal Operations Council Vice-Chair of the Consultative Committee
Italy	Postal Operations Council		
Liechtenstein			
Luxembourg		Vatican	

Zone 4 – Southern Asia, Oceania

Afghanistan		Iraq	
Australia		Israel	Postal Operations Council
Bahrain		Japan	Postal Operations Council Consultative Committee
Bangladesh	Council of Administration Postal Operations Council	Jordan	
Bhutan		Kiribati	
Brunei Darussalam		Kuwait	Council of Administration
Cambodia		Lao PDR	
China	Council of Administration Postal Operations Council	Lebanon	
		Malaysia	Council of Administration
DPRK		Maldives	
Fiji		Mongolia	
India	Council of Administration Postal Operations Council	Myanmar	
		Nauru	
Indonesia	Council of Administration Postal Operations Council	Nepal	
		New Zealand	Postal Operations Council
Iran		Oman	

Members	Membership of UPU bodies
Overseas Territories (of the UK)	
Pakistan	
Papua New Guinea	
Philippines	
Qatar	Council of Administration
ROK	Postal Operations Council
Samoa	
Singapore	Postal Operations Council
Solomon Islands	
Sri Lanka	

Zone 5 – Africa

Members	Membership of UPU bodies
Algeria	Council of Administration Postal Operations Council
Angola	
Benin	Council of Administration
Botswana	Council of Administration
Burkina Faso	
Burundi	
Cameroon	Council of Administration
Cape Verde	
Central African Republic	
Chad	
Comoros	
Congo	Council of Administration
Côte d'Ivoire	
DR Congo	
Djibouti	
Egypt	Council of Administration Postal Operations Council Consultative Committee
Equatorial Guinea	
Eritrea	
Ethiopia	
Gabon	
Gambia	
Ghana	
Guinea	
Guinea-Bissau	
Kenya[2]	Chair of the Council of Administration
Lesotho	
Liberia	

Members	Membership of UPU bodies
Syrian AR	
Thailand	Council of Administration
Timor-Leste	
Tonga	
Tuvalu	
UAE	Council of Administration Postal Operations Council
Vanuatu	
Viet Nam	
Yemen	

Members	Membership of UPU bodies
Libya	Council of Administration Postal Operations Council
Madagascar	
Malawi	
Mali	
Mauritania	
Mauritius	
Morocco	Postal Operations Council
Mozambique	
Namibia	
Niger	
Nigeria	Council of Administration Postal Operations Council
Rwanda	
Sao Tome and Principe	
Saudi Arabia	Council of Administration
Senegal	Council of Administration
Seychelles	
Sierra Leone	
Somalia	
South Africa	Postal Operations Council
South Sudan	
Sudan	
Swaziland	
Togo	
Tunisia	Council of Administration Postal Operations Council
Uganda	
UR of Tanzania	Council of Administration
Zambia	
Zimbabwe	

Notes

1   Netherlands Antilles was previously a Zone 1 member. On 10 October 2010, the five-island Dutch Caribbean dependency ceased to exist. Curaçao and Saint Maarten now have internal self-government within the Netherlands, joining Aruba, which gained similar status in 1986. Bonaire, Saint Eustatius and Saba have become part of the Netherlands. The Netherlands retains responsibility for defence and foreign policy and remains the subject of international law with which agreements are concluded.

2   Chair for 24th Congress.

International Telecommunication Union (ITU)

Palais des Nations
1211 Geneva 20
Switzerland
Telephone: (+41 22) 730 5111
Fax: (+41 22) 733 7256
Email: itumail@itu.int
Internet: www.itu.int
Secretary-General: Hamadoun Touré, Mali (elected by Member States in 2007 and re-elected in 2010)

Purpose

The International Telecommunication Union (ITU) brings together governments and industry to coordinate the establishment and operation of global telecommunication networks and services. It was founded in 1865 in Paris as the International Telegraph Union. The 1932 Madrid Plenipotentiary Conference decided the current name, which came into force on 1 January 1934. The purposes of the Union are to:

*   Extend international cooperation among Member States for the improvement and rational use of telecommunications of all kinds
*   Promote and enhance participation of entities and organisations in the activities of the Union and foster cooperation and partnership between them and Member States
*   Promote and offer technical assistance to developing countries in telecommunications
*   Promote the development of technical facilities and their most efficient operation
*   Promote the extension of the benefits of information and communication technologies to all the world's inhabitants
*   Promote the use of telecommunication services with the aim of facilitating peaceful relations
*   Harmonise the actions of Member States and promote cooperation and partnership between Member States and sector members
*   Promote internationally a broader approach to telecommunications issues by cooperating with other inter-governmental organisations and those non-governmental organisations concerned with telecommunications.

The Union's current areas of focus are:

*   Developing infrastructure for information and communication technologies (ICTs) to connect under-served and remote communities
*   Managing radio-frequency spectrum and orbital slots for satellites
*   Building cybersecurity and confidence in online transactions with a focus on protecting children online
*   Promoting ICTs as an aid to combat climate change
*   Strengthening emergency telecommunications
*   Facilitating implementation of the outcomes of the World Summit on the Information Society.

Structure

- Plenipotentiary Conference
- Council
- World conferences on international telecommunications
- General Secretariat

The Constitution provides that a Plenipotentiary Conference, the supreme organ of the Union, be convened every four years. Plenipotentiary Conferences are composed of delegations from the Union's Member States. They adopt the underlying policies of the organisation, determine its direction and activities, and make decisions relating to its structure through a treaty called the Constitution and Convention of the International Telecommunication Union.

The Council acts on behalf of the Plenipotentiary Conference. It comprises up to 25 percent of Member States elected by the Plenipotentiary Conference with due regard to the equitable distribution of Council seats among the five world regions (Americas, nine seats; Western Europe, eight seats; Eastern Europe and Northern Asia, five seats; Africa, 13 seats; Asia and Australasia, 13 seats). The current Council comprises 48 Member States and meets annually.

The role of the Council is to consider, in the interval between Plenipotentiary Conferences, broad telecommunication policy issues and ensure that the Union's activities, policies and strategies respond fully to the rapidly changing telecommunication environment. The Council is also responsible for ensuring the smooth day-to-day running of the Union, coordinating work programmes, approving budgets and controlling finances.

The ITU has three main sectors, encompassing its main conferences:
- Radiocommunication
- Telecommunication Standardization
- Telecommunication Development.

The ITU's General Secretariat is headed by the organisation's Secretary-General, assisted by a deputy secretary-general and three elected directors.

Meetings

The Conference meets every four years (most recently in Mexico in October 2010). The Council meets annually (most recently in July 2012 in Geneva). The ITU regularly convenes other international meetings, conferences and seminars. Details are on its website.

Membership

ITU membership consists of 193 Member States and around 700 sector members. Sector members are public and private companies and organisations with an interest in telecommunications that are entitled to participate, with specific rights and obligations, in the work of one or more ITU sectors. One hundred associates also take part in some ITU work under special arrangements with the sectors. It is up to each sector to admit associates as partners in their activities.

Current ITU Council members were elected at the Plenipotentiary Conference in October 2010. The next elections will be held in 2014.

The Americas

	Previous membership	Current membership
Antigua and Barbuda		
Argentina	1947–2010	2010–14
Bahamas	1994–98	
Barbados		
Belize		
Bolivia		
Brazil	1947–2010	2010–14
Canada	1947–2010	2010–14
Chile	1994–98	
Colombia	1982–94	
Costa Rica		2010–14
Cuba	1989–2010	2010–14
Dominica		
Dominican Republic		
Ecuador		
El Salvador		
Grenada		
Guatemala		
Guyana		
Haiti		
Honduras		
Jamaica	1989–94	
Mexico	1952–2010	2010–14
Nicaragua		
Panama		
Paraguay		2010–14
Peru	1982–89	
Saint Kitts and Nevis		
Saint Lucia	1998–2002	
Saint Vincent and the Grenadines		
Suriname	2006–10	
Trinidad and Tobago	1973–82 2006–10	
USA	1947–2010	2010–14
Uruguay		
Venezuela	1965–2010	2010–14

Western Europe

	Previous membership	Current membership
Andorra		
Austria		
Belgium		
Bosnia and Herzegovina		
Croatia		
Cyprus		
Denmark	1994–2002	
Estonia		
Finland		
France	1947–2010	2010–14
Germany	1959–2010	2010–14
Greece	1989–94	2010–14
Hungary	1973–82	
Iceland		
Ireland	1965–73	

OTHER BODIES

	Previous membership	Current membership
Italy	1947–2010	2010–14
Latvia		
Liechtenstein		
Lithuania		
Luxembourg		
Malta		
Monaco		
Netherlands		
Norway	2002–06	
Portugal	1947–52 1994–2010	
San Marino		
Slovenia		
Spain	1973–2010	2010–14
Sweden	1973–94 2006–10	2010–14
Switzerland	1947–2010	2010–14
Turkey	2002–10	2010–14
UK	1947–89 1994–2002	
Vatican		

Eastern Europe and Northern Asia[1, 2]

	Previous membership	Current membership
Albania		
Armenia		
Azerbaijan		
Belarus		
Bulgaria	1989–2010	2010–14
Czech Republic	1993–2010	2010–14
Georgia		
Kazakhstan		
Kyrgyzstan		
Montenegro		
Poland	1965–82 1994–2006	2010–14
Republic of Moldova		
Romania	1973–89 1994–2010	2010–14
Russian Federation	1947–2010	2010–14
Serbia		
Slovakia		
Tajikistan		
The former Yugoslav Republic of Macedonia		
Turkmenistan		
Ukraine	1994–98 2006–10	
Uzbekistan	1947–59	

Africa

	Previous membership	Current membership
Algeria	1965–2010	2010–14
Angola		
Benin	1982–98	
Botswana		
Burkina Faso	1989–2010	2010–14
Burundi		
Cameroon	1973–2010	2010–14
Cape Verde	1989–98	
Central African Republic		

	Previous membership	Current membership
Chad		
Comoros		
Congo		
Côte d'Ivoire	1998–2002	
DR Congo	1973–82	
Djibouti		
Egypt	1973–2010	2010–14
Equatorial Guinea		
Eritrea		
Ethiopia	1959–89	
Gabon	1998–2002	
Gambia		
Ghana	2002–10	2010–14
Guinea		
Guinea-Bissau		
Kenya	1982–2010	2010–14
Lesotho		
Liberia		
Libya		
Madagascar	1965–73	
Malawi		
Mali	1989–2010	2010–14
Mauritania		
Mauritius		
Morocco	1959–2010	2010–14
Mozambique		
Namibia		
Niger		
Nigeria	1965–98 2002–10	2010–14
Rwanda		2010–14
Sao Tome and Principe		
Senegal	1973–2010	2010–14
Seychelles		
Sierra Leone		
Somalia		
South Africa	1994–2010	2010–14
South Sudan		
Sudan		
Swaziland		
Togo		
Tunisia	1959–2010	2010–14
Uganda	1965–73 2002–06	
UR of Tanzania	1973–2002 06–10	
Zambia	1982–89	
Zimbabwe		

Asia and Australasia

Afghanistan		
Australia	1959–2010	2010–14
Bahrain		
Bangladesh		2010–14
Bhutan		
Brunei Darussalam		

	Previous membership	Current membership
Cambodia		
China	1947–2010	2010–14
DPRK		
Fiji		
India	1952–2010	2010–14
Indonesia	1982–98 2002–10	2010–14
Iran	1973–82 2002–06	
Iraq		
Israel		
Japan	1959–2010	2010–14
Jordan		
Kiribati		
Kuwait	1982–2002	2010–14
Lao PDR		
Lebanon	1965–89	
Malaysia	1973–82 1989–2010	2010–14
Maldives		
Marshall Islands		
Micronesia		
Mongolia		
Myanmar		
Nauru		
Nepal		
New Zealand		
Oman		
Pakistan	1982–2010	
Papua New Guinea		
Philippines	1982–2002 06–10	2010–14
Qatar		
ROK	1989–2010	2010–14
Samoa		
Saudi Arabia	1965–2010	2010–14
Singapore		
Solomon Islands		
Sri Lanka		
Syria		
Thailand	1973–2010	2010–14
Timor-Leste		
Tonga		
Tuvalu		
UAE	2006–10	2010–14
Vanuatu		
Viet Nam	1994–2006	
Yemen		

Notes

1   Czechoslovakia served on the Council from 1989–1992.

2   The former Socialist Federal Republic of Yugoslavia served on the Council from 1989–92.

World Meteorological Organization (WMO)

7 bis Avenue de la Paix
Case Postale 2300
1211 Geneva 2
Switzerland
Telephone: (+41 22) 730 8111
Fax: (+41 22) 730 8181
Email: wmo@wmo.int
Internet: www.wmo.int
Secretary-General: Michel Jarraud, France (appointed by the 14th WMO Congress; reappointed by the 16th Congress for a third four-year term from January 2012)

Purpose

The World Meteorological Organization (WMO) is the successor to the International Meteorological Organization, which was established in 1873. It formally came into existence in 1950 and became a UN specialised agency in 1951.

Article 2 of the WMO Convention, which was signed in Washington in 1947 and came into force on 23 March 1950, defined the Organization's purposes as being to:
- Facilitate worldwide cooperation in the establishment of networks of stations for making meteorological observations, as well as hydrological and other geophysical observations related to meteorology, and to promote the establishment and maintenance of centres charged with the provision of meteorological and related services
- Promote the establishment and maintenance of systems for rapid exchange of meteorological and related information
- Promote standardisation of meteorological and related observations, and ensure the uniform publication of observations and statistics
- Further the application of meteorology to aviation, shipping, water problems, agriculture and other human activities
- Promote activities in operational hydrology and further close cooperation between meteorological and hydrological services
- Encourage research and training in meteorology and, as appropriate, in related fields, and assist in coordinating the international aspects of such research and training.

Structure
- World Meteorological Congress
- Executive Council
- Six regional associations (Africa; Asia; South America; North America, Central America and the Caribbean; South-West Pacific; and Europe)
- Eight technical commissions (atmospheric sciences, aeronautical meteorology, agricultural meteorology, basic systems, hydrology, instruments and methods of observation, oceanography and marine meteorology, and climatology)
- Secretariat

Meetings

The World Meteorological Congress, the supreme body of the Organization, meets once every four years. The 16th Congress was held from 16 May to 3 June 2011.

Membership

Membership of the WMO comprises 183 Member States and six territories. Members of the Executive Council are elected in an individual capacity. The 37 members are the Organization's President and three Vice-Presidents, the six Presidents of the regional associations who are ex officio members, and 27 Directors of members' national meteorological or hydro-meteorological services. Elections to the Council are held at the World Meteorological Congress, except those for presidents of regional associations, who are elected by their respective associations. Apart from regional association presidents, the members of the Council serve from the end of one Congress to the end of the next. When a vacancy occurs among the 27 elected members between Congress sessions, an acting member is designated by the Executive Council. The members are:

President
D Grimes, Canada

First Vice-President
A D Moura, Brazil

Second Vice-President
M S Ostojski, Poland

Third Vice-President
A Mokssit, Morocco

Presidents of regional associations
Region I, Africa: M L Bah, Guinea
Region II, Asia: V E Chub, Uzbekistan
Region III, South America: J Báez Benítez, Paraguay (acting)
Region IV, North America, Central America and the Caribbean: A W Rolle, Bahamas
Region V, South-West Pacific: S W B Harijono, Indonesia
Region VI, Europe: I Čačić, Croatia

	Previous terms	Current terms*
Afghanistan		
Albania		
Algeria	1987–91	
Angola	1979–80	
Antigua and Barbuda		
Argentina	1975–2000 03–11	2011–15
Armenia		
Australia	1958–2011	2011–15
Austria	1994–98	
Azerbaijan		
Bahamas		2009–13
Bahrain	2000–08	
Bangladesh		
Barbados		
Belarus		
Belgium	1963–71	
Belize	2002–03 05–08	
Benin	1997–2001	
Bhutan		
Bolivia		

	Previous terms	Current terms*
Bosnia and Herzegovina		
Botswana	1995–2003	
Brazil	1974–99 2001–11	2011–15
British Caribbean Territories	1983–2011	2011–15
Brunei Darussalam		
Bulgaria		
Burkina Faso	2005	
Burundi	1993–97	
Cambodia		
Cameroon	1979–81 86–95 2001–03	
Canada	1975–2011	2011–15
Cape Verde		
Central African Republic		
Chad		
Chile	1980–82 89 2007 08–11	
China	1973–2011	2011–15
Colombia	1971–83 91–92 95–99	
Comoros		
Congo	1981–87 1999–2001	2011–15
Cook Islands	2005–10	
Costa Rica	1986–91 2003–11	2011–15
Côte d'Ivoire	1986–87 90–95	
Croatia		2009–13
Cuba	1983–84	
Curaçao and St Maarten[1]	1993–95 1997–2005	
Cyprus		
Czech Republic	1995–99 2004–07	
DPRK		
DR Congo		
Denmark	1999–2003	
Djibouti		
Dominica		
Dominican Republic		
Ecuador	1963–71 2000–03	2011–15
Egypt	1955–85 87–91 95–99 2003–06 07–11	
El Salvador		
Eritrea		
Estonia		
Ethiopia	1982–90 2003–05	
Fiji	1995–2003	2011–15
Finland	1983–90 2007–11	2011–15
France	1951–2006 07–11	2011–15
French Polynesia		
Gabon		
Gambia	1994–95	
Georgia		
Germany	1963–2011	2011–15
Ghana	1979–81 87–91 2003–06	
Greece	1989–94	
Guatemala	1973–77	
Guinea	2002–10	2011–14
Guinea-Bissau		
Guyana		

355

OTHER BODIES

	Previous terms	Current terms*
Haiti		
Honduras	1991–93	
Hong Kong, China		
Hungary	1979–81 2000–01	
Iceland		
India	1979–99 2002–11	2011–15
Indonesia	1993–99 2001–02 07–10	2010–14
Iran	1969–79 1991–2011	
Iraq	1979–82	
Ireland		
Israel	1995–2002	
Italy	1983–95 1998–2000 03–11 12	
Jamaica		
Japan	1967–2011	2011–15
Jordan	1987–91 2003–06	
Kazakhstan		
Kenya	1971–2011	2011–15
Kiribati		
Kuwait		
Kyrgyzstan		
Lao PDR		
Latvia		
Lebanon		
Lesotho	1994–95 2003–07	
Liberia		
Libya		
Lithuania	2002–05	
Luxembourg	1955–71	
Macau, China		
Madagascar		
Malawi	1981–82 91–95	
Malaysia	1979–86 95–96 1998–2001 03–05 06–11	2011–15
Maldives		
Mali	1990–2001 06–07	
Malta		
Mauritania	2007–11	
Mauritius	1975–79 2007–11	
Mexico	1979–85 1995–2002 07–09	
Micronesia		
Mongolia	1975 1994–2000	
Montenegro		
Morocco	1983–87 1999–2003	2011–15
Mozambique	2006–07	
Myanmar	1982–84	
Namibia	2007–11	
Nepal	1983–87	
Netherlands	1991–95	
New Caledonia	1962–71	
New Zealand	1986–88 2003–07 10–11	
Nicaragua		
Niger	1985–91	
Nigeria	1973–83 91–93 1995–2002 07–11	2011–15
Niue		

	Previous terms	Current terms*
Norway	1979–83 90–94	
Oman		
Pakistan	1971–91 2003–07	
Panama	1987–91 2008–09	
Papua New Guinea		
Paraguay	1959–63 91–99 2003–05	2011–14
Peru	1983–87 2007–11	
Philippines	1974–95 97–99	
Poland	1971–75 1991–2003 07–11	2011–15
Portugal	1984–87 2001–02	
Qatar	1986–95	
ROK	2000 07–11	2011–15
Republic of Moldova		
Romania		
Russian Federation	1951–2003 04–11	2011–15
Rwanda	1991–92 98–99 2006–07	
Saint Lucia		
Samoa		
Sao Tome and Principe		
Saudi Arabia	1983–2002 07–11	2011–15
Senegal	1975–85 95–97 2001–04 11–12	
Serbia[2]		
Seychelles		
Sierra Leone		
Singapore	1967–74 89–92 2002–06	
Slovakia		
Slovenia		
Solomon Islands		
Somalia		
South Africa	1995–2005 07–11	2011–15
Spain	1983–96 1999–2000 03–11	2011–15
Sri Lanka		
Sudan	1959–63 91–95 2010–12	
Suriname		
Swaziland		
Sweden	1955–79	
Switzerland	1971–75 2003–09	
Syrian AR	1979–84 2001–03	
Tajikistan		
Thailand		
The former Yugoslav Republic of Macedonia		
Timor-Leste		
Togo	1983–90	
Tonga		
Trinidad and Tobago	1994–97	
Tunisia	1975–79 91–95	
Turkey		
Turkmenistan		
Uganda	1971–79	
Ukraine		
UAE		
UK	1979–2011	2011–15

	Previous terms	Current terms*
UR of Tanzania	1975–79 1995–2007	
USA	1951–2011	2011–15
Uruguay	1982–91 1999–2000 03–05	
Uzbekistan	2008–12	
Vanuatu		
Venezuela	1971–79 86–88 94–95 1999–2003 06–10	
Viet Nam		
Yemen		
Zambia	1983–87	2011–15
Zimbabwe	1987–91	

Notes

*   Three seats vacant.

1   Netherlands Antilles was previously a member. On 10 October 2010, the five-island Dutch Caribbean dependency ceased to exist. Curaçao and Saint Maarten now have internal self-government within the Netherlands, joining Aruba, which gained similar status in 1986. Bonaire, Saint Eustatius and Saba have become part of the Netherlands. The Netherlands retains responsibility for defence and foreign policy, and remains the subject of international law with which agreements are concluded.

2   The former Socialist Federal Republic of Yugoslavia served on the Executive Council from 1963 to 1991.

International Maritime Organization (IMO)

4 Albert Embankment
London SE1 7SR
United Kingdom
Telephone: (+44 0) 20 7735 7611
Fax: (+44 0) 20 7587 3210
Email: info@imo.org
Internet: www.imo.org
Secretary-General: Koji Sekimizu, Japan (elected by the IMO Council in June 2011 for an initial four-year period beginning 1 January 2012)

Purpose

The International Maritime Organization (IMO) is the UN specialised agency responsible for the safety of life at sea, maritime security and the protection of the marine environment through prevention of sea pollution caused by ships. It facilitates cooperation among governments to achieve the highest practicable standards of maritime safety and security, and efficiency in navigation. It deals with legal matters connected with international shipping, including liability and compensation regimes, as well as with facilitation of international maritime traffic. It is also responsible for providing technical assistance in maritime matters to developing countries.

The IMO convenes international conferences on shipping matters and for drafting international conventions or agreements on this subject. The current emphasis is on ensuring relevant conventions and treaties are properly implemented by the countries that have accepted them.

Evolution

The Convention on the International Maritime Organization concluded at Geneva in 1948 and came into force in 1958. The first IMO Assembly was convened in London in 1959. Prior to 22 May 1982 (the date of entry into force of the 1975 amendments to the IMO Convention), the Organization's name was the Inter-governmental Maritime Consultative Organization (IMCO).

Structure

- Assembly
- Council
- Committees
- Secretariat

The 40-member Council is the IMO's executive organ. It is responsible, under the Assembly, for supervising the Organization's work. Between Assembly sessions, the Council performs all the Assembly's functions except for making recommendations to governments on maritime safety and pollution prevention. This function is reserved for the Assembly by article 15(j) of the Convention.

The IMO Council is also responsible for appointing its Secretary-General, subject to the approval of the Assembly. Council members are elected by the Assembly for two-year terms beginning after each regular session of the Assembly. Member States are elected from three categories:

- Category A: 10 states with the largest interest in providing international shipping services
- Category B: 10 other states with the largest interest in international seaborne trade
- Category C: 20 states not elected under either category (A) or (B) that have special interests in maritime transport or navigation and whose election will ensure the representation of all major areas of the world.

All IMO committees are open to all member governments on an equal basis.

The Maritime Safety Committee, established under the IMO Convention, is the highest IMO technical body. Much of its work is carried out through subsidiary bodies. Subjects dealt with include maritime security, flag state implementation, navigation safety, radio communications, life-saving appliances and arrangements, search and rescue, ship design and equipment, fire protection, standards of training and watch keeping, containers and cargoes, and the carriage of dangerous goods.

The Marine Environment Protection Committee was set up in 1973 to coordinate and administer IMO activities for the prevention and control of marine pollution from ships. All members of the IMO are entitled to take part, as are representatives of non-IMO states that are parties to treaties linked to Committee work. The Committee was institutionalised in 1982.

The Maritime Safety Committee and the Marine Environment Protection Committee are assisted by nine sub-committees, which are open to all Member States.

The Legal Committee was set up in 1967 to consider any legal matters within the IMO's scope and submit to the Council its drafts of international conventions and other international treaty instruments. It was institutionalised in 1982. Subjects dealt with include liability and compensation regimes for damage caused at sea by hazardous and noxious substances, wreck removal and seafarer claims.

The Technical Cooperation Committee was set up in 1969 to establish directives and guidelines for the IMO's programme of assistance to developing countries in maritime transport (particularly shipping and ports), to monitor the programme's progressive development and review the results. It was institutionalised in 1984.

The Facilitation Committee, established in 1972, is responsible for facilitating international maritime traffic through reducing the formalities and simplifying documentation required of ships when entering or leaving ports or other terminals. It became formally institutionalised on 7 December 2008, with the entry into force of the 1991 amendments to the IMO Convention.

The IMO also acts as a secretariat in respect of the Convention on the Prevention of Marine Pollution by Dumping of Wastes and Other Matter, adopted in London in 1972, which regulates the disposal into the sea of waste materials generated on land. Consultative meetings are normally held once a year. A Protocol amending the Convention was adopted in 1996 and entered into force on 24 March 2006. Forty-one states have now acceded to the Protocol, which is expected ultimately to replace the Convention.

Meetings
The Assembly, consisting of all Member States, usually meets every two years. The 28th session is scheduled to take place in London in November 2013.

Membership
The IMO has 170 members and three associate members. The Council has 40 members. The following list of all members shows their membership terms on the Council, which expire at the end of Assembly meetings. Elections were most recently held at the 27th session in November 2011.

	Previous terms	Current terms
African states		
Algeria	1971–79 83–99 2004–07	
Angola		
Benin		
Cameroon		
Cape Verde		
Comoros		
Congo		
Côte d'Ivoire		
DR Congo		
Djibouti		
Egypt[3]	1978–2011	2011–13
Equatorial Guinea		
Eritrea		
Ethiopia		
Gabon	1984–87	
Gambia		
Ghana	1986–87 96–97 2002–05	
Guinea		
Guinea-Bissau		
Kenya[3]	1978–79 2002–03 06–11	2011–13
Liberia[3]	1978–91 98–99	2011–13
Libya		
Madagascar	1964–71	
Malawi		
Mauritania		
Mauritius		
Morocco[3]	1980–81 84–87 89–97 2000–01	2011–13

	Previous terms	Current terms
Mozambique		
Namibia		
Nigeria	1974–85 88–95 2002–05 08–11	
Sao Tome and Principe		
Senegal		
Seychelles		
Sierra Leone		
Somalia		
South Africa[3]	1998–2011	2011–13
Sudan		
Togo		
Tunisia	1998–99	
Uganda		
UR of Tanzania		
Zimbabwe		

Asia–Pacific states

	Previous terms	Current terms
Bahrain		
Bangladesh[2]	1981–87 2002–11	2011–13
Brunei Darussalam		
Cambodia		
China[1]	1975–81 83–87 1989–2011	2011–13
Cyprus[3]	1991–2011	2011–13
DPRK		
Fiji		
India[2]	1959–83 1985–2011	2011–13
Indonesia[3]	1974–79 1985–2011	2011–13
Iran	1991–97	
Iraq		
Japan[1]	1959–2011	2011–13
Jordan		
Kazakhstan		
Kuwait	1978–91 93–95	
Lebanon	1981–91 2002–03	
Malaysia[3]	2006–11	2011–13
Maldives		
Marshall Islands		
Mongolia		
Myanmar		
Nepal		
Oman		
Pakistan	1978–81 87–93	
Palau		
Papua New Guinea		
Philippines[3]	1989–93 1998–2011	2011–13
Qatar		
ROK[1]	1991–2011	2011–13
Samoa		
Saudi Arabia	1982–97 2004–11	
Singapore[3]	1993–2011	2011–13
Solomon Islands		
Sri Lanka		
Syrian AR		
Thailand[3]	2008–11	2011–13

	Previous terms	Current terms

Timor-Leste
Tonga
Turkmenistan
Tuvalu
UAE
Vanuatu
Viet Nam
Yemen

Eastern European states

Albania
Azerbaijan
Bosnia and Herzegovina
Bulgaria 1984–85
Croatia
Czech Republic
Estonia
Georgia
Hungary
Latvia
Lithuania
Montenegro
Poland 1980–83 85–91 93–99 2002–05
Republic of Moldova
Romania 1978–79
Russian Federation[1] 1959–2011 2011–13
Serbia[4]
Slovakia
Slovenia
The former Yugoslav Republic
  of Macedonia
Ukraine

Latin American and Caribbean states

Antigua and Barbuda
Argentina[2] 1975–79 1983–2011 2011–13
Bahamas[3] 1991–95 2000–11 2011–13
Barbados 1989–91
Belize
Bolivia
Brazil[2] 1967–2011 2011–13
Chile[3] 1984–85 2002–11 2011–13
Colombia
Costa Rica
Cuba 1979–81 83–85
Dominica
Dominican Republic
Ecuador
El Salvador
Grenada
Guatemala
Guyana
Haiti
Honduras 2002–03
Jamaica[3] 1980–83 2008–11 2011–13

	Previous terms	Current terms
Mexico[3]	1978–79 82–83 86–87 1989–2011	2011–13
Nicaragua		
Panama[1]	1980–83 85–89 91–93 1995–2011	2011–13
Paraguay		
Peru	1978–81 87–89	
Saint Kitts and Nevis		
Saint Lucia		
Saint Vincent and the Grenadines		
Suriname		
Trinidad and Tobago	1983–89	
Uruguay		
Venezuela	2002–05	

Western European and Other states

Australia[3]	1985–2011	2011–13
Austria		
Belgium[3]	1959–75 2006–07 10–11	2011–13
Canada[2]	1959–2011	2011–13
Denmark[3]	2002–11	2011–13
Finland	1998–2001	
France[2]	1959–2011	2011–13
Germany[2]	1959–2011	2011–13
Greece[1]	1979–2011	2011–13
Iceland		
Ireland		
Israel		
Italy[1]	1982–83 1986–2011	2011–13
Luxembourg		
Malta[3]	1978–79 2000–11	2011–13
Monaco		
Netherlands[2]	1984–87 1991–2011	2011–13
New Zealand	2008–09	
Norway[1]	1959–2011	2011–13
Portugal	2004–07	
San Marino		
Spain[2]	1974–75 1980–2011	2011–13
Sweden[2]	1988–2011	2011–13
Switzerland		
Turkey[3]	2000–11	2011–13
UK[1]	1959–2011	2011–13

Members outside of UN General Assembly regional groupings

Cook Islands		
Kiribati		
USA[1]	1959–2011	2011–13

Associate IMO members

Faroe Islands, Denmark	Hong Kong, China	Macau, China

Notes

1   Category A: 10 states with the largest interest in providing international shipping services.

2   Category B: 10 other states with the largest interest in providing international seaborne trade.

3   Category C: 20 states not elected under category A or B that have special interests in maritime transport or navigation, and whose election would ensure the representation of all geographic areas of the world.

4   The former Socialist Federal Republic of Yugoslavia served on the Executive Council from 1963 to 1991.

World Intellectual Property Organization (WIPO)

34 Chemin des Colombettes
PO Box 18
CH 1211 Geneva 20
Switzerland
Telephone: (+41 22) 338 9111
Fax: (+41 22) 733 5428
Email: wipo.mail@wipo.int
Internet: www.wipo.int
Director-General: Francis Gurry, Australia (appointed by the General Assembly, upon nomination by the Coordination Committee, for 2008–14)

Purpose

The World Intellectual Property Organization (WIPO) is dedicated to developing a balanced and accessible international intellectual property (IP) system that rewards creativity, stimulates innovation and contributes to economic development while safeguarding the public interest.

It was established following the conclusion of the Convention Establishing the World Intellectual Property Organization in Stockholm in 1967. Its mandate is to promote the protection of IP through cooperation among states and in collaboration with other international organisations. The WIPO Convention entered into force on 26 April 1970. The Organization became a UN specialised agency in 1974.

WIPO administers 24 treaties that deal with different legal and administrative aspects of intellectual property, notably the Paris Convention for the Protection of Industrial Property (174 contracting parties as of May 2012), the Berne Convention for the Protection of Literary and Artistic Works (165 contracting parties) and the Patent Cooperation Treaty (146 contracting parties as of June 2012).

Structure

- General Assembly
- Conference
- Coordination Committee
- Secretariat

The General Assembly is the Organization's supreme decision-making body and has 176 members. The Conference has 185 members (see www.wipo.int/members). The Paris and Berne Unions elect executive committees from among their members. The joint membership of these two committees constitutes the WIPO Coordination Committee, which has 83 members.

Meetings

Member States of WIPO and the Unions established by the different WIPO Treaties meet in an ordinary session of the General Assembly once every two years and in extraordinary session every other year. Meetings are traditionally held in the northern hemisphere autumn for approximately 10 days. The 2012 Assemblies are scheduled to be held from 1 to 9 October.

All WIPO Member States, whether or not they are members of any of the Unions, are also entitled to participate in the WIPO Conference, which meets at the same time as the General Assembly. The Coordination Committee meets in ordinary session once a year.

International Fund for Agricultural Development (IFAD)

Via Paolo di Dono, 44
00142 Rome, Italy
Telephone: (+39 06) 54591
Fax: (+39 06) 5043 463
Email: ifad@ifad.org
Website: www.ifad.org
President: Kanayo F Nwanze, Nigeria (elected by the Governing Council for 2009–13)

Purpose

The International Fund for Agricultural Development (IFAD) is an international financial institution and UN specialised agency dedicated to eradicating poverty in rural areas of developing countries. The Fund was established in 1977 as one of the major outcomes of the 1974 World Food Conference.

IFAD provides low-interest loans and grants to developing countries to finance innovative agricultural and rural development programmes and projects. The Fund is among the top three multilateral institutions working in agriculture in Africa, and is the only institution that has focused exclusively on smallholder development.

IFAD-supported programmes and projects ensure that poor rural people have better access to, and the skills and organisation needed, to take advantage of:
* Natural resources, especially secure access to land and water, and improved natural resource management and conservation practices
* Improved agricultural technologies and effective production services
* A broad range of financial services
* Transparent and competitive markets for agricultural inputs and produce
* Opportunities for rural off-farm employment and enterprise development
* Local and national policy and programming processes.

The Millennium Development Goals (MDGs) have guided IFAD's work since 2000, in particular, the first goal to halve the proportion of people suffering from hunger and extreme poverty by 2015.

The great majority of IFAD's resources are provided to low-income countries on highly concessional terms, under which the loans are repayable over 40 years, with a 10-year grace period, at zero percent interest and a 0.75 percent service charge. In 2007, IFAD's Executive Board approved the Fund's debt sustainability framework (DSF), replacing loans with grants for poor countries unable to sustain debt. The framework is part of a unified effort by multilateral financial institutions to ensure that essential economic assistance does not cause undue financial hardship for countries most in need.

Since starting operations, IFAD has invested more than $13.7 billion in grants and low-interest loans, supporting 892 programmes and projects that have helped 405 million people achieve better lives for themselves and their families. Co-financing has been provided by governments, project participants, multilateral and bilateral donors, and other partners.

Structure

The Governing Council is IFAD's highest decision-making authority. Each Member State is represented on the Council by a governor and/or an alternate governor. The Executive Board is responsible for overseeing IFAD's general operations and approving the Fund's programme of work. The Board consists of 18 elected members and up to 18 alternate members, all of whom have three-year terms of office. The President chairs the Executive Board, is IFAD's legal representative, the head of staff and conducts the organisation's business under the direction of the Governing Council and Executive Board.

Executive Board membership is determined by the Governing Council, and comprises eight members and up to eight alternate members from List A, four members and four alternate members from List B, and six members and six alternate members from List C.

Following a change to IFAD's governance structure approved by the Governing Council at its 20th session in 1997 (IFAD res. 86/XVIII), countries in the former Category I (Organisation for Economic Co-operation and Development (OECD) members) were reclassified as List A, former Category II (Organization of the Petroleum Exporting Countries (OPEC) members) as List B, and former Category III (developing countries) as List C. The latter list has three sub-lists: C1 for countries in Africa; C2 for Europe, Asia and the Pacific; and C3 for Latin America and the Caribbean. Upon joining the Fund, new members decide which list they wish to be placed on, after consultation with the members of that list. States are also periodically allowed to withdraw from one list to be placed on another, with the approval of members on that list.

Meetings

The Governing Council meets once a year, usually in February. The Executive Board meets three times a year, usually in April, September and December.

Membership

IFAD membership is open to any state that is a member of the UN or its specialised agencies, or the International Atomic Energy Agency (IAEA). Countries may join the Fund after approval by IFAD's Governing Council and accession to the Agreement Establishing IFAD. IFAD has a total membership of 168 countries: 23 in List A, 12 in List B and 133 in List C.

The Executive Board members and alternate members for the three-year term of office approved by the Governing Council 53rd session in February 2012 are as follows. Terms that end at the 38th session in 2015 (other than where shown) are:

Members	Alternates
List A	
Canada	Finland
France	Belgium
Germany	Luxembourg (2012)/Switzerland (2013–14)
Italy	Portugal
Japan	Denmark
Netherlands (2012)/UK (2013–14)	UK (2012)/Netherlands (2013–14)
Norway	Sweden
USA	Spain

Members	Alternates
List B	
Kuwait	UAE
Nigeria	Qatar
Saudi Arabia	Indonesia
Venezuela	Algeria
List C	
Sub-list C1 Africa	
Cameroon (2012)/Egypt (2013–14)	Egypt (2012)/Equatorial Guinea (2013–14)
Angola	Mauritius
Sub-list C2 Europe, Asia and the Pacific	
China	Pakistan
India	Bangladesh (2012)/Turkey (2013)/ROK (2014)
Sub-list C3 Latin America and the Caribbean	
Brazil	Argentina
Mexico	Guatemala

UN Industrial Development Organization (UNIDO)

Vienna International Centre
PO Box 300
A–1400 Vienna
Austria
Telephone: (+43 1) 260 260
Fax: (+43 1) 269 2669
Email: unido@unido.org
Internet: www.unido.org
Director-General: Kandeh K Yumkella, Sierra Leone (elected by the General Conference, on the recommendation of the Industrial Development Board, in 2005; re-elected 2009)

Purpose

The UN Industrial Development Organization (UNIDO) is the UN specialised agency mandated to promote industrial development and international industrial cooperation. The Organization's mission statement is: *Partner for prosperity: UNIDO aspires to reduce poverty through sustainable industrial development. We want every country to have the opportunity to grow a flourishing productive sector, to increase their participation in international trade and to safeguard their environment.*

In order to achieve these objectives, UNIDO's constitution calls on the Organization to:
* Assist developing countries in the formulation of development, institutional, scientific and technological policies and programmes in the field of industrial development
* Analyse trends, disseminate information and coordinate activities in industrial development
* Act as a forum for consultations and negotiations directed towards the industrialisation of developing countries
* Provide technical cooperation to developing countries for the implementation of their development plans for sustainable industrialisation in their public and private sectors.

UNIDO's work focuses on three thematic priority areas: poverty reduction through productive activities; trade capacity-building; and energy and environment.

Activities under the thematic priorities are reflected in UNIDO's strategic long-term vision statement, medium-term programme frameworks (2010–13) and biennial programme documents (2012–13). Activities are strictly aligned with the priorities of the UN Decade for the Eradication of Poverty and relevant multilateral declarations, including the Millennium Declaration, Brussels Declaration and Programme of Action, World Summit Outcome and the Doha Ministerial Declaration. Of special importance for UNIDO's technical cooperation and programming priorities for Africa, is the New Partnership for Africa's Development (NEPAD), a strategic development framework of the African Union (AU).

UNIDO takes part in various UN system inter-agency coordination mechanisms and participates in programme-related task forces and management-related coordination groups. In its programmatic activities, UNIDO partners with UN organisations relevant to its thematic priorities and cooperates with the World Trade Organization (WTO) in the enhanced integrated framework for Aid for Trade. UNIDO is also an executing agency under the Global Environment Facility (GEF), a core agency of the UN Global Compact, and a major implementing agency for several multilateral environmental agreements, including the Montreal Protocol, Stockholm Convention and UN Framework Convention on Climate Change. UNIDO maintains direct collaboration agreements with civil society organisations, academia, government-owned institutions and transnational corporations.

Evolution

The origins of UNIDO can be traced back to a series of studies on the rapid industrialisation of developing countries carried out by the UN Secretariat during the early 1950s at the request of the Economic and Social Council (ECOSOC). In 1962, the Secretariat's Industry Section became the Industrial Development Centre. In 1966, the General Assembly created UNIDO as a special organ of the UN (GA res. 2152 (XXI)), and the Organization was formally established with headquarters in Vienna, Austria, in January 1967. UNIDO's second General Conference, in 1975, recommended the Organization be converted into a specialised agency, and this process was completed in December 1985.

Structure

- The General Conference is UNIDO's highest policy-making organ. It consists of all UNIDO Member States. The Conference appoints the Director-General for four years.
- The Industrial Development Board acts as a preparatory body for the Conference. It consists of 53 Member States elected for four-year terms.
- The Programme and Budget Committee consists of 27 Member States elected for two-year terms.

The UNIDO Secretariat is based in Vienna, Austria. Since 29 March 2011, UNIDO's organisational structure comprises: Office of the Director-General (ODG); Programme Development and Technical Cooperation Division (PTC); Strategic Research, Quality Assurance and Advocacy Division (SQA); Programme Support and General Management Division (PSM); and the independent offices of internal oversight, legal affairs, evaluation, ethics and accountability, and change and organisational renewal. UNIDO has a presence in 64 countries, including 10 regional offices, 19 country offices, 18 desks, five focal points, one regional centre and 11 Investment and Technology Promotion Offices.

Meetings

The General Conference meets every second year. Its 15th session is scheduled to be held in Vienna in December 2013 (tentative). The Industrial Development Board meets once in Conference years and twice in other years. The Programme and Budget Committee meets at least once a year.

Membership

The 174 UNIDO Member States are:

Afghanistan
Albania
Algeria[1, 3]
Angola[1]
Argentina
Armenia
Austria[1, 3]
Azerbaijan
Bahamas
Bahrain
Bangladesh
Barbados
Belarus
Belgium[2, 3]
Belize
Benin
Bhutan
Bolivia
Bosnia and Herzegovina
Botswana
Brazil[2]
Bulgaria
Burkina Faso
Burundi
Cambodia
Cameroon[1]
Cape Verde
Central African Republic
Chad
Chile[1]
China[2, 3]
Colombia
Comoros
Congo
Costa Rica[2]
Côte d'Ivoire[1, 3]
Croatia
Cuba[1, 3]
Cyprus
Czech Republic[2]
DPRK
DR Congo
Denmark
Djibouti
Dominica
Dominican Republic
Ecuador[2]

Egypt[2]
El Salvador
Equatorial Guinea
Eritrea
Ethiopia
Fiji
Finland[2]
France[2, 3]
Gabon
Gambia
Georgia
Germany[2, 3]
Ghana[2]
Greece[1]
Grenada
Guatemala[1]
Guinea
Guinea-Bissau
Guyana
Haiti
Honduras
Hungary[2]
India[1, 3]
Indonesia[1, 3]
Iran[1, 3]
Iraq[1]
Ireland[1]
Israel
Italy[2, 3]
Jamaica
Japan[2, 3]
Jordan
Kazakhstan[1]
Kenya[3]
Kuwait[2]
Kyrgyzstan
Lao PDR
Lebanon
Lesotho[2]
Liberia
Libya
Lithuania[4]
Luxembourg
Madagascar
Malawi
Malaysia
Maldives

Mali
Malta
Mauritania
Mauritius
Mexico[2, 3]
Monaco
Mongolia
Montenegro
Morocco
Mozambique
Myanmar
Namibia[1]
Nepal
Netherlands
New Zealand
Nicaragua
Niger
Nigeria[2, 3]
Norway[2]
Oman
Pakistan[3]
Panama
Papua New Guinea
Paraguay
Peru[1, 3]
Philippines
Poland[2, 3]
Portugal[1]
Qatar
ROK[2]
Republic of Moldova
Romania
Russian Federation[1, 3]
Rwanda
Saint Kitts and Nevis
Saint Lucia
Saint Vincent and the
    Grenadines
Samoa
Sao Tome and Principe
Saudi Arabia[1]
Senegal[1]
Serbia
Seychelles
Sierra Leone
Slovakia
Slovenia

continued next page

OTHER BODIES

Somalia	The former Yugoslav	UAE
South Africa[2, 3]	Republic of Macedonia	UK[5]
Spain[1, 3]	Timor-Leste	UR of Tanzania
Sri Lanka[2]	Togo	Uruguay[1]
Sudan[2, 3]	Tonga	Uzbekistan
Suriname	Trinidad and Tobago	Vanuatu
Swaziland	Tunisia	Venezuela[3]
Sweden[2]	Turkey[1, 3]	Viet Nam
Switzerland[1, 3]	Turkmenistan	Yemen
Syrian AR	Tuvalu	Zambia
Tajikistan	Uganda	Zimbabwe[1]
Thailand[2]	Ukraine[1, 3]	

Notes

1   Member of the Industrial Development Board whose term of office expires at the end of the 15th regular session of the General Conference in 2013 (decision GC.13/Dec.7 of 11 December 2009).

2   Member of the Industrial Development Board whose term of office expires at the end of the 16th regular session of the General Conference in 2015 (decision GC.14/Dec.10 of 2 December 2011).

3   Member of the Programme and Budget Committee whose term of office expires at the close of the 15th regular session of the General Conference in 2013 (decision GC.14/Dec.11 of 2 December 2011).

4   The Secretary-General received an instrument of denunciation of the Constitution from the Government of Lithuania on 29 December 2011. The effective date of the denunciation (withdrawal from UNIDO) is 31 December 2012.

5   The Secretary-General received an instrument of denunciation of the Constitution from the Government of the UK on 27 April 2011. The effective date of the denunciation (withdrawal from UNIDO) is 31 December 2012.

World Tourism Organization (UNWTO)

Capitán Haya, 42
28020 Madrid
Spain
Telephone: (+34) 91 567 81 00
Fax: (+34) 91 571 37 33
Email: omt@unwto.org
Internet: www.unwto.org
Secretary-General: Taleb Rifai, Jordan (elected by the UNWTO General Assembly in October 2009)

Purpose

UNWTO is the UN's specialised agency in the field of tourism. It provides leadership and support to the tourism sector in the advancement of sustainable policies, practices and actions. Through the promotion and development of responsible, sustainable and universally accessible tourism, UNWTO endeavours to maximise tourism's contribution to socio-economic growth, job creation, development, environmental conservation, cultural enrichment and international understanding, while minimising negative social or environmental impacts. It pays particular attention to the interests of developing countries.

UNWTO's general work programme comprises:
- Five regional programmes (Africa, the Americas, Asia and the Pacific, Europe, and the Middle East)
- Sustainable Development of Tourism
- Ethics and Social Dimensions of Tourism
- Technical Cooperation and Services
- Statistics and Tourism Satellite Account
- Market Trends and Marketing Strategies

- Education and Training
- Knowledge Network
- Risk and Crisis Management
- Destination Management
- Strategic Partnerships and Resource Mobilization
- Special field programmes/fairs
- Information Resources and Archives
- Communications
- Affiliate members.

UNWTO acts as an executing agency for the UN Development Programme (UNDP) and has cooperation agreements with the UN Environment Programme (UNEP); UN regional commissions, the Economic Commission for Africa (ECA) and the Economic and Social Commission for Asia and the Pacific (ESCAP); and other UN specialised agencies – the Food and Agriculture Organization (FAO), International Civil Aviation Organization (ICAO), International Maritime Organization (IMO), UN Educational, Scientific and Cultural Organization (UNESCO), World Meteorological Organization (WMO) and World Health Organization (WHO).

In the framework of the UN commitment of 'delivering as one' to ensure effective development assistance and accelerate progress towards the Millennium Development Goals (MDGs), UNWTO is leading an initiative with nine other UN agencies and programmes to coordinate their tourism-related work under the UN Steering Committee on Tourism for Development (SCTD). The other organisations are the International Labour Organization (ILO), International Trade Centre (ITC), UN Conference on Trade and Development (UNCTAD), UNDP, UNESCO, UN Industrial Development Organization (UNIDO), World Trade Organization (WTO) and UNEP.

Evolution

UNWTO was established on 2 January 1975 on the entry into force of statutes adopted on 27 September 1970 in Mexico City. Following a resolution adopted by its first General Assembly in May 1975, UNWTO established its headquarters in Madrid in January 1976, at the invitation of the Spanish Government. In GA res. 32/156 (1977), the General Assembly adopted an agreement on the relationship between the UN and UNWTO. The Organization became a UN specialised agency in December 2003 (GA res. 58/232).

World Tourism Day (WTD) has been commemorated on 27 September each year since 1980. The date marks the anniversary of the adoption of the UNWTO Statutes in 1970. WTD's purpose is to foster international awareness about the importance of tourism and its social, cultural, political and economic value. The event seeks to address global challenges outlined in the MDGs and highlight the contribution the tourism industry can make in reaching these goals. The 2012 theme is 'Tourism and Sustainable Energy: Powering Sustainable Development'.

Structure

- General Assembly
- Executive Council
- Regional Commissions
- Committees of the Executive Council and of the General Assembly
- Secretariat

The General Assembly, UNWTO's supreme body, has established six Regional Commissions covering Africa, the Americas, Europe, the Middle East, East Asia and the Pacific, and South Asia.

The Executive Council is UNWTO's governing body, and has one member elected on the basis of equitable geographical distribution for every five full members of UNWTO. There are 31 countries elected to the Council. A representative of UNWTO associate members and one of the affiliate members (Business Council) also participate. Neither has voting rights. Spain, the Organization's host country, sits on the Council as a permanent voting member.

Executive Council subsidiary bodies are the Programme Committee; Committee on Budget and Finance; Sustainable Development of Tourism Committee; Committee on Statistics and the Tourism Satellite Account; Market and Competitiveness Committee; and Committee for the Review of Applications for Affiliate Membership. The World Committee on Tourism Ethics is a subsidiary organ of the General Assembly.

The Secretariat, headed by UNWTO's Secretary-General, is responsible for implementing the work programme.

Meetings
The UNWTO General Assembly meets every two years to approve the Organization's budget and work programme. The 20th session is scheduled to be held in 2013 in Zambia/Zimbabwe. Regional commissions normally meet once a year. The Executive Council meets at least twice a year.

Membership
UNWTO has three categories of members:
- Full members: 154 Member States[1]
- Associate members: six territories or groups of territories not responsible for their external relations but whose membership is approved by the state assuming responsibility for their external relations[2]
- Affiliate members: more than 400 non-governmental entities with specialised interests in tourism, and commercial and non-commercial bodies and associations with activities related to the aims of UNWTO or falling within its competence.

Permanent Observer status, with the right to speak but without the right to vote, was given to the Holy See at the General Assembly in 1979. Palestine has Special Observer status, granted in 1999.

The term of office for Executive Council members is four years. Elections for half the members are held every two years. The Council elects one chair and two vice-chairs from among its members. The following list shows the year current Council terms end (on the final date of the General Assembly of that year).

Full members	Executive Council current term ends	Full members	Executive Council current term ends
Afghanistan		Argentina	2013
Albania		Armenia	
Algeria		Australia	
Andorra		Austria	
Angola		Azerbaijan	

Full members	Executive Council current term ends	Full members	Executive Council current term ends
Bahamas		Hungary	2013
Bahrain		India	2013
Bangladesh		Indonesia	2015
Belarus		Iran	2013
Benin		Iraq	
Bhutan		Israel	
Bolivia		Italy	2015
Bosnia and Herzegovina		Jamaica	2013
Botswana		Japan	
Brazil	2015	Jordan	
Brunei Darussalam		Kazakhstan	
Bulgaria	2013	Kenya	2013
Burkina Faso	2013	Kuwait	
Burundi		Kyrgyzstan	
Cambodia		Lao PDR	
Cameroon		Latvia	
Cape Verde		Lebanon	
Central African Republic		Lesotho	
Chad		Liberia	
Chile		Libya	
China	2015	Lithuania	
Colombia	2013	Madagascar	2015
Congo		Malawi	
Costa Rica		Malaysia	
Côte d'Ivoire		Maldives	
Croatia		Mali	
Cuba		Malta	
Cyprus		Mauritania	2015
Czech Republic		Mauritius	
DPRK		Mexico	2015
DR Congo		Monaco	
Djibouti		Mongolia	
Dominican Republic		Montenegro	
Ecuador		Morocco	
Egypt	2013	Mozambique	2015
El Salvador		Namibia	
Equatorial Guinea		Nepal	
Eritrea		Netherlands	
Ethiopia		Nicaragua	
Fiji		Niger	
France	2015	Nigeria	2015
Gabon		Norway	
Gambia	2015	Oman	
Georgia		Pakistan	
Germany	2013	Panama	
Ghana		Papua New Guinea	
Greece		Paraguay	
Guatemala		Peru	
Guinea		Philippines	
Guinea-Bissau		Poland	
Haiti		Portugal	
Honduras		Qatar	

OTHER BODIES

continued next page

Full members	Executive Council current term ends	Full members	Executive Council current term ends
ROK	2015	Tajikistan	
Republic of Moldova		Thailand	
Romania	2013	The former Yugoslav Republic of Macedonia	
Russian Federation	2015	Timor-Leste	
Rwanda		Togo	
San Marino		Tunisia	
Sao Tome and Principe		Turkey	
Saudi Arabia	2015	Turkmenistan	
Senegal		Uganda	
Serbia	2013	Ukraine	
Seychelles		UR of Tanzania	2015
Sierra Leone		Uruguay	
Slovakia		Uzbekistan	2015
Slovenia		Vanuatu	
South Africa	2013	Venezuela	
Spain	Permanent Member	Viet Nam	
Sri Lanka		Yemen	
Sudan		Zambia	
Swaziland		Zimbabwe	2013
Switzerland			
Syrian AR			

Associate members[2]

Aruba

Flemish Community of Belgium

Hong Kong, China

Macao, China

Madeira

Puerto Rico

Permanent Observer

Holy See

Special Observer

Palestine

Notes

1   On 12 May 2012, Canada ceased to be a full member (letter of resignation dated 12 May 2011).

2   Netherlands Antilles, as a territory, has ceased to exist. It was previously an associate member.

International Centre for the Study of the Preservation and Restoration of Cultural Property (ICCROM)

Via di San Michele, 13
I–00153 Rome
Italy
Telephone: (+39 06) 58 5531
Fax: (+39 06) 58 553349
Email: iccrom@iccrom.org
Internet: www.iccrom.org
Director-General: Stefano De Caro, Italy (appointed by the ICCROM General Assembly in November 2011 for a four-year term beginning January 2012)

Purpose

The International Centre for the Study of the Preservation and Restoration of Cultural Property (ICCROM) is an inter-governmental organisation founded by the ninth UN Education, Scientific and Cultural Organization (UNESCO) General Conference in New Delhi in 1956 and established in Rome in 1959. Its mandate is to promote the conservation of all types of cultural heritage, both movable and immovable, through its five main areas of activity: training, research, information, cooperation and advocacy.

Structure

* General Assembly
* Council
* Secretariat

ICCROM is governed by a General Assembly made up of delegates from its Member States. The General Assembly determines the Centre's general policies, including approving its biennial programme of activities and budget, electing Council members and appointing the Director-General. Other functions include approving reports on Council and ICCROM Secretariat activities, determining Member State contributions, adopting ICCROM's financial regulations and approving changes to the Statutes.

The ICCROM Council comprises 25 members elected by the General Assembly. The Council also has ex officio members with voting power: the Italian Government, Istituto Superiore per la Conservazione ed il Restauro (ISCR) and UNESCO. Ex officio members with no voting power are the International Council on Monuments and Sites (ICOMOS) and the International Council of Museums (ICOM).

Meetings

The General Assembly meets in ordinary session every two years and in extraordinary session if the Council, or at least one-third of its Member States, so request. The 28th session is scheduled to take place in November 2013 in Rome.

OTHER BODIES

Membership

There are 131 Member States as follows. Information about Council members and their terms is at www.iccrom.org (follow links from 'about us', 'governance' and 'Council Members').

Afghanistan
Albania
Algeria
Andorra
Angola
Argentina
Armenia
Australia
Austria
Azerbaijan
Bahrain
Bangladesh
Barbados
Belgium
Benin
Bolivia
Bosnia and Herzegovina
Botswana
Brazil
Brunei Darussalam
Bulgaria
Burkina Faso
Cambodia
Cameroon
Canada
Chad
Chile
China
Colombia
Congo
Côte d'Ivoire
Croatia
Cuba
Cyprus
Czech Republic
Denmark
Dominican Republic
Ecuador
Egypt
Estonia
Ethiopia
Finland
France
Gabon

Gambia
Georgia
Germany
Ghana
Greece
Guatemala
Guyana
Haiti
Honduras
Hungary
India
Iran
Iraq
Ireland
Israel
Italy
Japan
Jordan
Kenya
Kuwait
Lao PDR
Latvia
Lebanon
Lesotho
Libya
Lithuania
Luxembourg
Madagascar
Malaysia
Mali
Malta
Mauritania
Mauritius
Mexico
Monaco
Mongolia
Montenegro
Morocco
Mozambique
Myanmar
Namibia
Nepal
Netherlands
New Zealand

Nicaragua
Nigeria
Norway
Oman
Pakistan
Paraguay
Peru
Philippines
Poland
Portugal
ROK
Romania
Rwanda
Saudi Arabia
Senegal
Serbia
Seychelles
Slovakia
Slovenia
South Africa
Spain
Sri Lanka
Sudan
Swaziland
Sweden
Switzerland
Syrian AR
Thailand
The former Yugoslav
    Republic of Macedonia
Togo
Trinidad and Tobago
Tunisia
Turkey
UAE
UK
UR of Tanzania
USA
Uruguay
Venezuela
Viet Nam
Yemen
Zambia
Zimbabwe

The Sovereign Military Order of Malta is a permanent observer to ICCROM.

WORLD BANK GROUP

Headquarters
1818 H Street NW
Washington DC 20433
United States of America
Telephone: (+1 202) 473 1000
Fax: (+1 202) 477 6391
Email: pic@worldbank.org
Internet: www.worldbank.org

The World Bank Group comprises the:
- International Bank for Reconstruction and Development (IBRD)
- International Development Association (IDA)
- International Finance Corporation (IFC)
- Multilateral Investment Guarantee Agency (MIGA)
- International Centre for the Settlement of Investment Disputes (ICSID).

The term 'World Bank' refers specifically to the first two of these institutions, the IBRD and IDA.

International Bank for Reconstruction and Development (IBRD)

1818 H Street NW
Washington DC 20433
United States of America
Telephone: (+1 202) 473 1000
Fax: (+1 202) 477 6391
Internet: www.worldbank.org/ibrd
President: Jim Yong Kim, USA (since 1 July 2012)

Purpose

The International Bank for Reconstruction and Development (IBRD) was established to promote the international flow of capital for productive purposes and assist in financing the rebuilding of nations devastated by World War II. The IBRD articles were drawn up at the Bretton Woods Conference in 1944 and the Bank issued its first bond in 1947. The Bank's main objective now is to lend for productive projects or to finance reform programmes that will lead to economic growth in its less developed Member States. It is also attempting to increase the proportion of its lending that directly assists the poorest people in developing countries.

Capital and funding

The Bank obtains the bulk of its funds from borrowing on international capital markets, in effect using the callable capital as its security. No call has ever been made on IBRD capital. IBRD's lending and investment activities, as well as its general operations, are funded by equity and proceeds from debt issuance.

The Bank approved a selective capital and general capital increase in 2011. The capital increases, including share allocation for new members, increase IBRD's authorised capital to $278.4 billion.

Structure

The World Bank Group Board of Governors comprises one governor and one alternate appointed by each member country. Generally, the governors are member countries' ministers of finance or development.

World Bank Group member countries appoint or elect executive directors to the Boards of the IBRD, International Development Agency (IDA), International Finance Corporation (IFC) and Multilateral Investment Guarantee Agency (MIGA). While there are four boards, executive directors serving on these boards are usually the same.

The Joint Ministerial Committee of the World Bank Boards of Governors and the Fund on the Transfer of Real Resources to Developing Countries (Development Committee) meets in April and September each year. Each member country (or executive group of member countries) represented on the two boards appoints a member of the Development Committee.

Because the World Bank Governors only meet annually, they delegate specific duties to 25 executive directors who work at the Bank in Washington DC. Five of the executive directors are single country chairs. The other 20 executive directors are elected according to the wishes of their Constituency Offices.

Meetings

The World Bank Group Boards of Governors' annual meeting, in conjunction with the International Monetary Fund (IMF) Board of Governors, is scheduled to be held in Tokyo, Japan from 12 to 14 September 2012.

Membership

IBRD membership is restricted to members of the IMF that have ratified the articles of the Bank and accepted the terms laid down by it. As of May 2012, there were 187 members. A list is available on the website (www.worldbank.org/ibrd – click on the hyperlink '187 member countries').

International Development Association (IDA)

1818 H Street NW
Washington DC 20433
United States of America
Telephone: (+1 202) 473 1000
Fax: (+1 202) 477 6391
Internet: www.worldbank.org/ida
President: Jim Yong Kim, USA (since 1 July 2012)

Purpose

The International Development Association (IDA) began operations in 1960. Its task is to promote economic development by providing finance to the world's less developed areas on much more concessionary terms than conventional loans. It is designed specifically to finance projects or reform programmes in countries that are not able to service loans from the International Bank for Reconstruction and Development (IBRD).

Capital

The initial subscriptions of all members are proportioned to their subscriptions to the IBRD's capital stock, but under the Article of Agreement, members of the IDA are divided into two groups. Part One comprises the more economically advanced countries and Part Two comprises the less developed states. A Part One country pays its entire subscription in convertible currency, all of which may be used for IDA lending. A Part Two country pays only one-tenth of its subscriptions in convertible currency. The remaining portion is paid in the member's own currency and may not be used without the member's consent.

IDA lending resources have been supplemented since 1960 by a series of replenishments in which Part One and an increasing number of Part Two member countries contribute funds to IDA. Donors meet every three years to replenish IDA funds and review its policies. The most recent was the 16th replenishment (IDA16), which finances projects over the three-year period ending 30 June 2014. Fifty-one countries contributed to IDA16, which totalled $49.3 billion. This is up 18 percent on the previous round, and follows pledges not only from traditional donors but also funding from within the World Bank Group and current and former IDA borrowers.

Structure

The Association is affiliated to the IBRD. Each member country is represented by the same governor and executive director who represent it for the IBRD. The IDA shares the same president, management and staff as the IBRD.

Membership

Membership is open to IBRD member countries. A list of the 171 members is available on the website (www.worldbank.org/ida – follow link to 'What is IDA?' then hyperlink at the end of the page '171 member countries').

International Finance Corporation (IFC)

2121 Pennsylvania Ave NW
Washington DC 20433
United States of America
Telephone: (+1 202) 473 3800
Fax: (+1 202) 973 4384
Internet: www.ifc.org
Chair: Jim Yong Kim, USA (since 1 July 2012)

Purpose

The International Finance Corporation (IFC) is empowered to invest in productive private or part-government enterprises in association with private investors and without government guarantee of repayment, in cases where sufficient private capital is not available on reasonable terms. It also serves as a clearing-house to bring together investment opportunities, private capital (both foreign and domestic) and experienced management. Its primary purpose is to promote the growth of the private sector and to assist productive private enterprises in developing member countries, where such enterprises can advance economic development.

The IFC was established in 1956 and became a UN specialised agency in 1957. Although affiliated to the International Bank for Reconstruction and Development (IBRD), it is a separate legal entity and its capital is entirely separate from that of the Bank. The IFC's major source of borrowings is the international capital markets. Advisory services have become an important part of IFC's business, and a critical tool for extending its reach and impact in the private sector.

Capital

An increase in the IFC's authorised capital from $650 million to $1.3 billion was approved in 1985. This permitted it to expand its operations into more developing member countries, particularly lower-income countries, and into new sectors such as agro-business, energy and minerals.

In 2011, the IFC Board of Governors approved an increase in the authorised share capital of $130 million, to $2.58 billion, and the issue of $200 million of shares (including $70 million of unallocated shares).

Structure

Each member country is represented by the same governor and executive director who represent it for the IBRD. The IFC also shares the same president, but has its own management and staff.

Membership

A list of the 182 member countries is available on the IFC website (www.ifc.org – follow link from 'About IFC' and then the hyperlink '182 member countries').

Multilateral Investment Guarantee Agency (MIGA)

1818 H Street NW
Washington DC 20433
United States of America
Telephone: (+1 202) 473 1000
Fax: (+1 202) 522 0316
Email: migainquiry@worldbank.org
Internet: www.miga.org
Chair: Jim Yong Kim, USA (since 1 July 2012)

Purpose

The objective of the Multilateral Investment Guarantee Agency (MIGA) is to encourage the flow of productive investments among member countries, in particular, to developing countries, by insuring against political risk. MIGA guarantees or insures eligible investments against losses resulting from non-commercial risk such as unexpected restrictions on currency transfer, expropriation, contract repudiation by governments and armed conflict. It charges premiums for these services. MIGA also carries out research and promotional activities related to foreign direct investment.

The international Convention establishing MIGA took effect on 12 April 1988.

Capital

In the year ending 30 June 2011, MIGA issued $2.1 billion in investment guarantees (insurance) for 38 projects in developing countries. The results bring the total guarantee coverage issued since MIGA's inception in 1988 to $23.8 billion. The agency closed the year with an outstanding gross portfolio of $9.1 billion, surpassing the previous year's record high of $7.7 billion.

Membership

The agency's total membership stands at 175 (May 2012). The most recent new members are Iraq, Kosovo and Mexico. A list of members is available on the MIGA website (www.miga.org – follow links from 'Who we are' and 'Member countries').

International Centre for the Settlement of Investment Disputes (ICSID)

1818 H Street NW
Washington DC 20433
United States of America
Telephone: (+1 202) 458 1534
Fax: (+1 202) 522 2615
Internet: www.worldbank.org/icsid
Chair: Jim Yong Kim, USA (since 1 July 2012)

Membership of the International Centre for the Settlement of Investment Disputes (ICSID) is dependent on ratification of the Convention on the Settlement of Investment Disputes between States and Nationals of Other States, which was opened for signature in Washington DC on 18 March 1965. The Convention, serviced by the Centre, provides a voluntary mechanism for settling disputes between governments and foreign investors. As of June 2012, there were 158 signatory states to the Convention, of which 148 had deposited their instruments of ratification, acceptance or approval.

INTERNATIONAL MONETARY FUND (IMF)

700 19th Street NW
Washington DC 20431
United States of America
Telephone: (+1 202) 623 7300
Fax: (+1 202) 623 6278
Email: publicaffairs@imf.org
Internet: www.imf.org
Managing Director and Executive Board Chair: Christine Legarde, France (selected by the IMF Executive Board for a five-year term starting 5 July 2011)

Purpose

The International Monetary Fund (IMF) is an organisation of 187 countries that works to foster global monetary cooperation, secure financial stability, facilitate international trade, promote high employment and sustainable economic growth, and reduce poverty. As of May 2012, the IMF had $154.6 billion in credit outstanding.

The IMF Articles of Agreement were drawn up at the Bretton Woods Conference in 1944. Membership is open to all countries. Ratification of the articles and acceptance of conditions laid down by the Fund are conditions of membership.

The purposes of the Fund are to:
- Promote international monetary cooperation through consultation and collaboration
- Facilitate the expansion and balanced growth of international trade, and thereby contribute to the promotion and maintenance of high levels of employment and real income
- Promote exchange stability and orderly exchange arrangements
- Assist in the establishment of a multilateral system of payments and the elimination of foreign exchange restrictions
- Assist members through the temporary provision of financial resources to correct maladjustments in their balance of payments.

Quotas and drawing facilities

Each member has an assessed quota that is subscribed and determines voting power. Access to use of the Fund's resources is also determined in relation to quota, taking account of the member's balance of payments need and the strength of the policies it agrees to implement to restore balance of payments viability. The total of members' quotas, as of May 2012, was about $369 billion.

Members may draw on non-concessional terms from the general resources of the Fund, which are derived from quota subscriptions, under credit tranches (of 25 percent of quota each). Drawings (or 'purchases') in the upper credit tranches – in other words, beyond the first credit tranche – are subject to the terms of a stand-by arrangement agreed with the member. This arrangement specifies the precise economic policy conditions that the member must meet to qualify for each purchase, and the scheduling of purchases. Stand-by arrangements usually cover a 12- to 18-month period, but may be as long as three years. Members are expected to meet their repurchase deadlines, but the Fund may extend them on request if the Executive Board agrees that the member's external position is not sufficiently strong for it to repay early without undue hardship or risk.

There is also an Extended Fund Facility under which members with structural maladjustments and experiencing balance of payments difficulties can enter into extended arrangements for up to 36 months. These can be in amounts larger than is possible under the credit tranches.

A Flexible Credit Line (FCL) was announced on 24 March 2009, and subsequently expanded in August 2010, to address actual or potential balance of payments needs for countries with strong fundamentals, policies and track records of policy implementation. Countries seeking to use the FCL need to meet a set of up-front criteria, rather than facing ex-post or ongoing conditions. Having met the up-front criteria, a country then has the choice of drawing on the credit line at any time or to treat it as a precautionary instrument. At the time the FCL was expanded, a Precautionary Credit Line (PCL) was added to the toolkit for countries with sound fundamentals and policy track records but that face moderate vulnerabilities preventing them from meeting the high FCL qualification standards. The PCL combines some up-front criteria with ex-post conditions that focus on the vulnerabilities identified.

At the same time as the FCL was introduced, the Fund announced an enhanced framework for its Stand-By Arrangements (SBA). The enhanced framework allows countries ineligible for the FCL to have high access to the SBA funds on a precautionary basis, allows frontloading of access, reduces the frequency of reviews and provides greater flexibility for country-specific circumstances in determining the programme for reviews.

In September 1999, a new Poverty Reduction and Growth Facility (PRGF) replaced and strengthened the IMF's concessional lending under the former Enhanced Structural Adjustment Facility (ESAF). The ESAF had provided concessional loans to qualifying low-income countries, aimed at strengthening balance of payments and fostering growth. The PRGF has broadened this initiative to explicitly include lasting poverty reduction as well as to encourage sustainable growth. The PRGF provides a vehicle for integrating mutually reinforcing macroeconomic, structural and social policies, and is geared much more towards using social indicators to measure progress.

Under the PRGF, low-income countries may borrow on concessional terms through three main facilities: the Extended Credit Facility, which is designed to provide medium-term support to address protracted balance of payments problems; the Standby Credit Facility

(SCF), which addresses short-term balance of payments needs and includes an option to use the SCF on a precautionary basis; the Rapid Credit Facility (RCF), which is for emergency assistance with limited conditionality in the event of an urgent balance of payments need. These changes were agreed in tandem with commitments to enhance the Heavily Indebted Poor Countries (HIPCs) initiative.

Special Drawing Rights

The Fund has created and allocated Special Drawing Rights (SDRs) to supplement member countries' reserves and thereby improve the liquidity of the international monetary system. Members may use SDRs to acquire currency from other members for use in alleviating balance of payments difficulties and in a variety of other transactions. Members in strong balance of payments positions may be designated to accept SDRs from other members with a weak balance of payments in exchange for currency.

Allocations of SDRs are made over two basic periods that generally run to five years. The US dollar value of the SDR is posted daily on the IMF's website.

Evolution

The articles have been amended six times, in 1969, 1978, 1992, 2009 and twice in 2011. The first amendment provided for the creation and allocation of SDRs. The second amendment implemented a review of the Fund's responsibilities and operations that was conducted from 1972 to 1976 following the collapse of the fixed exchange rate system. The third empowers the Fund to suspend the voting and certain related rights of a member who fails to fulfil any of the obligations under the articles, other than obligations with respect to SDRs.

The fourth amendment was to provide for a special one-time allocation of SDRs so as to equalise members' ratio of cumulative allocations to their ninth review quotas. Amendments proposed in 2008 entered into effect in February and March 2011. The first expanded the IMF's investment authority, allowing the IMF a wider range of income sources than the previous reliance primarily on lending to member countries. The second strengthened the representation of emerging market and developing economies in the IMF and enhanced the voice and participation of low-income countries. Fifty-four countries received quota increases totalling around $33 billion.

In November 2010, the IMF agreed wide-ranging governance reforms to reflect the increasing importance of emerging market countries while protecting the voting shares of smaller developing countries in the Fund. The proposal was for a doubling of total quotas to about $756 billion, and for more than 6 percent of quota shares to shift to dynamic emerging market and developing economies and more than 6 percent from over-represented to under-represented countries in the Fund. The proposals would also lead to a more representative, all-elected executive board.

Structure

The Board comprises one governor appointed by each member country – typically a minister of finance or central bank governor. Substantive or policy matters are transmitted in the form of a report and draft resolution to the governors for their vote when one is required. An annual meeting of the Board, in conjunction with that of the World Bank Group, is held in late September/early October.

The Board's International Monetary and Financial Committee (IMFC) meets in April and September. Its terms of reference are the supervision of the international monetary system, including the operation of the adjustment process and global liquidity.

The Development Committee (the Joint Ministerial Committee of the Boards of Governors of the Bank and the Fund on the Transfer of Real Resources to Developing Countries) generally meets at the same time as the IMFC. It advises and reports to the World Bank and IMF Boards of Governors on all aspects of the real transfer of resources to developing countries. Each member country or group of member countries represented on the Executive Board appoints a member of the Committee. This board is responsible for the Fund's daily business, including requests for financial assistance, economic consultations with member countries and the development of Fund policies. It consists of the Managing Director, as Chair, and 24 executive directors. Of these, eight are appointed by members having the largest quotas – USA, Germany, Japan, UK, France, Russian Federation, China and Saudi Arabia – while the remainder are elected to represent the interests of constituencies made up of several countries. Elections can vary across the constituencies, with many being held every two years.

Membership

The IMF has 187 member countries (listed on the IMF website). The Executive Directors and alternates are listed here in order of voting power (as of June 2012).

Executive Directors/alternates

Meg Lundsager/Vacant, USA

Mitsuhiro Furusawa/Tomoyuki Shimoda, Japan

Hubert Temmeyer/Steffen Meyer, Germany

Ambroise Fayolle/Alice Terracol, France

Alexander Gibbs/Robert James Elder, UK

Willy Kiekens, Belgium/Johann Prader, Austria

Carlos Perez-Verdia, Mexico/Jose Rojas Ramirez, Venezuela

Menno Snel, Netherlands/Yuriy G Yakusha, Ukraine

Arrigo Sadun, Italy/Thanos Catsambas, Greece

Chia Der Jiun, Singapore/Aida S Budiman, Indonesia

Tao Zhang/Ping Sun, China

Christopher Y Legg, Australia/Hoseung Lee, ROK

Thomas Hockin, Canada/Mary T O'Dea, Ireland

Benny Andersen, Denmark/Audun Gronn, Norway

Moeketsi Majoro, Lesotho/Momodou Bamba Saho, Gambia

A Shakour Shaalan, Egypt/Sami Geadah, Lebanon

Arvind Virmani, India/P Nandalal Weerasinghe, Sri Lanka

Paulo Nogueira Batista Jr, Brazil/Maria Angelica Arbelaez, Colombia

Ahmed Abdulkarim Alkholifey/Fahad Ibrahim A Alshathri, Saudi Arabia

René Weber, Switzerland/Katarzyna Zajdel-Kurowska, Poland

Aleksei V Mozhin/Andrei Lushin, Russian Federation

Jafar Mojarrad, Iran/Mohammed Daïri, Morocco

Alfredo Mac Laughlin, Argentina/Pablo Garcia-Silva, Chile

Kossi Assimaidou, Togo/Nguéto Tiraina Yambaye, Chad

OTHER RELATED BODIES

International Atomic Energy Agency (IAEA)

Vienna International Centre
Wagramer Strasse 5
PO Box 100
A–1400 Vienna
Austria
Telephone: (+43 1) 2600 0
Fax: (+43 1) 2600 7
Email: official.mail@iaea.org
Internet: www.iaea.org
Director General: Yukiya Amano, Japan (appointed by the Board of Governors and confirmed by the General Conference in 2009)

Purpose

The purpose of the International Atomic Energy Agency (IAEA) is to promote and accelerate the contribution atomic energy makes to peace, health and prosperity throughout the world. At the same time, the Agency is charged with ensuring that the assistance it provides is not used to further states' military objectives, and that nuclear material is not diverted to non-peaceful activities.

Specifically, the IAEA seeks to act as a catalyst for the development and transfer of peaceful nuclear technologies, to build and maintain a global nuclear safety regime, and to assist in global efforts to prevent the proliferation of nuclear weapons. The IAEA groups its activities under three pillars:
1) Science and technology
2) Safety and security
3) Safeguards and verification.

The Agency is authorised to:
- Encourage and assist research on atomic energy for peaceful purposes worldwide
- Act as an intermediary in the supply of materials, services, equipment and facilities
- Foster the exchange of scientific and technical information
- Encourage the exchange and training of scientists and experts
- Establish and administer safeguards against the misuse of aid provided by the IAEA
- Establish safety standards.

Evolution

The IAEA Statute entered into force in 1957, making it an independent inter-governmental organisation under the aegis of the UN rather than a specialised agency.

The Agency is charged with drawing up and implementing the Nuclear Non-Proliferation Treaty (NPT) safeguards provisions, as well as those of the Treaty of Tlatelolco (the Latin American Nuclear Weapon Free Zone), the Treaty of Pelindaba (the African Nuclear Weapon Free Zone), the Treaty of Bangkok (the ASEAN Nuclear Weapon Free Zone), the Treaty of Rarotonga (the South Pacific Nuclear Free Zone) and the Central Asian Nuclear-Weapon-Free Zone (CANWFZ) Treaty.

The safeguard activities form one of the most important aspects of the IAEA's role and functions. The aim of the safeguards is to assist states in demonstrating their compliance with international obligations in the interest of preventing the further proliferation of nuclear weapons. There were 1212 nuclear installations under IAEA safeguards, with 373 inspectors conducting 2024 inspections by the end of 2011.

The IAEA's role in nuclear safety has increased as nuclear power programmes have grown and public attention has focused on the issue. The Agency helps its Member States improve nuclear safety by developing and promoting international safety standards and by supporting Member State efforts to implement safety regulations and manage nuclear activities.

In the security area, the focus is on helping states prevent, detect and respond to terrorist or other malicious acts, such as illegal possession, use, transfer and trafficking of nuclear materials, and to protect nuclear installations and transport against sabotage. Although the IAEA is not a regulatory body, many countries have used its recommendations as a basis for national standards and rules.

The Agency also has important functions under international conventions related to emergency response and preparedness in the event of a nuclear accident. These conventions (with party numbers as of May 2012) are: the Convention on Early Notification of a Nuclear Accident, which entered into force on 27 October 1986 (113 parties); and the Convention on Assistance in the Case of a Nuclear Accident or Radiological Emergency, which entered into force on 26 February 1987 (108 parties). In 1994, an IAEA Diplomatic Conference adopted the Convention on Nuclear Safety. It entered into force on 24 October 1996 (74 parties).

Other conventions adopted under the auspices of the IAEA (with numbers as of May 2012) are the:
- Convention on the Physical Protection of Nuclear Material, which entered into force on 8 February 1987 (145 parties). An amendment to this Convention was adopted on 8 July 2005 but has not yet entered into force (55 contracting states)
- Joint Convention on the Safety of Spent Fuel Management and on the Safety of Radioactive Waste Management, which entered into force on 18 June 2001 (63 parties)
- Vienna Convention on Civil Liability for Nuclear Damage, which entered into force on 12 November 1977 (38 parties)
- Joint Protocol relating to the Application of the Vienna Convention and the Paris Convention, which entered into force on 27 April 1992 (26 parties)
- Protocol to Amend the Vienna Convention on Civil Liability for Nuclear Damage, which entered into force on 4 October 2003 (nine parties)
- Optional Protocol concerning the Compulsory Settlement of Disputes to the Vienna Convention on Civil Liability for Nuclear Damage, which entered into force on 13 May 1999 (two parties)
- Convention on Supplementary Compensation for Nuclear Damage, which was adopted on 12 September 1997 but which has not yet entered into force (four parties).

The Agency also works to mobilise peaceful applications of nuclear science and technology for critical needs in developing countries through its Nuclear Applications and Technical Cooperation programmes. The aim is to promote tangible social and economic benefits through cooperative projects.

Structure

- General Conference
- Board of Governors
- Director General
- Secretariat
- Laboratories (Vienna, Seibersdorf, Monaco and Trieste), regional safeguards offices (Tokyo and Toronto) and UN liaison offices

The General Conference is composed of representatives of all IAEA Member States and is the Agency's highest policy-making body. The Board of Governors has 35 members. Thirteen members are designated each year by the Board to serve for one year, and 22 (11 each year) are elected by the General Conference to serve for two years. Article VI of the IAEA Statute requires the Board to designate the 10 members most advanced in the technology of atomic energy, including the production of source materials. It also requires the Board to designate the member most advanced in the technology of atomic energy, including the production of source materials, in each of the following areas: North America, Latin America, Western Europe, Eastern Europe, Africa, the Middle East and South Asia, South East Asia and the Pacific, and the Far East.

Board members are representatives from the following areas: five from Latin America, four from Western Europe, three from Eastern Europe, four from Africa, two from the Middle East and South Asia, one from South East Asia and the Pacific, and one from the Far East. In addition, one member is elected from the Middle East and South Asia, or South East Asia and the Pacific, or the Far East; and one other member from Africa, or the Middle East and South Asia, or South East Asia and the Pacific.

In 1999, the General Conference approved an amendment to the IAEA Statute concerning the size and distribution of seats on the Board of Governors, by which Board membership would be expanded from 35 to 43 seats. This amendment will enter into force when two-thirds of all IAEA Member States have accepted it and other conditions are met.

The Board of Governors Chair for 2011–12 is Filippo Formica, Italy, who succeeds Gianni Ghisi, Italy. Vice-Chairs for 2011–12 are Dana Drábová, Czech Republic, and Makram Mustafa Queisi, Jordan.

Meetings

The General Conference meets once a year. The 56th session is scheduled to be held from 17 to 21 September 2012 in Vienna, Austria. The Board of Governors generally meets five times a year, in March and June, twice in September (before and after the General Conference) and in December. Additional meetings can be scheduled.

Membership

The following table lists the IAEA's 154 Member States (as of April 2012) and Board member terms. Terms run from and to the end of General Conference regular sessions in the years stated.

	Previous terms	Current terms
Afghanistan	1963–65 2008–10	
Albania	2007–09	
Algeria	1967–69 73–74 81–83 85–87 88–90 91–93 94–96 1999–2001 04–06 07–09	
Angola		
Argentina	1957–11	2011–12
Armenia		
Australia	1957–11	2011–12
Austria	1965–67 77–79 83–85 90–92 1999–2001 06–08	
Azerbaijan	2009–11	
Bahrain		
Bangladesh	1975–77 81–83	
Belarus	1999–2001 05–07	
Belgium	1958–59 60–61 62–63 64–65 66–67 68–69 70–71 72–73 76–78 83–85 89–91 91–92 95–99 2003–06	2010–12
Belize		
Benin		
Bolivia	1999–2001 06–08	
Bosnia and Herzegovina		
Botswana		
Brazil	1957–2006 06–08 09–10	2010–12
Bulgaria	1959–61 67–69 73–75 77–79 82–84 86–88 91–93 95–97 2001–03	2011–13
Burundi		
Burkina Faso	2001–03 08–10	
Cambodia[1]		
Cameroon	1990–92 2009–11	
Canada	1957–2011	2011–12
Central African Republic		
Chad		
Chile	1964–66 70–72 73–74 75–77 79–81 83–85 86–88 89–91 92–94 95–97 1998–2000 01–03 06–08	2010–12
China	1984–2011	2011–12
Colombia	1961–63 65–67 71–73 75–77 81–83 87–89 93–95 96–98 2001–03 05–07	
Congo		
Costa Rica	1973–75	
Côte d'Ivoire	1984–86 88–90	
Croatia	2006–08	
Cuba	1983–85 87–89 90–92 93–95 96–98 1999–2001 02–07 08–10	2011–13
Cyprus		
Czech Republic	1996–98 2002–04	2010–12
DR Congo	1963–65 71–73 74–76 82–84 91–93	
Denmark	1958–59 62–63 66–67 70–71 73–74 75–77 82–84 88–90 95–97 2002–04 09–11	
Dominica		
Dominican Republic		
Ecuador	1977–79 84–86 91–93 2004–06 07–09	2010–12

	Previous terms	Current terms
Egypt	1957–60 64–66 71–73 76–97 1998–2007 08–10	2011–13
El Salvador	1960–62	
Eritrea		
Estonia		
Ethiopia	1993–95 2006–08	
Finland	1960–61 64–65 68–69 72–73 78–80 85–87 92–95 1999–2002 06–09	
France	1957–2011	2011–12
Gabon	1973–75	
Georgia		
Germany[2]	1960–62 66–68 1972–2011	2011–12
Ghana[3]	1962–63 65–67 73–74 77–79 88–90 94–96 97–99 2000–02 04–06 07–09	
Greece	1961–63 71–73 78–80 84–86 91–93 1998–2000 05–07	
Guatemala	1957–58 78–80 85–87	
Haiti		
Holy See		
Honduras		
Hungary	1961–63 69–71 73–75 78–80 83–85 87–89 92–94 97–99 2003–05	2011–13
Iceland		
India	1957–2011	2011–12
Indonesia	1957–60 62–64 66–68 72–74 75–77 78–80 81–83 84–86 87–89 90–92 93–95 1999–2001 05–07	2011–13
Iran	1962–64 68–70 74–76 77–79 90–92 2001–03	
Iraq	1960–62 74–76 80–82 83–85 86–88 89–91 2007–09	
Ireland	1973–74 79–81 86–88 93–95 2000–02 07–09	
Israel		
Italy	1957–58 62–64 68–70 73–86 89–91 93–94 97–99 2003–05 07–08 10–11	2011–13
Japan	1957–2011	2011–12
Jamaica		
Jordan	1984–86 1998–2000	2010–12
Kazakhstan		
Kenya	1979–81 82–84 2009–11	
Kuwait	1977–79 87–89 95–97 2001–03	
Kyrgyzstan		
Laos		
Latvia		
Lebanon	1966–68 73–74 80–82 93–95	
Lesotho		
Liberia		
Libya	1975–77 82–84 87–89 92–94 2000–02 05–07	
Liechtenstein		
Lithuania	2007–09	
Luxembourg		
Madagascar	1967–69 86–88	
Malawi		
Malaysia	1976–78 80–82 84–86 88–90 92–94 96–98 2002–04 08–10	

	Previous terms	Current terms
Mali		
Malta		
Marshall Islands		
Mauritania		
Mauritius		
Mexico	1959–61 62–64 66–68 72–74 76–78 79–81 82–84 85–87 88–90 91–93 94–96 97–99 2000–02 03–05 07–09	2011–13
Monaco		
Mongolia	1985–87 2009–11	
Montenegro		
Morocco	1963–65 69–71 78–80 84–86 90–92 94–96 97–99 2001–03 06–08	
Mozambique		
Myanmar		
Namibia	1996–98	
Nepal		
Netherlands	1958–60 64–66 70–72 75–77 81–83 88–90 95–98 2002–05 09–11	2011–12
New Zealand	1996–98 2002–04 08–10	
Nicaragua	1995–97	
Niger	1976–78 79–81	2010–12
Nigeria	1969–71 76–78 80–82 83–85 86–88 89–91 92–94 95–97 1999–2001 03–08	
Norway	1959–60 63–64 67–68 71–72 77–79 84–86 91–93 1998–2000 05–07	
Oman		
Pakistan	1957–59 61–63 65–67 69–71 73–75 76–78 79–81 82–84 85–87 88–90 91–93 94–96 97–99 2000–08 09–11	
Palau		
Panama	1976–78 81–83 2002–04	
Papua New Guinea		
Paraguay	1992–94	
Peru	1957–60 67–69 73–75 77–79 80–82 84–86 88–90 97–99 2000–05 09–11	
Philippines	1959–61 67–69 73–77 79–81 83–85 89–91 93–95 2001–03 07–09	
Poland	1958–59 60–61 62–63 64–65 66–67 68–69 70–71 72–73 75–77 80–82 85–87 89–91 93–95 1999–2001 03–05	
Portugal	1957–58 59–60 61–62 63–64 65–66 67–68 69–70 71–72 76–78 82–84 90–92 96–98 2004–06	2010–12
Qatar		
ROK	1957–59 65–67 73–75 77–79 81–83 85–89 91–93 1995–2001 03–07 09–11	2011–13
Republic of Moldova		
Romania	1957–59 63–65 71–73 77–79 81–83 91–93 95–97 2001–03 08–10	
Russian Federation	1957–2011	2011–12
Saudi Arabia	1972–74 78–80 86–88 89–91 92–94 95–97 1998–2000 02–04 07–09	2011–13
Senegal	1975–78 87–89	

	Previous terms	Current terms
Serbia		
Seychelles		
Sierra Leone		
Singapore	1968–70 1998–2000 04–06	2010–12
Slovakia	1994–96 1998–2000 04–06	
Slovenia	1997–99 2005–07	
South Africa	1957–77 1995–2011	2011–12
Spain	1959–61 69–71 74–76 81–83 86–89 92–93 94–96 2000–04 08–10	
Sri Lanka	1959–61 67–69 71–73 2004–06	
Sudan	1973–75 80–82 85–87 1998–2000 02–04	
Sweden	1957–58 61–62 65–66 69–70 73–75 80–82 85–94 1997–2000 04–07	2011–13
Switzerland	1963–65 73–75 79–81 86–89 93–95 96–97 2000–03 07–10	
Syrian AR	1970–72 83–85 92–94 1999–2001 05–07	
Tajikistan		
Thailand	1960–62 64–66 70–72 74–76 78–80 82–84 86–88 90–92 94–96 2000–02 06–08	
The former Yugoslav Republic of Macedonia		
Tunisia[3]	1962–63 65–67 77–79 83–85 89–91 93–95 96–98 2003–05	2010–12
Turkey	1957–59 67–69 74–76 80–82 87–89 94–96 2001–03 08–10	
Uganda		
Ukraine	1990–92 93–95 2000–02 09–11	
UAE	1996–98	2010–12
UK	1957–2011	2011–12
UR of Tanzania	1978–80	2011–13
USA	1957–2011	2011–12
Uruguay	1963–65 69–71 74–76 80–82 90–92 94–96 1998–2000 08–10	
Uzbekistan		
Venezuela	1958–60 68–70 74–76 78–80 82–84 86–88 89–91 2004–06 09–11	
Viet Nam	1961–63 69–71 91–93 97–99 2003–05	
Yemen	2004–06	
Zambia	1974–76 81–83	
Zimbabwe		

Notes

The former Socialist Federal Republic of Yugoslavia served on the Board from 1965–67, 1975–77, 1979–81, 1983–85 and 1987–89.

Czechoslovakia served on the Board from 1957–74, 1976–78, 1981–83, 1985–87 and 1989–91.

The DPRK, which joined the IAEA in 1974, withdrew its membership on 13 June 1994.

Membership has been approved by the IAEA General Conference for Togo (2004), Cape Verde (2007), Rwanda (2009), Tonga (2011) and Dominica (2011), and will take effect once the state deposits the necessary legal instruments with the IAEA.

1   Cambodia, which joined the IAEA in 1958, withdrew its membership on 26 March 2003. It rejoined on 23 November 2009.

2   Prior to 3 October 1990, the German Democratic Republic had been a member of the Board from 1974–76, 1979–81, 1984–86 and 1988–90.

3   One year as an observer.

International Criminal Court (ICC)

PO Box 19 519
2500 CM The Hague
The Netherlands
Telephone: (+31 70) 515 8515
Fax: (+31 70) 515 8555
Email: pio@icc-cpi.int
Internet: www.icc-cpi.int
Registrar: Silvana Arbia, Italy (elected by the judges for a five-year term 2008–13)

Purpose

The International Criminal Court (ICC) is a permanent international court with the power to exercise its jurisdiction over individuals who, since 1 July 2002, have committed the most serious crimes of concern to the international community as a whole. It is not a body of the UN, but an independent organisation. Its relationship with the UN is governed by a separate relationship agreement.

States decide to accept the jurisdiction of the Court by becoming party to the Rome Statute, to which there are 121 States Parties (as of June 2012). The Court may exercise jurisdiction only if either the state in which the suspected crime occurred or the state of nationality of the person suspected of having committed the crime is a party to the Rome Statute; and only when national legal systems are unable or unwilling to do so.

Evolution

The Court was established as a new international organisation by the Rome Statute, which was adopted on 17 July 1998 by the UN Diplomatic Conference of Plenipotentiaries on the Establishment of an International Criminal Court (1998). The Conference was convened pursuant to GA res. 51/207 (1996) and GA res. 52/160 (1997).

The Court issued its first verdict in March 2012. At the time, 14 other cases were before the Court, three of which were at trial stage.

Structure

The ICC is composed of the Presidency, Chambers, Office of the Prosecutor and Registry. The Assembly of States Parties, composed of representatives of states that have ratified and acceded to the Rome Statute, is the ICC's management oversight and legislative body (see www.icc-cpi.int and follow links from 'Assembly of States Parties'). Its seat is in The Hague, although the Court may sit elsewhere whenever it considers it desirable to do so.

The ICC's 18 judges are elected by the Assembly of States Parties and are chosen from two lists:
- Those with established competence in criminal law and procedure, and the necessary relevant experience – whether as judge, prosecutor, advocate or in other similar capacity in criminal proceedings
- Those with established competence in relevant areas of international law, such as international humanitarian law and the law of human rights, and extensive experience in a professional legal capacity that is relevant to the judicial work of the court.

In the selection of judges, States Parties must take into account the need for representation of the principal legal systems of the world, equitable geographical distribution and a fair representation of female and male judges.

Judges are elected for terms of nine years and may not be re-elected. The terms of one-third of the 18 judges expire every three years. The following list shows the members of the Court in order of precedence (as of May 2012). Terms end in March of the year shown.

Sang-Hyun Song, ROK (President[1]) 2015

Sanji Mmasenono Monageng, Botswana
(First Vice-President)................. 2018

Cuno Tarfusser, Italy
(Second Vice-President)................. 2018

Hans-Peter Kaul, Germany................. 2015

Akua Kuenyehia, Ghana................. 2015

Erkki Kourula, Finland................. 2015

Anita Ušacka, Latvia................. 2015

Ekaterina Trendafilova, Bulgaria................. 2015

Joyce Aluoch, Kenya................. 2018

Christine Van Den Wyngaert, Belgium.... 2018

Silvia Alejandra Fernandez de
Gurmendi, Argentina................. 2018

Kuniko Ozaki, Japan................. 2018

Miriam Defensor-Santiago, Philippines... 2021[2]

Howard Morrison, UK................. 2021[2]

Anthony T Carmona, Trinidad
and Tobago................. 2021[2]

Olga Herrera Carbuccia, Dominican
Republic................. 2021[2]

Robert Fremr, Czech Republic................. 2021[2]

Chile Eboe-Osuji, Nigeria................. 2021[2]

In addition, the following judges whose terms have expired will remain in office to complete their current trials:

Rene Blattmann, Bolivia................. 2009

Elizabeth Odio Benito, Costa Rica................. 2012

Fatoumata Dembele Diarra, Mali................. 2012

Adrian Fulford, UK................. 2012

Sylvia Steiner, Brazil................. 2012

Bruno Cotte, France................. 2012

Notes

1   Re-elected as President on 11 March 2012 for a three-year term with immediate effect.

2   Elected in December 2011 for terms beginning March 2012.

The Office of the Prosecutor is an independent organ of the Court headed by the Prosecutor, who can be assisted by one or more deputy prosecutors. The Prosecutor is elected by the Assembly of States Parties, and the Deputy Prosecutors are elected in the same way from a list of candidates provided by the Prosecutor. The Prosecutor and Deputy Prosecutors must be of different nationalities. Unless a shorter term is decided on at the time of election, the Prosecutor and Deputy Prosecutors hold office for nine years and are not eligible for re-election.

Deputy Prosecutor and Head of Prosecutions since September 2004, Fatou Bensouada, Gambia, was elected Prosecutor at the 10th session of the Assembly of States Parties in 2011. She replaced Luis Moreno Ocampo, Argentina, in June 2012.

The Registry is headed by the Registrar, who is the principal administrator of the Court. The Registrar is elected by the Judges of the Court, taking into account any recommendation by the Assembly of States Parties. If the need arises, and the Registrar so recommends, the Judges may also elect a deputy registrar. Silvana Arbia, Italy, was elected Registrar of the Court by the judges in a plenary meeting in February 2008 and holds office for five years.

Meetings

The Assembly of States Parties meets annually. The 11th session is scheduled to be held from 14 to 22 November 2012 in The Hague, Netherlands. Pursuant to article 123 of the Rome Statute, the first Review Conference took place in Kampala, Uganda, in June 2010.

Extraordinary Chambers in the Courts of Cambodia (ECCC)

National Road 4
Chaom Chau Commune
Dangkao District
Phnom Penh
PO Box 71
Cambodia
Telephone: (+855) 23 219814
Fax: (+855) 23 219841
Email: info@eccc.gov.kh
Internet: www.eccc.gov.kh/en
Acting Director of the Office of Administration: Tony Kranh, Cambodia (since 2009)
Deputy Director of the Office of Administration: Knut Rosandhaug, Norway (since 2008)

In 1997, the Royal Government of Cambodia requested the United Nations to assist in establishing a court for the prosecution under Cambodian law of crimes committed during the period of Democratic Kampuchea from 1975–79. In 2001, the Cambodian National Assembly passed a law to create the Extraordinary Chambers in the Courts of Cambodia (ECCC) to prosecute these crimes. An agreement concluded by Cambodia and the UN in June 2003 established that the international community would provide technical assistance to the ECCC through the UN Assistance to the Khmer Rouge Trials Mission (UNAKRT) (see www.unakrt-online.org). The ECCC is a Cambodian court with international participation.

The Tribunal consists of the Judicial Chambers (the Pre-Trial Chamber, the Trial Chamber and the Supreme Court Chamber), Office of the Co-Investigating Judges, Office of the Co-Prosecutors, Office of Administration, Defence Support Section and Victims Support Section. The Office of Administration provides support to the other organs of the Court.

Of the 27 judges, 15 are of Cambodian nationality and 12 are international judges nominated by the UN Secretary-General and appointed by the Cambodian Supreme Council of the Magistracy. In addition, there is a national Co-Prosecutor and reserve Co-Prosecutor, and an international Co-Prosecutor and reserve Co-Prosecutor.

The judges are:

Pre-Trial Chamber

Prak Kimsan, Cambodia (President)

Rowan Downing, Australia

Ney Thol, Cambodia

Chang Ho Chung, ROK

Huot Vuthy, Cambodia

Reserve

Pen Pichsaly, Cambodia

Steven Bwana, Tanzania

Trial Chamber

Nil Nonn, Cambodia (President)

Silvia Cartwright, New Zealand

Ya Sokhan, Cambodia

Jean-Marc Lavergne, France

You Ottara, Cambodia

Reserve

Thou Mony, Cambodia

Claudia Fenz, Austria

Supreme Court Chamber

Kong Srim, Cambodia (President)

Motoo Noguchi, Japan[1]

Som Sereyvuth, Cambodia

Agnieszka Klonowiecka-Milart, Poland

Mong Monichariya, Cambodia

Chandra Nihal Jayasinghe, Sri Lanka

Ya Narin, Cambodia

Reserve

Sin Rith, Cambodia

Florence Mumba, Zambia

Co-Investigating Judges[2]

You Bunleng, Cambodia

Reserve

Thong Ol, Cambodia

The Office of the Co-Prosecutors is led by Chea Leang, Cambodia, and Andrew T Cayley, UK.

Notes

1   Supreme Court Chamber Judge Motoo Noguchi, Japan, resigned effective 15 July 2012.
2   As of June 2012, the positions of International and Reserve International Co-Investigating Judges were vacant.

Special Court for Sierra Leone (SCSL)

Jomo Kenyatta Road
New England, Freetown
Sierra Leone
Telephone: (+232) 22 297000
Fax: (+232) 22 297001
Email: scsl-mail@un.org
Internet: www.sc-sl.org
Registrar: Binta Mansaray, Sierra Leone (appointed by the UN Secretary-General in 2010)

Purpose

The Special Court for Sierra Leone (SCSL), the first 'hybrid' international criminal tribunal, was established in January 2002 by an agreement between the UN and the Government of Sierra Leone, pursuant to SC res. 1315 (2000) of 14 August 2000. The Court began operations in July 2002 and the first indictments were issued in March 2003.

The Special Court's role is to prosecute those who bear the greatest responsibility for serious violations of international humanitarian law and Sierra Leonean law committed in the territory of Sierra Leone since 30 November 1996.

Structure

The Special Court consists of: the Chambers (Appeals Chamber, Trial Chamber I and Trial Chamber II); Registry (including the Office of the Principal Defender); and Office of the Prosecutor. The majority of judges, the Prosecutor and the Registrar are appointed by the UN Secretary-General. The remaining judges and the Deputy Prosecutor are appointed by the Government of Sierra Leone. As of 30 June 2012, the two Trial Chambers had completed their mandates and were dissolved.

As at 30 June 2012, the judges are:

Appeals Chamber
Shireen Avis Fisher, USA (President)
Emmanuel Ayoola, Nigeria (Vice President)
Jon Kamanda, Sierra Leone
George Gelaga King, Sierra Leone
Renate Winter, Austria

Alternate judge
Philip Nyamu Waki, Kenya

Judges who served on the two Trial Chambers were:

Trial Chamber II (dissolved in 2008)
Richard Lussick, Samoa (Presiding Judge)
Teresa Doherty, UK
Julia Sebutinde, Uganda

Alternate judge
El Hadji Malick Sow, Senegal

Trial Chamber I (dissolved in 2012)
Pierre G Boutet, Canada (Presiding Judge)
Rosolu John Bankole Thompson, Sierra Leone
Benjamin Mutanga Itoe, Cameroon

The Special Court's final appeal judgment is expected to be delivered in September 2013, after which the Special Court will transition to the Residual Special Court. The Residual Special Court, established by an agreement between the UN and the Government of Sierra Leone, will be responsible for the continuing legal obligations of the Special Court. These include ongoing functions such as the maintenance, preservation and management of the court's archive; witness protection and support; assistance to national prosecution authorities; supervision of prison sentences, pardons, commutations and early releases; and ad hoc functions, including review of convictions and acquittals, contempt of court proceedings, defence counsel and legal aid issues, claims for compensation, prevention of double jeopardy, and the trial of any indictee not brought before the court.

Organisation for the Prohibition of Chemical Weapons (OPCW)
Johan de Wittlaan 32
2517 JR The Hague
The Netherlands
Telephone: (+31 70) 416 3300
Fax: (+31 70) 306 3535
Email: media@opcw.org
Internet: www.opcw.org
Director-General: Ahmet Üzümcü, Turkey (appointed by the Conference, on the recommendation of the Executive Council, for 2010–14)

Purpose

The Organisation for the Prohibition of Chemical Weapons (OPCW) was created under the Convention on the Prohibition of the Development, Production, Stockpiling and Use of Chemical Weapons and on their Destruction (CWC), negotiated in the Conference on Disarmament and that entered into force on 29 April 1997. Its role is to ensure implementation of the Convention's provisions, including those for international compliance, and to provide a forum for consultation and cooperation. It is an independent inter-governmental organisation, not a UN specialised agency. An Agreement Concerning the Relationship between the UN and the OPCW was signed on 17 October 2000. It was approved by the Conference of States Parties in May 2001 and the UN General Assembly in GA res. 55/283 (2001).

The CWC is a global disarmament agreement that bans the development, production, stockpiling and use of chemical weapons, and provides for the destruction of existing chemical weapons stockpiles and related facilities within a specific timeframe. States Parties undertake never to:
* Develop, produce, otherwise acquire, stockpile or retain chemical weapons, or transfer, directly or indirectly, chemical weapons to anyone
* Use chemical weapons
* Engage in military preparations to use chemical weapons
* Assist, encourage or induce, in any way, anyone to engage in any activity prohibited to a State Party under the Convention.

States Parties also undertake:
* To destroy chemical weapons they own or possess, or that are located in any place under their jurisdiction or control, in accordance with the provisions of the Convention
* To destroy all chemical weapons they abandoned on the territory of another State Party
* To destroy any chemical weapons production facilities they own or possess, or that are located in any place under their jurisdiction or control
* Not to use riot control agents as a method of warfare.

The Convention also regulates the production, processing, consumption and, to some degree, the international transfer of toxic chemicals that can be converted into, or used to produce, chemical weapons. To this end, the OPCW monitors the chemical industry by means of compulsory annual national declarations by States Parties, controls the transfer of some chemicals listed in the Convention, and has a system of routine visits and challenge inspections by OPCW Technical Secretariat inspectors.

Structure
* Conference of States Parties
* Executive Council

The Conference of the States Parties is the plenary organ consisting of all members of the OPCW. It has the general power to oversee implementation of the Convention and, in this regard, the Conference may make recommendations and take decisions on any questions, matters or issues within the scope of the Convention. The Conference oversees the activities of the Council and Secretariat and may issue guidelines in accordance with the Convention to either of them.

The Conference Chair is Paul Arkwright, UK, who holds office until a successor is elected at the 17th session of the Conference in November 2012. Vice-Chairs are Algeria, Belgium, Cuba, Iran, Iraq, Russian Federation, Sudan, Ukraine, USA and Uruguay.

The Executive Council (EC) considers any issues or matters within its competence affecting the Convention and its implementation, including concerns regarding compliance. It brings non-compliance cases to the attention of the Conference as appropriate. The EC consists of 41 members sitting on a rotational basis with regard to equitable geographical distribution and the importance of the chemical industry, as well as to political and security interests. Its membership comprises nine African states, nine Asia–Pacific states, five Eastern European states, seven Latin American and Caribbean states, 10 Western European and Other states, plus one further seat rotating between Asia–Pacific and Latin America and the Caribbean. Nominations for election are made from within each region respectively.

The EC Chair is Bhaswati Mukherjee, India, for one year from 12 May 2012. Vice-Chairs are Ecuador, Russian Federation, Sudan and USA.

Meetings

The Conference of States Parties meets annually in The Hague, Netherlands. The 17th session is scheduled to be held from 26 to 30 November 2012. The EC holds three or four regular sessions annually.

Membership

As of May 2012, 188 countries are members of the OPCW. Two countries had signed but not yet ratified the Convention. Members' terms of appointment to the Executive Council are from May to May of the years shown.

	Previous terms	Current terms
Afghanistan		
Albania	2010–12	
Algeria	1997–2006 06–12	2012–14
Andorra		
Antigua and Barbuda		
Argentina	1997–2011	2011–13
Armenia		
Australia	1997–2000 06–10	
Austria	2000–02 08–10	
Azerbaijan		
Bahamas		
Bahrain		
Bangladesh	1997–2004	
Barbados		
Belarus	1997–98 2002–04 06–08	
Belgium	1998–2000 02–04 06–08	2012–14
Belize		
Benin	2002–04	
Bhutan		
Bolivia		2012–14
Bosnia and Herzegovina	2006–08	
Botswana	2001–03	
Brazil	1997–2011	2011–13
Brunei Darussalam		
Bulgaria	1997–98 2001–03 07–09	
Burkina Faso		
Burundi		

Cambodia

Cameroon 1997–2005 07–11 2011–13

Canada 2000–04 10–12 2012–14

Cape Verde

Central African Republic

Chad

Chile 1997–2004 06–10 2012–14

China 1997–2011 2011–13

Colombia 2002–07 10–12

Comoros

Congo

Cook Islands

Costa Rica 2008–12

Côte d'Ivoire 1997–2001

Croatia 2001–03 2011–13

Cuba 1998–2002 04–12

Cyprus

Czech Republic 1998–2000 03–05 07–09 2012–14

DR Congo

Denmark 2002–04 10–12

Djibouti

Dominica

Dominican Republic

Ecuador 1997–2000 10–12 2012–14

El Salvador

Equatorial Guinea

Eritrea

Estonia

Ethiopia 1997–2001

Fiji

Finland 1998–2000 06–08

France 1997–2011 2011–13

Gabon 2005–07

Gambia

Georgia

Germany 1997–2011 2011–13

Ghana 2005–09

Grenada

Greece

Guatemala

Guinea

Guinea-Bissau

Guyana

Haiti

Holy See

Honduras

Hungary 1997–99 2002–04 2011–13

Iceland

India 1997–2011 2011–13

Indonesia 2000–02

Iran 1998–2012 2012–14

Iraq 2010–12 2012–14

Ireland 2006–08 2012–14

	Previous terms	Current terms
Italy	1997–2011	2011–13
Jamaica		
Japan	1997–2011	2011–13
Jordan		
Kazakhstan		
Kenya	1997–2000 04–08 10–12	
Kiribati		
Kuwait	2003–05 08–10	
Kyrgyzstan		
Lao PDR		
Latvia		
Lebanon		
Lesotho	2005–09	
Liberia		
Libya	2008–12	2012–14
Liechtenstein		
Lithuania		
Luxembourg	2010–12	
Madagascar		
Malawi		
Malaysia	2004–06 07–09	2011–13
Maldives		
Mali		
Malta	1997–98	
Marshall Islands		
Mauritania		
Mauritius		
Mexico	1997–2011	2011–13
Micronesia		
Monaco		
Mongolia		
Montenegro		
Morocco	1999–2008 09–11	2011–13
Mozambique	2009–11	
Namibia	2000–02	2011–13
Nauru		
Nepal		
Netherlands	1997–98 2000–02 04–06 08–10	
New Zealand	2004–06	
Nicaragua		
Niger		
Nigeria	2001–05 08–10	2011–13
Niue		
Norway	1997–98 2004–06	2012–14
Oman	1997–98	
Pakistan	1998–2012	2012–14
Palau		
Panama	2000–06	
Papua New Guinea		
Paraguay		
Peru	1997–2010	2012–14
Philippines	1997–2000 06–08	
Poland	1997–2002 05–07 09–11	
Portugal	2002–04	2012–14

	Previous terms	Current terms
Qatar		2012–14
ROK	1997–2011	2011–13
Republic of Moldova		
Romania	1997–2001 05–07 10–12	
Russian Federation	1998–2012	2012–14
Rwanda		2011–13
Saint Kitts and Nevis		
Saint Lucia		
Saint Vincent and the Grenadines		
Samoa		
San Marino		
Sao Tome and Principe		
Saudi Arabia	1997–2011	2011–13
Senegal		
Serbia	2004–06	
Seychelles		
Sierra Leone		
Singapore		
Slovakia	1998–2000 03–05 08–10	
Slovenia	2000–02	
Solomon Islands		
South Africa	1997–2012	2012–14
Spain	1997–2002 04–06 08–12	
Sri Lanka	1997–2006 08–12	
Sudan	2001–11	2012–14
Suriname	1997–98	
Swaziland		
Sweden	2000–02 08–10	
Switzerland	1998–2000 06–08	
Tajikistan		
Thailand	2006–08	
The former Yugoslav Republic of Macedonia	2008–10	
Timor-Leste		
Togo		
Tonga		
Trinidad and Tobago		
Tunisia	1997–2011	
Turkey	2002–04 10–12	
Turkmenistan		
Tuvalu		
Uganda		
Ukraine	1999–2001 04–06 09–11	2012–14
UAE		
UK	1997–2011	2011–13
UR of Tanzania		
USA	1997–2011	2011–13
Uruguay	1997–98 2001–06 09–11	
Uzbekistan		
Vanuatu		
Venezuela	1998–2000	
Viet Nam		
Yemen		
Zambia	2003–05	
Zimbabwe	1997–2001	

Preparatory Commission for the Comprehensive Nuclear-Test-Ban Treaty Organization (CTBTO)

Vienna International Centre
PO Box 1200
A–1400 Vienna
Austria
Telephone: (+43 1) 26030 0
Fax: (+43 1) 26030 5823
Email: info@ctbto.org
Internet: www.ctbto.org
Executive Secretary: Tibor Tóth, Hungary (elected and appointed by Preparatory Commission in 2005; reappointed 2008 for 2009–13)

Purpose

The Preparatory Commission for the Comprehensive Nuclear-Test-Ban Treaty Organization (CTBTO), established by the States Signatories to the Comprehensive Nuclear-Test-Ban Treaty (CTBT) on 19 November 1996, is mandated to carry out the necessary preparations for the entry into force and effective implementation of the CTBT. This includes the establishment of a global verification regime to monitor Treaty compliance as well as the promotion of signatures and ratifications.

Evolution

The Treaty was adopted by the UN General Assembly on 10 September 1996 and opened for signature on 24 September 1996. Article I prohibits all nuclear weapons test explosions or any other nuclear explosions. Each State Party further undertakes to refrain from causing, encouraging or in any way participating in the carrying out of any such test or explosion.

The Treaty will enter into force after it has been signed and ratified by the 44 states listed in Annex 2 to the Treaty. These countries possessed nuclear reactors or research reactors and participated in negotiations for the Treaty. Under article XIV, if the Treaty had not entered into force three years after its opening for signature, a Conference on Facilitating the Entry into Force was to be convened. Seven such conferences have taken place, most recently in September 2011 in New York. The next conference is scheduled to take place in September 2013.

Structure

The CTBTO consists of two main organs:
- A plenary, or executive, body composed of all States Signatories
- The Provisional Technical Secretariat (PTS).

The plenary body has three subsidiary organs:
- Working Group A on budgetary and administrative matters
- Working Group B on verification issues
- An Advisory Group consisting of financial experts from States Signatories.

The verification regime is made up of a 337-facility International Monitoring System (IMS) – 321 monitoring stations supported by 16 radionuclide laboratories around the world that monitor the earth for signs of a nuclear explosion. Seismic, infrasound and hydroacoustic stations monitor underground, the atmosphere and oceans respectively. Radionuclide stations detect radioactive debris emanating from an explosion. The IMS stations send data to the International Data Centre (IDC) in Vienna where it is processed, analysed and forwarded to

Member States for their evaluation and judgement. When the Democratic People's Republic of Korea (DPRK) conducted nuclear tests in 2006 and 2009, Member States received initial estimates of the time, location and magnitude of the tests in less than two hours. As of May 2012, 287 monitoring facilities were operational.

Once the Treaty has entered into force, the verification regime will be complemented by on-site inspections in the event of a nuclear explosion, a consultation and clarification process, as well as confidence-building measures.

IMS data can be used in a variety of civil areas, including scientific research, meteorological and climate forecasting and disaster mitigation, such as tsunami warnings. Since November 2006, the CTBTO has been providing real-time and continuous data to tsunami warning organisations in the Indo-Pacific region. After the March 2011 Fukushima nuclear power plant accident, CTBTO radionuclide data provided a first-hand source of information on the composition and dispersal of radioactive emissions on a global scale.

Membership

A state becomes a member of the CTBTO upon signing the CTBT. Member States oversee the CTBTO's work and fund its activities.

As of May 2012, there were 183 States Signatories. Of these, 157 had deposited their instruments of ratification. Thirty-six of the 44 Annex 2 states (whose signature and ratification is required for the Treaty to enter into force) had ratified the Treaty, including three nuclear weapon states: France, Russian Federation and the UK.

The most recent Annex 2 state to ratify the Treaty was Indonesia, which did so on 6 February 2012. As of May 2012, eight Annex 2 states had not yet ratified the Treaty: China, DPRK, Egypt, India, Iran, Israel, Pakistan and the USA. The DPRK, India and Pakistan have also yet to sign the Treaty.

International Narcotics Control Board (INCB)

PO Box 500
A–1400 Vienna
Austria
Telephone: (+43 1) 26060 4277
Fax: (+43 1) 26060 5867/5868
Email: secretariat@incb.org
Internet: www.incb.org
Secretary: Andrés Finguerut, UK (appointed by the UN Secretary-General, in consultation with the Board, in 2011)

Purpose

The International Narcotics Control Board (INCB) is the independent and quasi-judicial control organ monitoring and supporting implementation of the international drug control conventions. It was established in 1968 in accordance with the 1961 Single Convention on Narcotic Drugs. It had predecessors under the former drug control treaties as far back as the time of the League of Nations.

The functions of INCB are laid down in the following treaties: the Single Convention on Narcotic Drugs of 1961 as amended by the 1972 Protocol; the Convention on Psychotropic Substances of 1971; and the UN Convention against Illicit Traffic in Narcotic Drugs and Psychotropic Substances of 1988.

In regard to the manufacture of, trade in and use of drugs, INCB:

- Endeavours, in cooperation with governments, to ensure that adequate supplies of licit drugs are available for medical and scientific uses, and that the diversion of drugs from licit sources to illicit channels does not occur. INCB also monitors governments' control over chemicals used in the illicit manufacture of drugs and assists them in preventing the diversion of those chemicals into the illicit traffic
- Identifies weaknesses in national and international control systems of narcotic drugs, psychotropic substances and precursor chemicals, and contributes to correcting such situations. INCB is also responsible for assessing chemicals used in the illicit manufacture of drugs to determine whether they should be placed under international control.

In the discharge of its responsibilities, INCB:

- Administers a system of estimates for narcotic drugs and a voluntary assessment system for psychotropic substances, and monitors licit activities involving drugs through a statistical returns system, with a view to assisting governments in achieving, amongst other things, a balance between supply and demand
- Monitors and promotes measures taken by governments to prevent the diversion of substances frequently used in the illicit manufacture of narcotic drugs and psychotropic substances. It also assesses such substances to determine whether there is need for change in the scope of control of Tables I and II of the 1988 Convention (which list substances frequently used in the illicit manufacture of narcotic drugs and psychotropic substances)
- Analyses information provided by governments, UN bodies, specialised agencies or other competent international organisations, with a view to ensuring that the provisions of the international drug control treaties are adequately carried out by governments, and recommends remedial measures
- Maintains a permanent dialogue with governments to assist them in complying with their obligations under the international drug control treaties, and recommends technical or financial assistance to be provided.

If measures necessary to remedy a serious situation have not been taken, INCB may call the matter to the attention of the parties concerned, the Commission on Narcotic Drugs and the Economic and Social Council (ECOSOC). As a last resort, the treaties empower INCB to recommend to parties that they stop importing drugs from a defaulting country, exporting drugs to it or both. In all cases, INCB acts in close cooperation with governments.

Structure

INCB consists of 13 members, elected by ECOSOC, who serve in their personal capacity. Three members with medical, pharmacological or pharmaceutical experience are elected from a list of people nominated by the World Health Organization (WHO) and 10 are elected from a list of people nominated by governments.

The INCB Secretariat is an administrative entity of the UN Office on Drugs and Crime (UNODC), but it reports solely to the Board on matters of substance. INCB collaborates closely with UNODC and also cooperates with other international bodies concerned with drug control, including ECOSOC and its Commission on Narcotic Drugs, and other relevant specialised agencies of the UN, particularly WHO. It also cooperates with bodies outside the UN system, especially the International Criminal Police Organization (INTERPOL) and the World Customs Organization.

INCB publishes an annual report containing an analysis of the drug control situation worldwide so that governments are kept aware of existing and potential situations that may endanger the objectives of the international drug control treaties. The annual report is supplemented by detailed technical reports on narcotic drugs and psychotropic substances. Under the provisions of article 12 of the 1988 Convention, INCB also publishes a report each year that gives an account of the results of the monitoring of precursors and chemicals frequently used in the illicit manufacture of narcotic drugs and psychotropic substances.

Meetings

INCB sessions are held in February, May and November each year.

Members

The following list shows current INCB members and the year in which their terms expire (on the eve of the Board's May session).

Hamid Ghodse, Iran*	2017	Lochan Naidoo, South Africa	2015
Wayne Hall, Australia*	2017	Rajat Ray, India*	2015
David Johnson, US	2017	Ahmed Kamal Eldin Samak, Egypt	2017
Galina Aleksandrovna Korchagina, Russian Federation	2015	Viroj Sumyai, Thailand	2015
		Werner Sipp, Germany	2017
Marc Moinard, France	2015	Raymond Yans, Belgium	2017
Jorge Montaño, Mexico	2017	Francisco Thoumi, Colombia**	2015

Notes

* Elected by ECOSOC from a list of people nominated by the World Health Organization.

** Elected by ECOSOC in April 2012 to replace Camilo Uribe Granja, Colombia, who had resigned.

International Trade Centre (ITC)

Palais des Nations
1211 Geneva 10
Switzerland
Telephone: (+41 22) 730 0111
Fax: (+41 22) 733 4439
Email: itcreg@intracen.org
Internet: www.intracen.org
Executive Director: Patricia Francis, Jamaica (since June 2006, reappointed by the UN Secretary-General for 2009 to June 2013)

Purpose

The International Trade Centre (ITC) is the joint technical cooperation agency of the UN Conference on Trade and Development (UNCTAD) and the World Trade Organization (WTO). ITC improves small business export success in developing countries by providing, with partners, sustainable and inclusive trade development solutions to exporters, trade support institutions and policy-makers. ITC's strategic objectives are:

- Exporters: Strengthen the international competitiveness of enterprises in developing countries and transition economies
- Trade support institutions: Develop the capabilities of trade service providers to support exporters
- Policy-makers: Support policy-makers in integrating the private sector into the global economy.

ITC is active in five major areas:
- Business and trade policy
- Export strategy
- Strengthening institutions
- Trade intelligence
- Exporter competitiveness.

ITC's regular programme is financed in equal parts by the WTO and UN. ITC also implements projects, at the demand of beneficiary countries, with voluntary contributions from donor governments and civil society institutions.

Evolution

ITC was created in 1964 through a decision of the General Agreement on Tariffs and Trade (GATT) contracting parties. In 1968, UNCTAD joined GATT as co-sponsor of ITC. Its legal status was formally confirmed by the General Assembly in 1974 as a joint subsidiary organ of the GATT and the UN, the latter acting through UNCTAD.

Structure

ITC's annual inter-governmental gathering is called the Joint Advisory Group (JAG) meeting. The JAG is open to all members of the WTO and UNCTAD, as well as to UN specialised agencies and bodies, other inter-governmental organisations with observer status and non-governmental organisations with an interest in trade promotion. This meeting, held in Geneva, reviews ITC's technical cooperation programme over the preceding year and makes recommendations for its future work programme.

Meetings

The JAG meets annually. Its 46th session was held in Geneva from 21 to 22 May 2012.

Membership

Because of its legal status, ITC does not have a membership of its own. Its de facto members are WTO and UNCTAD Member States.

International Union for the Protection of New Varieties of Plants (UPOV)

34 Chemin des Colombettes
1211 Geneva 20
Switzerland
Telephone: (+41 22) 338 9111
Fax: (+41 22) 733 0336
Email: upov.mail@upov.int
Internet: www.upov.int
Secretary-General: Francis Gurry, Australia (the UPOV Council appoints the Director-General of WIPO as Secretary-General of UPOV; current term 2008–14)

Purpose

The International Union for the Protection of New Varieties of Plants (UPOV) is an independent inter-governmental organisation. Its purpose is to ensure members:
- Recognise and secure an intellectual property right to breeders of new varieties of plants
- Encourage cooperation between members in their administration of such rights on the basis of a set of uniform and clearly defined principles.

Evolution

UPOV was established by the International Convention for the Protection of New Varieties of Plants, which was adopted in Paris in 1961 and entered into force in 1968. The Convention was revised in 1972, 1978 and 1991. The 1991 Act entered into force on 24 April 1998.

Structure

* Council
* Committees
* Secretariat

The UPOV Council is responsible for safeguarding the Union's interests, encouraging its development and adopting its work programme and budget. The Council consists of representatives of all members and meets annually. Each State Member has one vote in the Council.

Three committees assist the Council with its work – the Consultative Committee (which prepares the sessions of the Council), the Administrative and Legal Committee, and the Technical Committee. Several working groups have been established under the Technical Committee.

The Secretariat is called the Office of the Union and is directed by UPOV's Secretary-General. Information about upcoming meetings is on the UPOV website under 'Meetings'.

Membership

The 70 members are:

Albania	Georgia	Portugal
Argentina	Germany	ROK
Australia	Hungary	Republic of Moldova
Austria	Iceland	Romania
Azerbaijan	Ireland	Russian Federation
Belarus	Israel	Singapore
Belgium	Italy	Slovakia
Bolivia	Japan	Slovenia
Brazil	Jordan	South Africa
Bulgaria	Kenya	Spain
Canada	Kyrgyzstan	Sweden
Chile	Latvia	Switzerland
China	Lithuania	The former Yugoslav
Colombia	Mexico	Republic of Macedonia
Costa Rica	Morocco	Trinidad and Tobago
Croatia	Netherlands	Tunisia
Czech Republic	New Zealand	Turkey
Denmark	Nicaragua	Ukraine
Dominican Republic	Norway	UK
Ecuador	Oman	USA
Estonia	Panama	Uruguay
European Union	Paraguay	Uzbekistan
Finland	Peru	Viet Nam
France	Poland	

REGIONAL DEVELOPMENT BANKS

REGIONAL DEVELOPMENT BANKS

African Development Bank (AfDB)

Temporary Headquarters
15 Avenue du Ghana
PO Box 323-1002
Tunis-Belvedère
Tunisia
Telephone: (+216) 71 10 39 00
Fax: (+216) 71 35 19 33

Statutory Headquarters
Rue Joseph Anoma
01 BP 1387 Abidjan 01
Côte d'Ivoire
Telephone: (+225) 2020 4444
Fax: (+225) 2020 4959

Email: afdb@afdb.org
Internet: www.afdb.org
President: Donald Kaberuka, Rwanda (elected by the Board of Governors, on the recommendation of the
Board of Directors, in 2005)

Purpose

The African Development Bank (AfDB) is a regional multilateral development bank that promotes the economic development and social progress of its regional member countries (RMCs) in Africa. The AfDB is dedicated to combating poverty and improving living conditions across the continent.

The agreement establishing the AfDB was drawn up under the auspices of the Economic Commission for Africa and entered into force in 1964. The Bank began operations in 1966. Its principal functions are to:
- Make loans and equity investments for the economic and social advancement of the RMCs
- Provide technical assistance for the preparation and execution of development projects and programmes
- Promote investment of public and private capital for development purposes
- Respond to requests for assistance in coordinating development policies and plans of RMCs.

The Bank is also required to give special attention to national and multinational projects and programmes that promote regional integration.

The AfDB is working to play a leading role in the New Partnership for Africa's Development (NEPAD) initiative, which aims to reduce the gaps that exist between Africa and the developed world, and to achieve the Millennium Development Goals. The Bank is coordinating activities in the area of infrastructure, banking and finance, and corporate governance.

Structure

The shareholders are the 53 countries in Africa, as well as 24 countries in the Americas, Europe and Asia. Turkey was admitted in the latter category at the annual meeting on 15 May 2008.

The Board of Governors is the Bank's supreme organ and mostly comprises the ministers of finance and economy of Member State governments. It issues general directives concerning the Bank's operational policies.

The Board of Directors comprises 20 members holding the title of executive director. They are elected by the Board of Governors for a period of three years, renewable once. Regional members have 13 directors while states outside the region have seven.

The President is elected by the Bank's Board of Governors, on the recommendation of the Board of Directors, for a five-year term, renewable once. The President acts as the Bank's Chief Executive and conducts the current business of the Bank, as well as being its legal representative.

Membership

Any African country that has the status of an independent state may become a member of the Bank. The agreement defines 'Africa' or 'African' as comprising the continent of Africa and African islands. The 53 regional members are:

Algeria	Ethiopia	Niger
Angola	Gabon	Nigeria
Benin	Gambia	Rwanda
Botswana	Ghana	Sao Tome and Principe
Burkina Faso	Guinea	Senegal
Burundi	Guinea-Bissau	Seychelles
Cameroon	Kenya	Sierra Leone
Cape Verde	Lesotho	Somalia
Central African Republic	Liberia	South Africa
Chad	Libya	Sudan
Comoros	Madagascar	Swaziland
Congo	Malawi	Togo
Côte d'Ivoire	Mali	Tunisia
DR Congo	Mauritania	Uganda
Djibouti	Mauritius	UR of Tanzania
Egypt	Morocco	Zambia
Equatorial Guinea	Mozambique	Zimbabwe
Eritrea	Namibia	

There are 24 non-regional members:

Argentina	France	Portugal
Austria	Germany	ROK
Belgium	India	Saudi Arabia
Brazil	Italy	Spain
Canada	Japan	Sweden
China	Kuwait	Switzerland
Denmark	Netherlands	UK
Finland	Norway	USA

Inter-American Development Bank (IDB)

1300 New York Avenue NW
Washington DC 20577
United States of America
Telephone: (+1 202) 623 1000
Fax: (+1 202) 623 3096
Email: pic@iadb.org
Internet: www.iadb.org
President (Executive Head): Luis Alberto Moreno, Colombia (re-elected by the Board of Governors in 2010)

Purpose

Established in December 1959, the Inter-American Development Bank (IDB) is the main source of multilateral financing and expertise for sustainable economic, social and institutional development in Latin America and the Caribbean.

The Bank's Charter states that its principal functions are to:
- Use its own capital, funds raised in financial markets and other resources for financing the development of borrowing member countries
- Supplement private investment when private capital is unavailable on reasonable terms and conditions
- Provide technical assistance for the preparation, financing and implementation of development plans and projects.

The IDB obtains financial resources from its 48 member countries, borrowings on financial markets, trust funds it administers and through co-financing ventures.

Evolution

In recent years, the IDB has approved an average of $10 billion annually to finance projects in key sectors such as infrastructure, energy, water, education and health. Most of the IDB's loans finance public sector projects although a significant proportion of its operations are directed to the private sector.

In March 2010, the IDB's Board of Governors agreed to increase the Bank's capital by $70 billion to more than $170 billion. This ninth capital increase, the largest in the IDB's history, allowed it to increase lending capacity to an average of $12 billion a year. The Governors also agreed to provide an unprecedented relief package for Haiti, which included forgiveness of all the country's debt with the Bank and the provision of $2 billion of grants through to 2020. The March 2010 agreement also included a replenishment of the Fund for Special Operations, which finances operations in the region's poorest nations.

Structure

The IDB is an official observer to the UN. It has country offices in 26 borrowing countries, as well as Paris and Tokyo. Headquarters are in Washington DC.

The Bank is headed by its Board of Governors, which delegates oversight of Bank operations to the Board of Executive Directors. Each member country appoints a governor, whose voting power is proportional to the Bank's capital subscribed to by the country. The 26 Latin American and Caribbean countries in the IDB hold 50.02 percent of the voting power. The single largest shareholder is the USA, with 30.01 percent. Members of the Board of Executive Directors serve three-year terms. The President is elected by the Board of Governors for a five-year term.

The Office of Institutional Integrity (OII) plays a key role in the IDB Group's integrity efforts. OII investigates allegations of fraud and corruption within IDB Group-financed activities and performs prevention work.

Membership

Forty-eight countries are members of the Bank:

Argentina	China	Germany
Austria	Colombia	Guatemala
Bahamas	Costa Rica	Guyana
Barbados	Croatia	Haiti
Belgium	Denmark	Honduras
Belize	Dominican Republic	Israel
Bolivia	Ecuador	Italy
Brazil	El Salvador	Jamaica
Canada	Finland	Japan
Chile	France	Mexico

continued next page

Netherlands	Portugal	Switzerland
Nicaragua	ROK	Trinidad and Tobago
Norway	Slovenia	UK
Panama	Spain	USA
Paraguay	Suriname	Uruguay
Peru	Sweden	Venezuela

Associated organisations

The IDB Group includes three organisations based in Washington DC: the Inter-American Development Bank, the Inter-American Investment Corporation (IIC) and the Multilateral Investment Fund (MIF). The Institute for the Integration of Latin America and the Caribbean (INTAL) is an IDB affiliate based in Buenos Aires, Argentina, while the Inter-American Institute for Economic and Social Development is an IDB unit based in Washington DC.

Inter-American Investment Corporation (IIC)

1350 New York Avenue NW
Washington DC 20577
United States of America
Telephone: (+1 202) 623 3900
Fax: (+1 202) 623 3815
Internet: www.iic.int
General Manager: Jacques Rogozinski, Mexico (since 2000)

The Inter-American Investment Corporation (IIC) is a multilateral financial institution that is an autonomous affiliate of the Inter-American Development Bank (IDB). It began operations in 1989 to promote the economic development of its Latin American and Caribbean member countries by financing private enterprise, preferably small and medium in scale. It provides financing in the form of equity investments, loans and guarantees, and provides advisory services to private enterprise in the region. The IIC has 44 member countries.

The Corporation works directly with the private sector and neither seeks nor requires government guarantees for its loans, equity investments or lines of credit. IIC investments leverage significant capital flows to Latin America.

Multilateral Investment Fund (MIF)

1300 New York Avenue NW
Washington DC 20577
United States of America
Telephone: (+1 202) 942 8211
Fax: (+1 202) 942 8100
Internet: www.iadb.org/mif
General Manager: Nancy Lee, USA (since 2011)

The Multilateral Investment Fund (MIF) is a special fund administered by the Inter-American Development Bank (IDB) that promotes private sector development and private investment in Latin America and the Caribbean. The MIF began operations in 1993 with funds committed by 20 countries amounting to $1.145 billion. MIF operations are concentrated in three areas:
- Fostering efficient institutions and regulatory frameworks
- Raising the productivity of human resources
- Improving smaller enterprises' access to sources of finance and technical assistance.

There are 39 donating member countries.

Institute for the Integration of Latin America and the Caribbean (INTAL)

Esmeralda 130
Casilla de Correo 39
Buenos Aires
Argentina
Telephone: (+54 11) 4320 2350
Fax: (+54 11) 4323 2365
Internet: www.iadb.org/intal
Director: Ricardo Carciofi (since 2005)

The Institute for the Integration of Latin America and the Caribbean (INTAL) has been in operation since 1964. It provides services of specialised technical cooperation, conferences, policy research and publications in the field of integration and trade to Inter-American Development Bank (IDB) member countries and regional organisations.

Inter-American Institute for Economic and Social Development (INDES)

1350 New York Avenue NW
Washington DC 20577
United States of America
Telephone: (+1 202) 623 2420
Fax: (+1 202) 623 2008
Email: indes@iadb.org
Internet: www.iadb.org/indes
Director: Graciela Schamis, Argentina (since 2007)

The Inter-American Institute for Economic and Social Development (INDES) is part of the Inter-American Development Bank (IDB). It was created in 1994 as a training institute and forum dedicated to developing knowledgeable social policy-makers and public managers committed to sustainable social reform. INDES trains public sector decision-makers and managers as well as staff of non-governmental organisations and other civil society organisations. Training is held at IDB headquarters in Washington, in specially customised programmes in Latin America and the Caribbean, and online.

Asian Development Bank (ADB)

6 ADB Avenue, Mandaluyong City
1550 Metro Manila
Philippines
Telephone: (+63 2) 632 4444
Fax: (+63 2) 636 2444
Email: information@adb.org
Internet: www.adb.org
President and Chair of the Board of Directors: Haruhiko Kuroda, Japan (re-elected by the Board of Governors in August 2011 for a five-year term commencing in November 2011)

Purpose

The mission of the Asian Development Bank (ADB) is "an Asia–Pacific free of poverty", as articulated in its Strategy 2020, which provides a long-term strategic framework for 2009 to 2020. Established in 1966 through a multilateral agreement ratified then by 31 countries but now with 67 member countries, ADB has a strategic agenda that focuses on inclusive and environmentally sustainable economic growth and regional integration. To achieve this, ADB focuses on five drivers of change: private sector development, good governance and capacity development, gender equity, knowledge solutions and partnerships.

REGIONAL
DEVELOPMENT BANKS

ADB's main instruments in assisting its developing member countries (DMCs) are policy dialogue and technical assistance, sovereign and non-sovereign (state-owned and private sector enterprise) loans and guarantees, grants and non-sovereign equity investments. ADB also leverages off its own long-term financing and knowledge of, and relationship with, DMCs to attract supporting official and commercial co-financing to enhance development efforts.

Operations

At the end of 2011, ADB's subscribed capital stock, which is denominated in the International Monetary Fund's (IMF's) Special Drawing Rights (SDRs) translated into US dollars for its financial statements, was $162.49 billion, of which $5.32 billion was paid-in, the balance remaining callable.

In April 2009, ADB's Board of Governors authorised a 200 percent increase in capital stock, subscriptions to which were closed at the end of September 2011, following Board approvals for extensions from the original closing date of December 2010. With all but one of ADB's member countries fully subscribing to the capital increase, the actual increase amounted to 199.3 percent.

ADB has a triple A credit rating and funds its operations from borrowings and the repayments by DMCs of past loans. In 2011, net borrowings, largely through bond issues, reached $6.44 billion. ADB also mobilises financial resources through co-financing operations, tapping official, commercial and export credit sources.

In this way ADB's capital resources, reserves accumulated from net income and borrowings (ordinary capital resources or OCR), are used to fund a range of lending modalities to its middle-income DMCs on terms that would be better than they could achieve by borrowing directly from capital markets. In 2011, ADB disbursed $6.3 billion in loans and liquidated a net $0.15 billion in equity investments, for a net resource transfer (after loan and interest payments by DMCs) of $2.69 billion. At the end of 2011, OCR loans and equity investments outstanding were $50.8 billion, of which 7.3 percent was for non-sovereign operations. During 2011, loans of $10.65 billion and equity investments of $0.24 billion were approved, together with $2.38 billion approved for short-term arrangements under the Trade Finance Facilitation Program (which has an exposure limit of $1 billion at any one time).

ADB manages the Asian Development Fund (ADF), which is a special fund for DMCs with low per capita incomes and limited access to capital markets, providing sovereign lending on concessional terms and grants to DMCs in unsustainable debt situations. The ADF is financed by periodic contributions from donors and the repayment of earlier loans. In April 2011, the 10th replenishment of the ADF was concluded, to an aggregate value of $12.4 billion. In 2011, a gross $1.39 billion in loans and grants was disbursed, with a net resource flow of negative $0.04 billion after loan repayments and interest. Loans of $1.96 billion and grants of $0.60 billion were approved. Total loans outstanding at the end of 2011 were $29.51 billion.

Technical assistance is provided through the Technical Assistance Special Fund and Japan Special Fund, while grant funding can be provided through the Japan Fund for Poverty Reduction. Other funds managed by the ADB include the ADB Institute Special Fund, Japan Scholarship Program, Japan Fund for Information and Communication Technology, Korean Fund for E-Government, Regional Cooperation and Integration Fund, Climate Change Fund, and the Asia Pacific Disaster Response Fund.

ADB also manages grant funds and loans financed by bilateral donors to pursue objectives mutually agreed between the donor and ADB, and has a channel financing facility for grants provided by bilateral donors to support technical assistance and soft components of loans.

Most technical assistance grants are used for preparing projects and supporting advisory activities in areas such as law and policy reform, fiscal strengthening, good governance, capacity-building, climate change and regional integration.

Structure

ADB has its headquarters in the Philippines and missions in Afghanistan, Armenia, Azerbaijan, Bangladesh, Cambodia, China, Georgia, India, Indonesia, Kazakhstan (spread over two offices, in Astana and Almaty), Kyrgyz Republic, Lao PDR, Mongolia, Nepal, Pakistan, Papua New Guinea, Sri Lanka, Tajikistan, Thailand, Turkmenistan, Uzbekistan and Viet Nam. ADB maintains two sub-regional offices for the Pacific, one in Suva, Fiji, and the other in Sydney, Australia, and a special office in Timor-Leste. It also has a country office for the Philippines in Manila. It has representative offices for Europe (based in Frankfurt), Japan (Tokyo) and North America (Washington DC). The ADB Institute is located in Tokyo, Japan.

ADB's highest policy-making body is its Board of Governors, which meets annually and comprises one representative from each member. The Governors elect the 12-member resident Board of Directors, with each director appointing an alternate. The President is elected by the Board of Governors for a five-year term and is Chair of the Board of Directors. The President, assisted by five vice-presidents, manages the ADB's business under the general oversight of the Board of Directors.

The total voting power of each ADB member consists of basic votes (distributed equally among all members) plus proportional votes (allocated according to the number of shares of ADB capital stock held by the member). In total, the number of basic votes allocated comprises 25 percent of all votes.

ADB's Board of Directors and constituencies (as of 30 April 2012) are:

Executive Director	Alternate	Members represented
Phil Bowen	Andrew Collins	Australia; Azerbaijan; Cambodia; Georgia; Hong Kong, China; Kiribati; Micronesia; Nauru; Palau; Solomon Islands; Tuvalu
Micheline Aucoin	Jacob Rooimans	Canada; Denmark; Finland; Ireland; Netherlands; Norway; Sweden
Eduard Westreicher	Cedric Crelo	Austria; Germany; Luxembourg; Turkey; UK
Maurin Sitorus	C J (Stan) Vandersyp	Armenia; Cook Islands; Fiji; Indonesia; Kyrgyz Republic; New Zealand; Samoa; Tonga
Yeo Kwon Yoon	Wilson Kamit	ROK; Papua New Guinea; Sri Lanka; Taipei, China; Uzbekistan; Vanuatu; Viet Nam
Gaudencio Hernandez, Jr	Siraj S Shamsuddin	Kazakhstan; Maldives; Marshall Islands; Mongolia; Pakistan; Philippines; Timor-Leste
Jérôme Destombes	Jose Miguel Cortes	Belgium; France; Italy; Portugal; Spain; Switzerland
Kazuhiko Koguchi	Hideo Fukushima	Japan
Ashok K Lahiri	Bounleua Sinxayvolavong	Afghanistan; Bangladesh; Bhutan; India; Lao PDR; Tajikistan; Turkmenistan
Robert M Orr	Maureen Grewe	USA
Chaiyuth Sudthitanakom	Govinda Bahadur Thapa	Brunei; Malaysia; Myanmar; Nepal; Singapore; Thailand
Yingming Yang	Guoqi Wu	China

Membership

Membership is open to members and associate members of the UN Economic and Social Commission for Asia and the Pacific (UNESCAP), and other regional countries and non-regional developed countries that are members of the UN or any of its specialised agencies. The ADB has 67 members, of which 48 are in Asia and the Pacific and 19 are from elsewhere. The 48 regional members, with year of joining, are:

Afghanistan	1966	Micronesia	1990
Armenia	2005	Mongolia	1991
Australia	1966	Myanmar	1973
Azerbaijan	1999	Nauru	1991
Bangladesh	1973	Nepal	1966
Bhutan	1982	New Zealand	1966
Brunei Darussalam	2006	Pakistan	1966
Cambodia	1966	Palau	2003
China	1986	Papua New Guinea	1971
Cook Islands	1976	Philippines	1966
Fiji	1970	Samoa	1966
Georgia	2007	Singapore	1966
Hong Kong, China	1969	Solomon Islands	1973
India	1966	Sri Lanka	1966
Indonesia	1966	Taipei, China	1966
Japan	1966	Tajikistan	1998
Kazakhstan	1994	Thailand	1966
Kiribati	1974	Timor-Leste	2002
Korea	1966	Tonga	1972
Kyrgyz Republic	1994	Turkmenistan	2000
Lao PDR	1966	Tuvalu	1993
Malaysia	1966	Uzbekistan	1995
Maldives	1978	Vanuatu	1981
Marshall Islands	1990	Viet Nam	1966

The 19 non-regional members, with year of joining, are:

Austria	1966	Netherlands	1966
Belgium	1966	Norway	1966
Canada	1966	Portugal	2002
Denmark	1966	Spain	1986
Finland	1966	Sweden	1966
France	1970	Switzerland	1967
Germany	1966	Turkey	1991
Ireland	2006	UK	1966
Italy	1966	USA	1966
Luxembourg	2003		

Caribbean Development Bank (CDB)

PO Box 408
Wildey, St Michael
Barbados BB11000
Telephone: (+1 246) 431 1600
Fax: (+1 246) 426 7269
Email: info@caribank.org
Internet: www.caribank.org
President and Chair of Board of Directors: Warren Smith, Jamaica (appointed by the Board of
Governors, for 2011–16)

Purpose

The Caribbean Development Bank (CDB) was established in 1970. It aims to contribute to the economic growth and development of member countries in the Caribbean and promote economic cooperation and integration among them. The needs of the less developed member countries are a particular concern.

Special operations are financed from the Bank's Special Development Fund (SDF) and other special funds. The SDF is used to make or guarantee loans of high developmental priority that call for longer maturities, longer deferred commencement of repayment of principal, and lower interest rates than those determined for ordinary operations. The Fund amounted to $875.1 million at 31 December 2011.

The Bank can also accept contributions or loans for other special funds that it may administer on terms agreed with its donors, as long as the purposes are consistent with its objectives and functions. Other special funds in active operation include the Basic Needs Trust Fund, which finances small social and economic infrastructure projects geared to the alleviation of poverty in the less developed borrowing member countries.

At 31 December 2011, the Bank's subscribed capital was $1,501.892 million of which $331.005 million was paid-up and $1,170.887 million callable. Subscribed capital is held or available for subscription in the proportion of not less than 60 percent by regional members and not more than 40 percent by non-regional members.

Non-member contributors to the Bank's resources have included Netherlands, New Zealand, Nigeria, Sweden and USA.

Evolution

A resolution adopted by the Inter-American Development Bank (IDB) Board of Governors in 1974 provided for an amendment to the IDB Charter to enable the IDB to lend through the CDB to all of the latter's borrowing member countries, whether or not those countries were members of the IDB. The resolution entered into force in 1977.

Structure

The CDB Board of Governors comprises one governor and one alternate governor for each member country. For this purpose, the member territories of Anguilla, British Virgin Islands, Cayman Islands, Montserrat, and Turks and Caicos Islands are regarded as one member. Voting power is approximately proportional to shares subscribed, with a slight weighting in favour of the smaller member territories.

The Board of Directors comprises 17 members, 12 representing regional members and five representing non-regional members. Directors hold office for a term of two years and are eligible for reappointment. The Board meets five times a year. The members are (as of May 2012):

Director	Alternate Director	Country or group of countries
Regional		
Isaac Anthony	Rosamund Edwards	Dominica and Saint Lucia
Beatriz Bolívar	José Alexander Mendoza López	Venezuela
Ehurd Cunningham	Anthony Woodside	Bahamas
Jorge Alberto Mendoza Sanchez	Maria Isabel Lozano Santin	Mexico
Alberto de Brigard Perez	Adolfo Meisel Roca	Colombia
Whitfield Harris	Janet Harris	Antigua and Barbuda, and Saint Kitts and Nevis
Mervin Haynes	Maurice Edwards	Grenada, Saint Vincent and the Grenadines
Neil Smith	Yvonne Hyde	Anguilla, Belize, British Virgin Islands, Cayman Islands, Montserrat, and Turks and Caicos Islands
Rose Lemonius-Stewart	Carol Nelson	Jamaica
Vidiah Ramkhelawan	Michael Mendez	Trinidad and Tobago
Neermal Rekha	Keith Burrowes	Guyana
Juanita Thorington-Powlett	Seibert Frederick	Barbados
Non-regional		
Henry Hagan	Cherianne Clarke	UK
Holger Illi	Vacant	Germany
Stefania Bazzoni	Pablo Facchinei	Italy
Louise Clément	Zheng Zhang	Canada
He Jianxiong	Wang Lin	China

Membership

CDB membership is open to regional states and territories and non-regional states that are members of the UN, its specialised agencies or the International Atomic Energy Agency (IAEA). As of May 2012, the members are:

Borrowing member countries		Other
Anguilla	Guyana	Columbia
Antigua and Barbuda	Haiti	Mexico
Bahamas	Jamaica	Venezuela
Barbados	Montserrat	
Belize	Saint Kitts and Nevis	**Non-regional**
British Virgin Islands	Saint Lucia	Canada
Cayman Islands	Saint Vincent and the	China
Dominica	Grenadines	Germany
Grenada	Trinidad and Tobago	Italy
	Turks and Caicos Islands	UK

BUDGET AND
SCALES OF ASSESSMENT

BUDGET AND SCALES OF ASSESSMENT

UN BUDGET

The budget for the two calendar years 2012–13 continued to implement the budget process set in train by GA res. 41/213 (1986). The budget outline for 2012–13 was approved by GA res.65/262.

By its resolution 66/248, the General Assembly approved the budget for the biennium 2012–13. The total was allocated amongst principal expenditure sections as follows.

Appropriation section*   (thousands of US dollars)

Part I. Overall policymaking, direction and coordination
1. Overall policymaking, direction and coordination 105,133,800
2. General Assembly and Economic and Social Council affairs and
   conference management 616,654,500
   Total, Part I **721,788,300**

Part II. Political affairs
3. Political affairs 1,193,700,800
4. Disarmament 22,422,000
5. Peacekeeping operations 109,725,100
6. Peaceful uses of outer space 8,001,400
   Total, Part II **1,333,849,300**

Part III. International justice and law
7. International Court of Justice 47,766,400
8. Legal affairs 45,388,700
   Total, Part III **93,155,100**

Part IV. International cooperation for development
9. Economic and social affairs 148,979,300
10. Least developed countries, landlocked developing countries
    and small island developing states 7,264,900
11. United Nations support for the New Partnership for Africa's Development 12,587,700
12. Trade and development 136,524,600
13. International Trade Centre 41,337,700
14. Environment 13,925,500
15. Human settlements 20,631,500
16. International drug control, crime and terrorism prevention and criminal justice 40,902,200
17. UN-Women 14,482,300
    Total, Part IV **436,635,700**

Part V. Regional cooperation for development

Part VI. Human rights and humanitarian affairs

Part VII. Public information

Part VIII. Common support services

Part IX. Internal oversight

Part X. Jointly financed administrative activities and special expenses

Part XI. Capital expenditures

Part XII. Safety and security

Part XIII. Development Account

Part XIV. Staff assessment

By the same resolution, the General Assembly approved estimates of income other than assessments on Member States totalling 507,751,200 as follows.

Income section

1. Income from staff assessment.............455,366,000
2. General income............52,500,600
3. Services to the public............(115,400)
   Total, Income Section............**507,751,200**

Note

*   In line with resolution 66/246, the General Assembly decided that the proposed section 30 would be renamed section (29 H). Accordingly, there is no section 30 for the biennium 2012–13.

SCALES OF ASSESSMENT

UN Regular Budget

Contributions from Member States to the UN regular budget are determined by reference to a scale of assessments approved by the General Assembly on the basis of advice from the Committee on Contributions.

GA res. 55/5B (2000) substantially revised the scale of assessments, lowering the ceiling on the maximum contribution by any Member State to the regular budget to 22 percent. It reaffirmed the floor for the minimum contribution at 0.001 percent and the maximum contribution from Least Developed Countries at 0.01 percent. It also reaffirmed the low per capita income adjustment with a threshold per capita income limit of the average per capita gross national product of all Member States and a gradient of 80 percent.

GA res. 64/248(2010) set out the scale of assessments for 2010, 2011 and 2012. The scale of assessments will be reviewed by the General Assembly before the end of 2012.

The following table lists the scale of assessments for contributions to the regular budget for the period 2010–12.

Member States	Percentage contribution	Member States	Percentage contribution
Afghanistan	0.004	Bangladesh	0.010
Albania	0.010	Barbados	0.008
Algeria	0.128	Belarus	0.042
Andorra	0.007	Belgium	1.075
Angola	0.010	Belize	0.001
Antigua and Barbuda	0.002	Benin	0.003
Argentina	0.287	Bhutan	0.001
Armenia	0.005	Bolivia	0.007
Australia	1.933	Bosnia and Herzegovina	0.014
Austria	0.851	Botswana	0.018
Azerbaijan	0.015	Brazil	1.611
Bahamas	0.018	Brunei Darussalam	0.028
Bahrain	0.039	Bulgaria	0.038

Member States	Percentage contribution	Member States	Percentage contribution
Burkina Faso	0.003	Guatemala	0.028
Burundi	0.001	Guinea	0.002
Cambodia	0.003	Guinea-Bissau	0.001
Cameroon	0.011	Guyana	0.001
Canada	3.207	Haiti	0.003
Cape Verde	0.001	Honduras	0.008
Central African Republic	0.001	Hungary	0.291
Chad	0.002	Iceland	0.042
Chile	0.236	India	0.534
China	3.189	Indonesia	0.238
Colombia	0.144	Iran	0.233
Comoros	0.001	Iraq	0.020
Congo	0.003	Ireland	0.498
Costa Rica	0.034	Israel	0.384
Côte d'Ivoire	0.010	Italy	4.999
Croatia	0.097	Jamaica	0.014
Cuba	0.071	Japan	12.530
Cyprus	0.046	Jordan	0.014
Czech Republic	0.349	Kazakhstan	0.076
DPRK	0.007	Kenya	0.012
DR Congo	0.003	Kiribati	0.001
Denmark	0.736	Kuwait	0.263
Djibouti	0.001	Kyrgyzstan	0.001
Dominica	0.001	Lao PDR	0.001
Dominican Republic	0.042	Latvia	0.038
Ecuador	0.040	Lebanon	0.033
Egypt	0.094	Lesotho	0.001
El Salvador	0.019	Liberia	0.001
Equatorial Guinea	0.008	Libya	0.129
Eritrea	0.001	Liechtenstein	0.009
Estonia	0.040	Lithuania	0.069
Ethiopia	0.008	Luxembourg	0.090
Fiji	0.004	Madagascar	0.003
Finland	0.566	Malawi	0.001
France	6.123	Malaysia	0.253
Gabon	0.014	Maldives	0.001
Gambia	0.001	Mali	0.003
Georgia	0.006	Malta	0.017
Germany	8.018	Marshall Islands	0.001
Ghana	0.006	Mauritania	0.001
Greece	0.691	Mauritius	0.011
Grenada	0.001	Mexico	2.356

Member States	Percentage contribution	Member States	Percentage contribution
Micronesia	0.001	Sierra Leone	0.001
Monaco	0.003	Singapore	0.355
Mongolia	0.002	Slovakia	0.142
Montenegro	0.004	Slovenia	0.103
Morocco	0.058	Solomon Islands	0.001
Mozambique	0.003	Somalia	0.001
Myanmar	0.006	South Africa	0.385
Namibia	0.008	Spain	3.177
Nauru	0.001	Sri Lanka	0.019
Nepal	0.006	Sudan	0.010
Netherlands	1.855	Suriname	0.003
New Zealand	0.273	Swaziland	0.003
Nicaragua	0.003	Sweden	1.064
Niger	0.002	Switzerland	1.130
Nigeria	0.078	Syrian AR	0.025
Norway	0.871	Tajikistan	0.002
Oman	0.086	Thailand	0.209
Pakistan	0.082	The former Yugoslav Republic of Macedonia	0.007
Palau	0.001	Timor-Leste	0.001
Panama	0.022	Togo	0.001
Papua New Guinea	0.002	Tonga	0.001
Paraguay	0.007	Trinidad and Tobago	0.044
Peru	0.090	Tunisia	0.030
Philippines	0.090	Turkey	0.617
Poland	0.828	Turkmenistan	0.026
Portugal	0.511	Tuvalu	0.001
Qatar	0.135	Uganda	0.006
ROK	2.260	Ukraine	0.087
Republic of Moldova	0.002	UAE	0.391
Romania	0.177	UK	6.604
Russian Federation	1.602	UR of Tanzania	0.008
Rwanda	0.001	USA	22.000
Saint Kitts and Nevis	0.001	Uruguay	0.027
Saint Lucia	0.001	Uzbekistan	0.010
Saint Vincent and the Grenadines	0.001	Vanuatu	0.001
Samoa	0.001	Venezuela	0.314
San Marino	0.003	Viet Nam	0.033
Sao Tome and Principe	0.001	Yemen	0.010
Saudi Arabia	0.830	Zambia	0.004
Senegal	0.006	Zimbabwe	0.003
Serbia	0.037	**Grand Total**	**100.00**
Seychelles	0.002		

In accordance with GA res. 58/1B (2003) the Holy See, which is not a member of the UN but which participates in some of its activities, is called upon to contribute towards the expenses of the organisation on the basis of 50 percent of the notional assessment rate of 0.001 percent that would have been charged if it were a member.

AD HOC SCALE OF ASSESSMENTS FOR UN PEACEKEEPING BUDGETS

By GA res. 55/235 (2000), the General Assembly reformed its methodologies for apportioning the expenses of peacekeeping operations, replacing the ad hoc arrangements in place since GA res. 3101 XXVIII (1973). The Assembly took into account that the financing of peacekeeping operations was the collective responsibility of Member States and a different procedure was required from that used under the regular budget. The economically more developed countries were in a position to make relatively larger contributions and the economically less developed countries had a relatively limited capacity to contribute towards such operations. It also reaffirmed the special responsibilities of the Security Council's permanent Member States, as indicated in GA res. 1874 (S–IV) (1963), in connection with their contributions to the financing of peace and security operations.

To reflect these principles, the Assembly decided on the parameters of a new set of 10 levels for Member States for the purposes of apportioning the costs of peacekeeping, to be implemented on a phased basis from 1 July 2001. The resulting distribution of Member States among the 10 levels was set out in an annex to the resolution. The apportionments range from a premium payable by permanent Member States of the Security Council (Level A), to a 90 percent discount for Least Developed Countries (Level J).

GA res. 64/249 (2009) established the updated composition of levels of contribution for peacekeeping operations for the period 2010–12, as outlined in the report to the Secretary-General (see A/64/220/Add1). The scale of assessments for peacekeeping will be reviewed by the General Assembly before the end of 2012.

The membership of the 10 groups is as follows.*

Assignment of contribution levels for 2010–12

Level A

Permanent Members of the Security Council

China	Russian Federation	USA
France	UK	

Level B

Andorra	Germany	Monaco
Australia	Greece	Netherlands
Austria	Hungary	New Zealand
Bahamas[2]	Iceland	Norway
Bahrain[2]	Ireland	Portugal
Belgium	Israel	ROK
Canada	Italy	San Marino
Cyprus	Japan	Slovenia
Denmark	Liechtenstein	Spain
Estonia	Luxembourg	Sweden
Finland	Malta	Switzerland

Level C

Brunei Darussalam	Qatar	UAE
Kuwait	Singapore	

Level D

(None)

Level E

Barbados	Saudi Arabia

Transition to Level E

Czech Republic	Trinidad and Tobago

Level F

Antigua and Barbuda	Oman	Seychelles
Hungary		

Level G

Slovakia

Level H*1

Bulgaria	Lithuania	Romania
Latvia	Poland	

Level H1

Croatia	Mexico	Saint Kitts and Nevis
Libya	Palau	

Level I

Albania	Ghana	Papua New Guinea
Algeria	Grenada	Paraguay
Argentina	Guatemala	Peru
Armenia	Guyana	Philippines
Azerbaijan	Honduras	Republic of Moldova
Belarus	India	Saint Lucia
Belize	Indonesia	Saint Vincent and
Bolivia	Iran	the Grenadines
Bosnia and Herzegovina	Iraq	Serbia
Botswana	Jamaica	South Africa
Brazil	Jordan	Sri Lanka
Cameroon	Kazakhstan	Suriname
Cape Verde	Kenya	Swaziland
Chile	Kyrgyzstan	Syrian AR
Colombia	Lebanon	Tajikistan
Congo	Malaysia	Thailand
Costa Rica	Marshall Islands	The former Yugoslav
Côte d'Ivoire	Mauritius	Republic of Macedonia
Cuba	Micronesia	Tonga
DPRK	Mongolia	Tunisia
Dominica	Montenegro	Turkey
Dominican Republic	Morocco	Turkmenistan
Ecuador	Namibia	Ukraine
Egypt	Nauru	Uruguay
El Salvador	Nicaragua	Uzbekistan
Fiji	Nigeria	Venezuela
Gabon	Pakistan	Viet Nam
Georgia	Panama	Zimbabwe

Level J

Least Developed Countries

Afghanistan	Guinea	Samoa
Angola	Guinea-Bissau	Sao Tome and Principe
Bangladesh	Haiti	Senegal
Benin	Kiribati	Sierra Leone
Bhutan	Lao PDR	Solomon Islands
Burkina Faso	Lesotho	Somalia
Burundi	Liberia	Sudan
Cambodia	Madagascar	Timor-Leste
Central African Republic	Malawi	Togo
Chad	Maldives	Tuvalu
Comoros	Mali	Uganda
DR Congo	Mauritania	UR of Tanzania
Djibouti	Mozambique	Vanuatu
Equatorial Guinea	Myanmar	Yemen
Eritrea	Nepal	Zambia
Ethiopia	Niger	
Gambia	Rwanda	

Notes

*   As at 31 May 2012, no formal decision had been taken on which group South Sudan would be included in.

1   Category H* comprises countries that have voluntarily moved to category H.

2   Before the adoption of General Assembly resolution 64/249, the Chair of the Fifth Committee and the President of the General Assembly stated that it is the understanding of the Assembly that, as an exception, the Bahamas and Bahrain shall be treated as Level C for the scale of assessments for the period 2010–12.

UN BUDGET
AND SCALES

LIST OF ACRONYMS

GUIDE TO THE INDICES

The United Nations Handbook 2012–13 includes a list of acronyms found in the text and a separate index. The index is intended to help the reader locate bodies and programmes by full name, acronym and key word.

LIST OF ACRONYMS

A

ACABQ	Advisory Committee on Administrative and Budgetary Questions
ACC	Administrative Committee on Coordination
ACPR	Advisory Committee of Permanent Representatives
ADB	Asian Development Bank
ADF	Asian Development Fund
ADN	European Agreement Concerning the International Carriage of Dangerous Goods by Inland Waterways
ADR	European Agreement Concerning the International Carriage of Dangerous Goods by Road
AfDB	African Development Bank
AMIS	African Union Mission in Sudan (also see UNMIS and UNMISS)
AMISOM	African Union Mission in Somalia
APCICT	Asian and Pacific Training Centre for Information and Communications Technology for Development
APCTT	Asian and Pacific Centre for Transfer of Technology
ASPAC	Asia and the Pacific countries

B

BINUB	UN Integrated Office in Burundi (now BNUB)
BINUCA	UN Integrated Peacebuilding Office in the Central African Republic
BNUB	UN Office in Burundi
BONUCA	UN Peace-building Support Office in the Central African Republic (now BINUCA)

C

CA	Council of Administration
CAAC	Working Group on Children and Armed Conflict
CANWFZ	Central Asian Nuclear-Weapon-Free Zone Treaty
CAPSA	Centre for Alleviation of Poverty through Sustainable Agriculture
CAT	Committee Against Torture
CBD	Convention on Biological Diversity
CC	Consultative Committee
CCE	Committee on Central American Economic Cooperation
CCO	Committee of Cosponsoring Organizations
CCPCJ	Commission on Crime Prevention and Criminal Justice
CD	Conference on Disarmament
CDB	Caribbean Development Bank
CDCC	Caribbean Development and Cooperation Committee
CDP	Committee for Development Policy
CEB	UN System Chief Executives Board for Coordination
CED	Committee on Enforced Disappearances
CEDAW	Committee on the Elimination of Discrimination against Women
CEGAN	Committee of High-Level Government Experts
CEPA	Committee of Experts on Public Administration
CERD	Committee on the Elimination of Racial Discrimination
CESCR	Committee on Economic, Social and Cultural Rights
CFA	Committee on Food Aid Policies and Programmes
CHR	Commission on Human Rights
CIGEPS	Intergovernmental Committee for Physical Education and Sport
CIS	Commonwealth of Independent States

CITES	Convention on International Trade in Endangered Species of Wild Fauna and Flora
CMS	Convention on the Conservation of Migratory Species of Wild Animals
CMW	Committee on the Protection of the Rights of All Migrant Workers and Members of Their Families
CND	Commission on Narcotic Drugs
CNGO	Committee on Non-Governmental Organizations
COP	Conference of the Parties
COPUOS	Committee on the Peaceful Uses of Outer Space
CPA	Comprehensive Peace Agreement
CPC	Committee for Programme and Coordination
CPD	Commission on Population and Development
CPF	Collaborative Partnership on Forests
CPR	Committee of Permanent Representatives
CRC	Committee on the Rights of the Child
CRIC	Committee for the Review of the Implementation of the Convention (to Combat Desertification in Countries Experiencing Serious Drought and/or Desertification, particularly in Africa)
CRPD	Committee on the Rights of Persons with Disabilities
CSD	Commission on Sustainable Development
CSocD	Commission for Social Development
CST	Committee on Science and Technology
CSTD	Commission on Science and Technology for Development
CSW	Commission on the Status of Women
CTBT	Comprehensive Nuclear-Test-Ban Treaty
CTBTO	Comprehensive Nuclear-Test-Ban Treaty Organization
CTC	Counter-Terrorism Committee
CTED	Counter-Terrorism Committee Executive Directorate
CTITF	Counter-Terrorism Implementation Task Force
CWC	Convention on the Prohibition of the Development, Production, Stockpiling and Use of Chemical Weapons and on their Destruction

D

DAW	Division for the Advancement of Women (now UN Women)
DDPA	Durban Declaration and Programme of Action
DESA	Department of Economic and Social Affairs
DFS	Department of Field Support
DGACM	Department for General Assembly and Conference Management
DHA	Department of Humanitarian Affairs
DM	Department of Management
DMCs	Developing member countries
DOCO	Development Operations Coordination Office
DPA	Department of Political Affairs
DPI	Department of Public Information
DPKO	Department of Peacekeeping Operations
DPRK	Democratic People's Republic of Korea
DRR	Disaster risk reduction
DSS	Department of Safety and Security

E

EBRD	European Bank for Reconstruction and Development
EC	European Community or European Commission
ECA	Economic Commission for Africa
ECAFE	Economic Commission for Asia and the Far East (now ESCAP)
ECCAS	Economic Community of Central African States
ECCC	Extraordinary Chambers in the Courts of Cambodia
ECE	Economic Commission for Europe

ECHA	Executive Committee for Humanitarian Affairs
ECLAC	Economic Commission for Latin America and the Caribbean
ECOSOC	Economic and Social Council
ECOWAS	Economic Community of West African States
ECWA	Economic Commission for Western Asia (now ESCWA)
EMRIP	Expert Mechanism on the Rights of Indigenous Peoples
EOSG	Executive Office of the Secretary-General
ERC	Emergency Relief Coordinator
ESAF	Enhanced Structural Adjustment Facility
ESCAP	Economic and Social Commission for Asia and the Pacific
ESCWA	Economic and Social Commission for Western Asia
EULEX	European Union Rule of Law Mission in Kosovo

F

FAO	Food and Agriculture Organization
FCL	Flexible Credit Line

G

GA	General Assembly
GATT	General Agreement on Tariffs and Trade
GEF	Global Environment Facility
GHS	Globally Harmonized System of Classification and Labelling of Chemicals
GM	Global mechanism
GRULAC	Latin America and Caribbean countries

H

HFA	Hyogo Framework for Action
HIPCs	Heavily Indebted Poor Countries
HLCM	High-Level Committee on Management
HLCP	High-Level Committee on Programmes
HONLEA	Heads of National Drug Law Enforcement Agencies
HRCAC	Human Rights Council Advisory Committee
HRC	Human Rights Council

I

IAAC	Independent Audit Advisory Committee
IAEA	International Atomic Energy Agency
IASC	Inter-Agency Standing Committee
IBRD	International Bank for Reconstruction and Development
ICAO	International Civil Aviation Organization
ICC	International Criminal Court
ICCROM	International Centre for the Study of the Preservation and Restoration of Cultural Property
ICJ	International Court of Justice
ICOM	International Council of Museums
ICOMOS	International Council on Monuments and Sites
ICPD	International Conference on Population and Development
ICSC	International Civil Service Commission
ICSID	International Centre for the Settlement of Investment Disputes
ICTs	Information communication technologies
ICTR	International Criminal Tribunal for Rwanda
ICTY	International Criminal Tribunal for the former Yugoslavia

IDA	International Development Association
IDB	Inter-American Development Bank
IDC	International Data Centre
IEE	Group of Independent Eminent Experts
IEFR	International Emergency Food Reserve
IFAD	International Fund for Agricultural Development
IFAP	Intergovernmental Council for the Information for All Programmes
IFC	International Finance Corporation
IGBC	Intergovernmental Bioethics Committee
IGCP	International Geoscience Programme
IHP	Intergovernmental Council of the International Hydrological Programme
IIC	Inter-American Investment Corporation
ILC	International Law Commission
ILO	International Labour Organization
ILPES	Latin American and Caribbean Institute for Economic and Social Planning
IMCO	Inter-governmental Maritime Consultative Organization
IMF	International Monetary Fund
IMFC	International Monetary and Financial Committee
IMO	International Maritime Organization
IMS	International Monitoring System
INCB	International Narcotics Control Board
INDES	Inter-American Institute for Economic and Social Development
INSTRAW	International Research and Training Institute for the Advancement of Women (now UN Women)
INTAL	Institute for the Integration of Latin America and the Caribbean
INTERPOL	International Criminal Police Organization
IOC	Intergovernmental Oceanographic Commission
IPCC	Intergovernmental Panel on Climate Change
IPDC	Intergovernmental Council of the International Programme for the Development of Communication
IPPC	International Plant Protection Convention
ISA	International Seabed Authority
ISDR	International Strategy for Disaster Reduction (see also UNISDR)
ITC	International Trade Centre
ITLOS	International Tribunal for the Law of the Sea
ITU	International Telecommunication Union
IUCN	International Union for Conservation of Nature
IWMI	International Water Management Institute

J

JAG	Joint Advisory Group
JECFA	Joint FAO/WHO Expert Committee on Food Additives
JEMRA	Joint FAO/WHO Expert Meetings on Microbiological Risk Assessment
JIU	Joint Inspection Unit
JMPR	Joint FAO/WHO Meetings on Pesticide Residues
JPOI	Johannesburg Plan of Implementation

L

LDCs	Least Developed Countries

M

MAB	International Coordinating Council of the Programme on Man and the Biosphere
MAC	Military Armistice Commission
MDGs	Millennium Development Goals
MIF	Multilateral Investment Fund
MIF	Multinational Interim Force

MIGA	Multilateral Investment Guarantee Agency
MINUCI	UN Mission in Côte d'Ivoire (now UNOCI)
MINURSO	UN Mission for the Referendum in Western Sahara
MINUSTAH	UN Stabilization Mission in Haiti
MONUC	UN Organization Mission in the Democratic Republic of the Congo (now MONUSCO)
MONUSCO	UN Organization Stabilization Mission in the Democratic Republic of the Congo
MOST	Management of Social Transformations Programme

N

NEPAD	New Partnership for Africa's Development
NGO	Non-governmental organisation
NPT	Nuclear Non-Proliferation Treaty

O

OCHA	Office for the Coordination of Humanitarian Affairs
OCR	ordinary capital resources
ODA	Office for Disarmament Affairs
OECD	Organization for Economic Cooperation and Development
OHCHR	Office of the UN High Commissioner for Human Rights
OIE	World Organisation for Animal Health
OII	Office of Institutional Integrity
OIOS	Office of Internal Oversight Services
OLA	Office of Legal Affairs
OPCAT	Optional Protocol to the Convention Against Torture
OPCW	Organisation for the Prohibition of Chemical Weapons
OPEC	Organisation of the Petroleum Exporting Countries
OSAA	Office of the Special Adviser on Africa
OSAGI	Office of the Special Adviser on Gender Issues (now UN Women)
OSG	Office of the Secretary-General
OSRSG-CAAC	Office of the Special Representative of the Secretary-General for Children and Armed Conflict

P

PCL	Precautionary Credit Line
PBC	Peacebuilding Commission
PFII	Permanent Forum on Indigenous Issues
POC	Postal Operations Council
POPs	Persistent Organic Pollutants
PRGF	Poverty Reduction and Growth Facility
PTS	Provisional Technical Secretariat

R

RCF	Rapid Credit Facility
RMCs	Regional member countries
RID	Regulations concerning the International Carriage of Dangerous Goods by Rail

S

SARPs	Standards and Recommended Practices
SBA	Stand-By Arrangements
SBC	Secretariat of the Basel Convention on the Control of Transboundary Movements of Hazardous Wastes and their Disposal

SC	Security Council
SCF	Standby Credit Facility
SCTD	UN Steering Committee on Tourism for Development
SDF	Special Development Fund
SDRs	Special Drawing Rights
SIAP	Statistical Institute for Asia and the Pacific
SIDS	Small Island Developing States
SPT	Subcommittee on Prevention of Torture
STAP	Scientific and Technical Advisory Panel
STL	Special Tribunal for Lebanon
STRP	Scientific and Technical Review Panel

T

| TDB | Trade and Development Board |

U

UN Women	UN Entity for Gender Equality and the Empowerment of Women
UNAIDS	UN Programme on HIV/AIDS, Joint
UNAKRT	UN Assistance to the Khmer Rouge Trials
UNAMA	UN Assistance Mission in Afghanistan
UNAMI	UN Assistance Mission for Iraq
UNAMID	UN African Union Mission in Darfur
UNAMIS	UN Advance Mission in Sudan (now UNMISS)
UNAMSIL	UN Assistance Mission in Sierra Leone (now UNIPSIL)
UNAPCAEM	UN Asian and Pacific Centre for Agricultural Engineering and Machinery
UNAT	UN Appeals Tribunal
UNC	UN Command (in Korea)
UNCC	UN Compensation Commission
UNCCD	UN Convention to Combat Desertification in Countries Experiencing Serious Drought and/or Desertification, particularly in Africa
UNCCT	UN Counter-Terrorism Centre
UNCDF	UN Capital Development Fund
UNCIP	UN Commission for India and Pakistan
UNCITRAL	UN Commission on International Trade Law
UNCLOS	UN Convention on the Law of the Sea
UNCTAD	UN Conference on Trade and Development
UNDC	UN Disarmament Commission
UNDCP	UN International Drug Control Programme (now UNODC)
UNDEF	UN Democracy Fund
UNDG	UN Development Group
UNDOF	UN Disengagement Observer Force
UNDP	UN Development Programme
UNDSS	UN Department of Safety and Security
UNDT	UN Dispute Tribunal
UNECE	UN Economic Commission for Europe
UNEP	UN Environment Programme
UNESCAP	UN Economic and Social Commission for Asia and the Pacific
UNESCO	UN Educational, Scientific and Cultural Organization
UNFCCC	UN Framework Convention on Climate Change
UNFF	UN Forum on Forests
UNFICYP	UN Force in Cyprus
UNFIP	UN Fund for International Partnerships
UNFPA	UN Population Fund
UNGEGN	UN Group of Experts on Geographical Names
UN-HABITAT	UN Human Settlements Programme

UNHCR	UN High Commissioner for Refugees, Office of the
UNICEF	UN Children's Fund
UNICRI	UN Interregional Crime and Justice Research Institute
UNIDIR	UN Institute for Disarmament Research
UNIDO	UN Industrial Development Organization
UNIFEM	UN Development Fund for Women (now UN Women)
UNIFIL	UN Interim Force in Lebanon
UN-INSTRAW	UN International Research and Training Institute for the Advancement of Women (now UN Women)
UNIOGBIS	UN Integrated Peace-Building Office in Guinea-Bissau
UNIOSIL	UN Integrated Office in Sierra Leone (now UNIPSIL)
UNIPOM	UN India–Pakistan Observation Mission
UNIPSIL	UN Integrated Peacebuilding Office in Sierra Leone
UNIS	UN International School
UNISDR	UN International Strategy for Disaster Reduction (see also ISDR)
UNISFA	UN Interim Security Force for Abyei
UNITAR	UN Institute for Training and Research
UNLB	UN Logistics Base
UN-LiREC	UN Regional Centre for Peace, Disarmament and Development in Latin America and the Caribbean
UNMAS	UN Mine Action Service
UNMIK	UN Interim Administration Mission in Kosovo
UNMIL	UN Mission in Liberia
UNMIS	UN Mission in Sudan (now UNMISS)
UNMISS	UN Mission in the Republic of South Sudan
UNMIT	UN Mission in Timor-Leste
UNMOGIP	UN Military Observer Group in India and Pakistan
UNOAU	UN Office to the African Union
UNOCA	UN Regional Office for Central Africa
UNOCI	UN Operations in Côte d'Ivoire
UNODA	UN Office for Disarmament Affairs
UNODC	UN Office on Drugs and Crime
UNOG	UN Office at Geneva
UNOGBIS	UN Peace-Building Support Office in Guinea-Bissau (now UNIOGBIS)
UN-OHRLLS	Office of the High Representative for the Least Developed Countries, Landlocked Developing Countries and Small Island Developing States
UNOL	UN Peace-building Support Office in Liberia (now UNMIL)
UNON	UN Office at Nairobi
UNOP	UN Office for Partnerships
UNOPS	UN Office for Project Services
UNOSDP	UN Office on Sport for Development and Peace
UNOV	UN Office at Vienna
UNOWA	UN Office for West Africa
UNPFII	UN Permanent Forum on Indigenous Issues
UNPOS	UN Political Office for Somalia
UNRCCA	UN Regional Centre for Preventive Diplomacy for Central Asia
UNRCPD	UN Regional Centre for Peace and Disarmament in Asia and the Pacific
UNREC	UN Regional Centre for Peace and Disarmament in Africa
UNRISD	UN Research Institute for Social Development
UNRoD	UN Register of Damage
UNRWA	UN Relief and Works Agency for Palestine Refugees in the Near East
UNSCEAR	UN Scientific Committee on the Effects of Atomic Radiation
UNSCO	UN Special Coordinator for the Middle East Peace Process, Office of the
UNSCOL	UN Special Coordinator for Lebanon, Office of the
UNSDRI	UN Social Defense Research Institute (now UNICRI)
UNSMA	UN Special Mission to Afghanistan (now UNAMA)
UNSMIL	UN Support Mission in Libya
UNSMIS	UN Supervision Mission in Syria

UNSSC	UN System Staff College
UNTSO	UN Truce Supervision Organization
UNU	United Nations University
UNV	UN Volunteers
UNWTO	UN World Tourism Organization
UPOV	International Union for the Protection of New Varieties of Plants
UPR	Universal Periodic Review
UPU	Universal Postal Union

W

WEOG	Western European and Other States Group
WFP	World Food Programme
WGC	Working Group on Communications
WGS	Working Group on Situations
WHC	World Heritage Committee
WHO	World Health Organization
WIPO	World Intellectual Property Organization
WMDs	Weapons of mass destruction
WMO	World Meteorological Organization
WSIS	World Summit on the Information Society
WSSD	World Summit on Sustainable Development
WTO	World Trade Organization

INDEX

INDEX

Bold entries denote the main entry for the organisations.